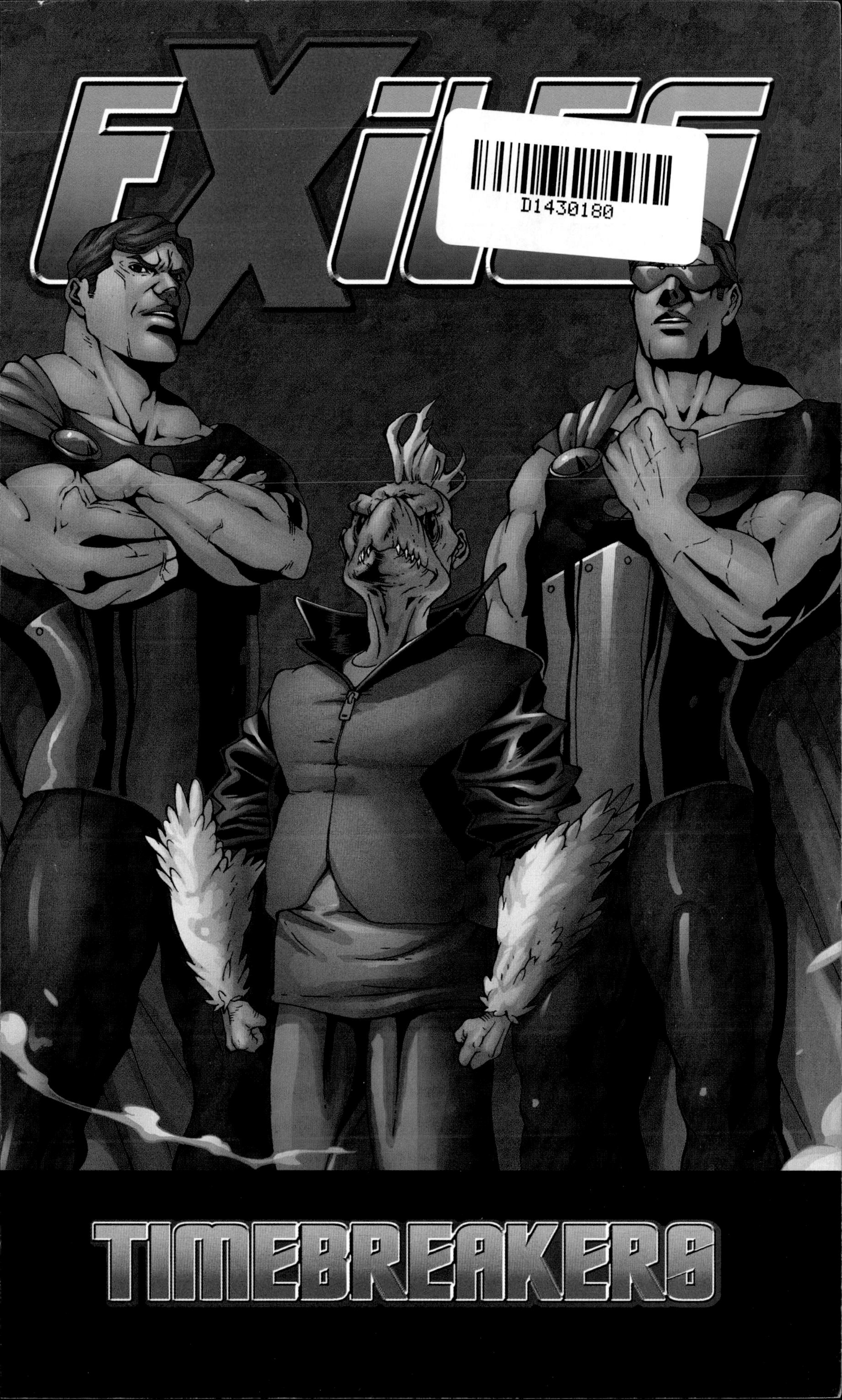
EXILES
TIMEBREAKERS

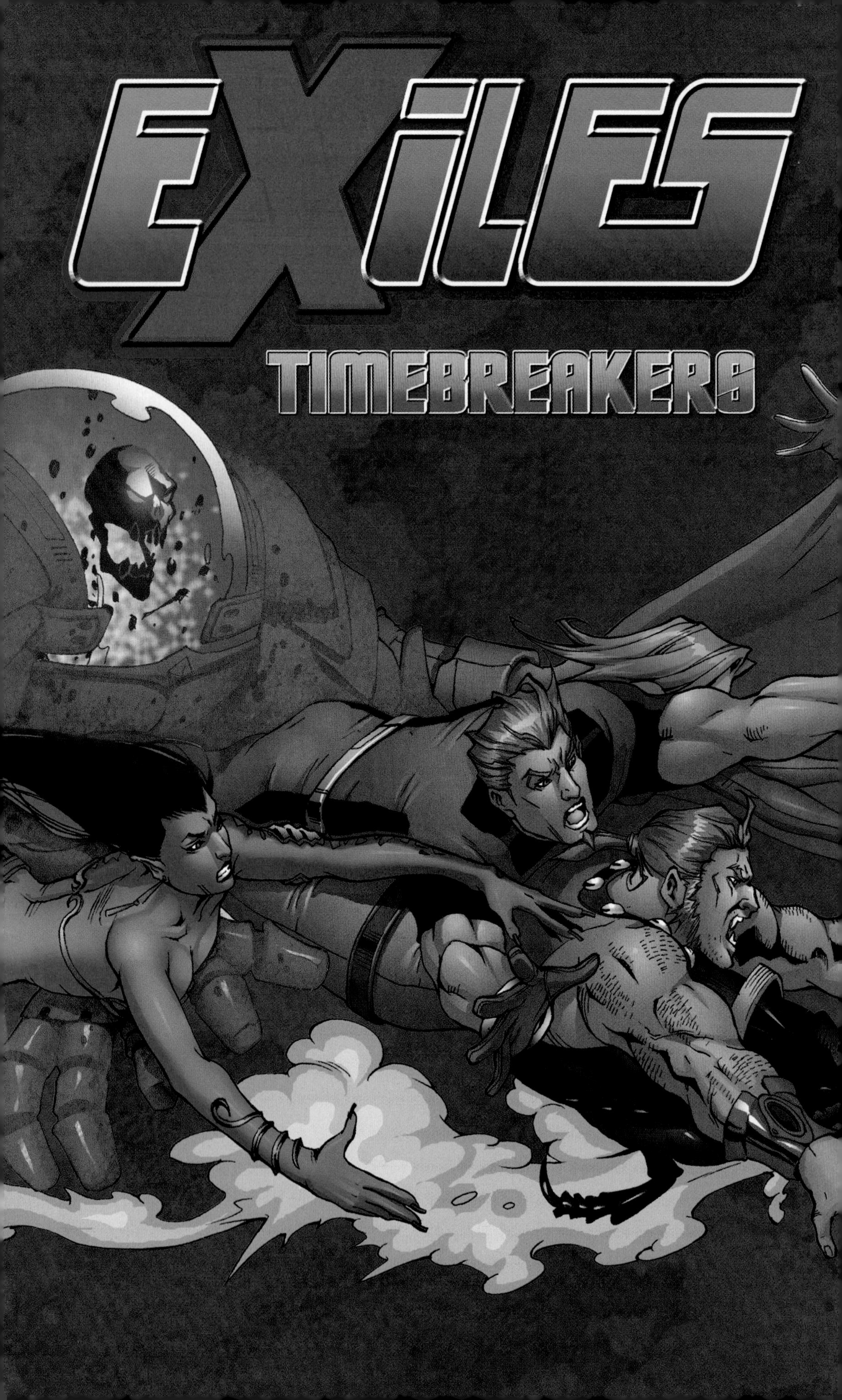
EXILES
TIMEBREAKERS

Writer:
Tony Bedard
Art:
Mizuki Sakakibara (Timebreakers) & Jim Calafiore & Mark McKenna
Colors:
JC
Letters:
Dave Sharpe
Covers:
Jim Calafiore
Assistant Editor:
Sean Ryan
Associate Editor:
Nick Lowe
Editor:
Mike Marts

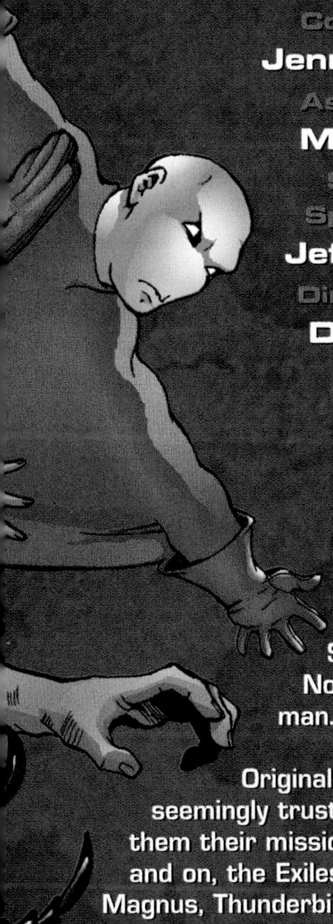

Collection Editor:
Jennifer Grünwald
Assistant Editor:
Michael Short
Senior Editor, Special Projects:
Jeff Youngquist
Director of Sales:
David Gabriel

Production:
Loretta Krol
Book Designer:
Carrie Beadle
Creative Director:
Tom Marvelli

Editor in Chief:
Joe Quesada
Publisher:
Dan Buckley

PREVIOUSLY

Six strangers, each an X-Man from a different reality, have been brought together to insure that life as we know it doesn't cease to exist! Blink, Teleporter; Mimic, Powered by his reality's X-Men; Magnus, Son of Magneto and Rogue; Thunderbird, Super-strength and senses; Nocturne, Daughter of Nightcrawler; and Morph, Shape-changing funny man. Destined to fix the kinks in the chains of reality. Things have changed.

Originally these six members were brought together by the mysterious, but seemingly trustworthy, TIMEBROKER. They were given a "TALLUS," a guide that told them their mission on each new earth they journeyed to. As the months went on and on and on, the Exiles faced numerous challenges and team members were lost and gained. Magnus, Thunderbird, Nocturne, Magik and Sunfire, have all been maimed, killed, or simply left behind.

And though things were never easy, at least there was some rationale to their job. But recently that has begun to change as well. Recent missions have been vague, irrational, and sometimes non-existent. Even the Timebroker himself has been appearing angry, evil, and down right sadistic — even going so far as giving the Exiles the mission to kill Mimic, one of their teammates.

So now, with the recent disappearance of Sasquatch and Beak, and the unrelenting jerking around, he Exiles have had enough. The team — now consisting of original members Mimic, Blink, and Morph, long with Namora, and two mutants from the Age of Apocalypse timeline — Sabretooth and Holocaust - has used the reality-bending M'KRAAN CRYSTAL to travel to the home of the Timebroker and take ack their lives or die trying. Things are about to change again.

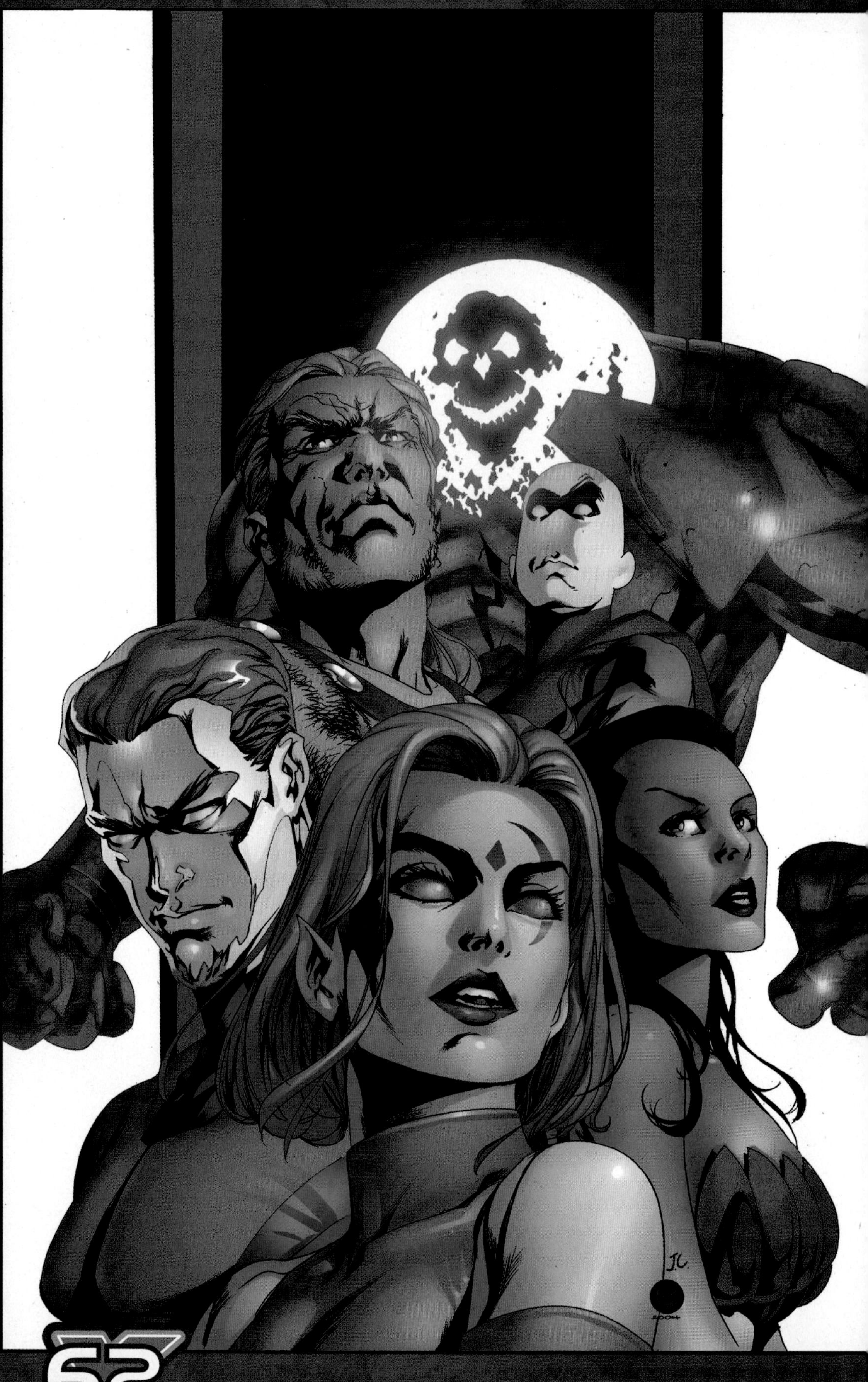

62

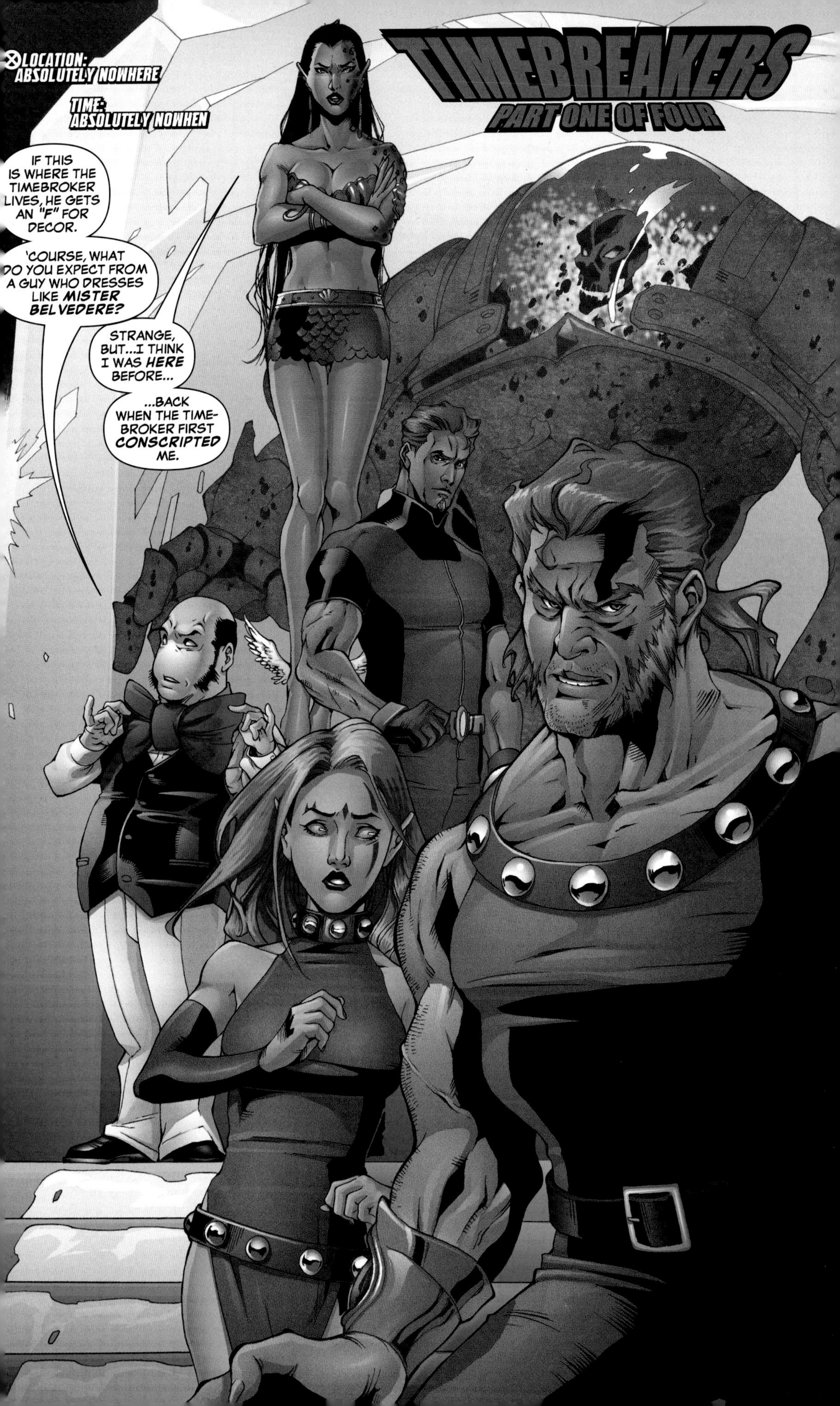
LOCATION: ABSOLUTELY NOWHERE
TIME: ABSOLUTELY NOWHEN
TIMEBREAKERS
PART ONE OF FOUR
IF THIS IS WHERE THE TIMEBROKER LIVES, HE GETS AN "F" FOR DECOR.
'COURSE, WHAT DO YOU EXPECT FROM A GUY WHO DRESSES LIKE MISTER BELVEDERE?
STRANGE, BUT...I THINK I WAS HERE BEFORE...
...BACK WHEN THE TIME-BROKER FIRST CONSCRIPTED ME.

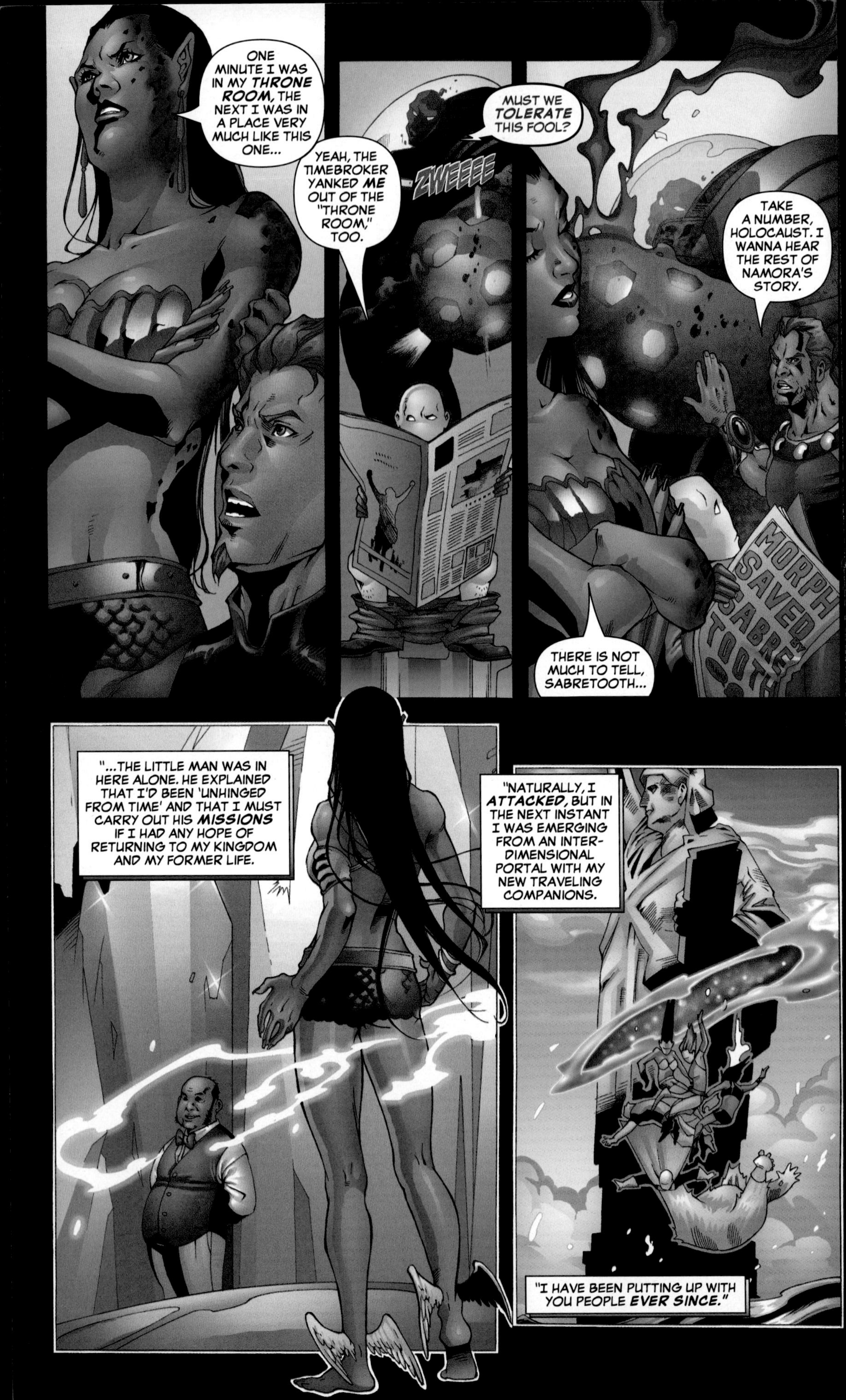
ONE MINUTE I WAS IN MY THRONE ROOM, THE NEXT I WAS IN A PLACE VERY MUCH LIKE THIS ONE...
YEAH, THE TIMEBROKER YANKED ME OUT OF THE "THRONE ROOM," TOO.
MUST WE TOLERATE THIS FOOL?
ZWEEEE
TAKE A NUMBER, HOLOCAUST. I WANNA HEAR THE REST OF NAMORA'S STORY.
MORPH SAVED BY SABRETOOTH
THERE IS NOT MUCH TO TELL, SABRETOOTH...
"...THE LITTLE MAN WAS IN HERE ALONE. HE EXPLAINED THAT I'D BEEN 'UNHINGED FROM TIME' AND THAT I MUST CARRY OUT HIS MISSIONS IF I HAD ANY HOPE OF RETURNING TO MY KINGDOM AND MY FORMER LIFE.
"NATURALLY, I ATTACKED, BUT IN THE NEXT INSTANT I WAS EMERGING FROM AN INTER-DIMENSIONAL PORTAL WITH MY NEW TRAVELING COMPANIONS.
"I HAVE BEEN PUTTING UP WITH YOU PEOPLE EVER SINCE."

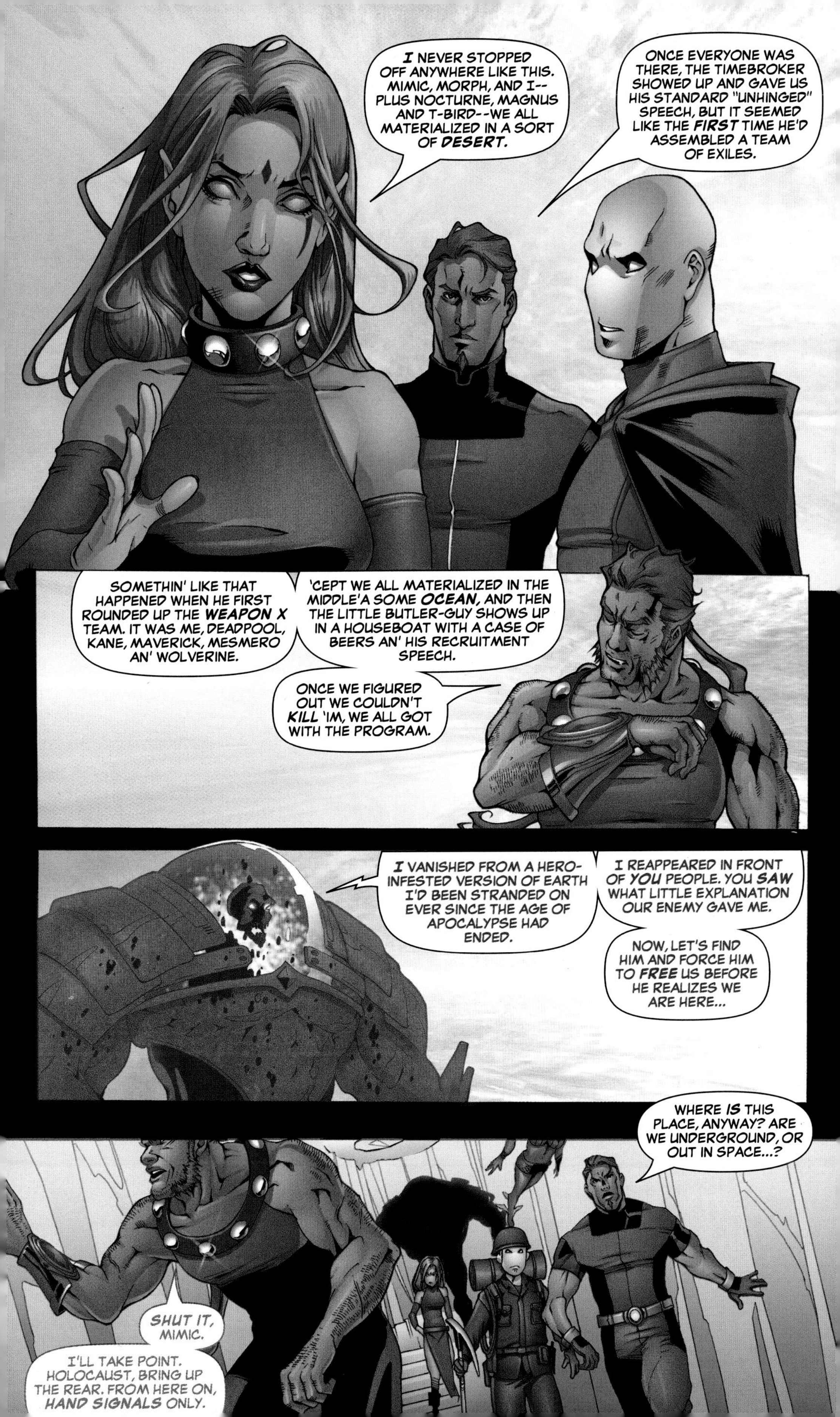
I NEVER STOPPED OFF ANYWHERE LIKE THIS. MIMIC, MORPH, AND I-- PLUS NOCTURNE, MAGNUS AND T-BIRD--WE ALL MATERIALIZED IN A SORT OF DESERT.
ONCE EVERYONE WAS THERE, THE TIMEBROKER SHOWED UP AND GAVE US HIS STANDARD "UNHINGED" SPEECH, BUT IT SEEMED LIKE THE FIRST TIME HE'D ASSEMBLED A TEAM OF EXILES.
SOMETHIN' LIKE THAT HAPPENED WHEN HE FIRST ROUNDED UP THE WEAPON X TEAM. IT WAS ME, DEADPOOL, KANE, MAVERICK, MESMERO AN' WOLVERINE.
'CEPT WE ALL MATERIALIZED IN THE MIDDLE'A SOME OCEAN, AND THEN THE LITTLE BUTLER-GUY SHOWS UP IN A HOUSEBOAT WITH A CASE OF BEERS AN' HIS RECRUITMENT SPEECH.
ONCE WE FIGURED OUT WE COULDN'T KILL 'IM, WE ALL GOT WITH THE PROGRAM.
I VANISHED FROM A HERO-INFESTED VERSION OF EARTH I'D BEEN STRANDED ON EVER SINCE THE AGE OF APOCALYPSE HAD ENDED.
I REAPPEARED IN FRONT OF YOU PEOPLE. YOU SAW WHAT LITTLE EXPLANATION OUR ENEMY GAVE ME.
NOW, LET'S FIND HIM AND FORCE HIM TO FREE US BEFORE HE REALIZES WE ARE HERE...
WHERE IS THIS PLACE, ANYWAY? ARE WE UNDERGROUND, OR OUT IN SPACE...?
SHUT IT, MIMIC.
I'LL TAKE POINT. HOLOCAUST, BRING UP THE REAR. FROM HERE ON, HAND SIGNALS ONLY.

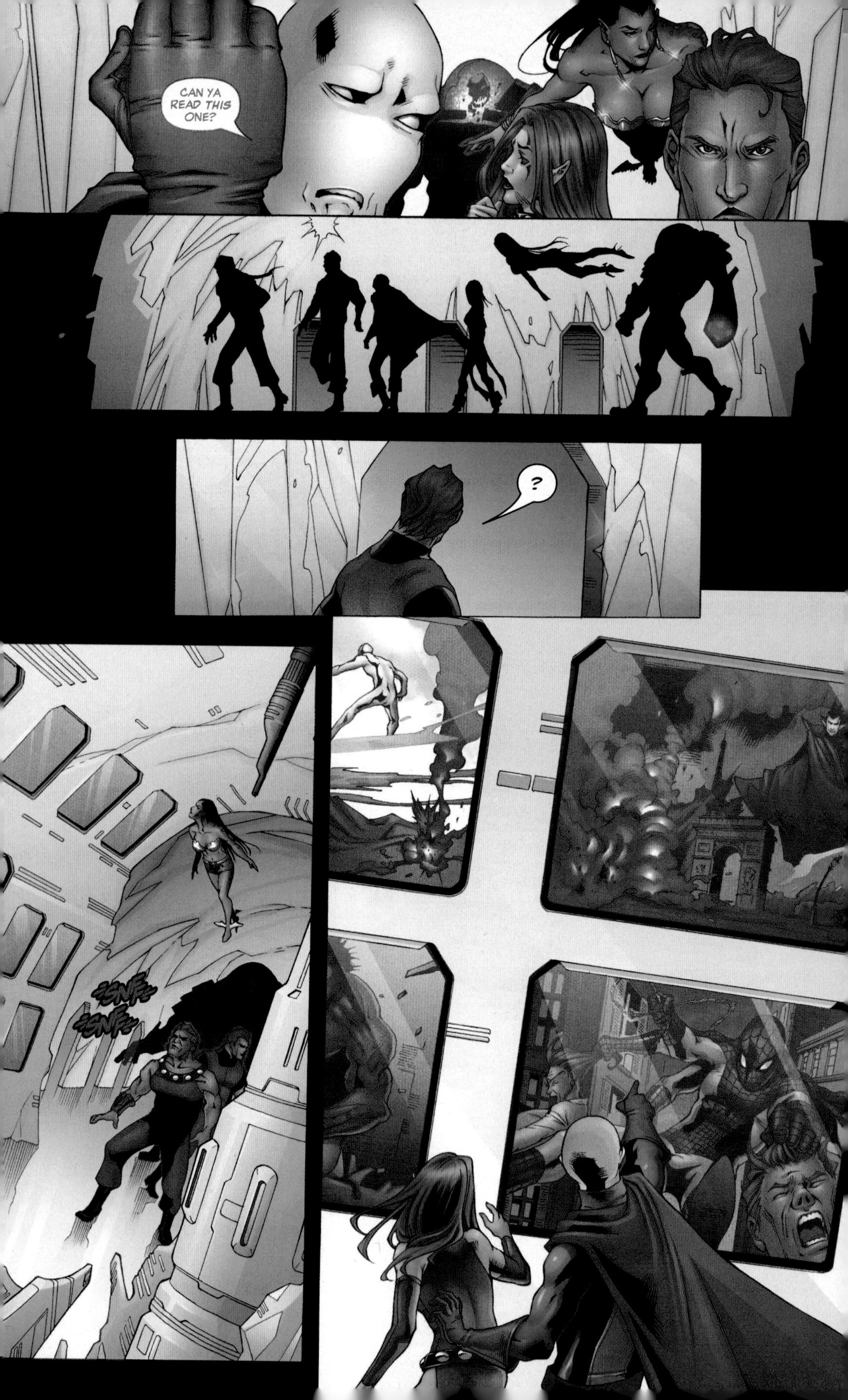
CAN YA READ THIS ONE?
?
SNF
SNF

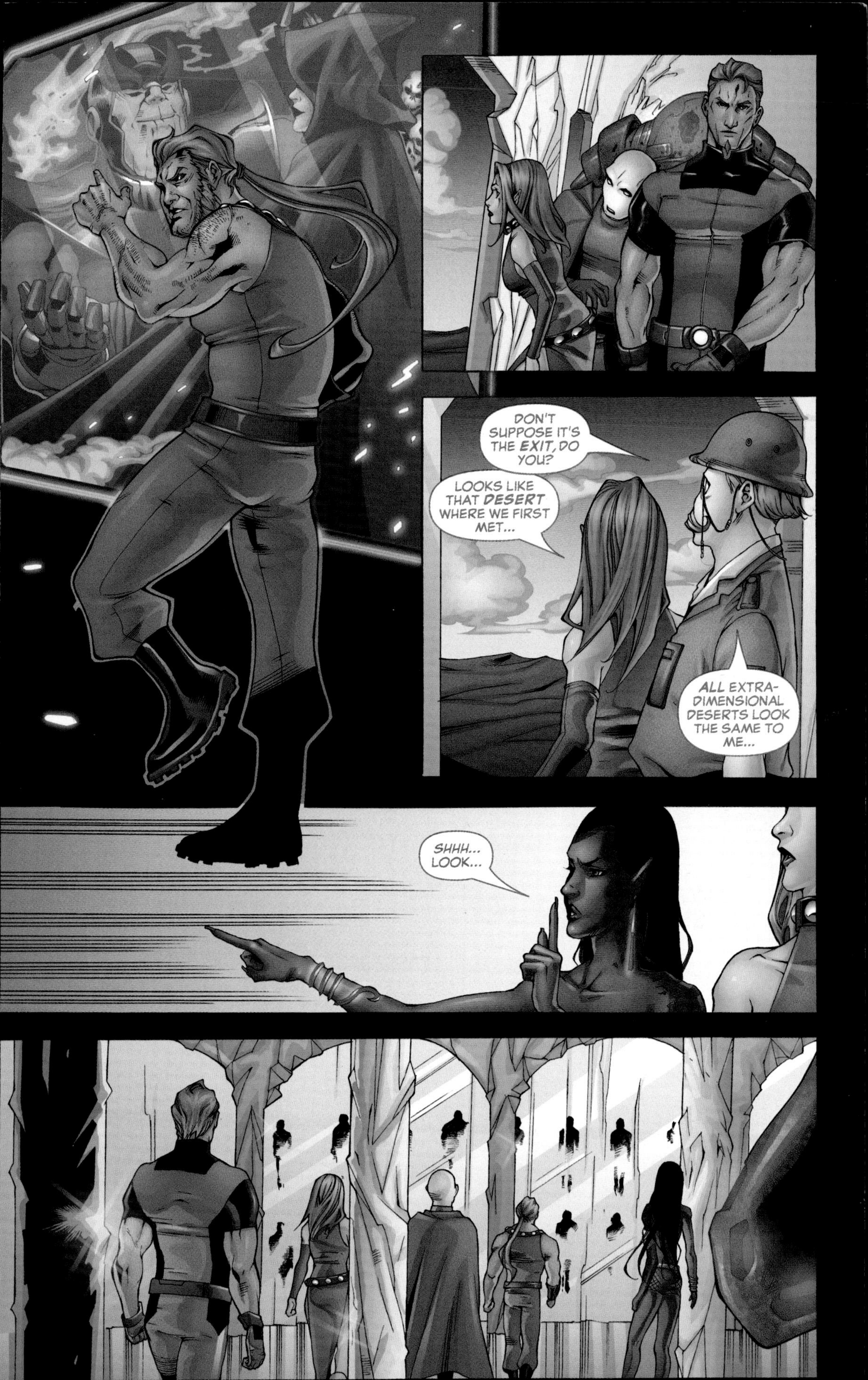
DON'T SUPPOSE IT'S THE EXIT, DO YOU?
LOOKS LIKE THAT DESERT WHERE WE FIRST MET...
ALL EXTRA-DIMENSIONAL DESERTS LOOK THE SAME TO ME...
SHHH... LOOK...

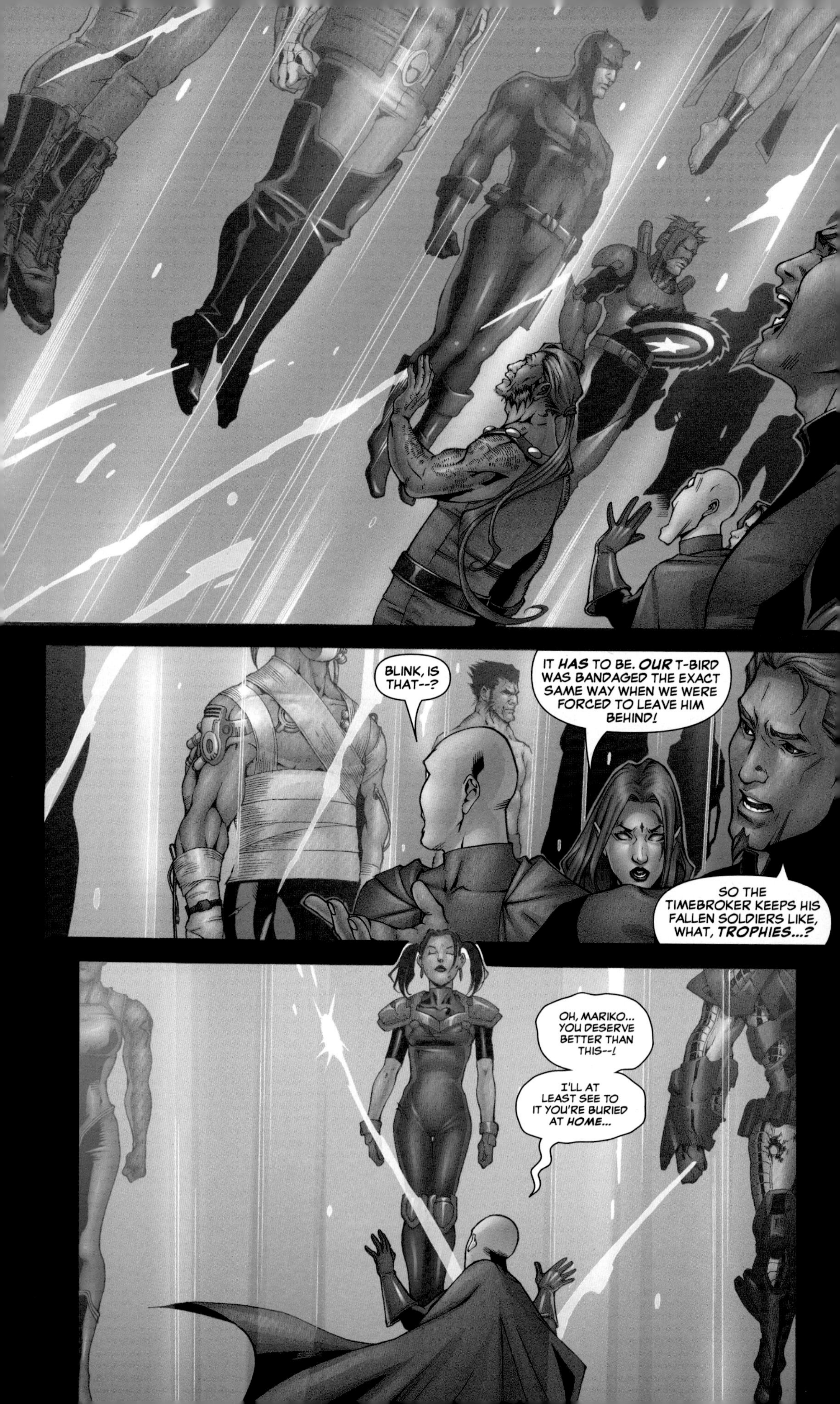
BLINK, IS THAT--?
IT **HAS** TO BE. **OUR** T-BIRD WAS BANDAGED THE EXACT SAME WAY WHEN WE WERE FORCED TO LEAVE HIM BEHIND!
SO THE TIMEBROKER KEEPS HIS FALLEN SOLDIERS LIKE, WHAT, **TROPHIES...?**
OH, MARIKO... YOU DESERVE BETTER THAN THIS--!
I'LL AT LEAST SEE TO IT YOU'RE BURIED AT **HOME...**

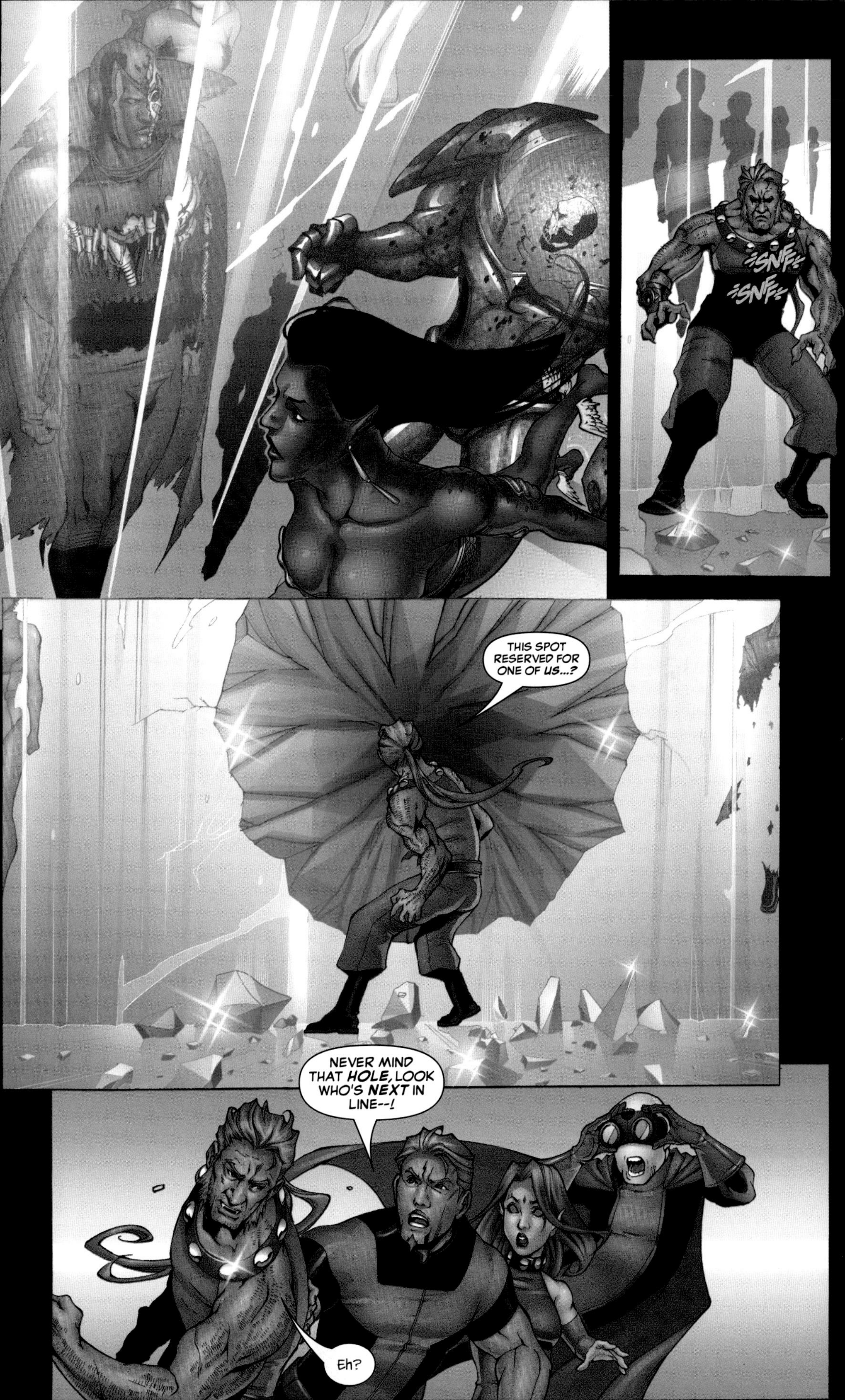
SNF
SNF
THIS SPOT RESERVED FOR ONE OF US...?
NEVER MIND THAT HOLE, LOOK WHO'S NEXT IN LINE--!
Eh?

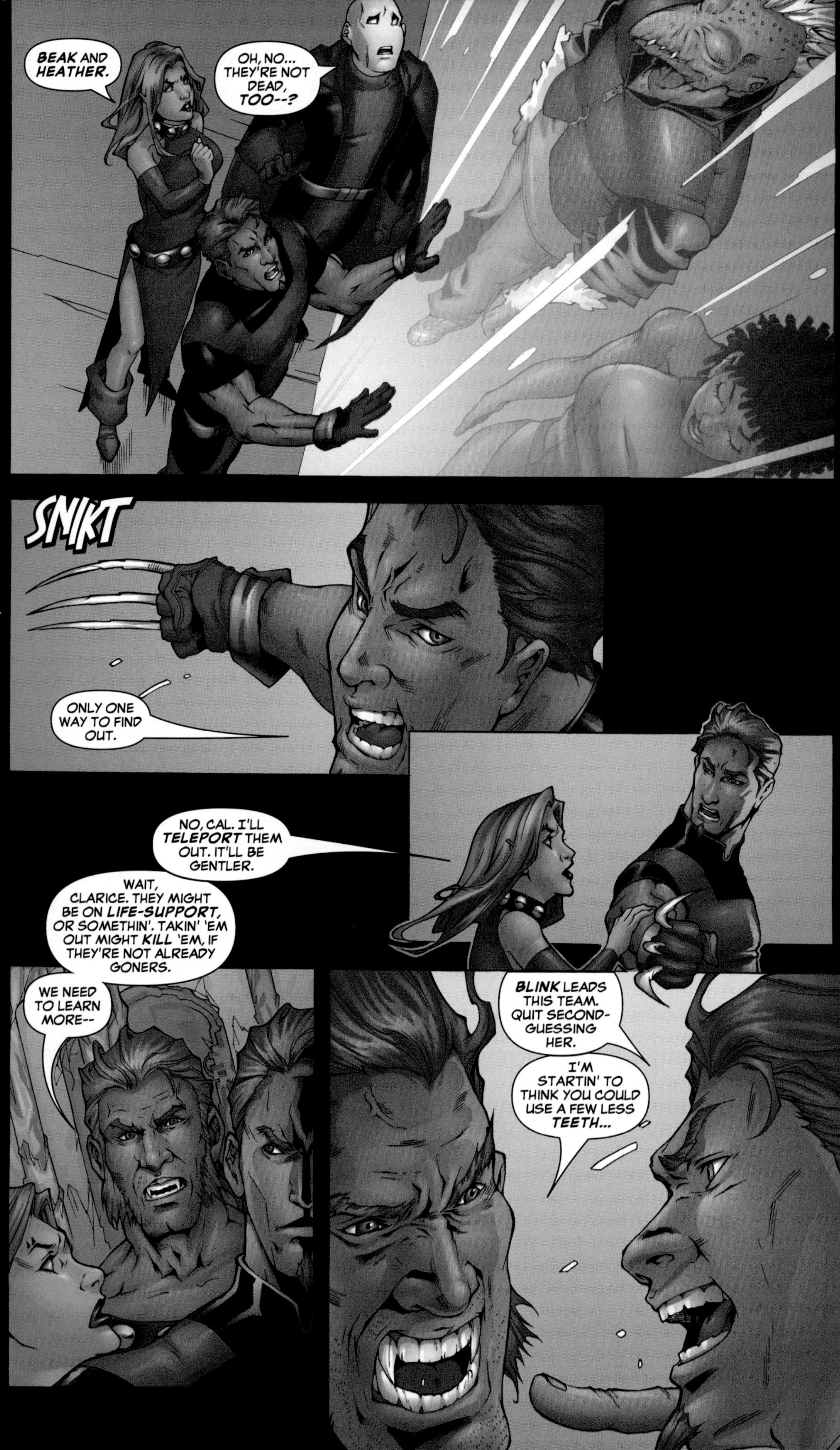
BEAK AND HEATHER.
OH, NO... THEY'RE NOT DEAD, TOO--?
SNIKT
ONLY ONE WAY TO FIND OUT.
NO, CAL. I'LL TELEPORT THEM OUT. IT'LL BE GENTLER.
WAIT, CLARICE. THEY MIGHT BE ON LIFE-SUPPORT, OR SOMETHIN'. TAKIN' 'EM OUT MIGHT KILL 'EM, IF THEY'RE NOT ALREADY GONERS.
WE NEED TO LEARN MORE--
BLINK LEADS THIS TEAM. QUIT SECOND-GUESSING HER.
I'M STARTIN' TO THINK YOU COULD USE A FEW LESS TEETH...

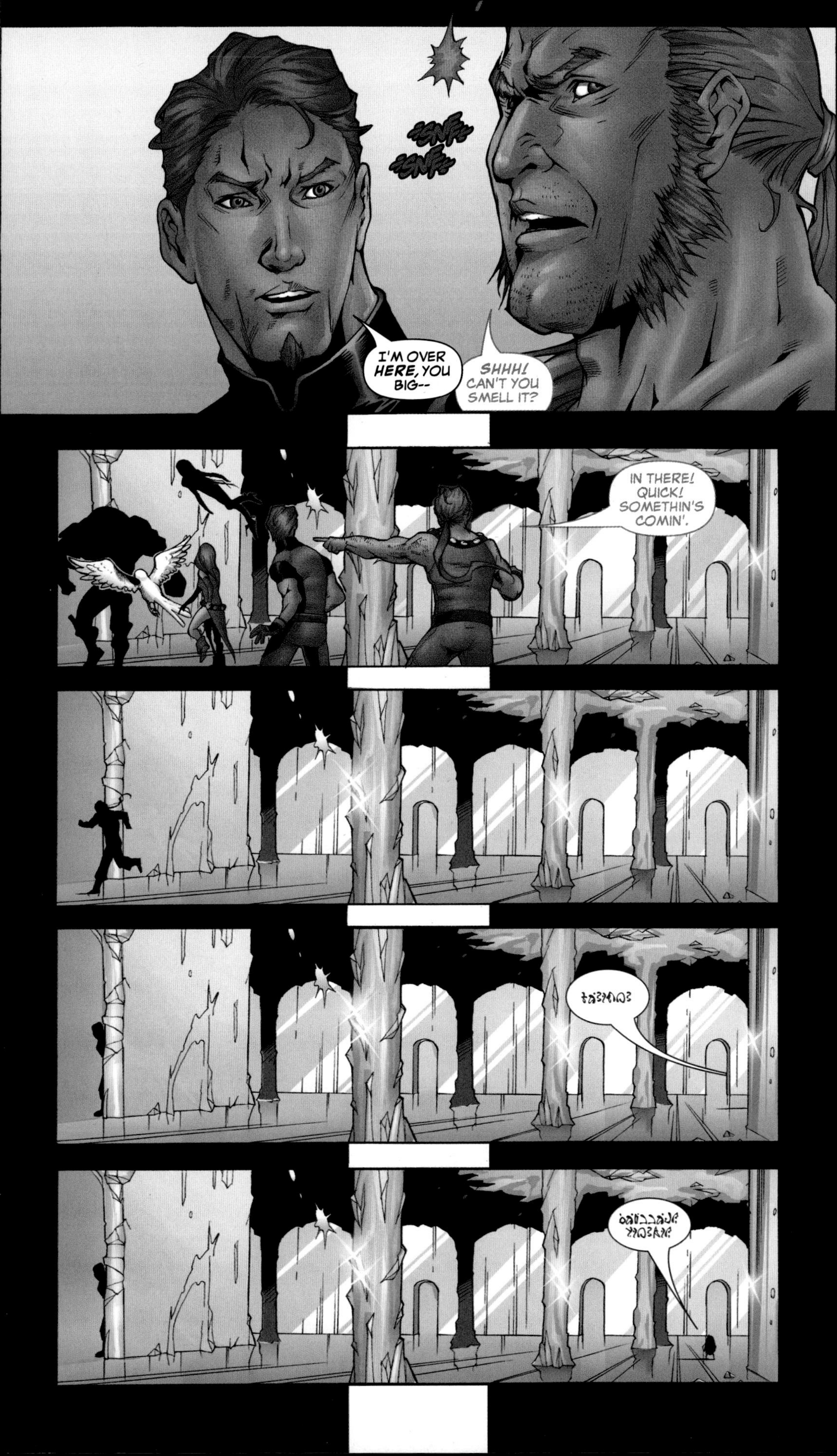
SNF SNF
I'M OVER HERE, YOU BIG--
SHHH! CAN'T YOU SMELL IT?
IN THERE! QUICK! SOMETHIN'S COMIN'.

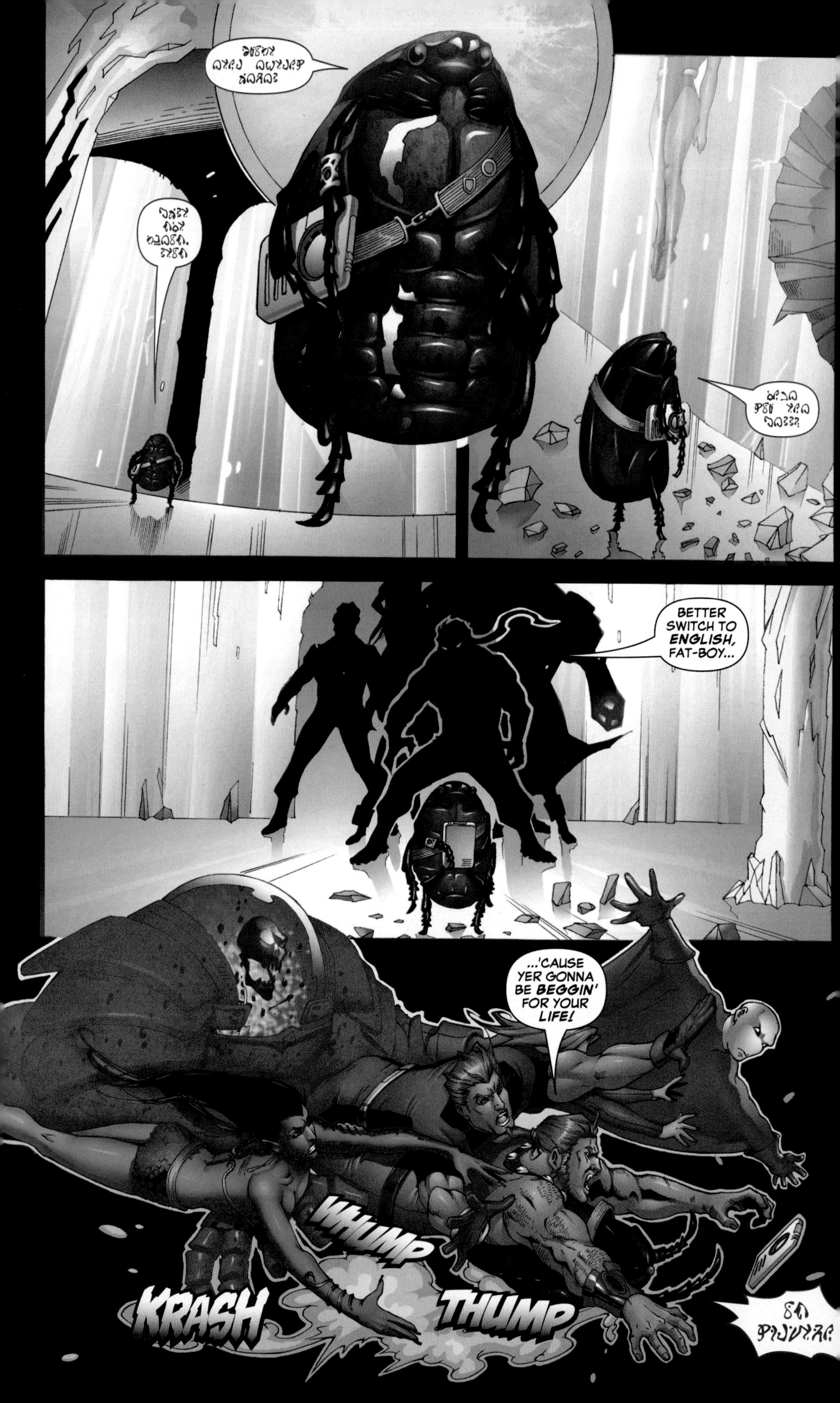

BETTER SWITCH TO ENGLISH, FAT-BOY...
...'CAUSE YER GONNA BE BEGGIN' FOR YOUR LIFE!
WHUMP
KRASH
THUMP

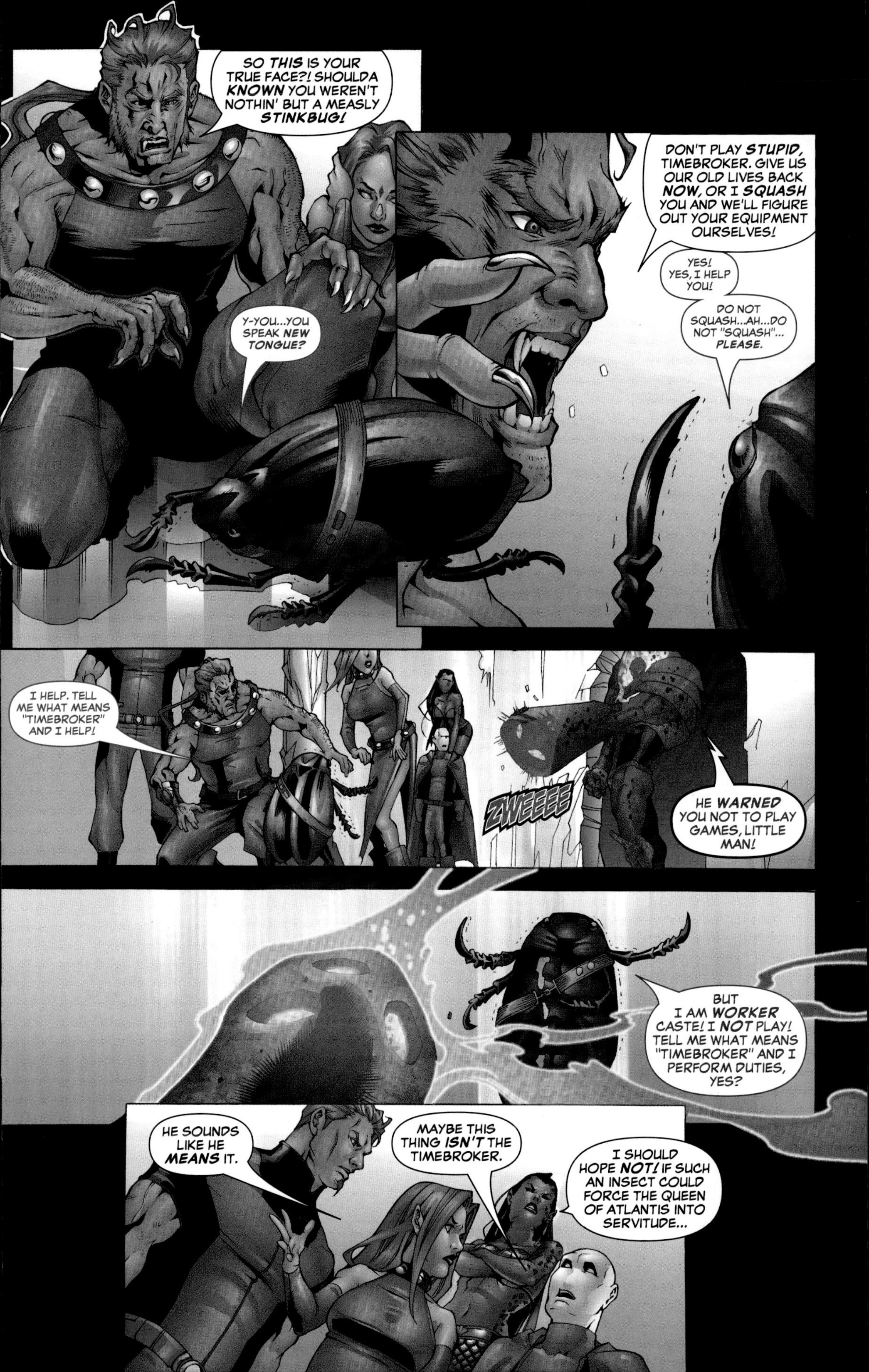
SO THIS IS YOUR TRUE FACE?! SHOULDA KNOWN YOU WEREN'T NOTHIN' BUT A MEASLY STINKBUG!
Y-YOU...YOU SPEAK NEW TONGUE?
DON'T PLAY STUPID, TIMEBROKER. GIVE US OUR OLD LIVES BACK NOW, OR I SQUASH YOU AND WE'LL FIGURE OUT YOUR EQUIPMENT OURSELVES!
YES! YES, I HELP YOU!
DO NOT SQUASH...AH...DO NOT "SQUASH"... PLEASE.
I HELP. TELL ME WHAT MEANS "TIMEBROKER" AND I HELP!
ZWEEEE
HE WARNED YOU NOT TO PLAY GAMES, LITTLE MAN!
BUT I AM WORKER CASTE! I NOT PLAY! TELL ME WHAT MEANS "TIMEBROKER" AND I PERFORM DUTIES, YES?
HE SOUNDS LIKE HE MEANS IT.
MAYBE THIS THING ISN'T THE TIMEBROKER.
I SHOULD HOPE NOT! IF SUCH AN INSECT COULD FORCE THE QUEEN OF ATLANTIS INTO SERVITUDE...

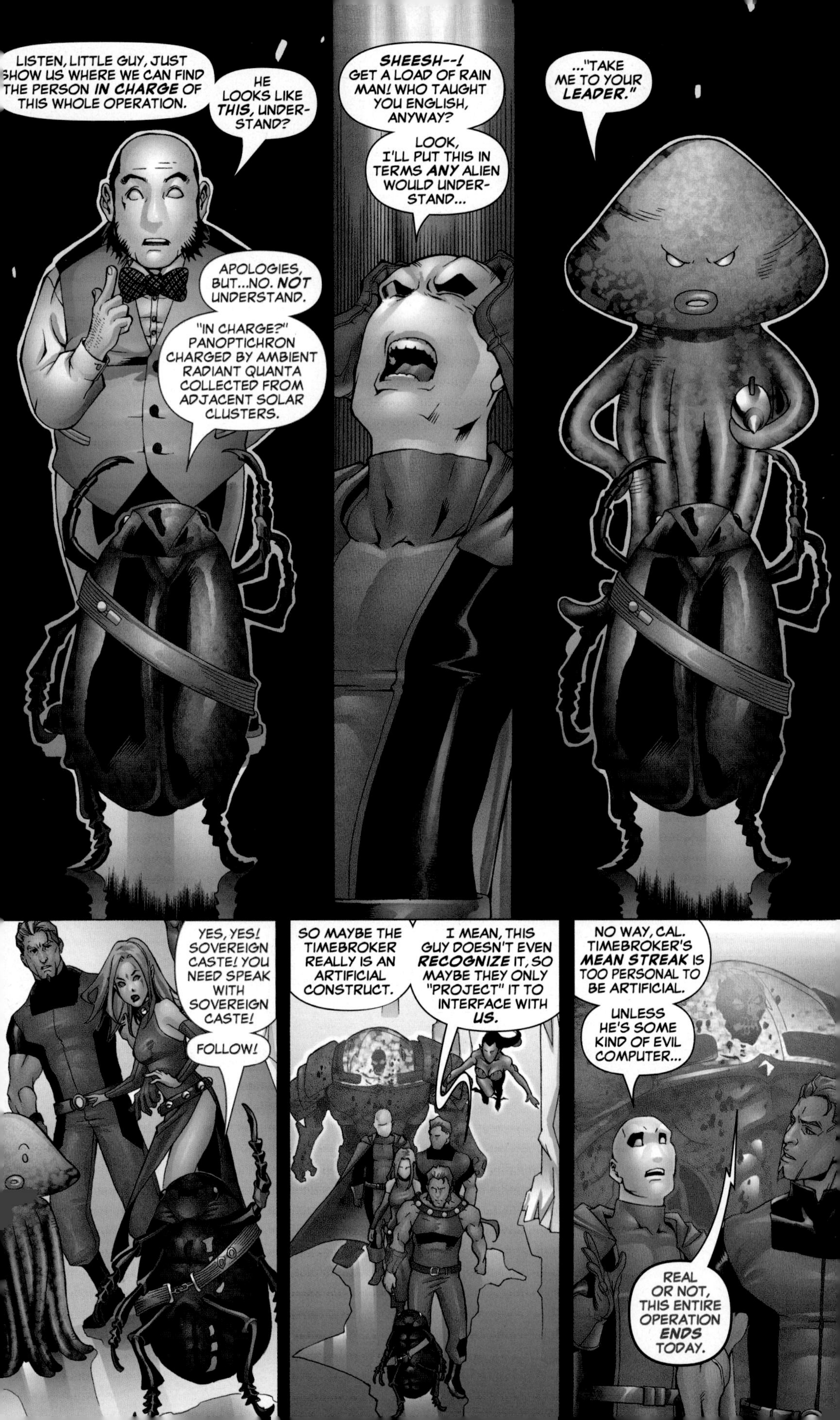
LISTEN, LITTLE GUY, JUST SHOW US WHERE WE CAN FIND THE PERSON IN CHARGE OF THIS WHOLE OPERATION.
HE LOOKS LIKE THIS, UNDER-STAND?
APOLOGIES, BUT...NO. NOT UNDERSTAND.
"IN CHARGE?" PANOPTICHRON CHARGED BY AMBIENT RADIANT QUANTA COLLECTED FROM ADJACENT SOLAR CLUSTERS.
SHEESH--! GET A LOAD OF RAIN MAN! WHO TAUGHT YOU ENGLISH, ANYWAY?
LOOK, I'LL PUT THIS IN TERMS ANY ALIEN WOULD UNDER-STAND...
..."TAKE ME TO YOUR LEADER."
YES, YES! SOVEREIGN CASTE! YOU NEED SPEAK WITH SOVEREIGN CASTE!
FOLLOW!
SO MAYBE THE TIMEBROKER REALLY IS AN ARTIFICIAL CONSTRUCT.
I MEAN, THIS GUY DOESN'T EVEN RECOGNIZE IT, SO MAYBE THEY ONLY "PROJECT" IT TO INTERFACE WITH US.
NO WAY, CAL. TIMEBROKER'S MEAN STREAK IS TOO PERSONAL TO BE ARTIFICIAL.
UNLESS HE'S SOME KIND OF EVIL COMPUTER...
REAL OR NOT, THIS ENTIRE OPERATION ENDS TODAY.

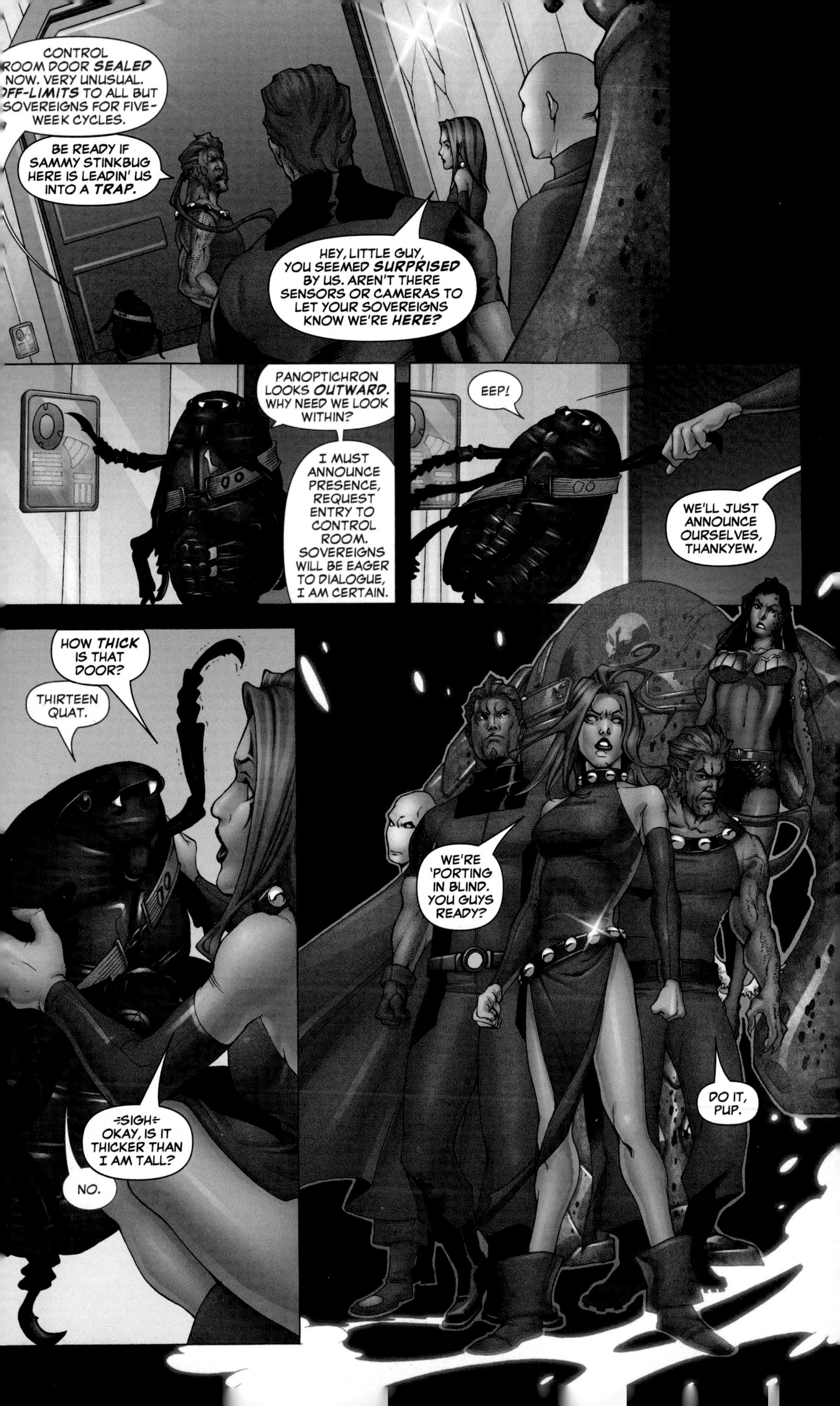

CONTROL ROOM DOOR SEALED NOW. VERY UNUSUAL. OFF-LIMITS TO ALL BUT SOVEREIGNS FOR FIVE-WEEK CYCLES.
BE READY IF SAMMY STINKBUG HERE IS LEADIN' US INTO A TRAP.
HEY, LITTLE GUY, YOU SEEMED SURPRISED BY US. AREN'T THERE SENSORS OR CAMERAS TO LET YOUR SOVEREIGNS KNOW WE'RE HERE?
PANOPTICHRON LOOKS OUTWARD. WHY NEED WE LOOK WITHIN?
I MUST ANNOUNCE PRESENCE, REQUEST ENTRY TO CONTROL ROOM. SOVEREIGNS WILL BE EAGER TO DIALOGUE, I AM CERTAIN.
EEP!
WE'LL JUST ANNOUNCE OURSELVES, THANKYEW.
HOW THICK IS THAT DOOR?
THIRTEEN QUAT.
=SIGH= OKAY, IS IT THICKER THAN I AM TALL?
NO.
WE'RE 'PORTING IN BLIND. YOU GUYS READY?
DO IT, PUP.

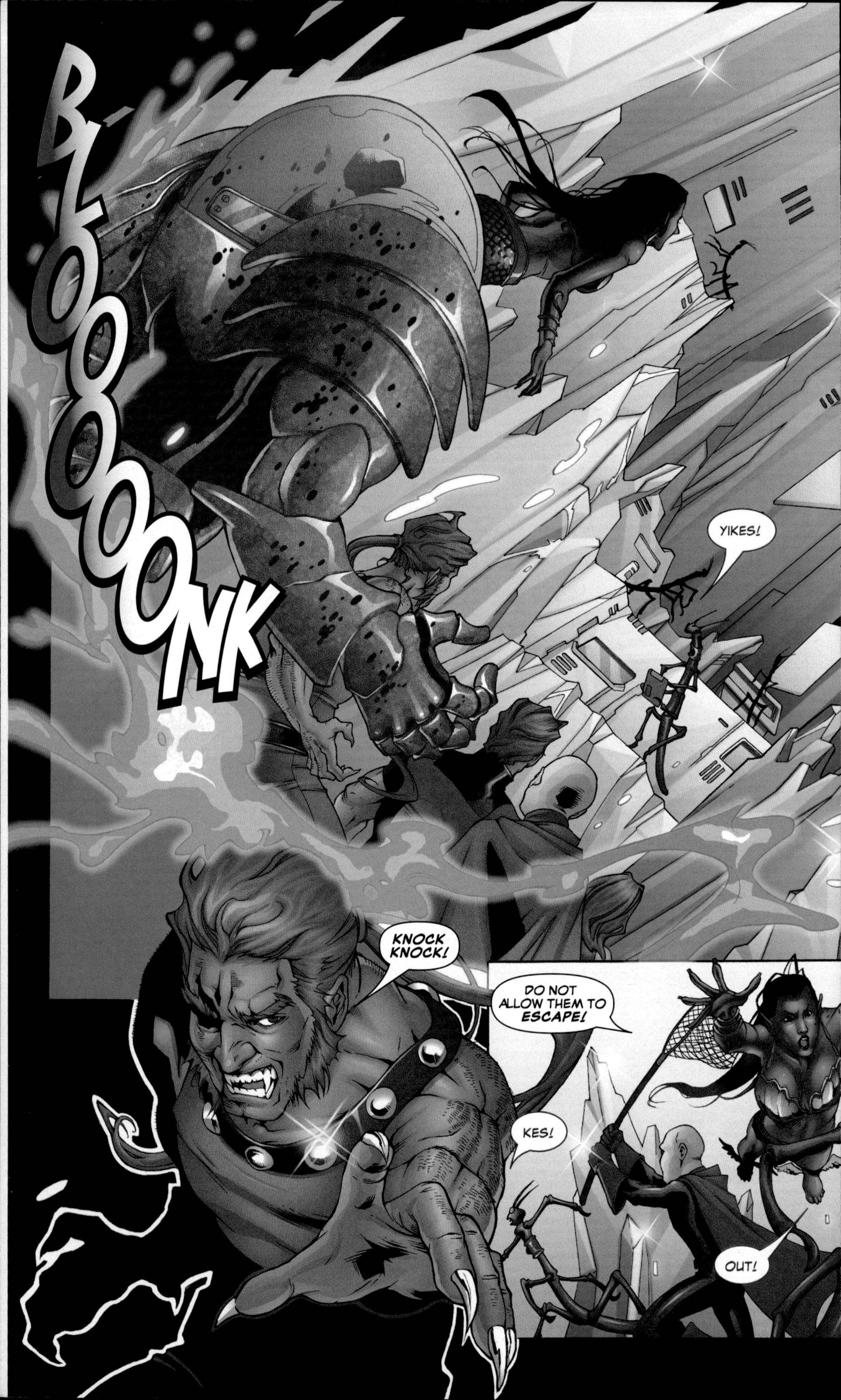
BLOOOOOONK
YIKES!
KNOCK KNOCK!
DO NOT ALLOW THEM TO *ESCAPE!*
KES!
OUT!

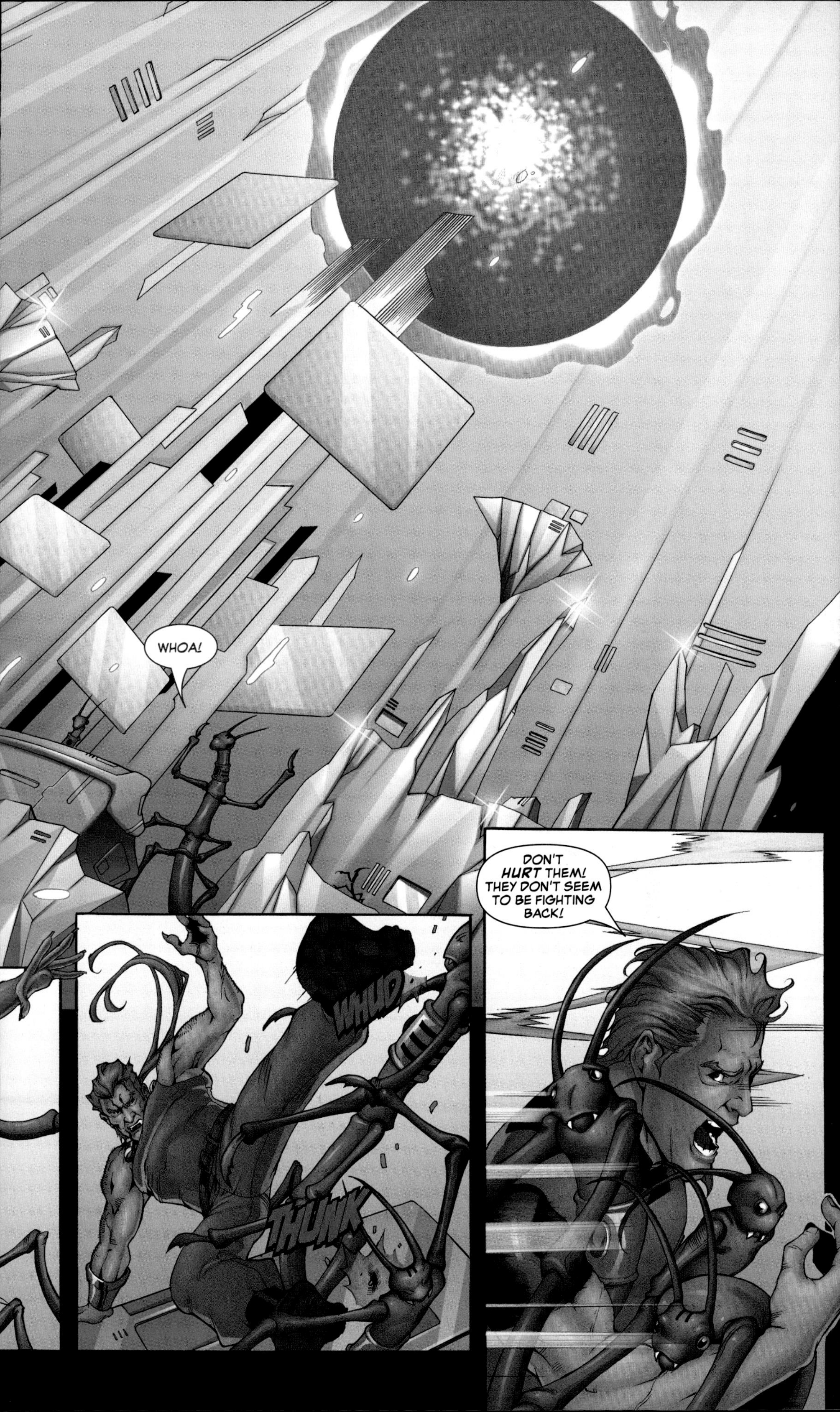
WHOA!
DON'T HURT THEM! THEY DON'T SEEM TO BE FIGHTING BACK!
WHUD
THUNK

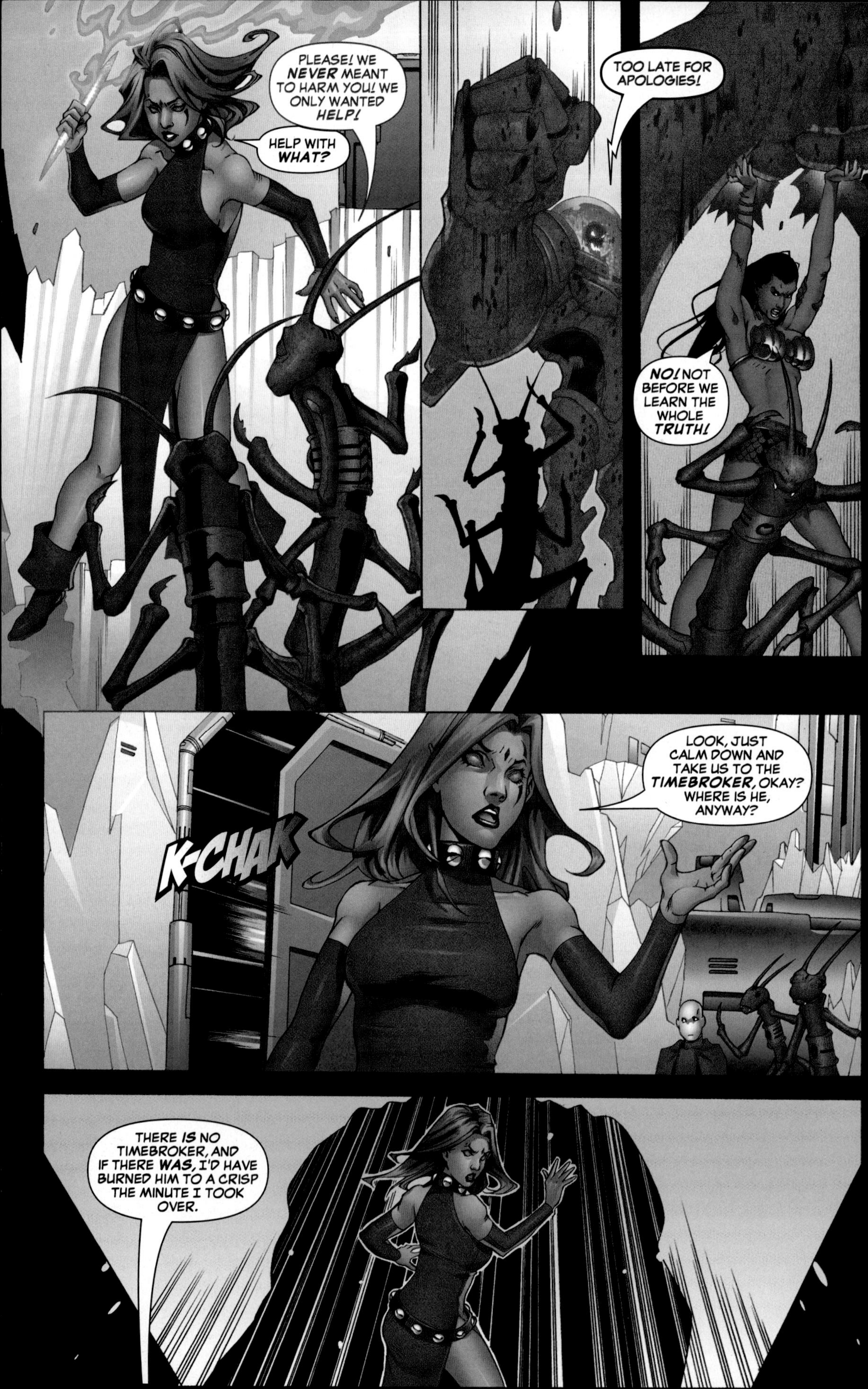
PLEASE! WE NEVER MEANT TO HARM YOU! WE ONLY WANTED HELP!
HELP WITH WHAT?
TOO LATE FOR APOLOGIES!
NO! NOT BEFORE WE LEARN THE WHOLE TRUTH!
LOOK, JUST CALM DOWN AND TAKE US TO THE TIMEBROKER, OKAY? WHERE IS HE, ANYWAY?
K-CHAK
THERE IS NO TIMEBROKER, AND IF THERE WAS, I'D HAVE BURNED HIM TO A CRISP THE MINUTE I TOOK OVER.

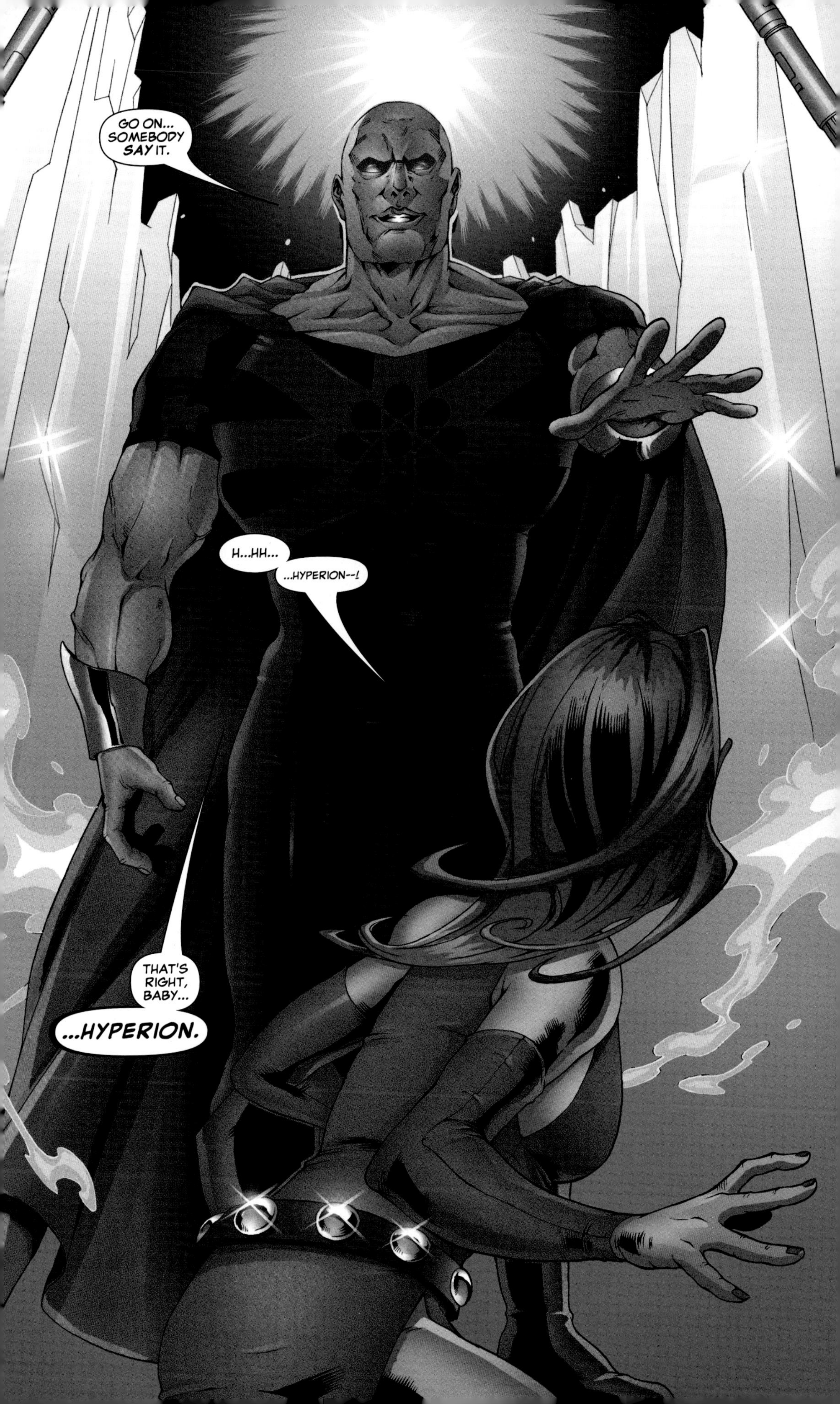
GO ON... SOMEBODY SAY IT.
H...HH...
...HYPERION--!
THAT'S RIGHT, BABY...
...HYPERION.

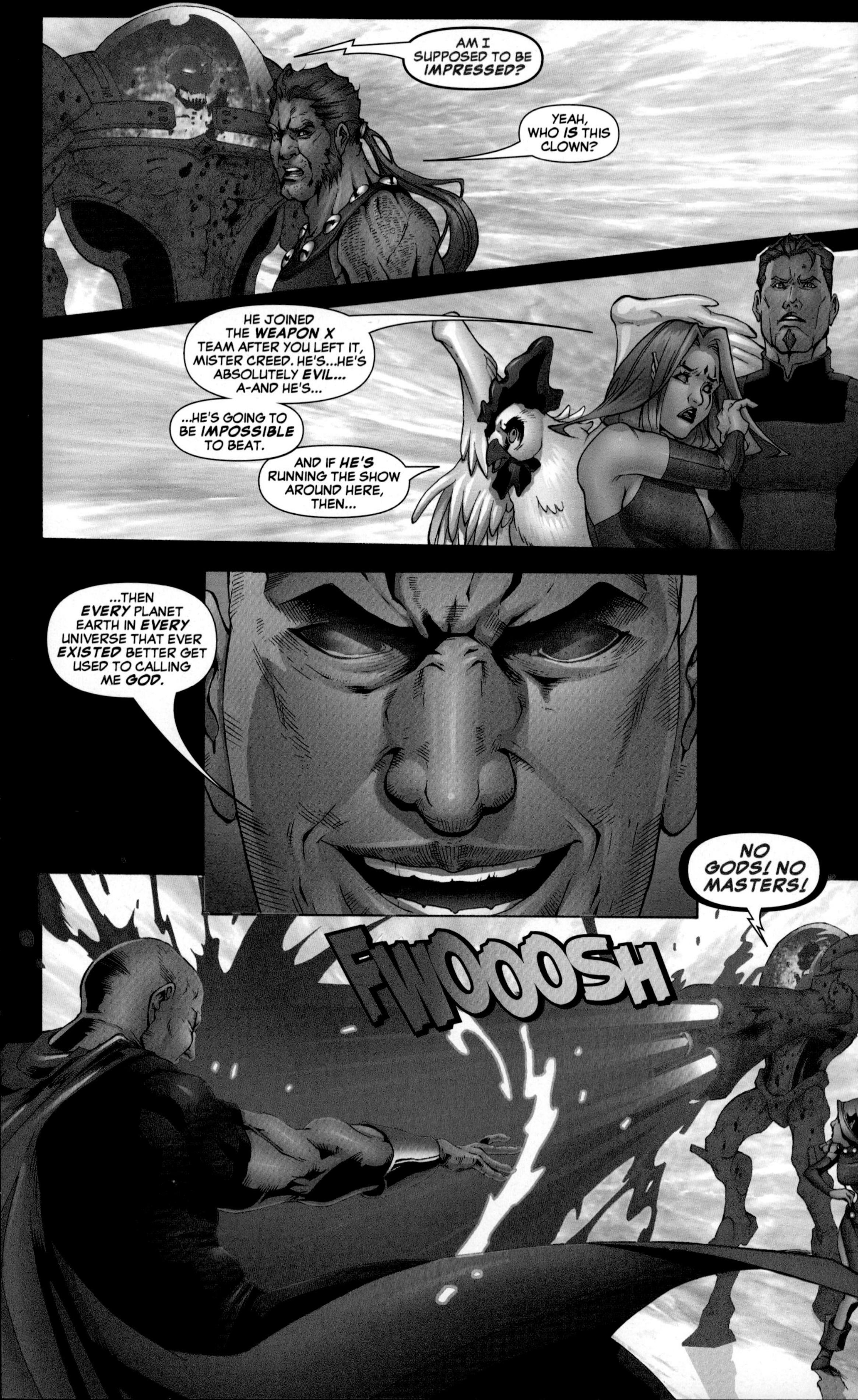
AM I SUPPOSED TO BE IMPRESSED?
YEAH, WHO IS THIS CLOWN?
HE JOINED THE WEAPON X TEAM AFTER YOU LEFT IT, MISTER CREED. HE'S...HE'S ABSOLUTELY EVIL... A-AND HE'S...
...HE'S GOING TO BE IMPOSSIBLE TO BEAT.
AND IF HE'S RUNNING THE SHOW AROUND HERE, THEN...
...THEN EVERY PLANET EARTH IN EVERY UNIVERSE THAT EVER EXISTED BETTER GET USED TO CALLING ME GOD.
NO GODS! NO MASTERS!
FWOOOSH

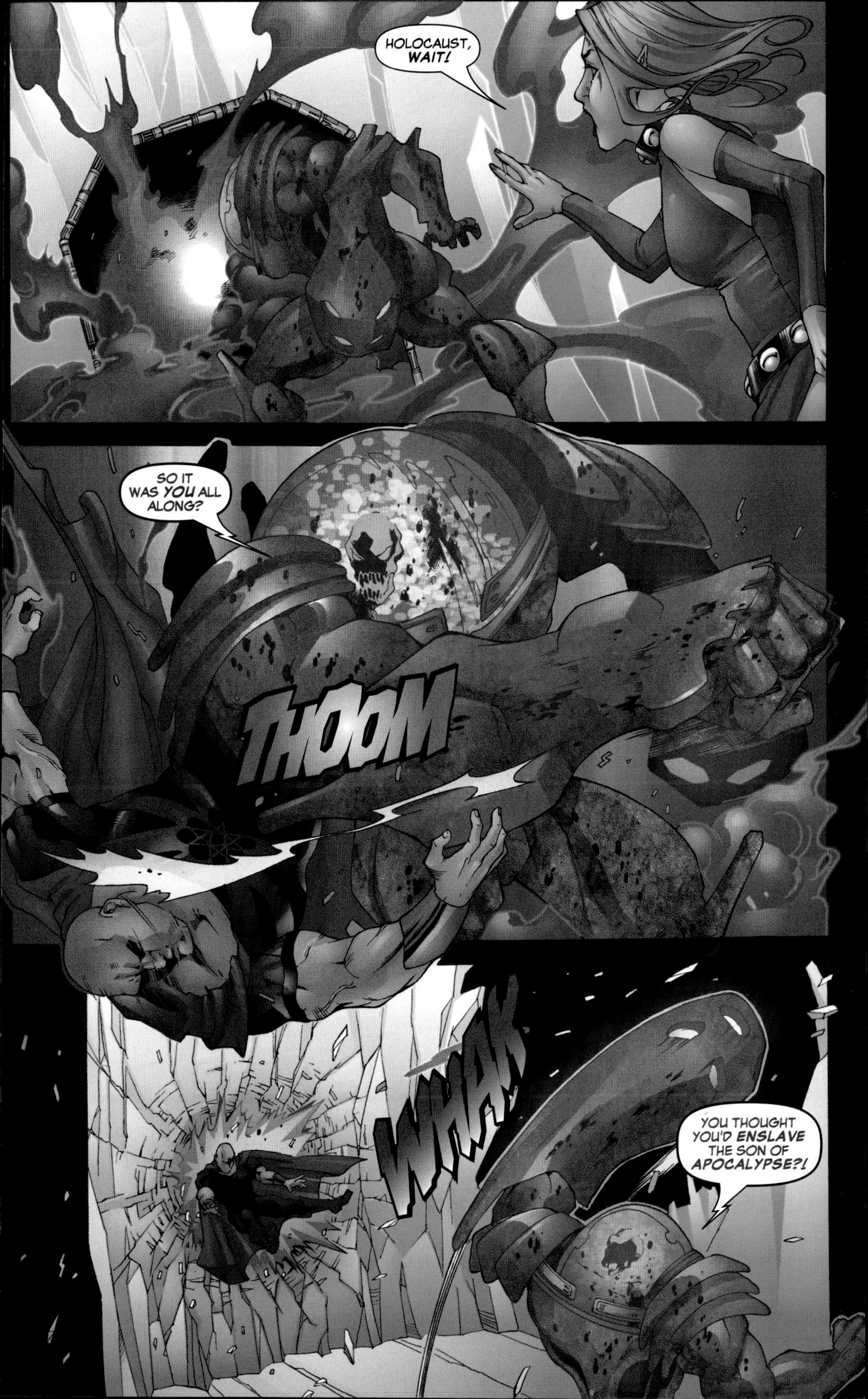
HOLOCAUST, WAIT!
SO IT WAS YOU ALL ALONG?
THOOM
WHAK
YOU THOUGHT YOU'D ENSLAVE THE SON OF APOCALYPSE?!

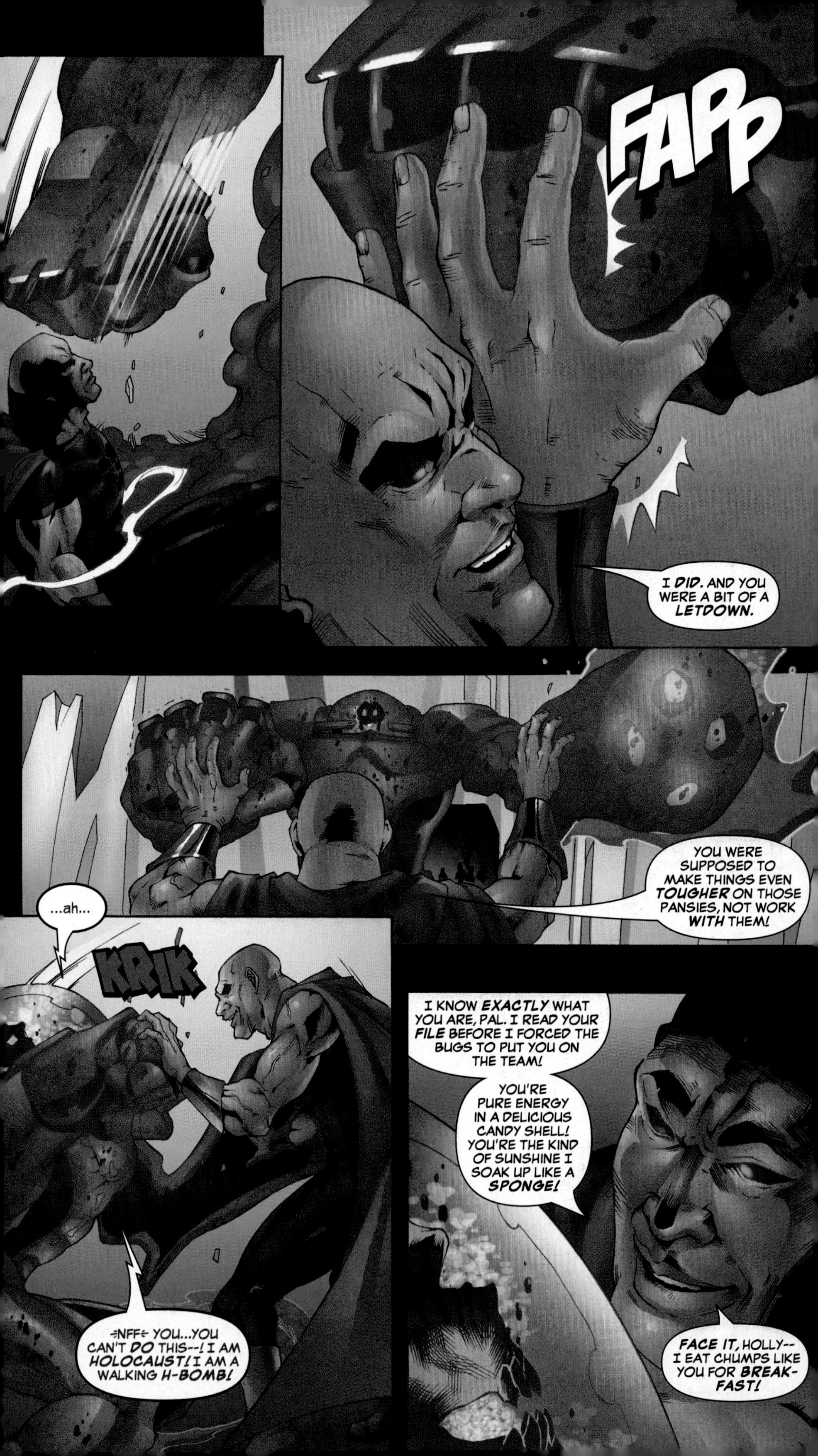
FAPP
I DID. AND YOU WERE A BIT OF A LETDOWN.
YOU WERE SUPPOSED TO MAKE THINGS EVEN TOUGHER ON THOSE PANSIES, NOT WORK WITH THEM!
...ah...
KRIK
=NFF= YOU...YOU CAN'T DO THIS--! I AM HOLOCAUST! I AM A WALKING H-BOMB!
I KNOW EXACTLY WHAT YOU ARE, PAL. I READ YOUR FILE BEFORE I FORCED THE BUGS TO PUT YOU ON THE TEAM!
YOU'RE PURE ENERGY IN A DELICIOUS CANDY SHELL! YOU'RE THE KIND OF SUNSHINE I SOAK UP LIKE A SPONGE!
FACE IT, HOLLY-- I EAT CHUMPS LIKE YOU FOR BREAK-FAST!

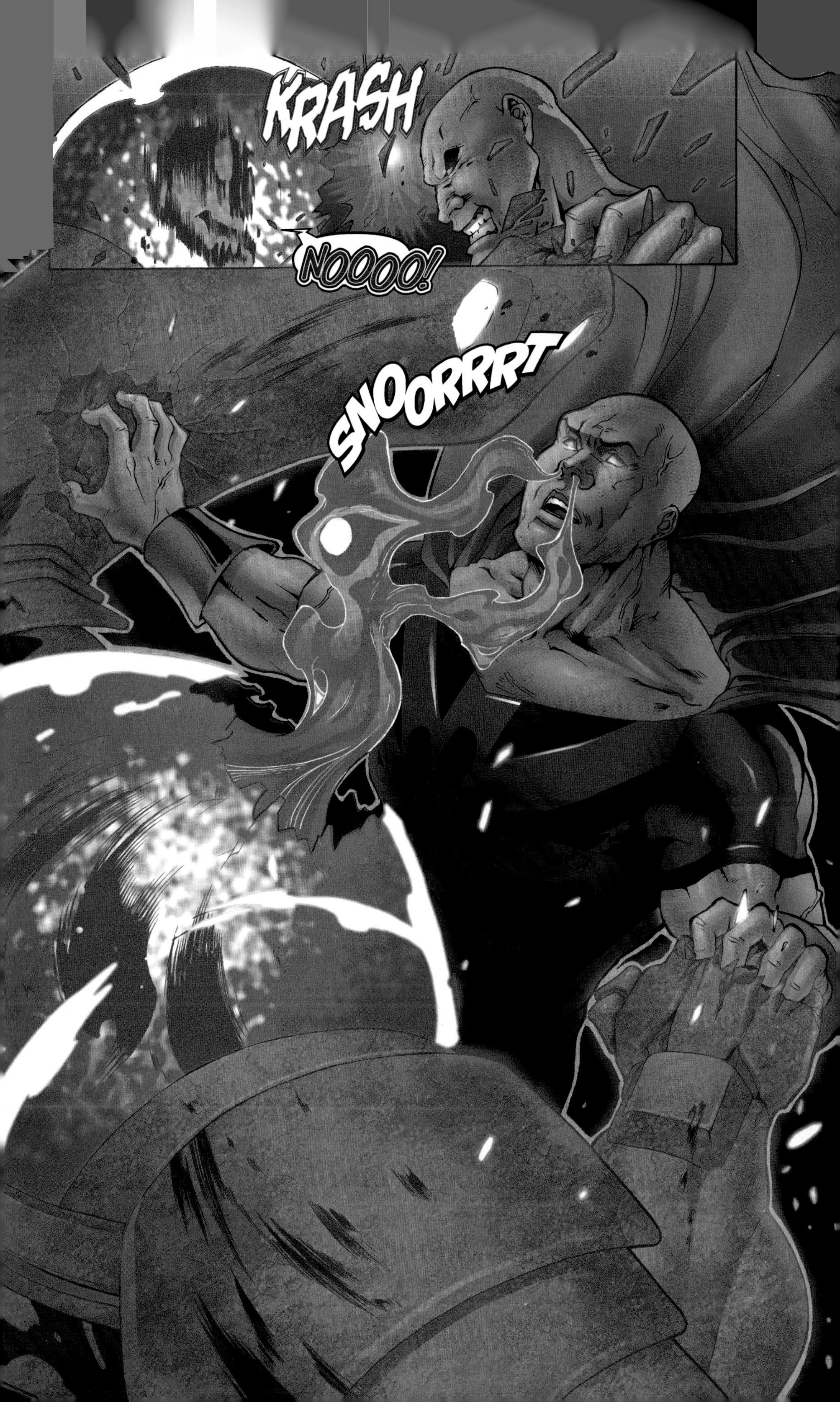
KRASH
NOOOO!
SNOORRRT

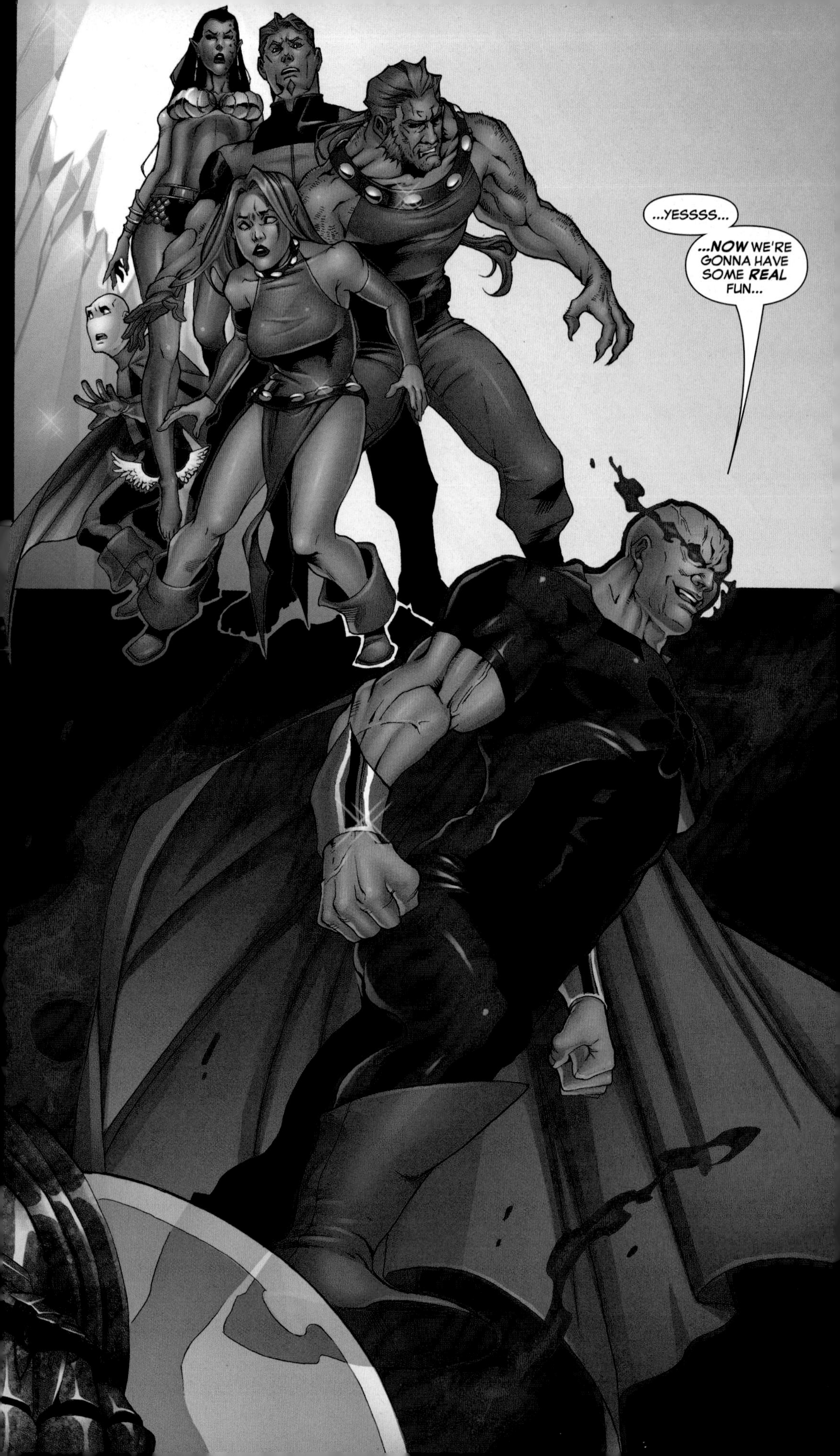
...YESSSS...
...NOW WE'RE GONNA HAVE SOME REAL FUN...

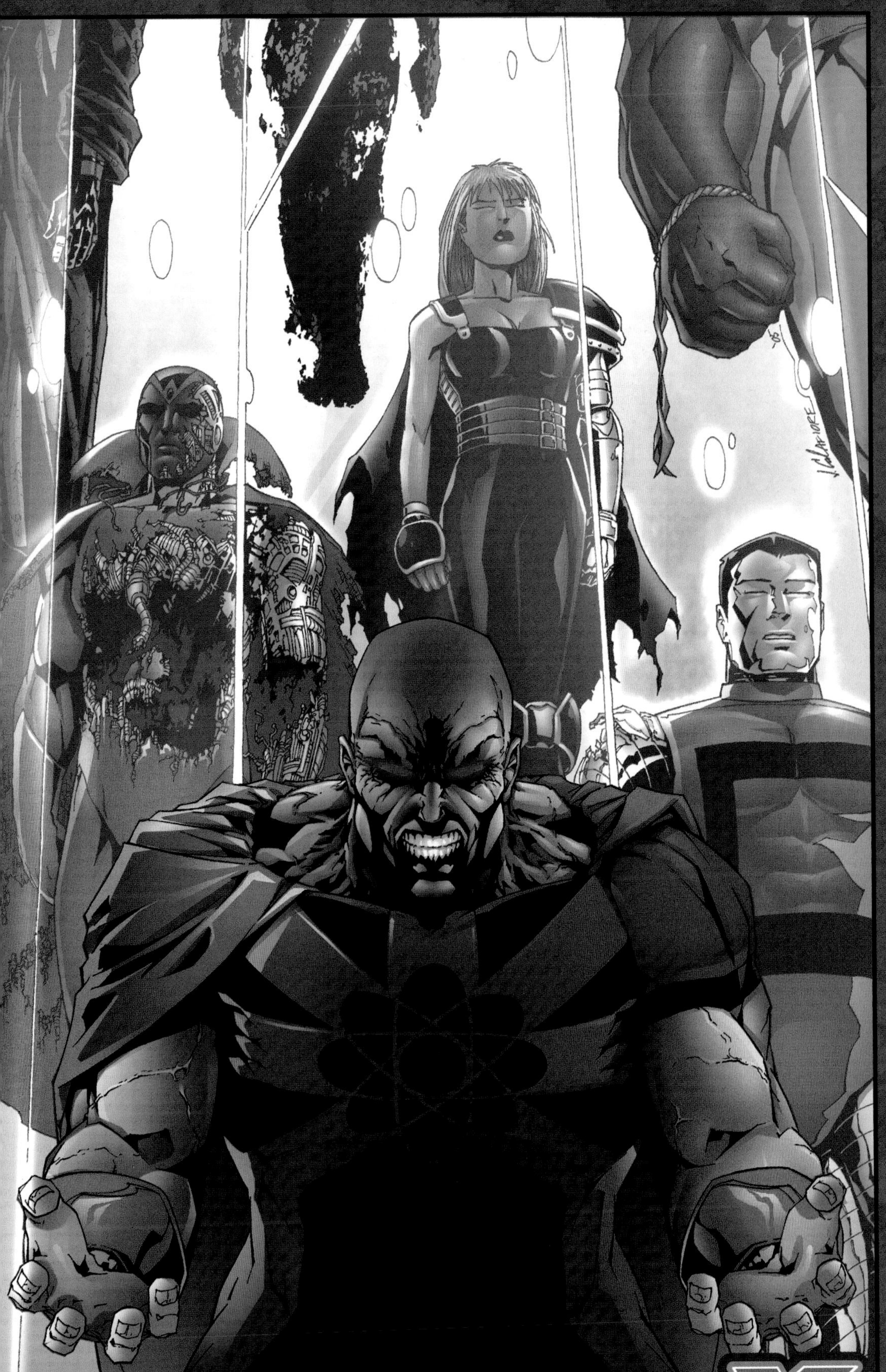

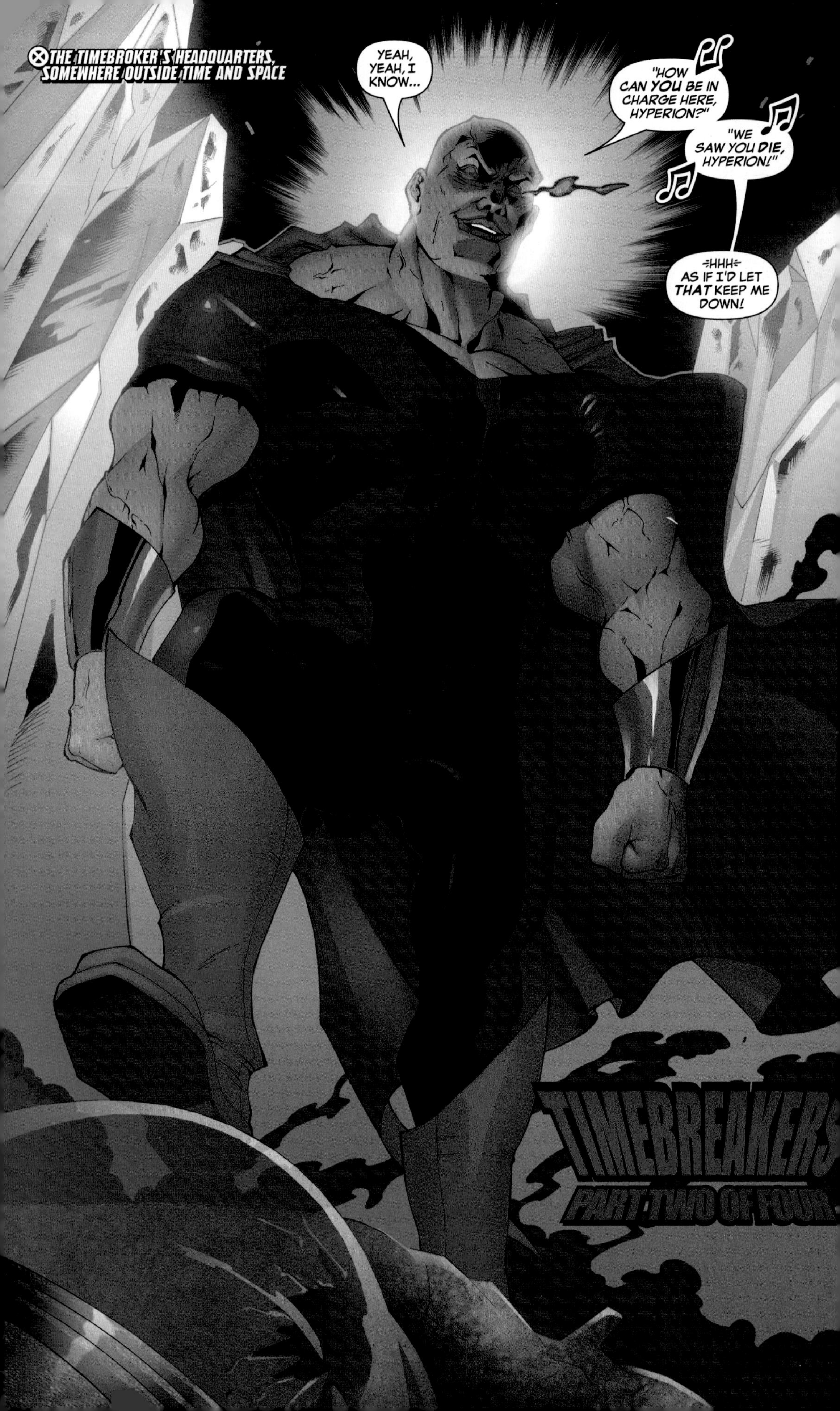
THE TIMEBROKER'S HEADQUARTERS, SOMEWHERE OUTSIDE TIME AND SPACE
YEAH, YEAH, I KNOW...
"HOW CAN YOU BE IN CHARGE HERE, HYPERION?"
"WE SAW YOU DIE, HYPERION!"
=HHH= AS IF I'D LET THAT KEEP ME DOWN!
TIMEBREAKERS
PART TWO OF FOUR

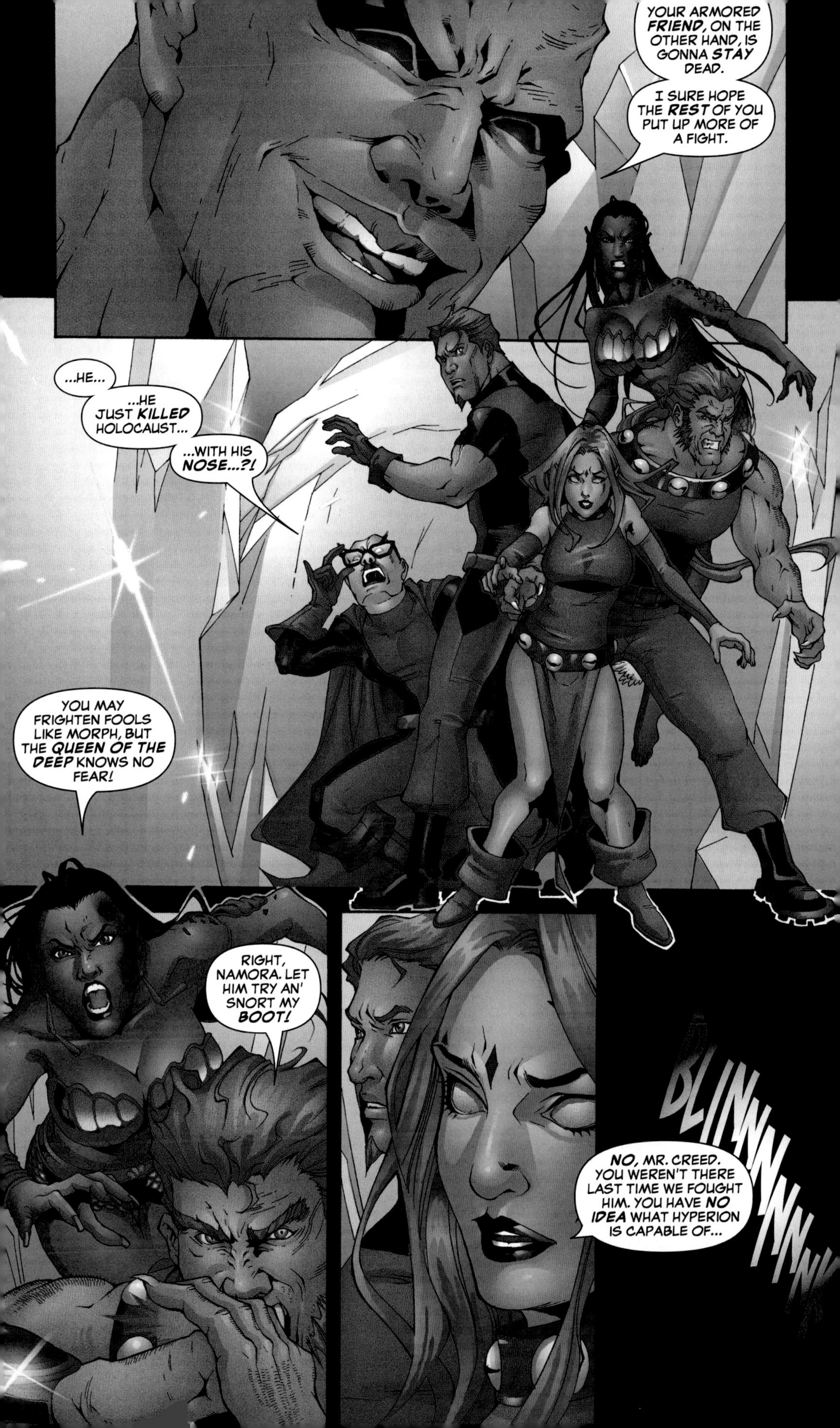
YOUR ARMORED FRIEND, ON THE OTHER HAND, IS GONNA STAY DEAD.
I SURE HOPE THE REST OF YOU PUT UP MORE OF A FIGHT.
...HE...
...HE JUST KILLED HOLOCAUST...
...WITH HIS NOSE...?!
YOU MAY FRIGHTEN FOOLS LIKE MORPH, BUT THE QUEEN OF THE DEEP KNOWS NO FEAR!
RIGHT, NAMORA. LET HIM TRY AN' SNORT MY BOOT!
BLINNNNNNK
NO, MR. CREED. YOU WEREN'T THERE LAST TIME WE FOUGHT HIM. YOU HAVE NO IDEA WHAT HYPERION IS CAPABLE OF...

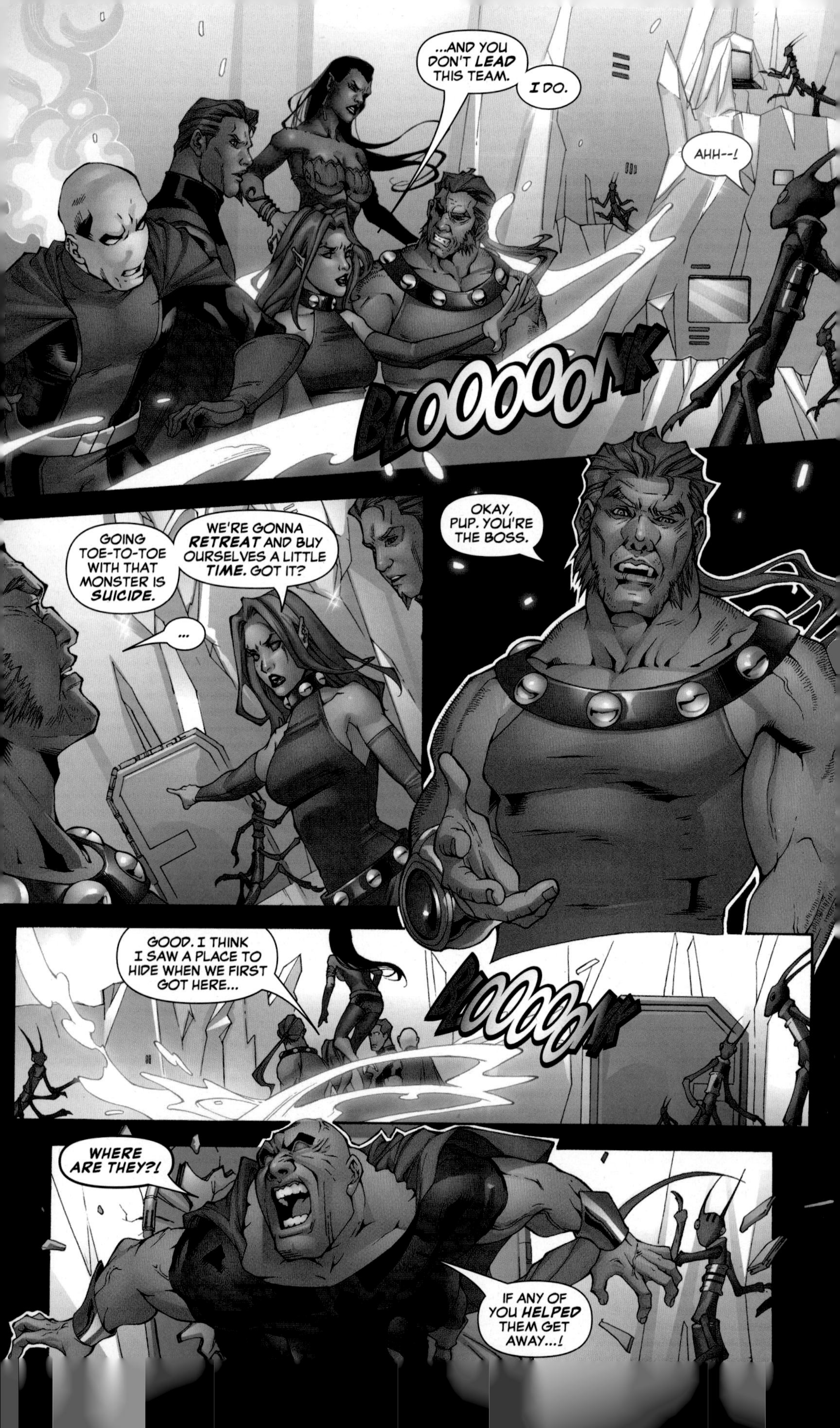
...AND YOU DON'T LEAD THIS TEAM.
I DO.
AHH--!
BLOOOOOOM
GOING TOE-TO-TOE WITH THAT MONSTER IS SUICIDE.
WE'RE GONNA RETREAT AND BUY OURSELVES A LITTLE TIME. GOT IT?
...
OKAY, PUP. YOU'RE THE BOSS.
GOOD. I THINK I SAW A PLACE TO HIDE WHEN WE FIRST GOT HERE...
WHERE ARE THEY?!
IF ANY OF YOU HELPED THEM GET AWAY...!

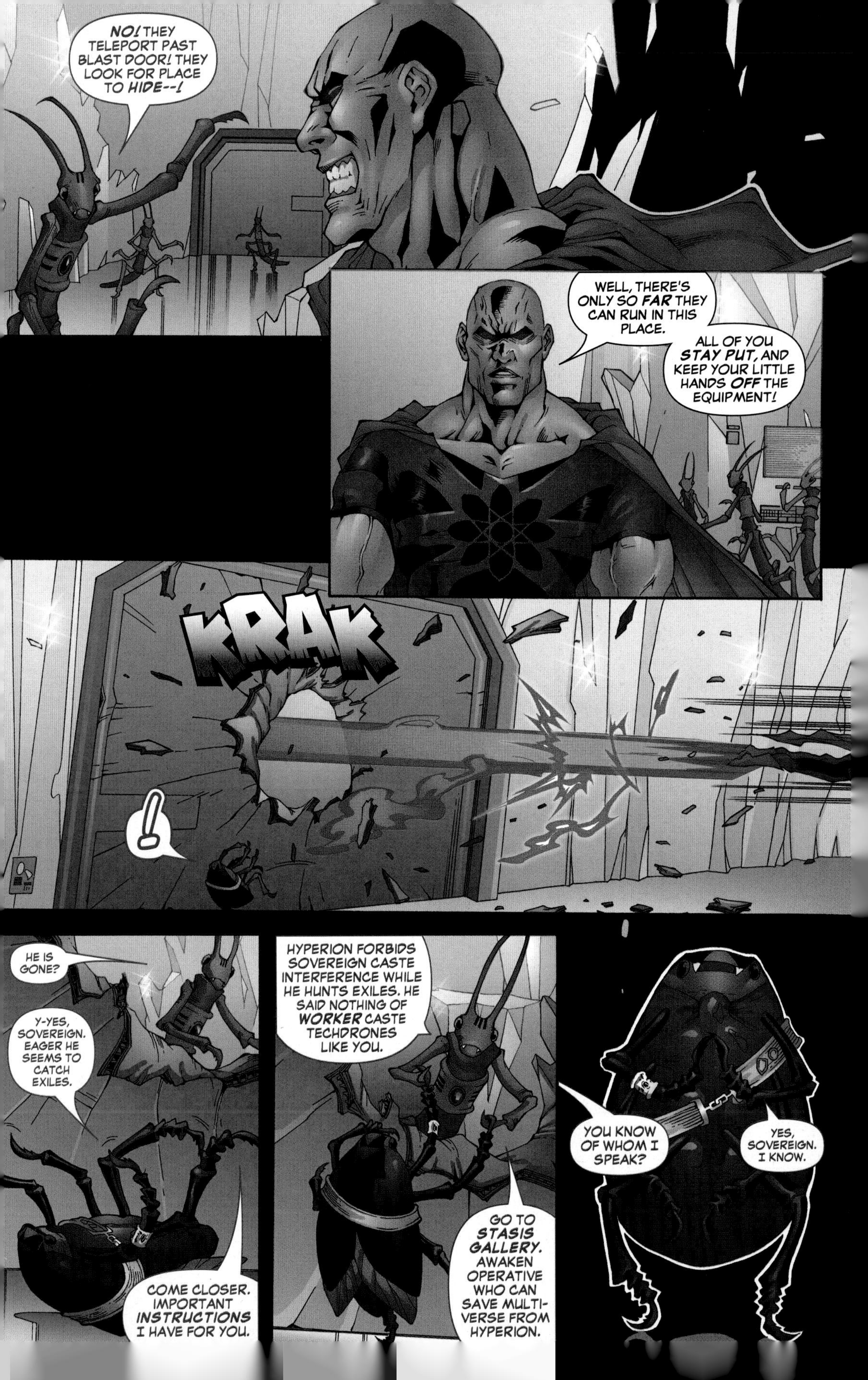
NO! THEY TELEPORT PAST BLAST DOOR! THEY LOOK FOR PLACE TO HIDE--!
WELL, THERE'S ONLY SO FAR THEY CAN RUN IN THIS PLACE.
ALL OF YOU STAY PUT, AND KEEP YOUR LITTLE HANDS OFF THE EQUIPMENT!
KRAK
!
HE IS GONE?
Y-YES, SOVEREIGN. EAGER HE SEEMS TO CATCH EXILES.
COME CLOSER. IMPORTANT INSTRUCTIONS I HAVE FOR YOU.
HYPERION FORBIDS SOVEREIGN CASTE INTERFERENCE WHILE HE HUNTS EXILES. HE SAID NOTHING OF WORKER CASTE TECHDRONES LIKE YOU.
GO TO STASIS GALLERY. AWAKEN OPERATIVE WHO CAN SAVE MULTI-VERSE FROM HYPERION.
YOU KNOW OF WHOM I SPEAK?
YES, SOVEREIGN. I KNOW.

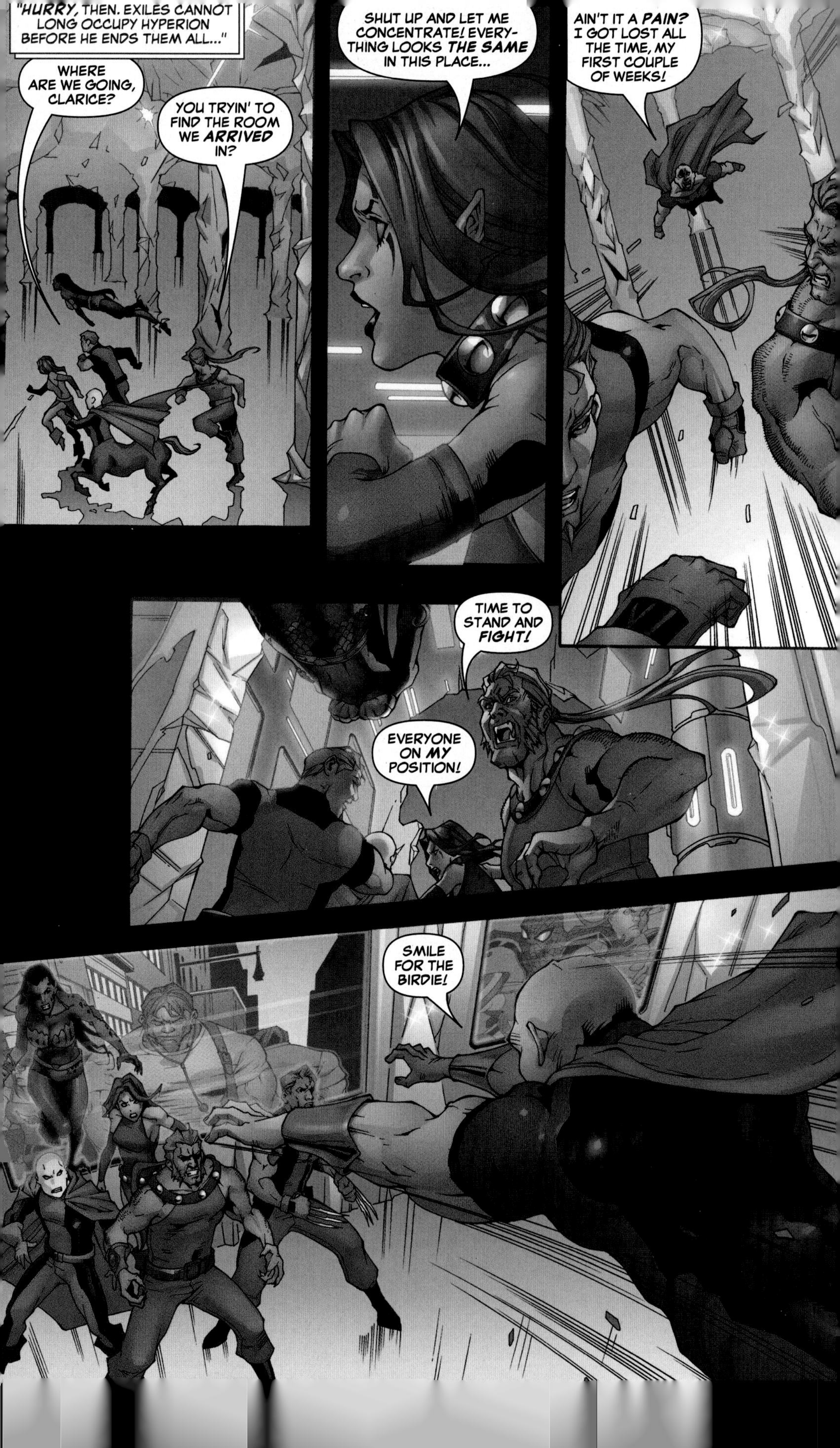
"HURRY, THEN. EXILES CANNOT LONG OCCUPY HYPERION BEFORE HE ENDS THEM ALL..."
WHERE ARE WE GOING, CLARICE?
YOU TRYIN' TO FIND THE ROOM WE ARRIVED IN?
SHUT UP AND LET ME CONCENTRATE! EVERY-THING LOOKS THE SAME IN THIS PLACE...
AIN'T IT A PAIN? I GOT LOST ALL THE TIME, MY FIRST COUPLE OF WEEKS!
TIME TO STAND AND FIGHT!
EVERYONE ON MY POSITION!
SMILE FOR THE BIRDIE!

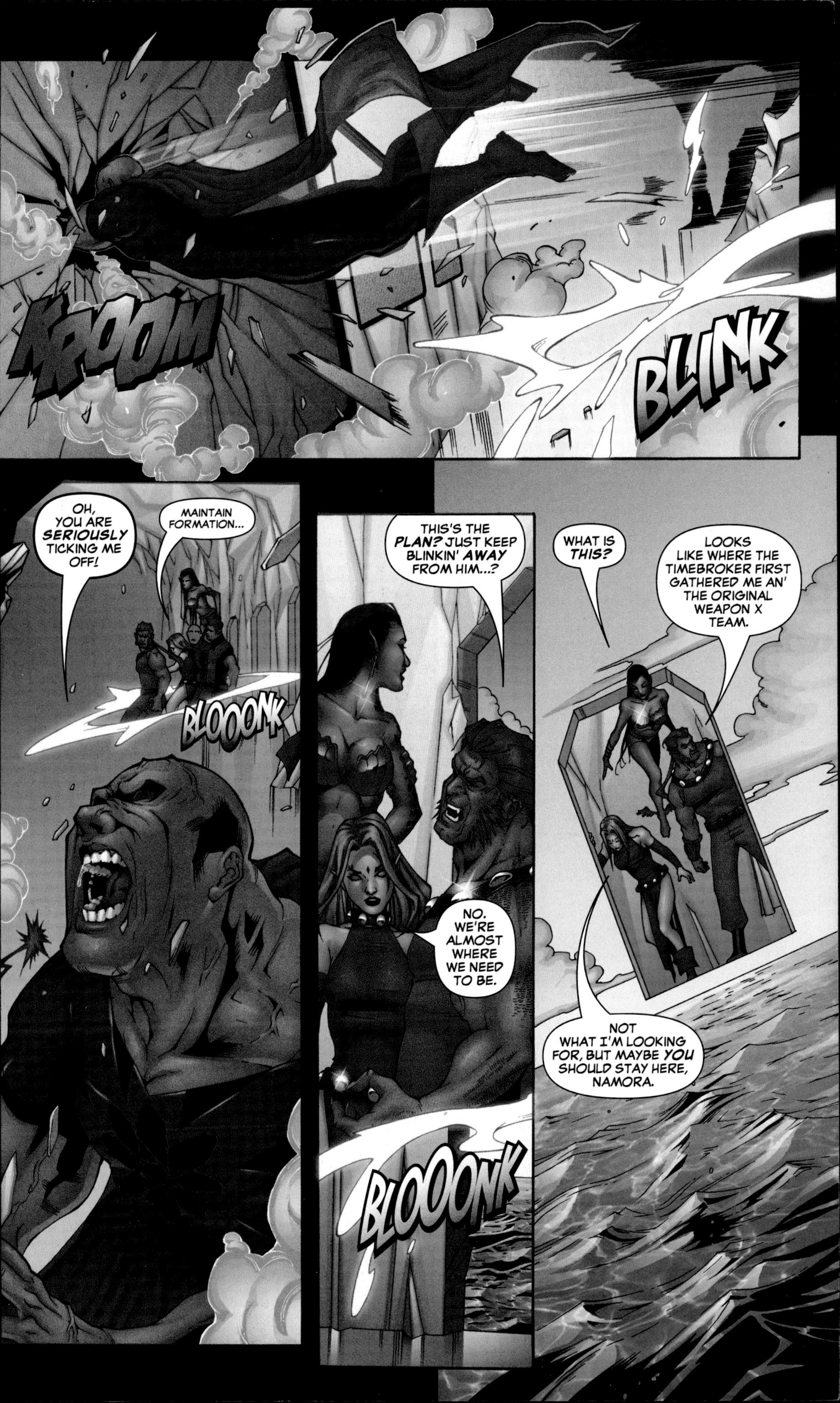
KROOM
BLINK
OH, YOU ARE SERIOUSLY TICKING ME OFF!
MAINTAIN FORMATION...
BLOOONK
THIS'S THE PLAN? JUST KEEP BLINKIN' AWAY FROM HIM...?
NO. WE'RE ALMOST WHERE WE NEED TO BE.
BLOOONK
WHAT IS THIS?
LOOKS LIKE WHERE THE TIMEBROKER FIRST GATHERED ME AN' THE ORIGINAL WEAPON X TEAM.
NOT WHAT I'M LOOKING FOR, BUT MAYBE YOU SHOULD STAY HERE, NAMORA.

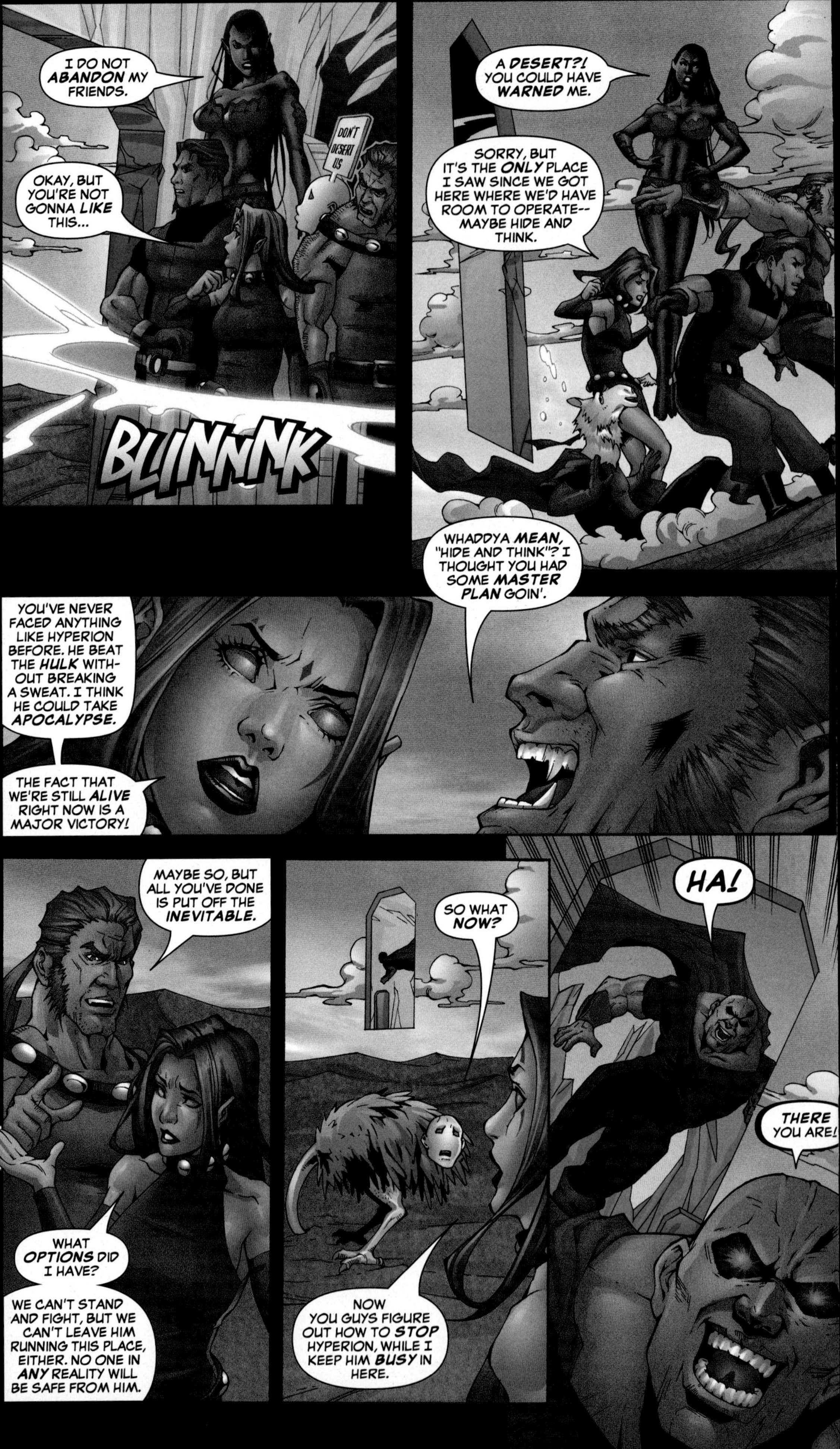
I DO NOT ABANDON MY FRIENDS.
DON'T DESERT US
OKAY, BUT YOU'RE NOT GONNA LIKE THIS...
BLINNNK
A DESERT?! YOU COULD HAVE WARNED ME.
SORRY, BUT IT'S THE ONLY PLACE I SAW SINCE WE GOT HERE WHERE WE'D HAVE ROOM TO OPERATE-- MAYBE HIDE AND THINK.
WHADDYA MEAN, "HIDE AND THINK"? I THOUGHT YOU HAD SOME MASTER PLAN GOIN'.
YOU'VE NEVER FACED ANYTHING LIKE HYPERION BEFORE. HE BEAT THE HULK WITH-OUT BREAKING A SWEAT. I THINK HE COULD TAKE APOCALYPSE.
THE FACT THAT WE'RE STILL ALIVE RIGHT NOW IS A MAJOR VICTORY!
MAYBE SO, BUT ALL YOU'VE DONE IS PUT OFF THE INEVITABLE.
WHAT OPTIONS DID I HAVE?
WE CAN'T STAND AND FIGHT, BUT WE CAN'T LEAVE HIM RUNNING THIS PLACE, EITHER. NO ONE IN ANY REALITY WILL BE SAFE FROM HIM.
SO WHAT NOW?
NOW YOU GUYS FIGURE OUT HOW TO STOP HYPERION, WHILE I KEEP HIM BUSY IN HERE.
HA!
THERE YOU ARE!

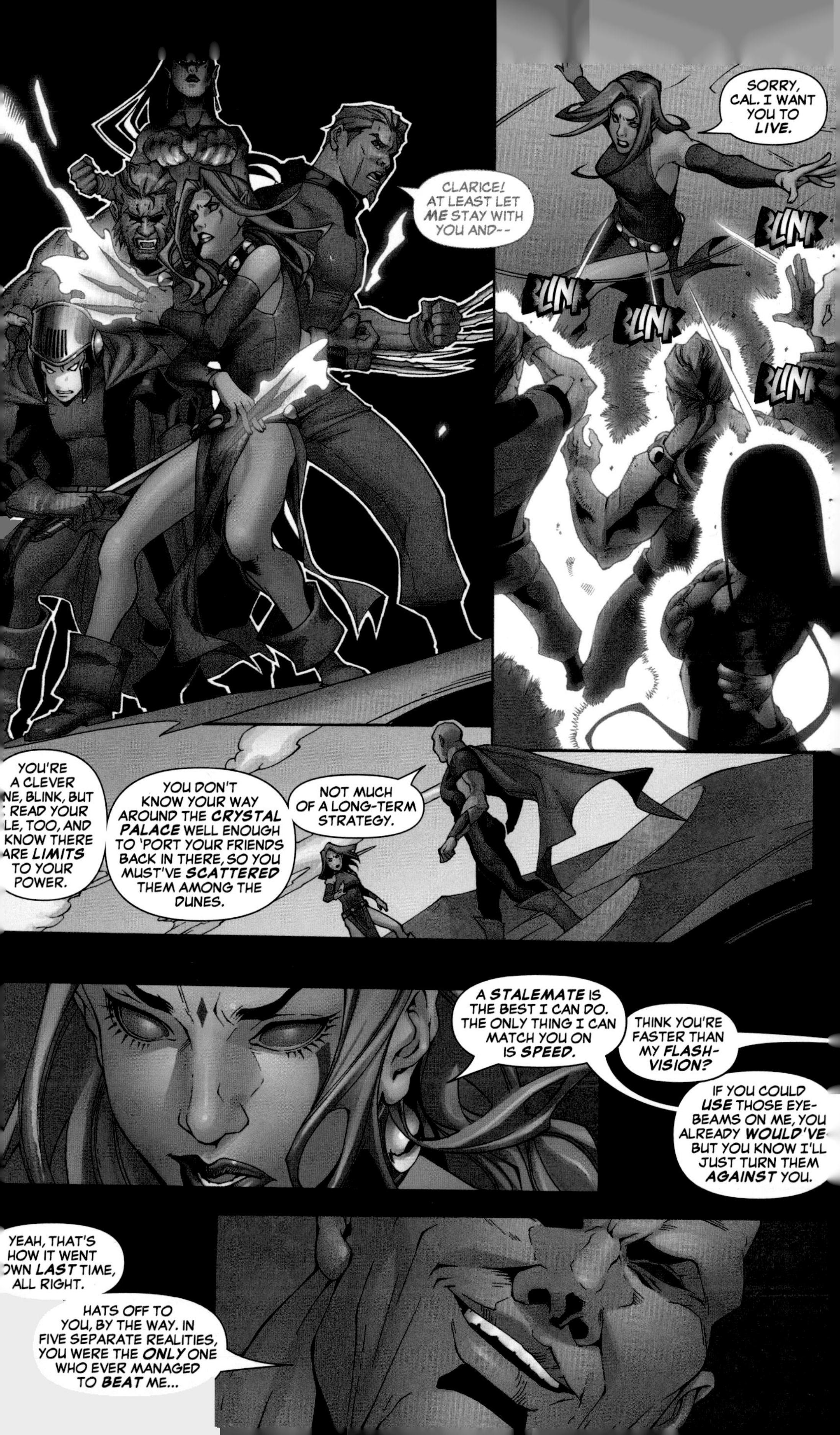

CLARICE! AT LEAST LET ME STAY WITH YOU AND--
SORRY, CAL. I WANT YOU TO LIVE.
BLINK
BLINK
BLINK
BLINK
YOU'RE A CLEVER NE, BLINK, BUT READ YOUR LE, TOO, AND KNOW THERE ARE LIMITS TO YOUR POWER.
YOU DON'T KNOW YOUR WAY AROUND THE CRYSTAL PALACE WELL ENOUGH TO 'PORT YOUR FRIENDS BACK IN THERE, SO YOU MUST'VE SCATTERED THEM AMONG THE DUNES.
NOT MUCH OF A LONG-TERM STRATEGY.
A STALEMATE IS THE BEST I CAN DO. THE ONLY THING I CAN MATCH YOU ON IS SPEED.
THINK YOU'RE FASTER THAN MY FLASH-VISION?
IF YOU COULD USE THOSE EYE-BEAMS ON ME, YOU ALREADY WOULD'VE BUT YOU KNOW I'LL JUST TURN THEM AGAINST YOU.
YEAH, THAT'S HOW IT WENT WN LAST TIME, ALL RIGHT.
HATS OFF TO YOU, BY THE WAY. IN FIVE SEPARATE REALITIES, YOU WERE THE ONLY ONE WHO EVER MANAGED TO BEAT ME...

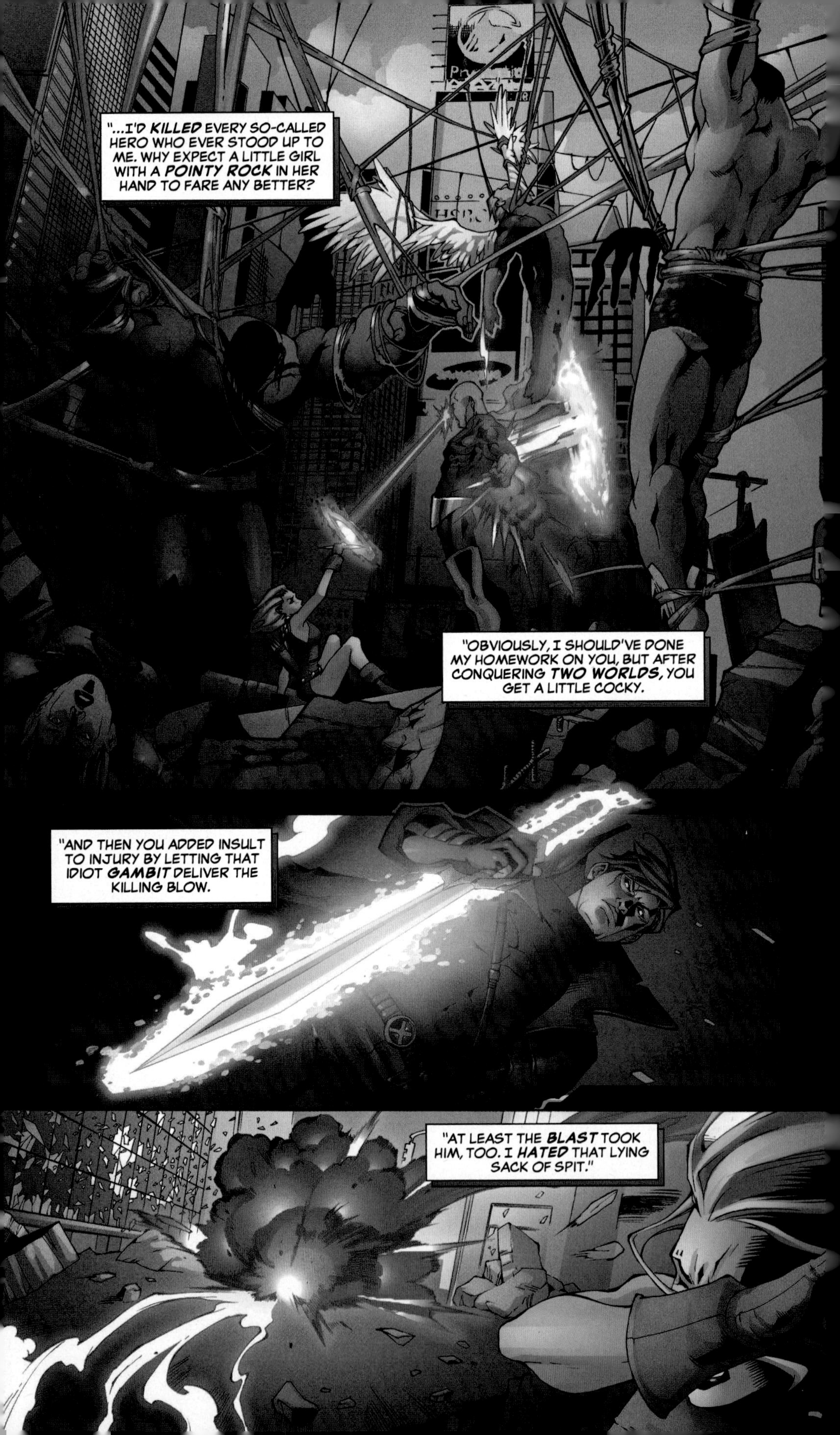
"...I'D KILLED EVERY SO-CALLED HERO WHO EVER STOOD UP TO ME. WHY EXPECT A LITTLE GIRL WITH A POINTY ROCK IN HER HAND TO FARE ANY BETTER?
"OBVIOUSLY, I SHOULD'VE DONE MY HOMEWORK ON YOU, BUT AFTER CONQUERING TWO WORLDS, YOU GET A LITTLE COCKY.
"AND THEN YOU ADDED INSULT TO INJURY BY LETTING THAT IDIOT GAMBIT DELIVER THE KILLING BLOW.
"AT LEAST THE BLAST TOOK HIM, TOO. I HATED THAT LYING SACK OF SPIT."

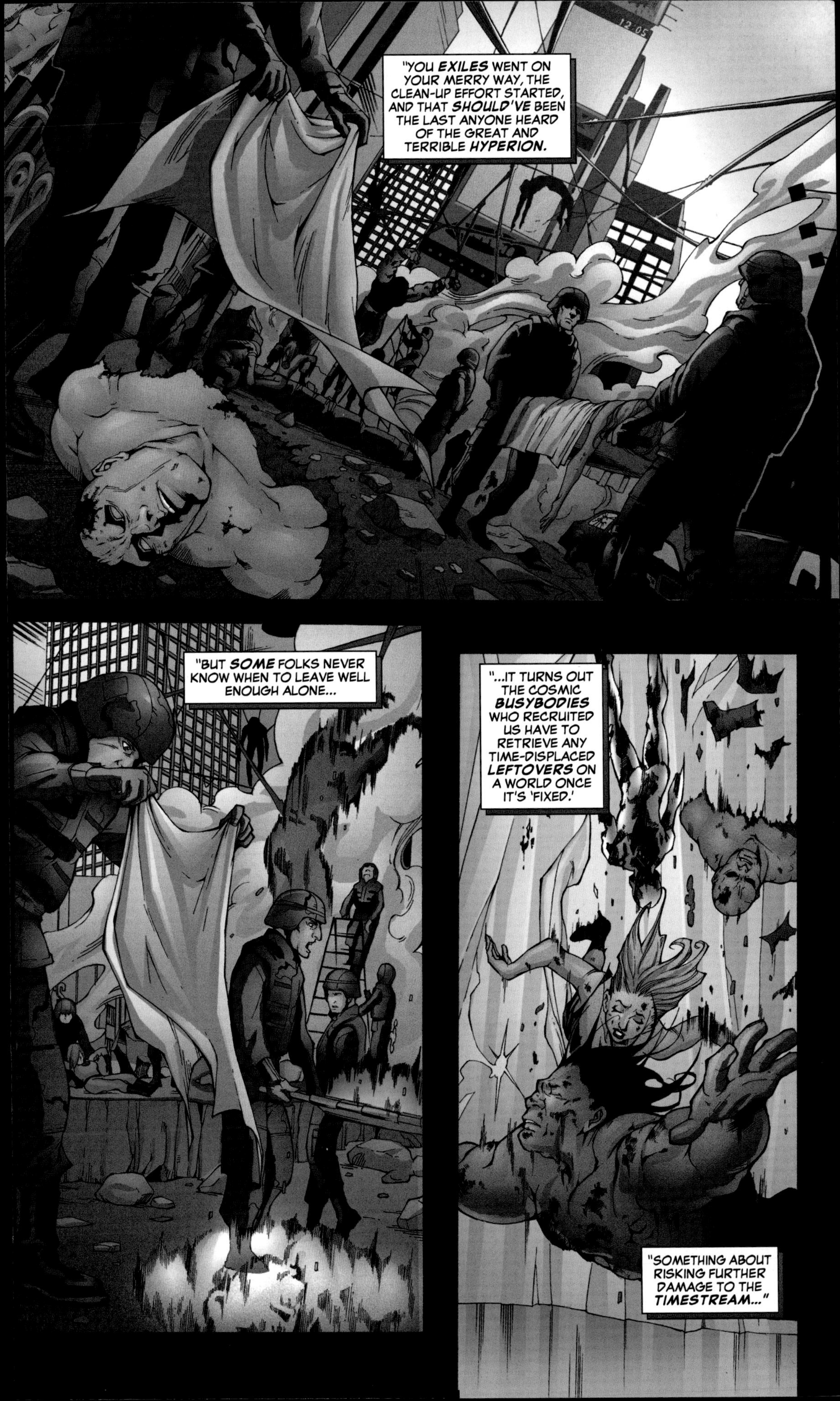
"YOU EXILES WENT ON YOUR MERRY WAY, THE CLEAN-UP EFFORT STARTED, AND THAT SHOULD'VE BEEN THE LAST ANYONE HEARD OF THE GREAT AND TERRIBLE HYPERION.
"BUT SOME FOLKS NEVER KNOW WHEN TO LEAVE WELL ENOUGH ALONE...
"...IT TURNS OUT THE COSMIC BUSYBODIES WHO RECRUITED US HAVE TO RETRIEVE ANY TIME-DISPLACED LEFTOVERS ON A WORLD ONCE IT'S 'FIXED.'
"SOMETHING ABOUT RISKING FURTHER DAMAGE TO THE TIMESTREAM..."

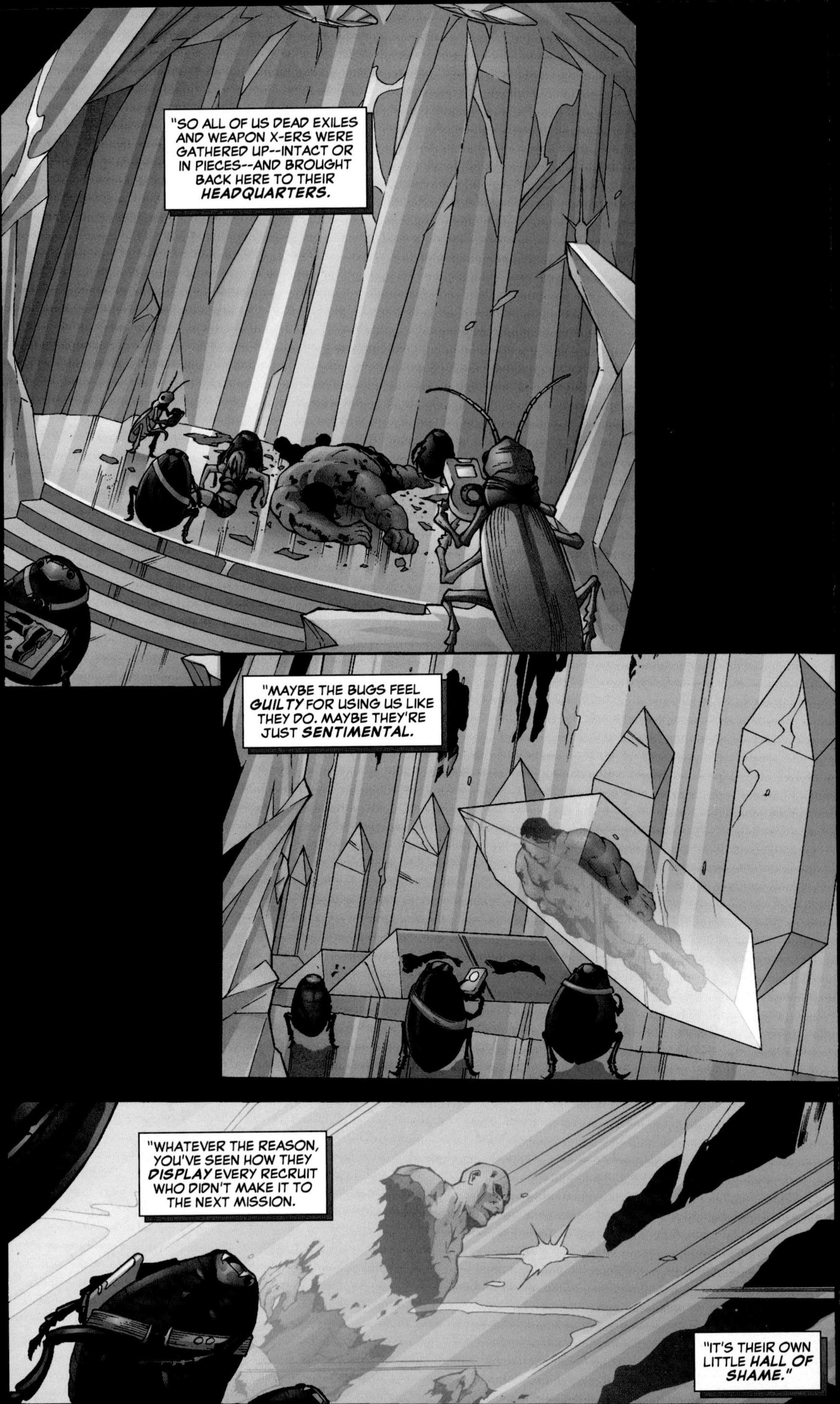

"SO ALL OF US DEAD EXILES AND WEAPON X-ERS WERE GATHERED UP--INTACT OR IN PIECES--AND BROUGHT BACK HERE TO THEIR HEADQUARTERS.
"MAYBE THE BUGS FEEL GUILTY FOR USING US LIKE THEY DO. MAYBE THEY'RE JUST SENTIMENTAL.
"WHATEVER THE REASON, YOU'VE SEEN HOW THEY DISPLAY EVERY RECRUIT WHO DIDN'T MAKE IT TO THE NEXT MISSION.
"IT'S THEIR OWN LITTLE HALL OF SHAME."

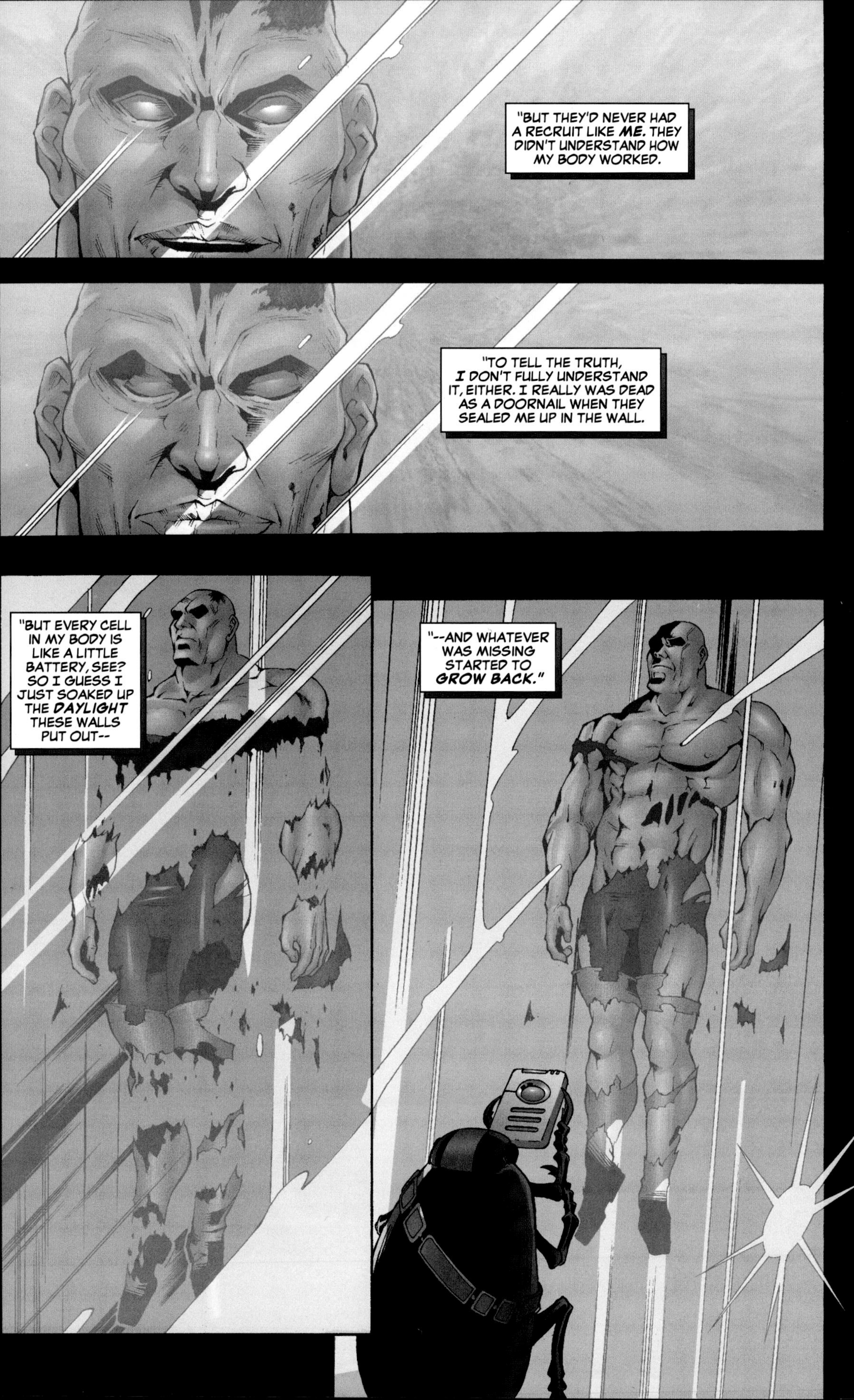
"BUT THEY'D NEVER HAD A RECRUIT LIKE ME. THEY DIDN'T UNDERSTAND HOW MY BODY WORKED.
"TO TELL THE TRUTH, I DON'T FULLY UNDERSTAND IT, EITHER. I REALLY WAS DEAD AS A DOORNAIL WHEN THEY SEALED ME UP IN THE WALL.
"BUT EVERY CELL IN MY BODY IS LIKE A LITTLE BATTERY, SEE? SO I GUESS I JUST SOAKED UP THE DAYLIGHT THESE WALLS PUT OUT--
"--AND WHATEVER WAS MISSING STARTED TO GROW BACK."

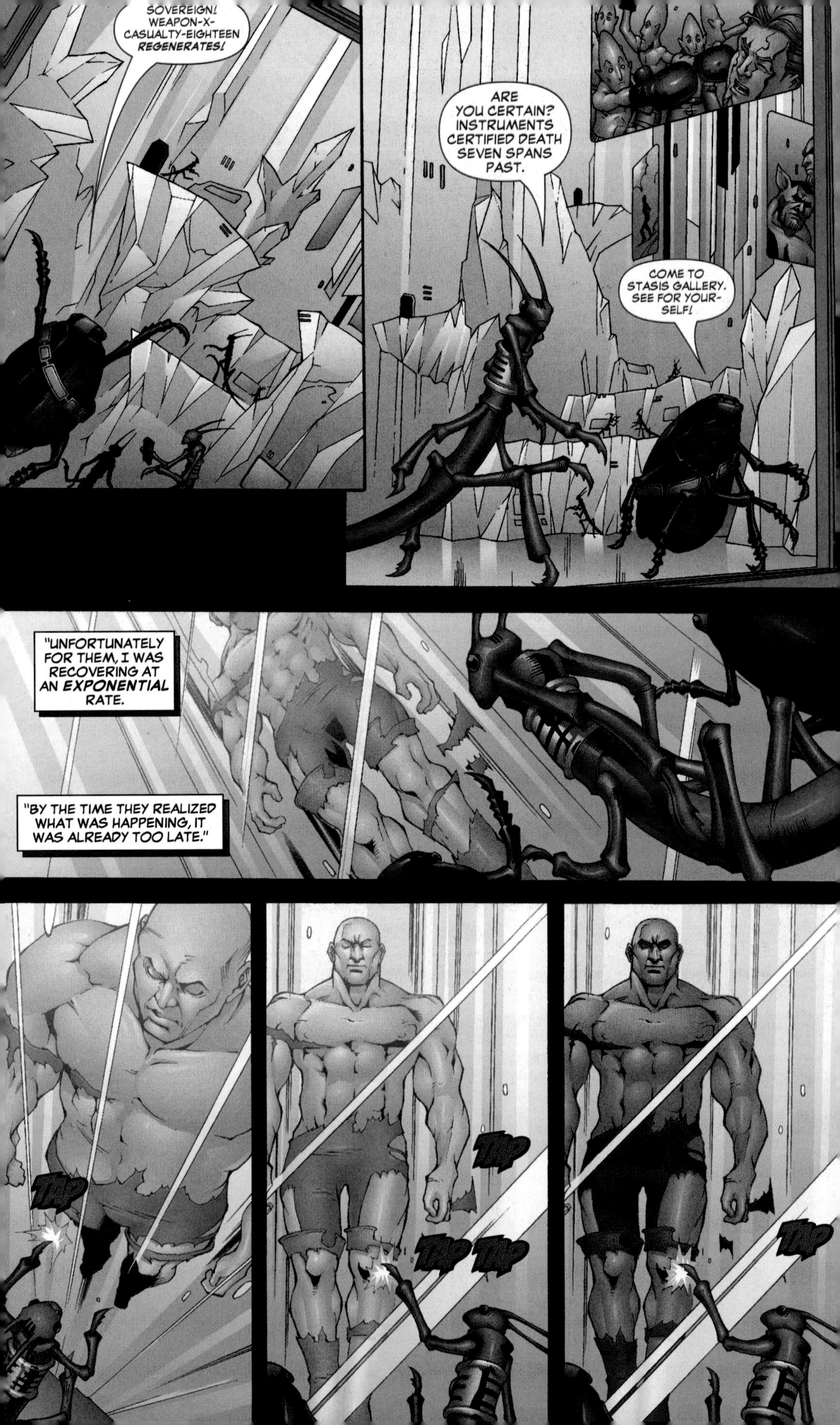
SOVEREIGN! WEAPON-X-CASUALTY-EIGHTEEN REGENERATES!
ARE YOU CERTAIN? INSTRUMENTS CERTIFIED DEATH SEVEN SPANS PAST.
COME TO STASIS GALLERY. SEE FOR YOURSELF!
"UNFORTUNATELY FOR THEM, I WAS RECOVERING AT AN EXPONENTIAL RATE.
"BY THE TIME THEY REALIZED WHAT WAS HAPPENING, IT WAS ALREADY TOO LATE."
TAP
TAP
TAP TAP
TAP

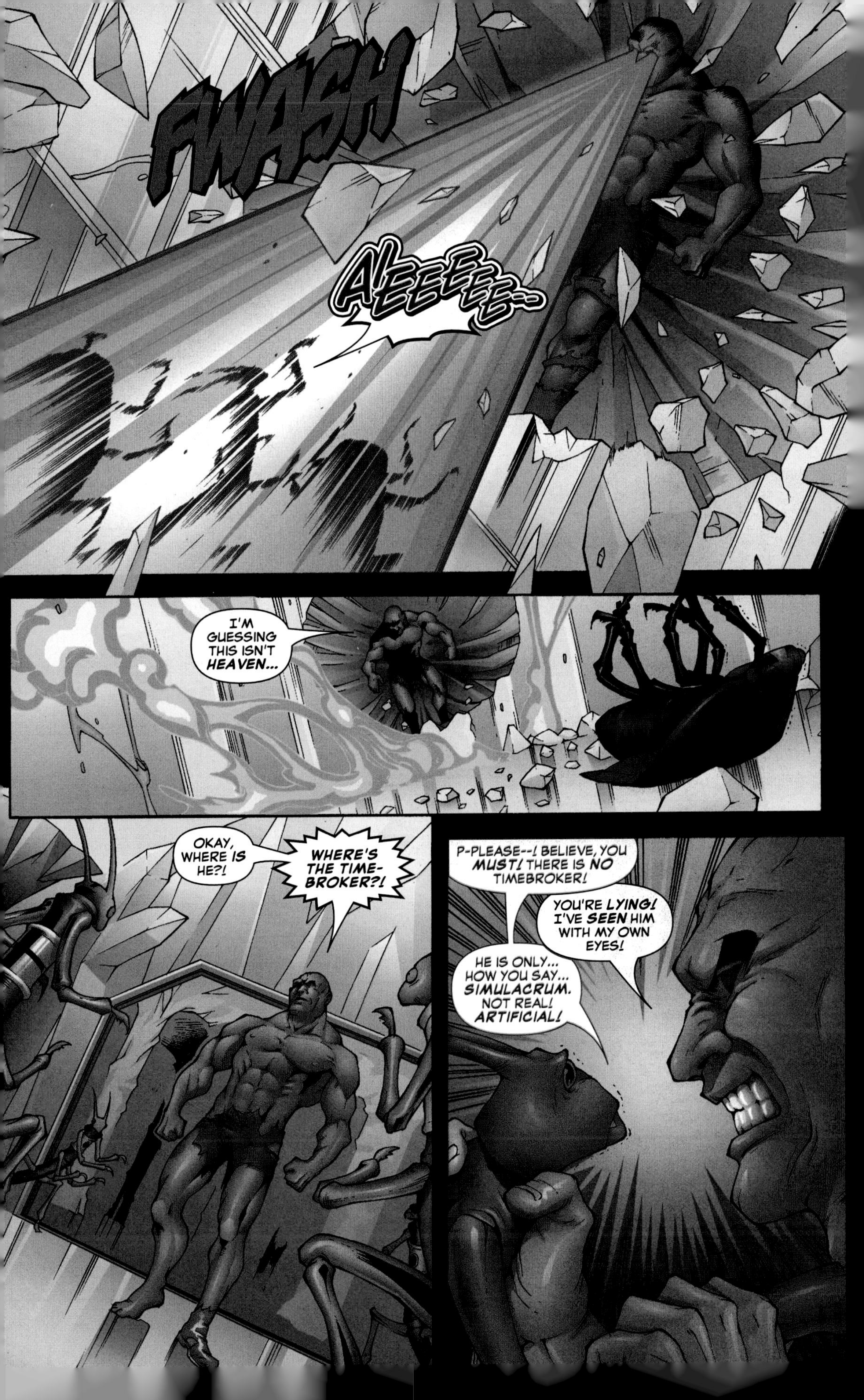
FWASH
AIEEEEEE--
I'M GUESSING THIS ISN'T HEAVEN...
OKAY, WHERE IS HE?!
WHERE'S THE TIME-BROKER?!
P-PLEASE--! BELIEVE, YOU MUST! THERE IS NO TIMEBROKER!
YOU'RE LYING! I'VE SEEN HIM WITH MY OWN EYES!
HE IS ONLY... HOW YOU SAY... SIMULACRUM. NOT REAL! ARTIFICIAL!

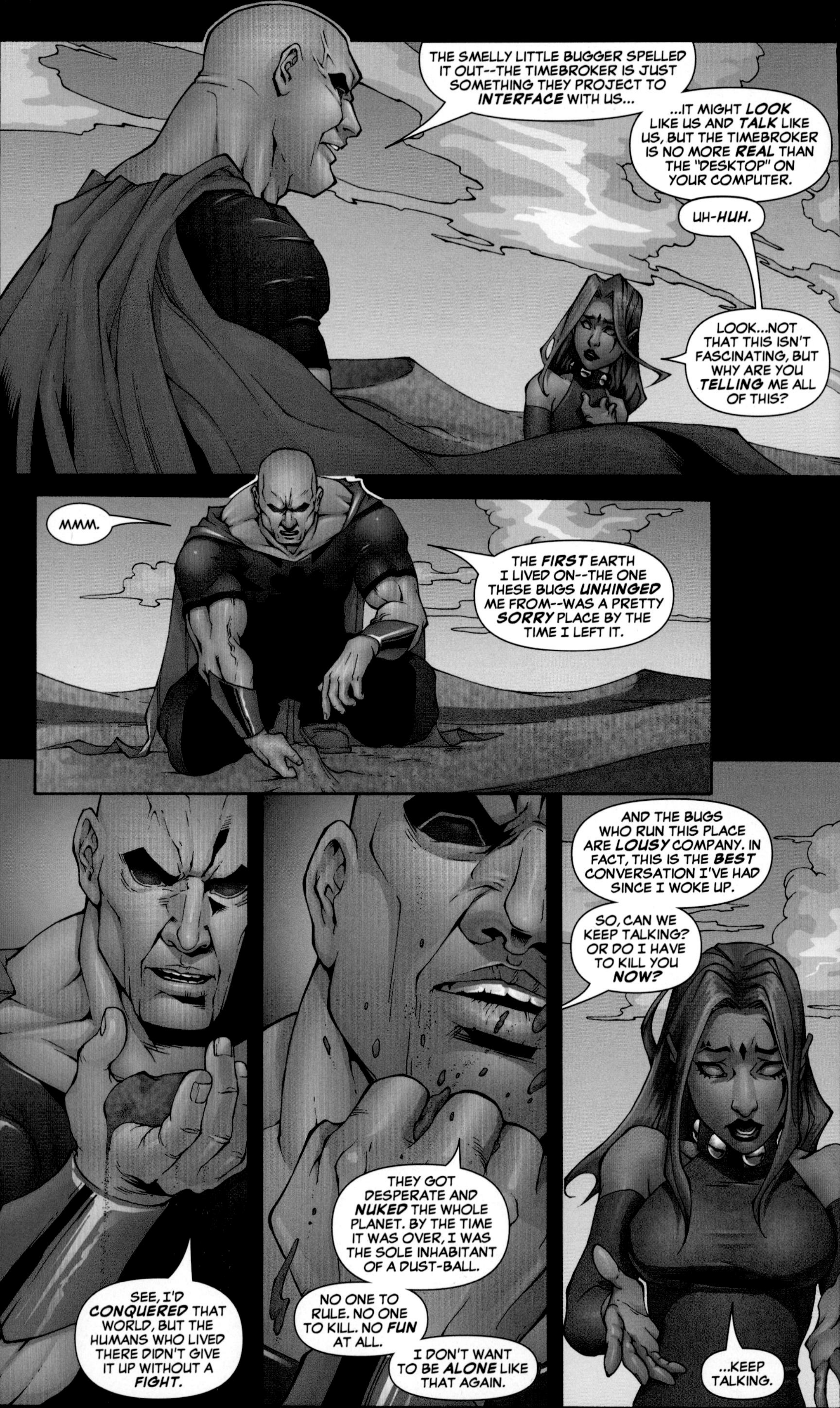
THE SMELLY LITTLE BUGGER SPELLED IT OUT--THE TIMEBROKER IS JUST SOMETHING THEY PROJECT TO INTERFACE WITH US...
...IT MIGHT LOOK LIKE US AND TALK LIKE US, BUT THE TIMEBROKER IS NO MORE REAL THAN THE "DESKTOP" ON YOUR COMPUTER.
UH-HUH.
LOOK...NOT THAT THIS ISN'T FASCINATING, BUT WHY ARE YOU TELLING ME ALL OF THIS?
MMM.
THE FIRST EARTH I LIVED ON--THE ONE THESE BUGS UNHINGED ME FROM--WAS A PRETTY SORRY PLACE BY THE TIME I LEFT IT.
SEE, I'D CONQUERED THAT WORLD, BUT THE HUMANS WHO LIVED THERE DIDN'T GIVE IT UP WITHOUT A FIGHT.
THEY GOT DESPERATE AND NUKED THE WHOLE PLANET. BY THE TIME IT WAS OVER, I WAS THE SOLE INHABITANT OF A DUST-BALL.
NO ONE TO RULE. NO ONE TO KILL. NO FUN AT ALL.
I DON'T WANT TO BE ALONE LIKE THAT AGAIN.
AND THE BUGS WHO RUN THIS PLACE ARE LOUSY COMPANY. IN FACT, THIS IS THE BEST CONVERSATION I'VE HAD SINCE I WOKE UP.
SO, CAN WE KEEP TALKING? OR DO I HAVE TO KILL YOU NOW?
...KEEP TALKING.

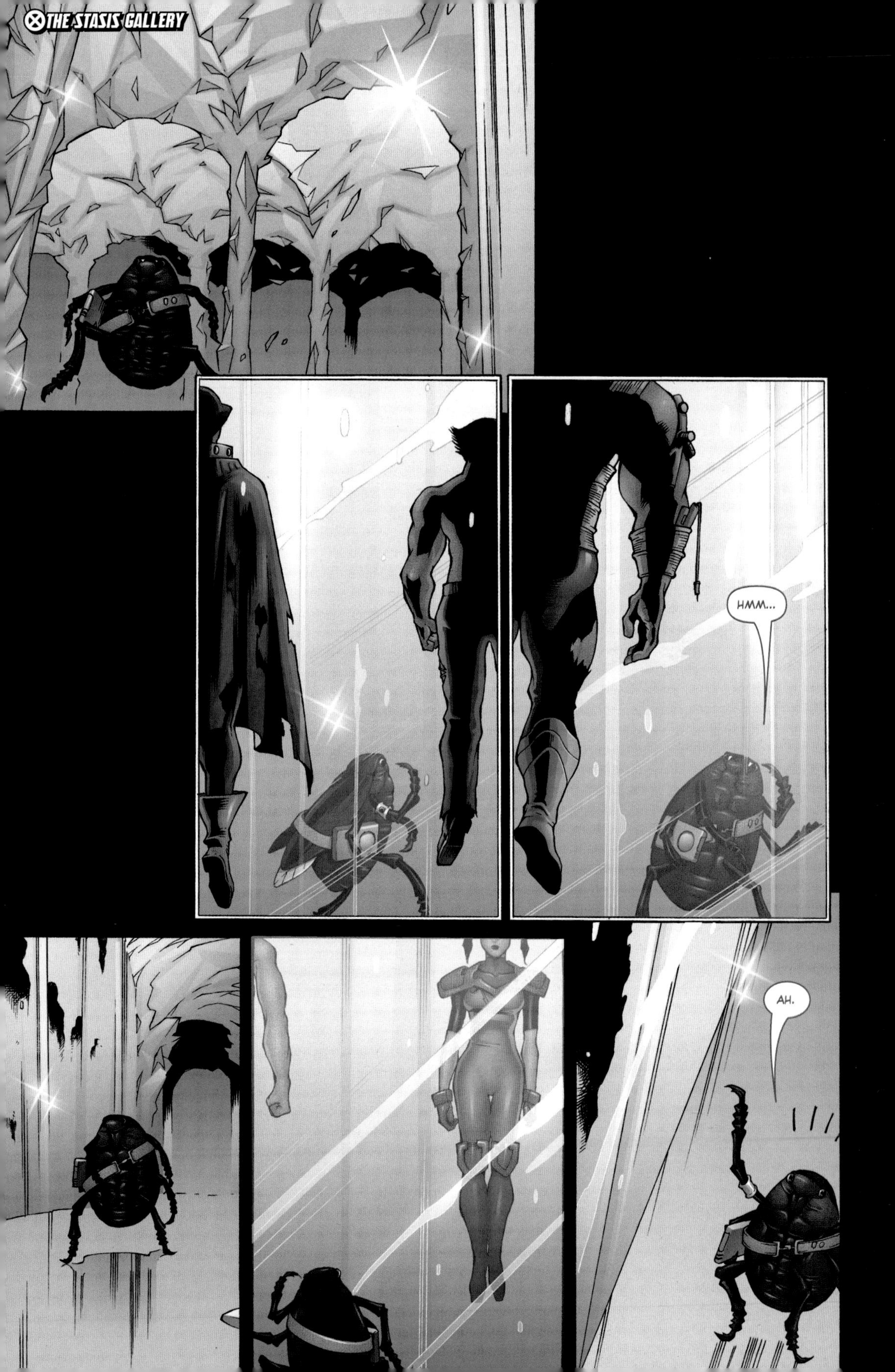
HMM...
AH.

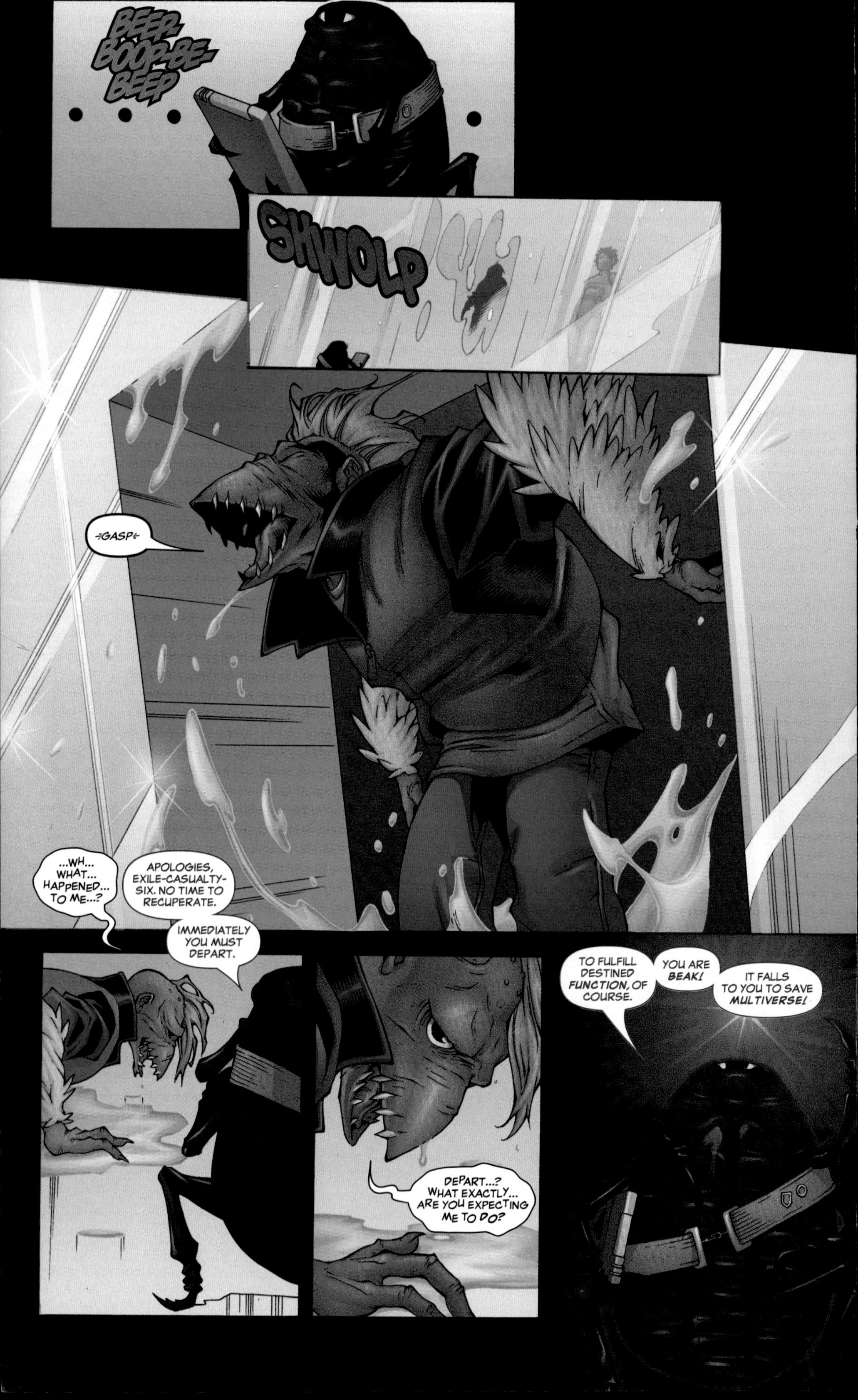
BEEP BOOP-BE-BEEP
SHWOLP
≠GASP≠
...WH... WHAT... HAPPENED... TO ME...?
APOLOGIES, EXILE-CASUALTY-SIX. NO TIME TO RECUPERATE.
IMMEDIATELY YOU MUST DEPART.
DEPART...? WHAT EXACTLY... ARE YOU EXPECTING ME TO DO?
TO FULFILL DESTINED FUNCTION, OF COURSE.
YOU ARE BEAK!
IT FALLS TO YOU TO SAVE MULTIVERSE!

THIS DESERT GOES ON FOR *MILES*, BUT IT'S STILL JUST A BIG ROOM, MORE OR LESS...A POCKET DIMENSION WITHIN THIS WHOLE COMPLEX.

THERE'S ANOTHER ROOM DOWN THE HALL WITH AN *OCEAN* IN IT, IF YOU CAN BELIEVE IT!

I FIGURED STRAIGHTAWAY THAT THE BUGS COULDN'T HAVE BUILT IT, AND SURE ENOUGH, THEY CONFESSED THEY *HADN'T.*

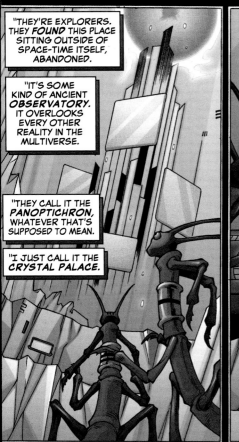

"THEY'RE EXPLORERS. THEY *FOUND* THIS PLACE SITTING OUTSIDE OF SPACE-TIME ITSELF, ABANDONED.

"IT'S SOME KIND OF ANCIENT *OBSERVATORY.* IT OVERLOOKS EVERY OTHER REALITY IN THE MULTIVERSE.

"THEY CALL IT THE *PANOPTICHRON,* WHATEVER THAT'S SUPPOSED TO MEAN.

"I JUST CALL IT THE *CRYSTAL PALACE.*

"THEY'RE BORN SCIENTISTS, THESE BUGS. THEY FIGURED OUT THE EQUIPMENT AND LAUNCHED *EXPEDITIONS* TO OTHER REALITIES...

"...BUT ONLY TO *MAP* THEM. THEY'RE GENETICALLY NONVIOLENT-- COULDN'T HURT ANOTHER LIVING THING IF THEY *WANTED* TO.

"IN OTHER WORDS, *PATHETIC.*"

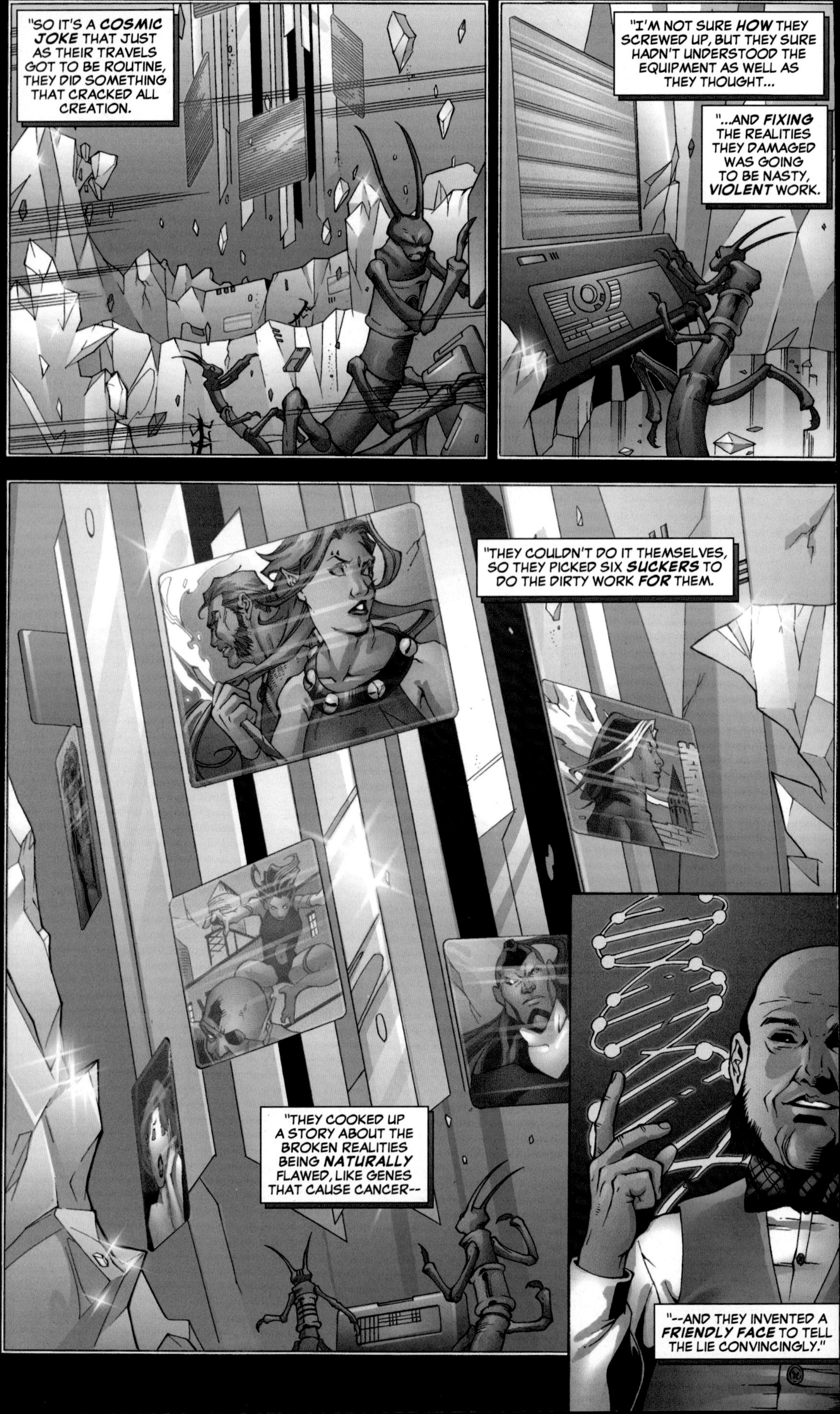
"SO IT'S A COSMIC JOKE THAT JUST AS THEIR TRAVELS GOT TO BE ROUTINE, THEY DID SOMETHING THAT CRACKED ALL CREATION.
"I'M NOT SURE HOW THEY SCREWED UP, BUT THEY SURE HADN'T UNDERSTOOD THE EQUIPMENT AS WELL AS THEY THOUGHT...
"...AND FIXING THE REALITIES THEY DAMAGED WAS GOING TO BE NASTY, VIOLENT WORK.
"THEY COULDN'T DO IT THEMSELVES, SO THEY PICKED SIX SUCKERS TO DO THE DIRTY WORK FOR THEM.
"THEY COOKED UP A STORY ABOUT THE BROKEN REALITIES BEING NATURALLY FLAWED, LIKE GENES THAT CAUSE CANCER--
"--AND THEY INVENTED A FRIENDLY FACE TO TELL THE LIE CONVINCINGLY."

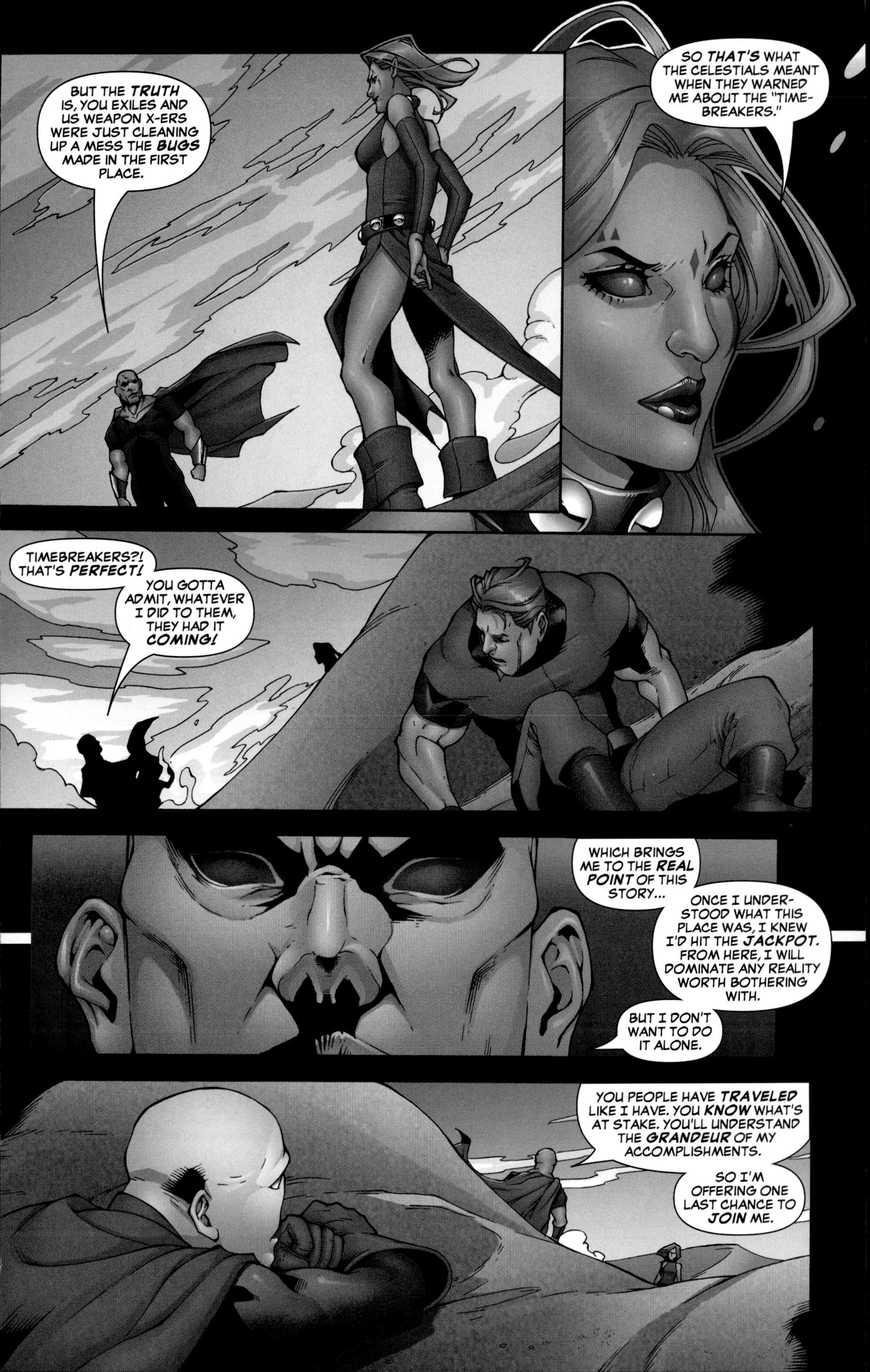
BUT THE TRUTH IS, YOU EXILES AND US WEAPON X-ERS WERE JUST CLEANING UP A MESS THE BUGS MADE IN THE FIRST PLACE.
SO THAT'S WHAT THE CELESTIALS MEANT WHEN THEY WARNED ME ABOUT THE "TIME-BREAKERS."
TIMEBREAKERS?! THAT'S PERFECT!
YOU GOTTA ADMIT, WHATEVER I DID TO THEM, THEY HAD IT COMING!
WHICH BRINGS ME TO THE REAL POINT OF THIS STORY...
ONCE I UNDER-STOOD WHAT THIS PLACE WAS, I KNEW I'D HIT THE JACKPOT. FROM HERE, I WILL DOMINATE ANY REALITY WORTH BOTHERING WITH.
BUT I DON'T WANT TO DO IT ALONE.
YOU PEOPLE HAVE TRAVELED LIKE I HAVE. YOU KNOW WHAT'S AT STAKE. YOU'LL UNDERSTAND THE GRANDEUR OF MY ACCOMPLISHMENTS.
SO I'M OFFERING ONE LAST CHANCE TO JOIN ME.

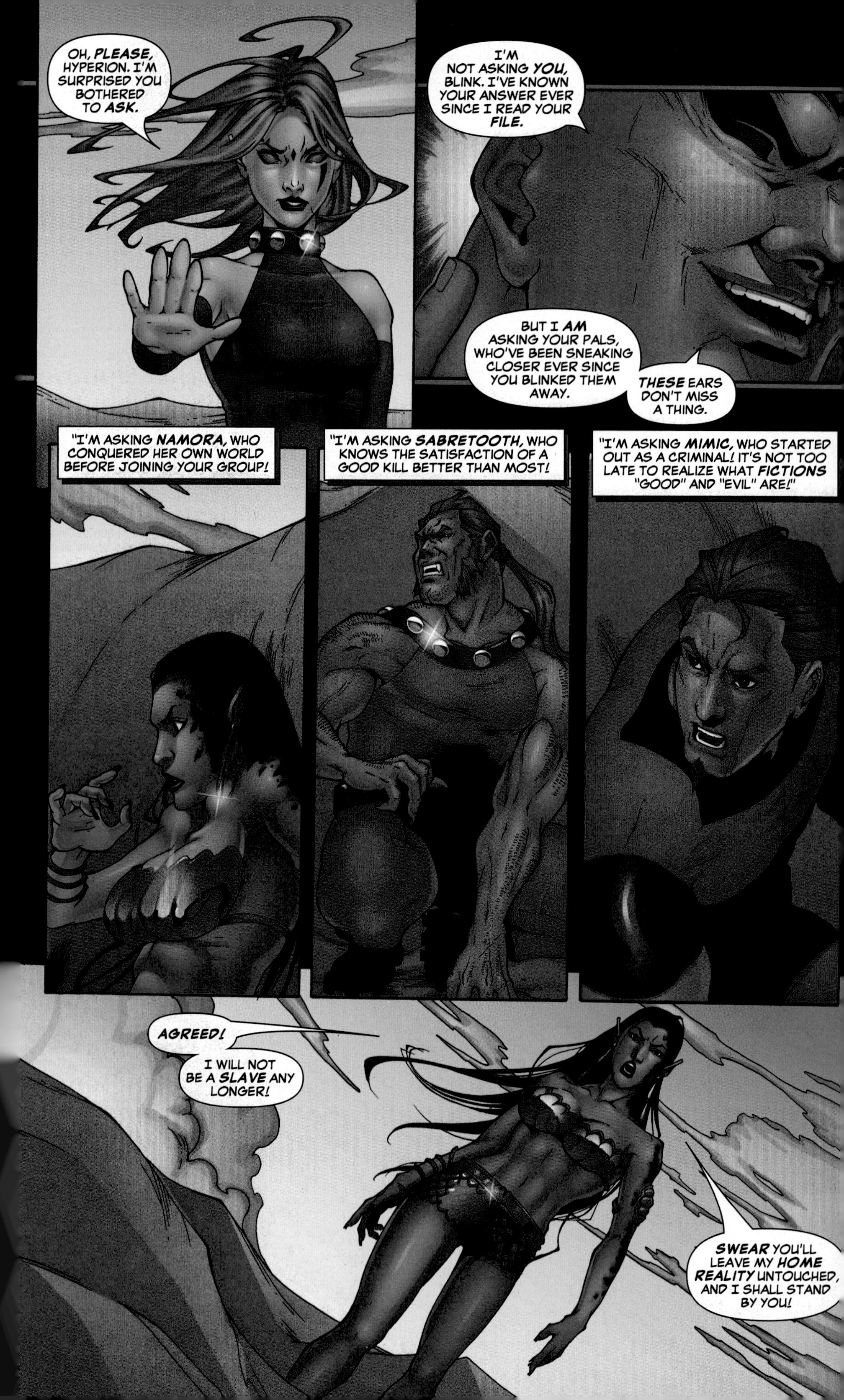

OH, PLEASE, HYPERION. I'M SURPRISED YOU BOTHERED TO ASK.
I'M NOT ASKING YOU, BLINK. I'VE KNOWN YOUR ANSWER EVER SINCE I READ YOUR FILE.
BUT I AM ASKING YOUR PALS, WHO'VE BEEN SNEAKING CLOSER EVER SINCE YOU BLINKED THEM AWAY.
THESE EARS DON'T MISS A THING.
"I'M ASKING NAMORA, WHO CONQUERED HER OWN WORLD BEFORE JOINING YOUR GROUP!
"I'M ASKING SABRETOOTH, WHO KNOWS THE SATISFACTION OF A GOOD KILL BETTER THAN MOST!
"I'M ASKING MIMIC, WHO STARTED OUT AS A CRIMINAL! IT'S NOT TOO LATE TO REALIZE WHAT FICTIONS "GOOD" AND "EVIL" ARE!"
AGREED!
I WILL NOT BE A SLAVE ANY LONGER!
SWEAR YOU'LL LEAVE MY HOME REALITY UNTOUCHED, AND I SHALL STAND BY YOU!

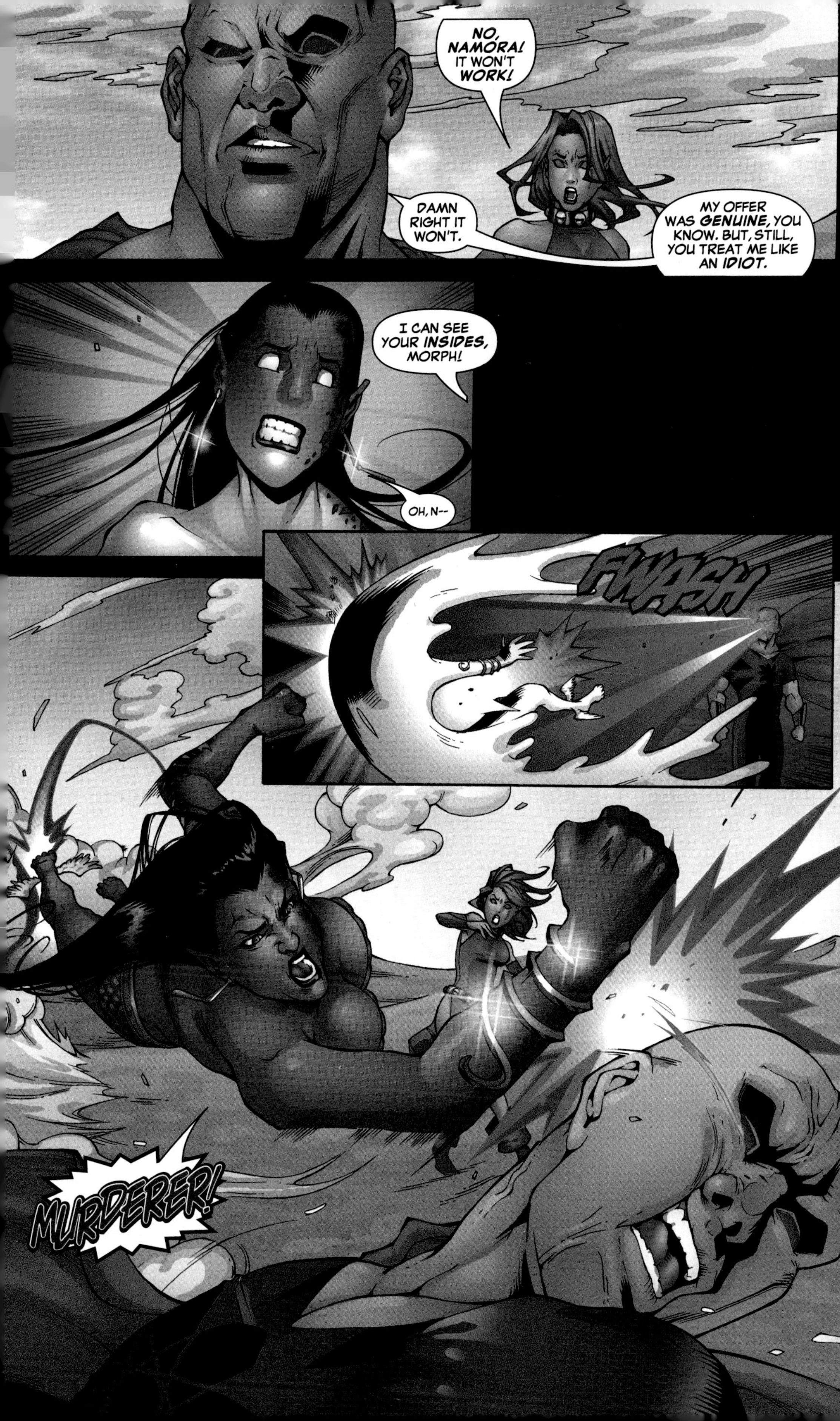
NO, NAMORA! IT WON'T WORK!
DAMN RIGHT IT WON'T.
MY OFFER WAS GENUINE, YOU KNOW. BUT, STILL, YOU TREAT ME LIKE AN IDIOT.
I CAN SEE YOUR INSIDES, MORPH!
OH, N--
FWASH
MURDERER!

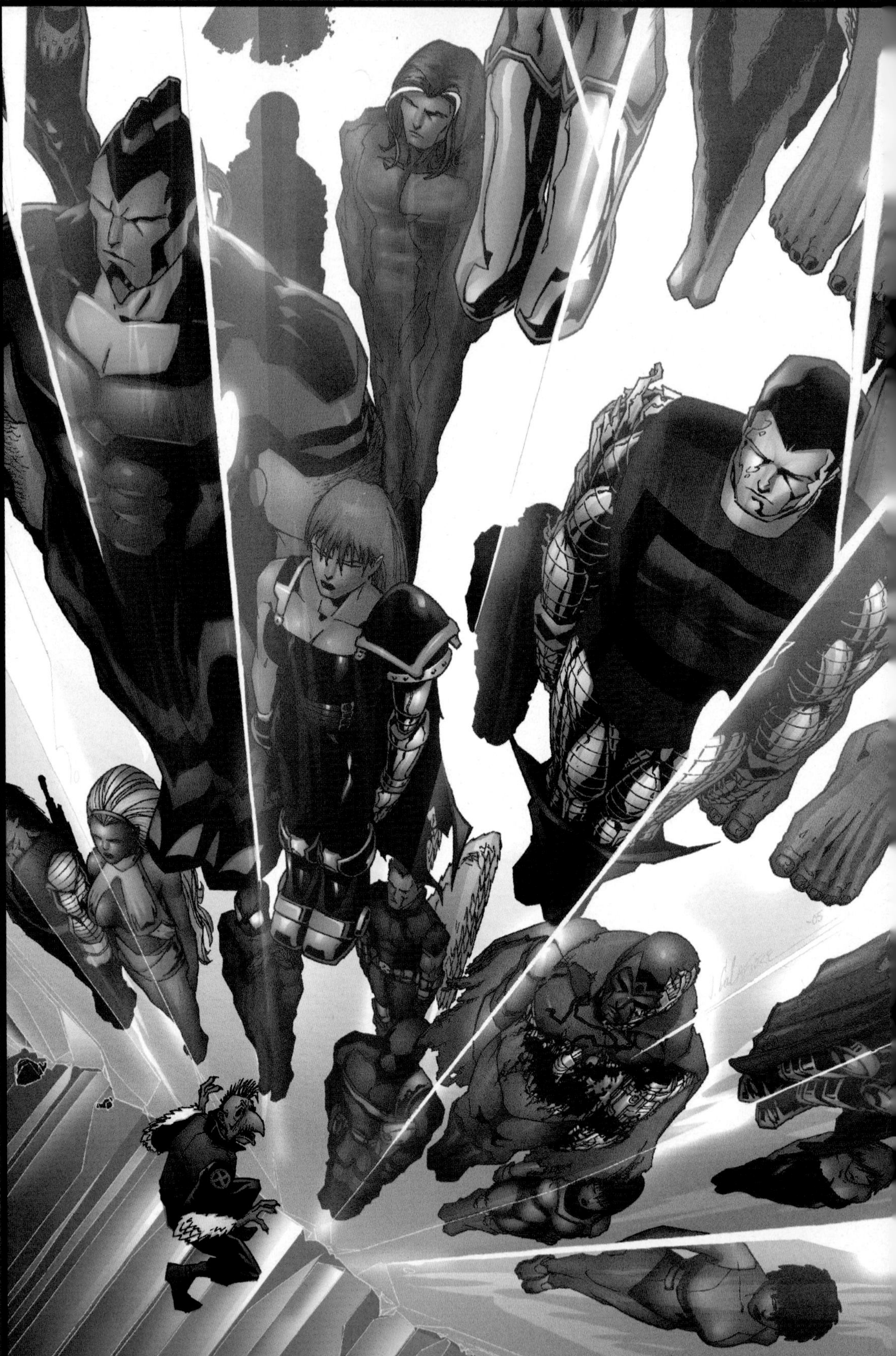

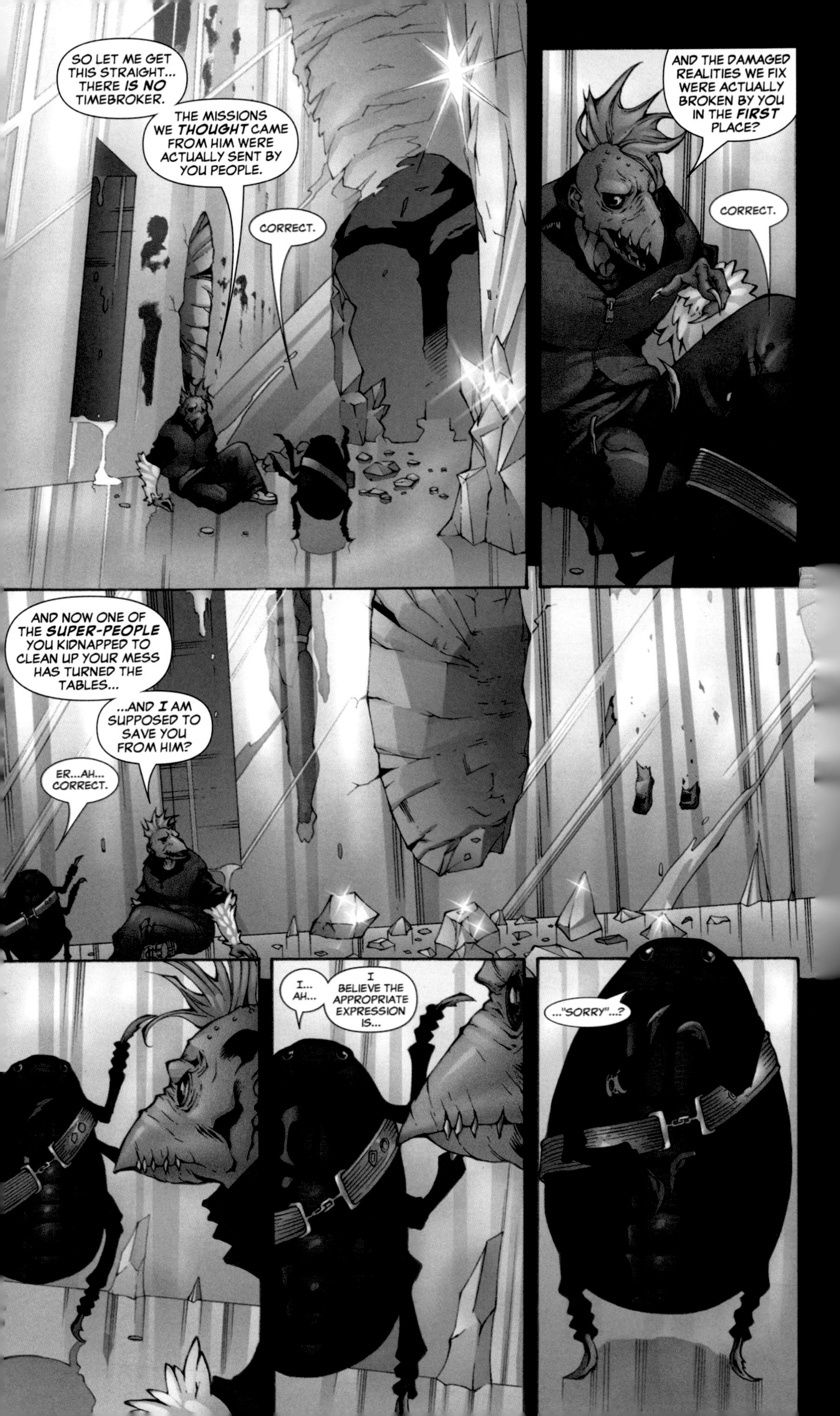
SO LET ME GET THIS STRAIGHT... THERE IS NO TIMEBROKER.
THE MISSIONS WE THOUGHT CAME FROM HIM WERE ACTUALLY SENT BY YOU PEOPLE.
CORRECT.
AND THE DAMAGED REALITIES WE FIX WERE ACTUALLY BROKEN BY YOU IN THE FIRST PLACE?
CORRECT.
AND NOW ONE OF THE SUPER-PEOPLE YOU KIDNAPPED TO CLEAN UP YOUR MESS HAS TURNED THE TABLES...
...AND I AM SUPPOSED TO SAVE YOU FROM HIM?
ER...AH... CORRECT.
I... AH...
I BELIEVE THE APPROPRIATE EXPRESSION IS...
..."SORRY"...?

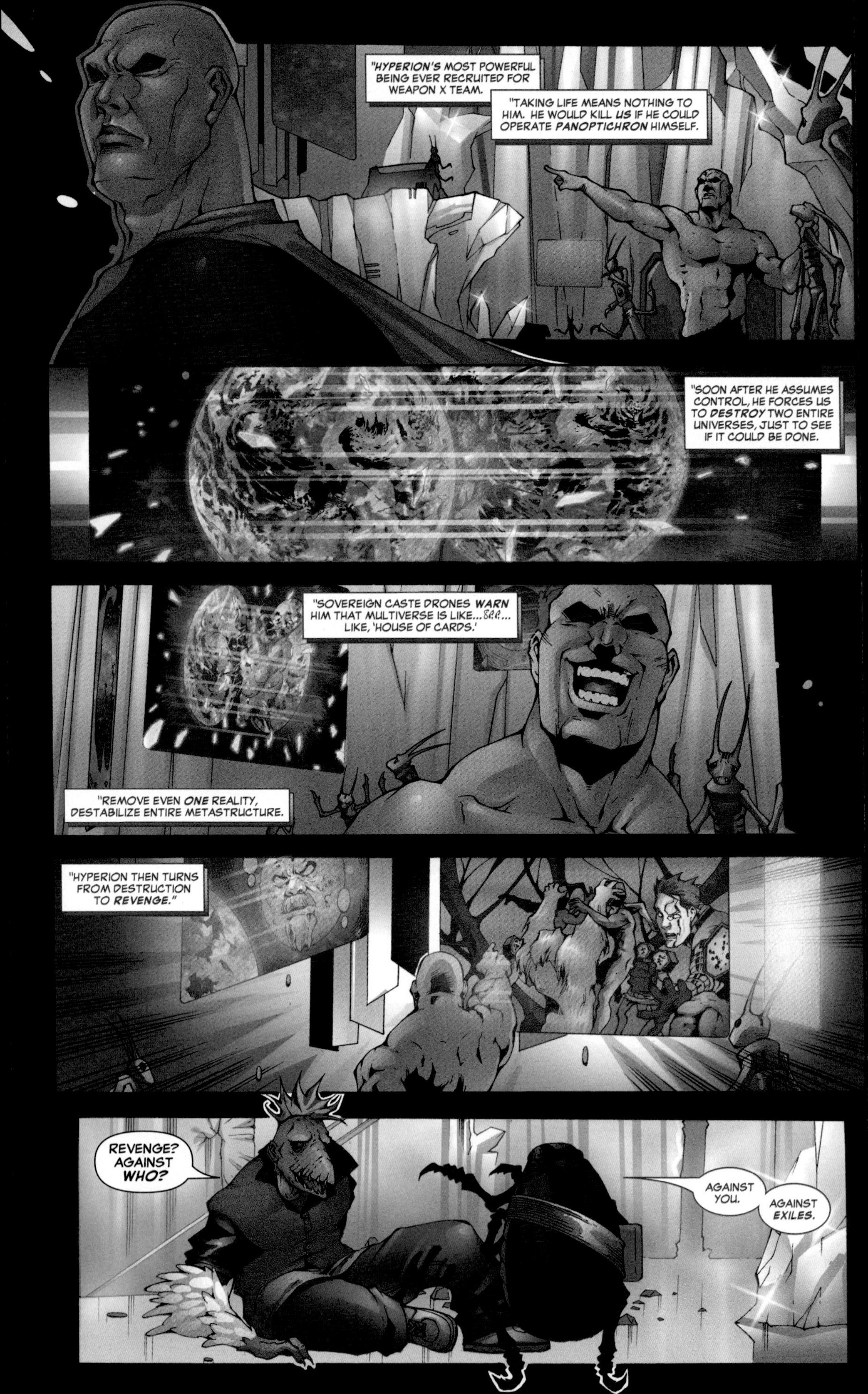
"*HYPERION'S* MOST POWERFUL BEING EVER RECRUITED FOR WEAPON X TEAM.
"TAKING LIFE MEANS NOTHING TO HIM. HE WOULD KILL *US* IF HE COULD OPERATE *PANOPTICHRON* HIMSELF.
"SOON AFTER HE ASSUMES CONTROL, HE FORCES US TO *DESTROY* TWO ENTIRE UNIVERSES, JUST TO SEE IF IT COULD BE DONE.
"SOVEREIGN CASTE DRONES *WARN* HIM THAT MULTIVERSE IS LIKE... ... LIKE, 'HOUSE OF CARDS.'
"REMOVE EVEN *ONE* REALITY, DESTABILIZE ENTIRE METASTRUCTURE.
"HYPERION THEN TURNS FROM DESTRUCTION TO *REVENGE*."
REVENGE? AGAINST *WHO?*
AGAINST YOU.
AGAINST *EXILES*.

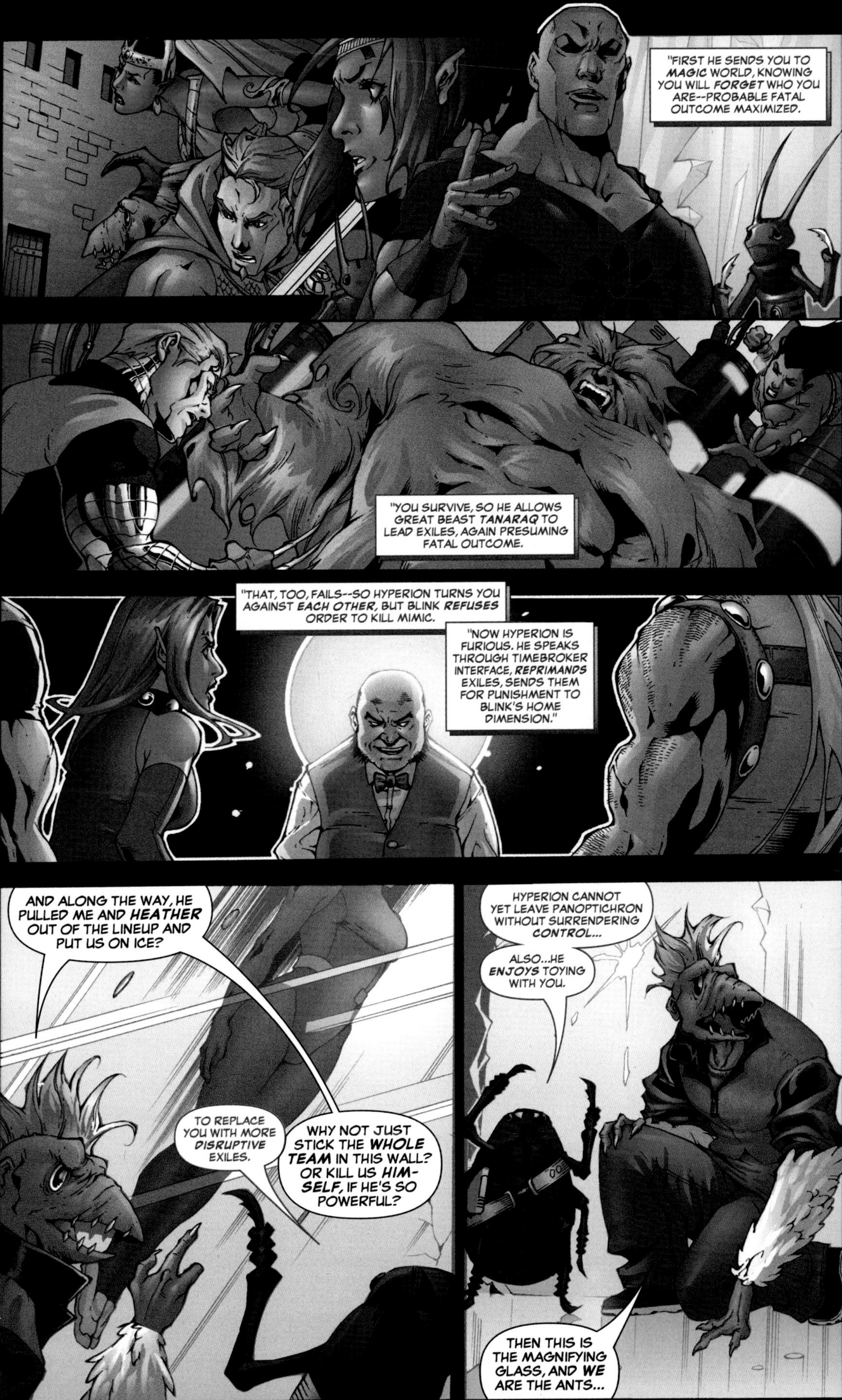
"FIRST HE SENDS YOU TO MAGIC WORLD, KNOWING YOU WILL FORGET WHO YOU ARE--PROBABLE FATAL OUTCOME MAXIMIZED.
"YOU SURVIVE, SO HE ALLOWS GREAT BEAST TANARAQ TO LEAD EXILES, AGAIN PRESUMING FATAL OUTCOME.
"THAT, TOO, FAILS--SO HYPERION TURNS YOU AGAINST EACH OTHER, BUT BLINK REFUSES ORDER TO KILL MIMIC.
"NOW HYPERION IS FURIOUS. HE SPEAKS THROUGH TIMEBROKER INTERFACE, REPRIMANDS EXILES, SENDS THEM FOR PUNISHMENT TO BLINK'S HOME DIMENSION."
AND ALONG THE WAY, HE PULLED ME AND HEATHER OUT OF THE LINEUP AND PUT US ON ICE?
TO REPLACE YOU WITH MORE DISRUPTIVE EXILES.
WHY NOT JUST STICK THE WHOLE TEAM IN THIS WALL? OR KILL US HIM-SELF, IF HE'S SO POWERFUL?
HYPERION CANNOT YET LEAVE PANOPTICHRON WITHOUT SURRENDERING CONTROL...
ALSO...HE ENJOYS TOYING WITH YOU.
THEN THIS IS THE MAGNIFYING GLASS, AND WE ARE THE ANTS...

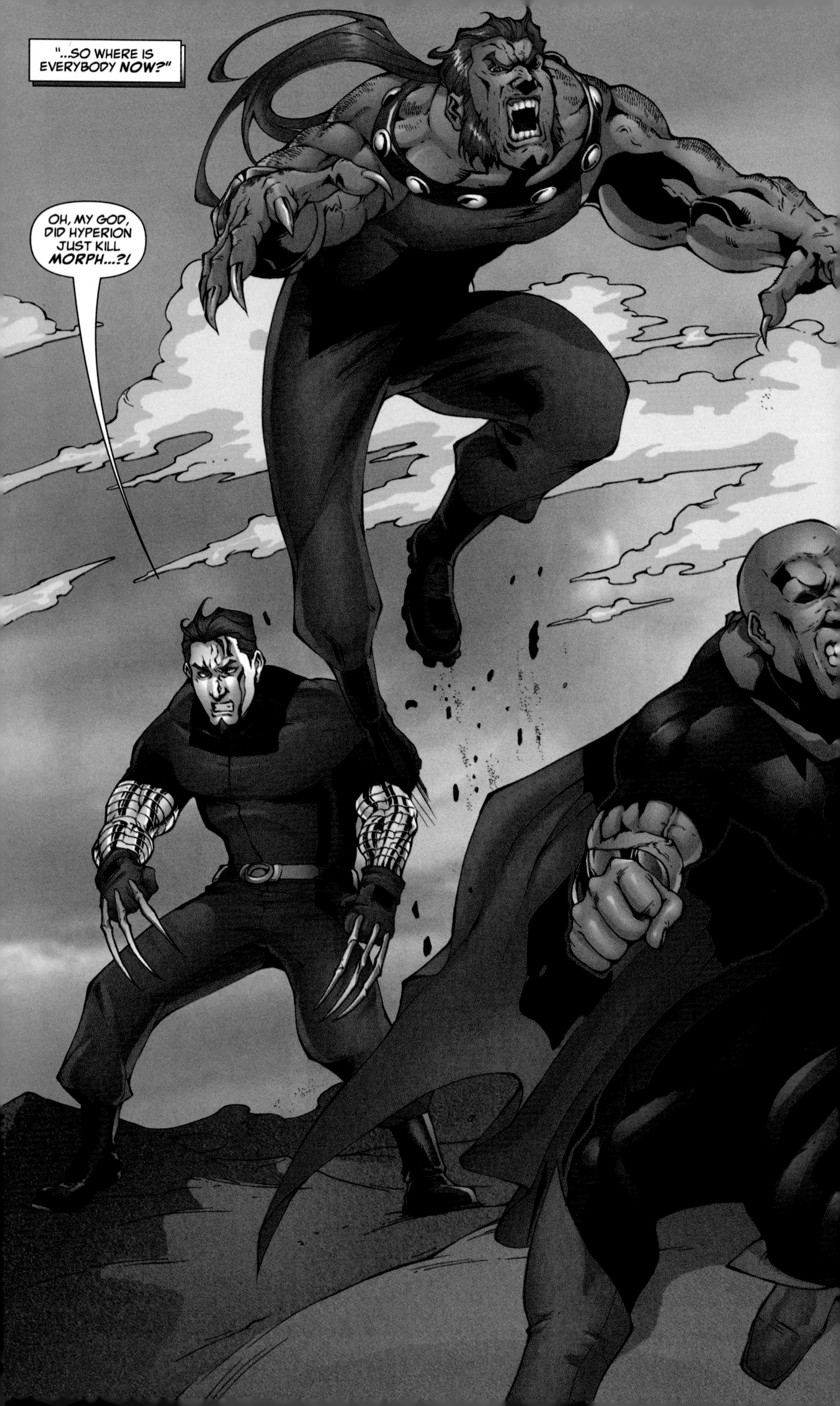
"...SO WHERE IS EVERYBODY NOW?"
OH, MY GOD, DID HYPERION JUST KILL MORPH...?!

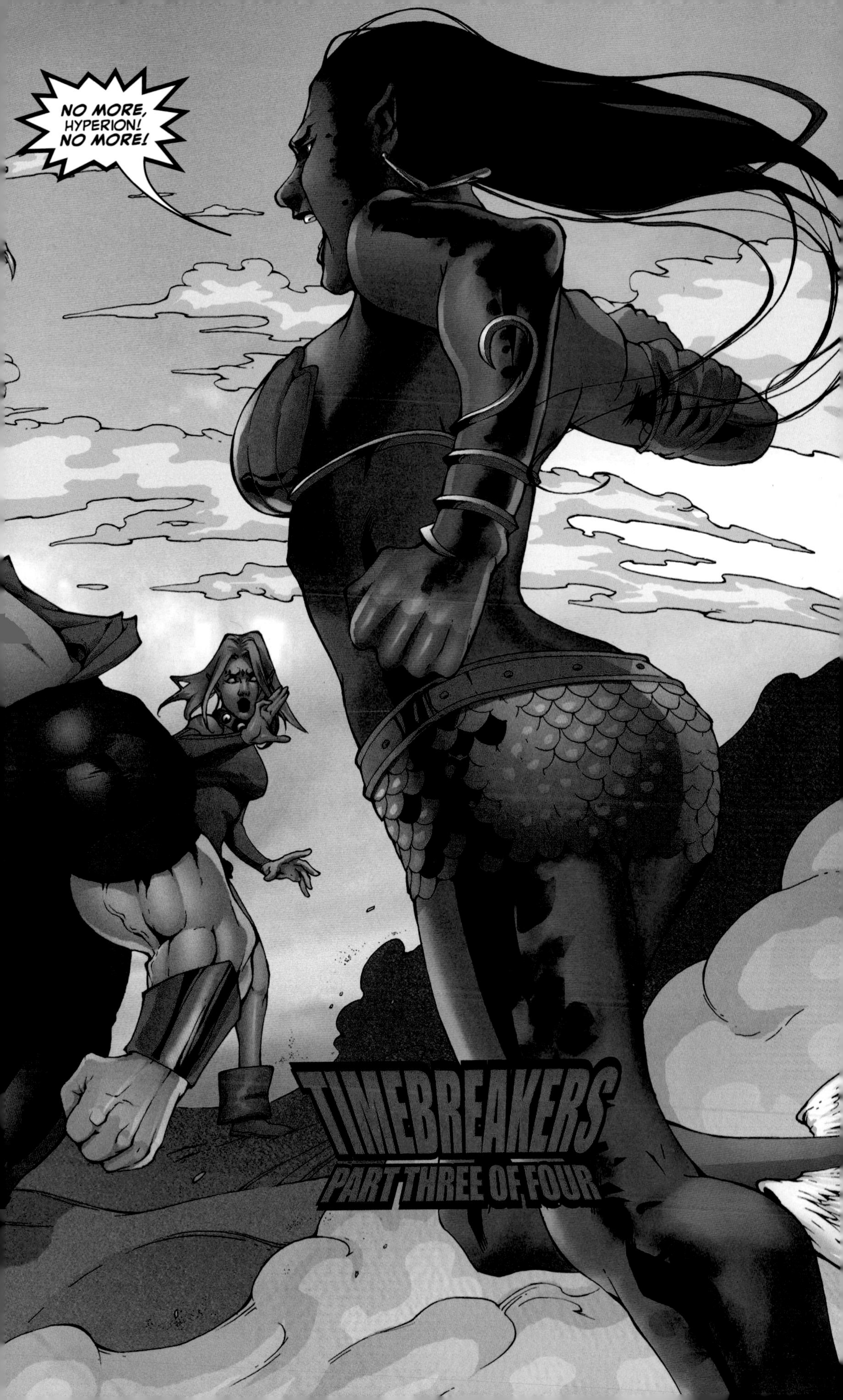
NO MORE, HYPERION! NO MORE!
TIMEBREAKERS
PART THREE OF FOUR

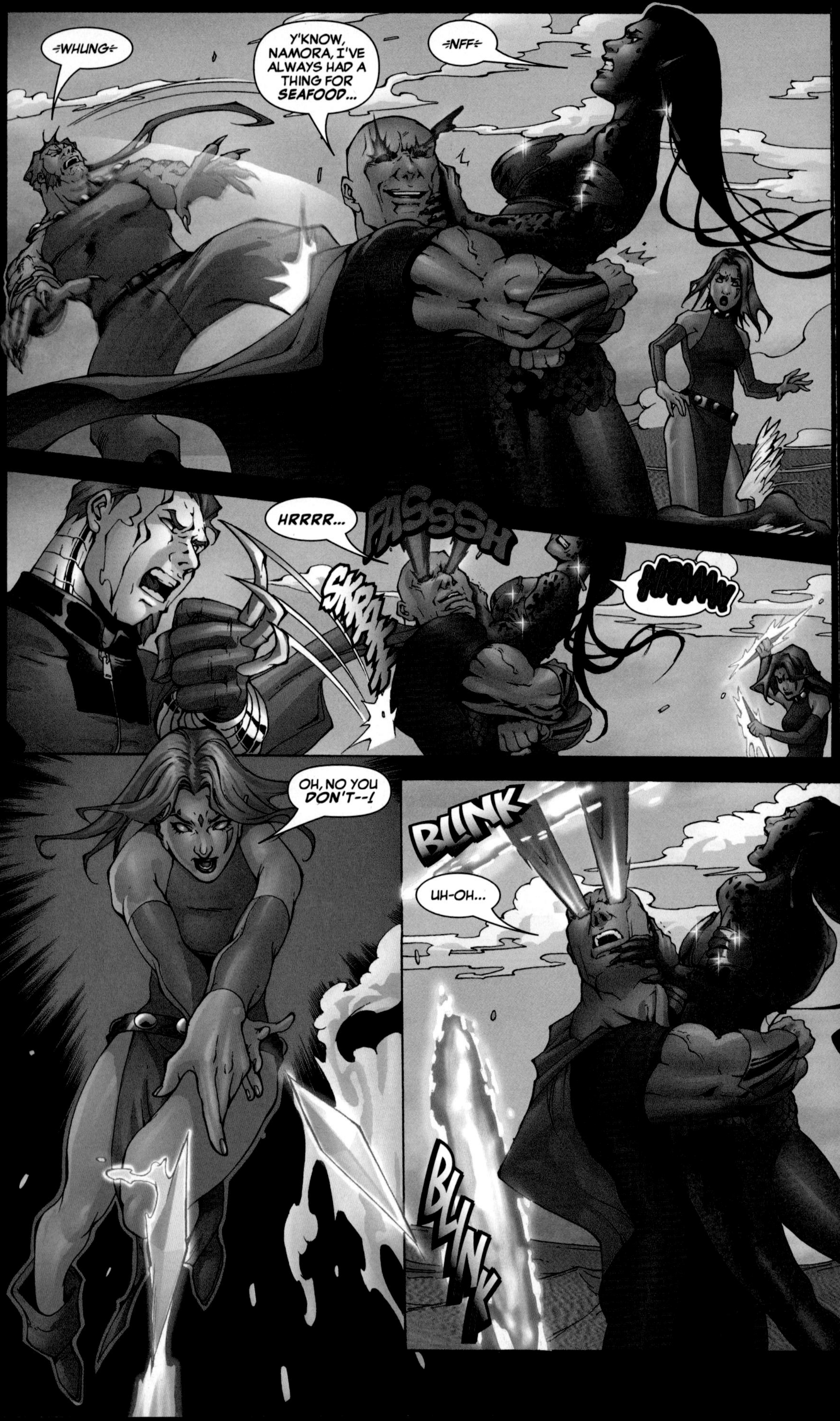

WHUNG
Y'KNOW, NAMORA, I'VE ALWAYS HAD A THING FOR *SEAFOOD*...
NFF
HRRRR...
FASSSH
OH, NO YOU *DON'T*--!
BLINK
UH-OH...

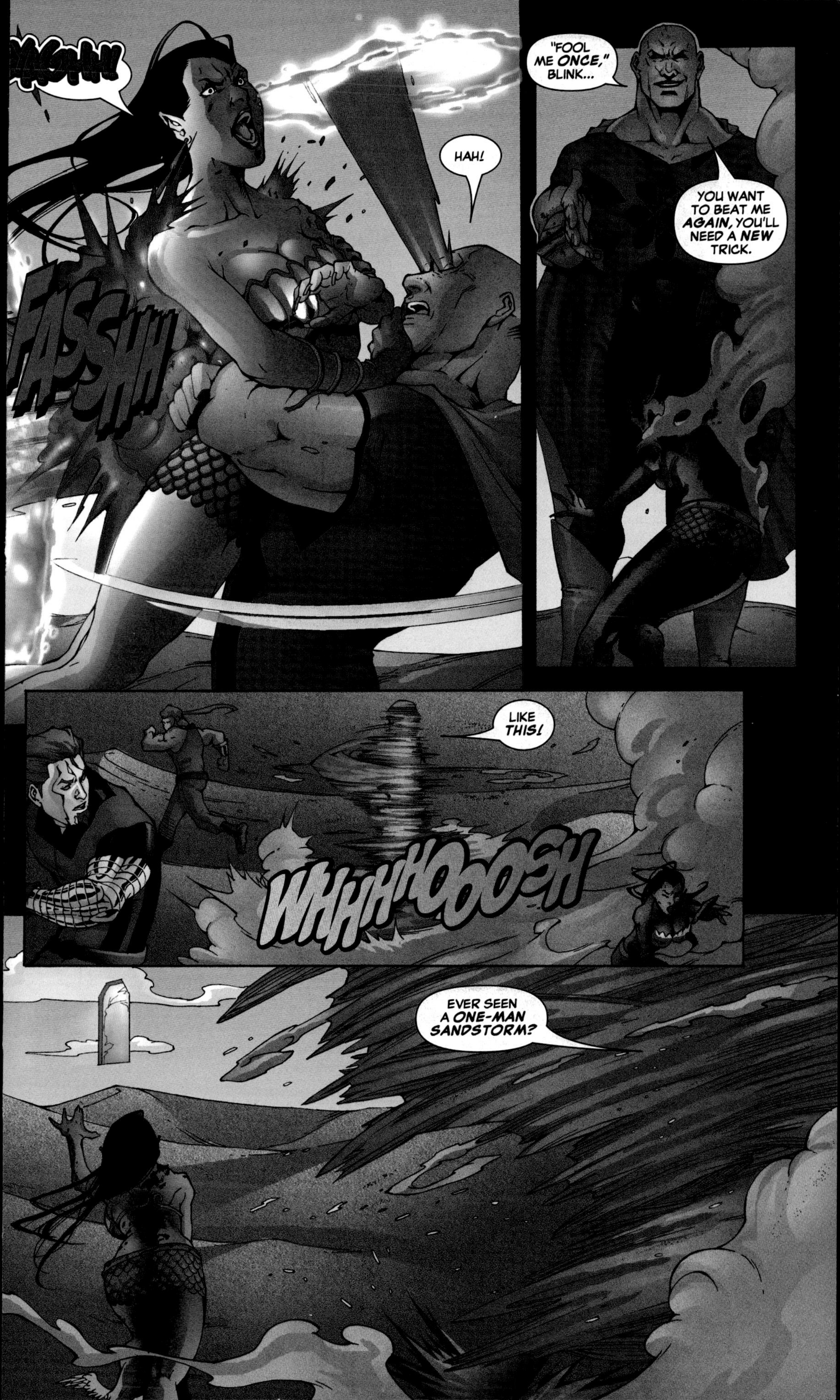

YAAGHH!
FASSHH
HAH!
"FOOL ME ONCE," BLINK...
YOU WANT TO BEAT ME AGAIN, YOU'LL NEED A NEW TRICK.
LIKE THIS!
WHHHHOOOOSH
EVER SEEN A ONE-MAN SANDSTORM?

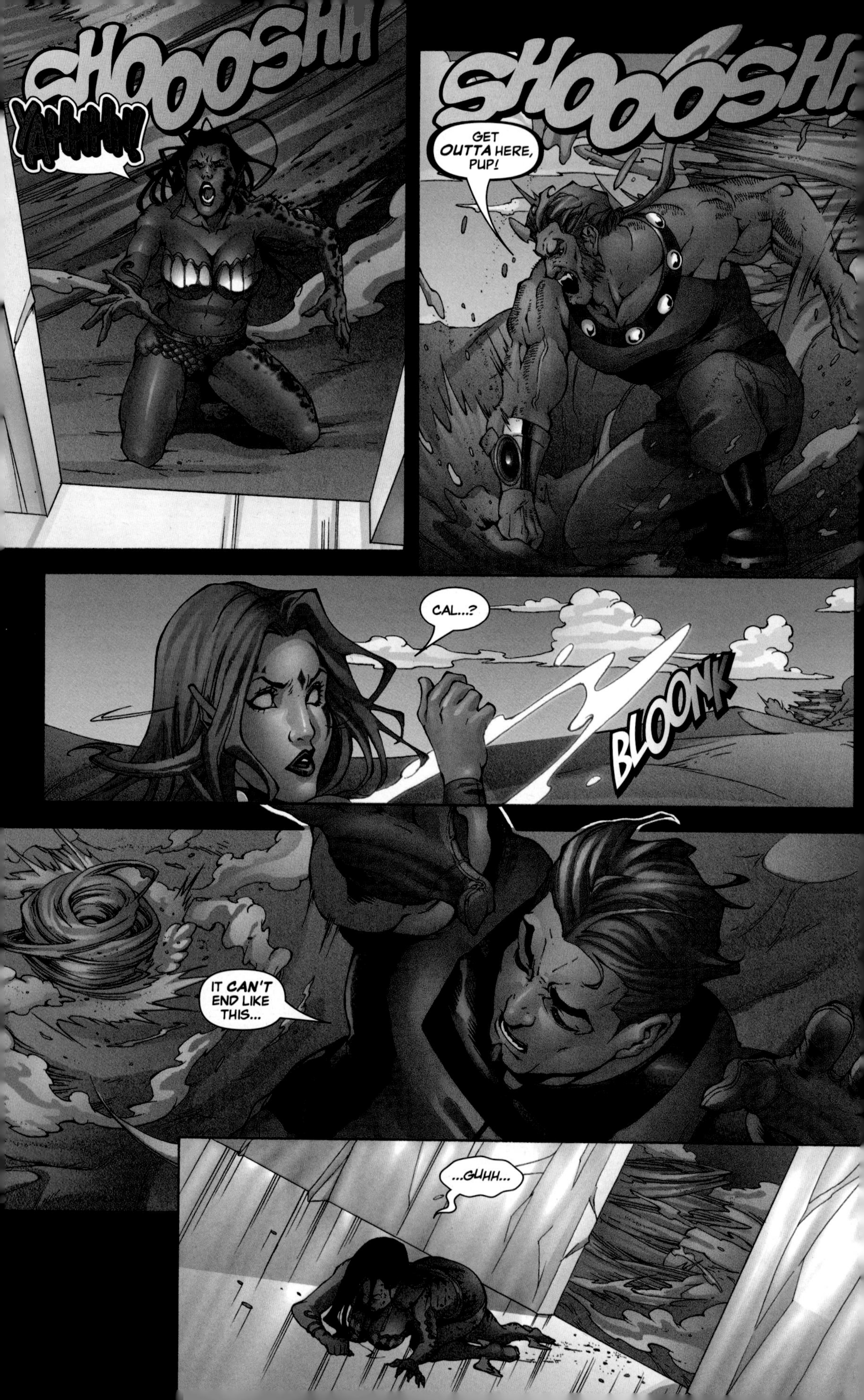
SHOOOSHH
YAHHHH!
SHOOOSHH
GET OUTTA HERE, PUP!
CAL...?
BLOONK
IT CAN'T END LIKE THIS...
...GUHH...

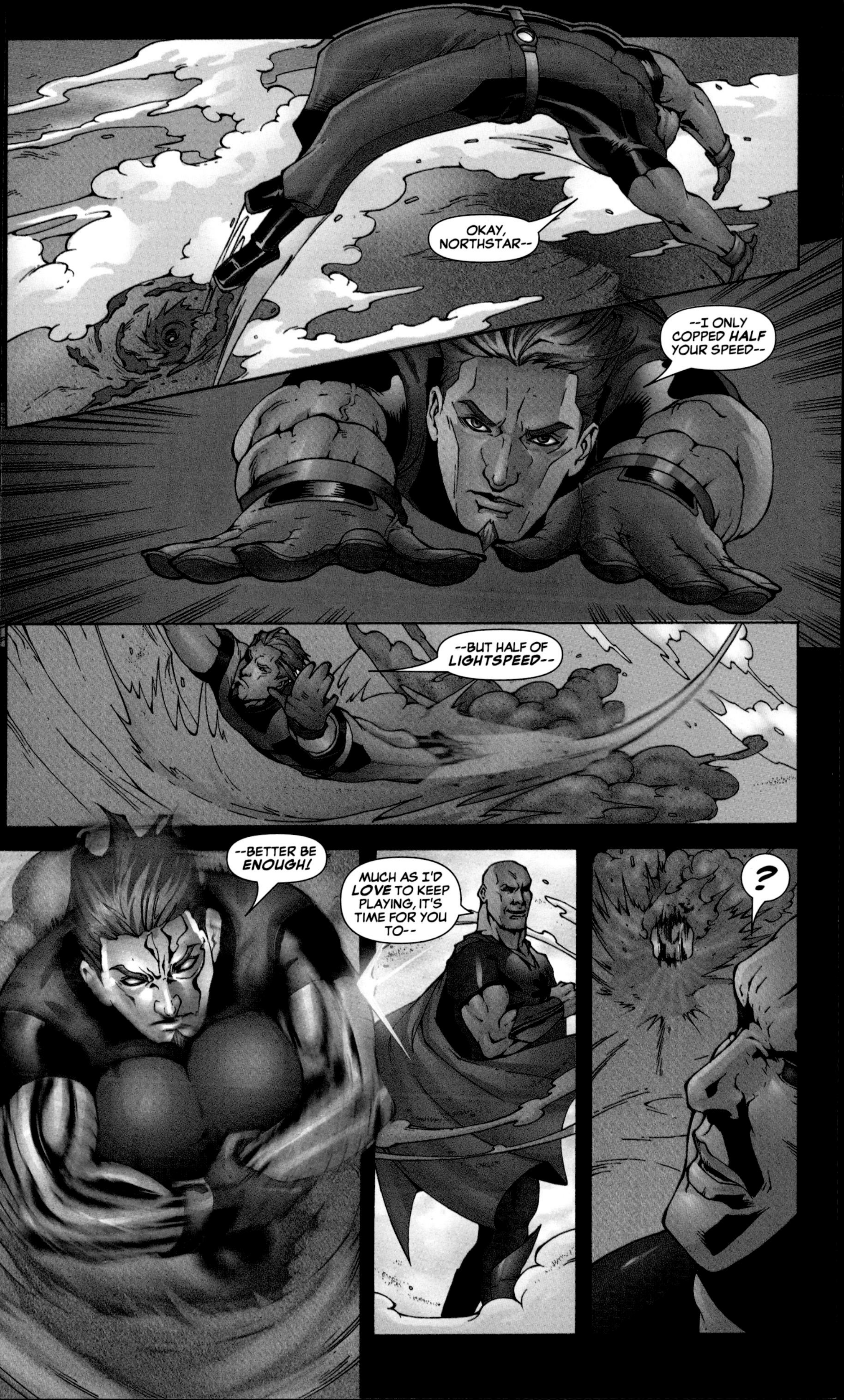
OKAY, NORTHSTAR--
--I ONLY COPPED HALF YOUR SPEED--
--BUT HALF OF LIGHTSPEED--
--BETTER BE ENOUGH!
MUCH AS I'D LOVE TO KEEP PLAYING, IT'S TIME FOR YOU TO--
?

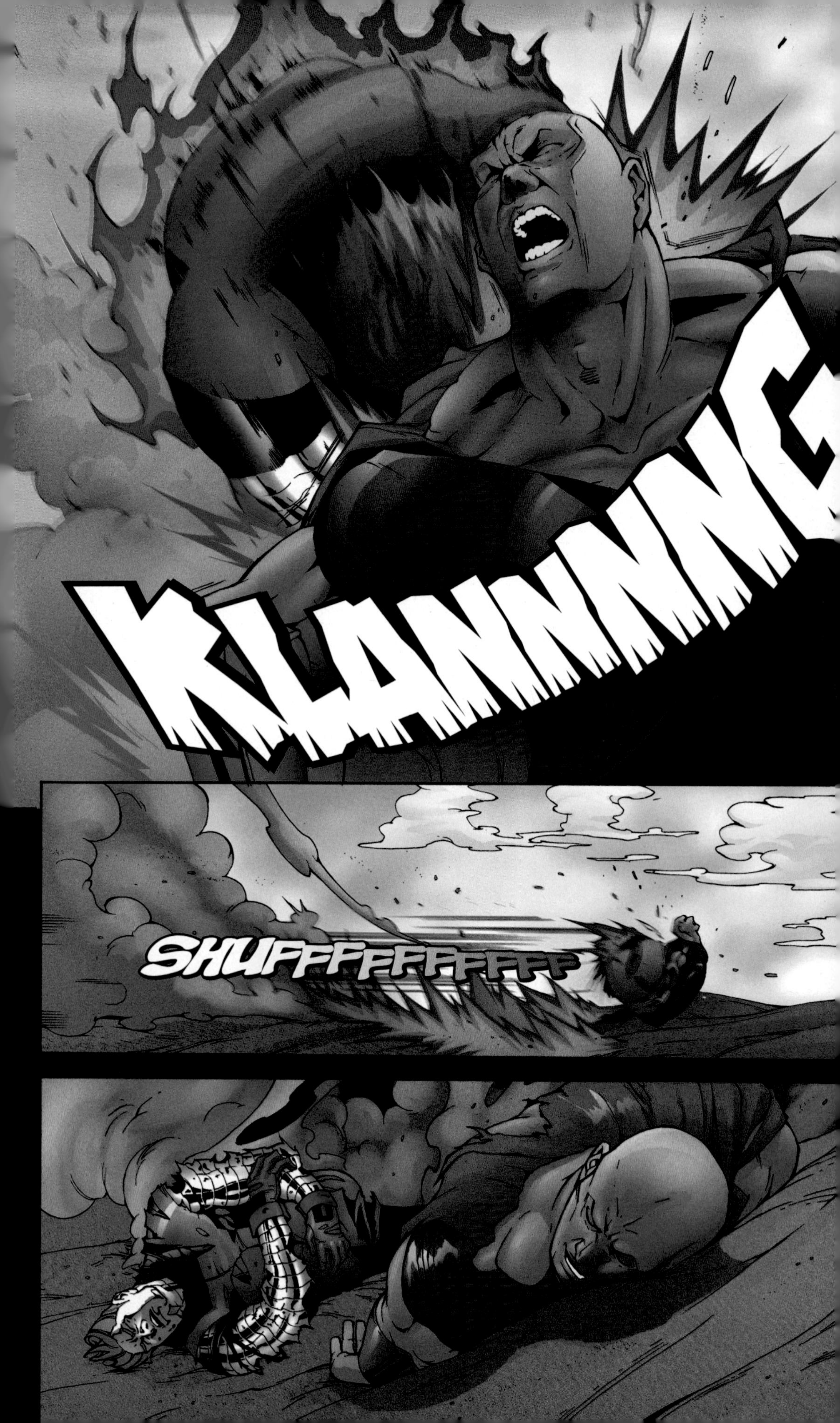
KLANNNNNG
SHUFFFFFFFFFFFF

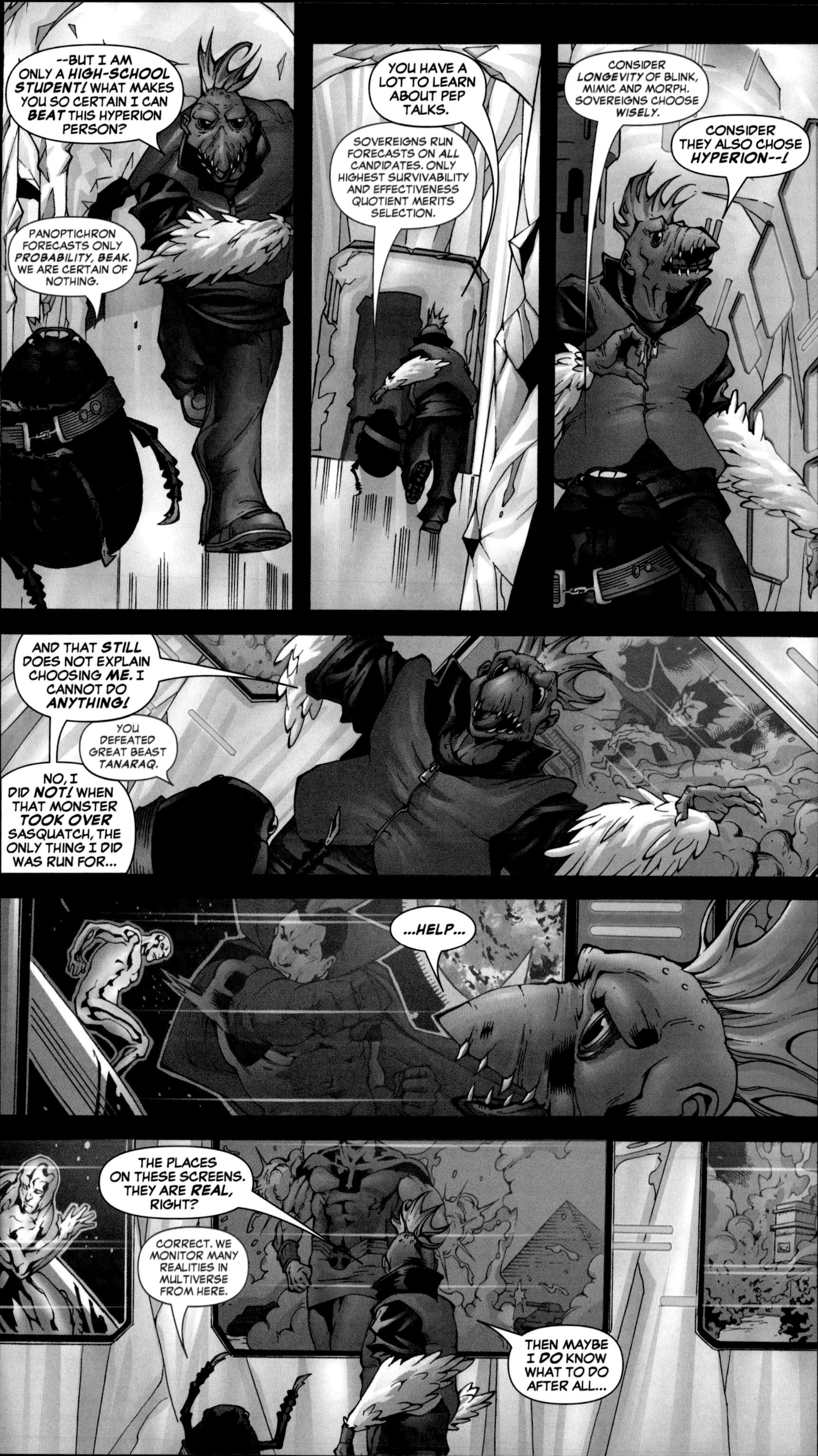
--BUT I AM ONLY A HIGH-SCHOOL STUDENT! WHAT MAKES YOU SO CERTAIN I CAN BEAT THIS HYPERION PERSON?
PANOPTICHRON FORECASTS ONLY PROBABILITY, BEAK. WE ARE CERTAIN OF NOTHING.
YOU HAVE A LOT TO LEARN ABOUT PEP TALKS.
SOVEREIGNS RUN FORECASTS ON ALL CANDIDATES. ONLY HIGHEST SURVIVABILITY AND EFFECTIVENESS QUOTIENT MERITS SELECTION.
CONSIDER LONGEVITY OF BLINK, MIMIC AND MORPH. SOVEREIGNS CHOOSE WISELY.
CONSIDER THEY ALSO CHOSE HYPERION--!
AND THAT STILL DOES NOT EXPLAIN CHOOSING ME. I CANNOT DO ANYTHING!
YOU DEFEATED GREAT BEAST TANARAQ.
NO, I DID NOT! WHEN THAT MONSTER TOOK OVER SASQUATCH, THE ONLY THING I DID WAS RUN FOR...
...HELP...
THE PLACES ON THESE SCREENS. THEY ARE REAL, RIGHT?
CORRECT. WE MONITOR MANY REALITIES IN MULTIVERSE FROM HERE.
THEN MAYBE I DO KNOW WHAT TO DO AFTER ALL...

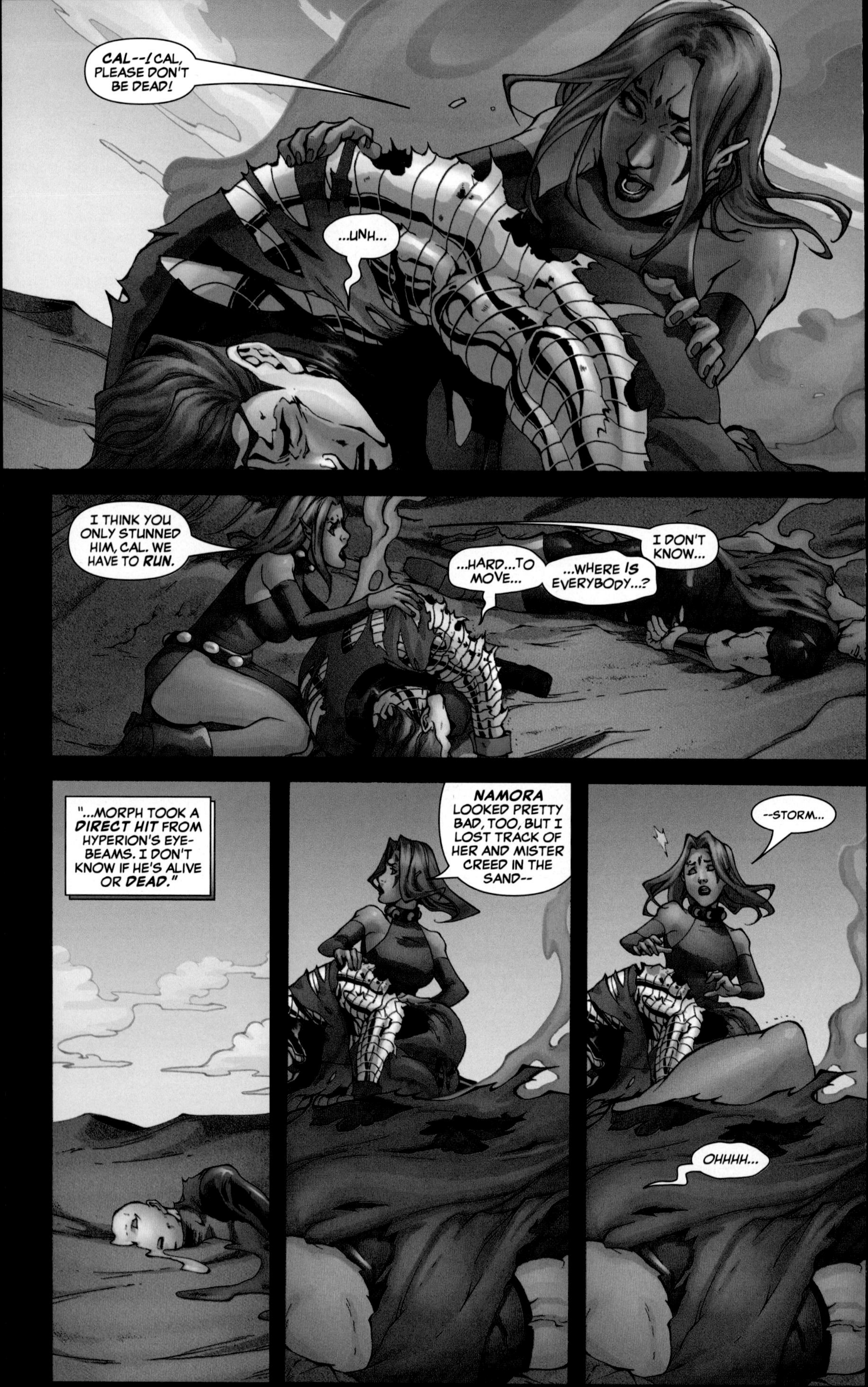
CAL--! CAL, PLEASE DON'T BE DEAD!
...UNH...
I THINK YOU ONLY STUNNED HIM, CAL. WE HAVE TO RUN.
...HARD...TO MOVE...
...WHERE IS EVERYBODY...?
I DON'T KNOW...
"...MORPH TOOK A DIRECT HIT FROM HYPERION'S EYE-BEAMS. I DON'T KNOW IF HE'S ALIVE OR DEAD."
NAMORA LOOKED PRETTY BAD, TOO, BUT I LOST TRACK OF HER AND MISTER CREED IN THE SAND--
--STORM...
OHHHH...

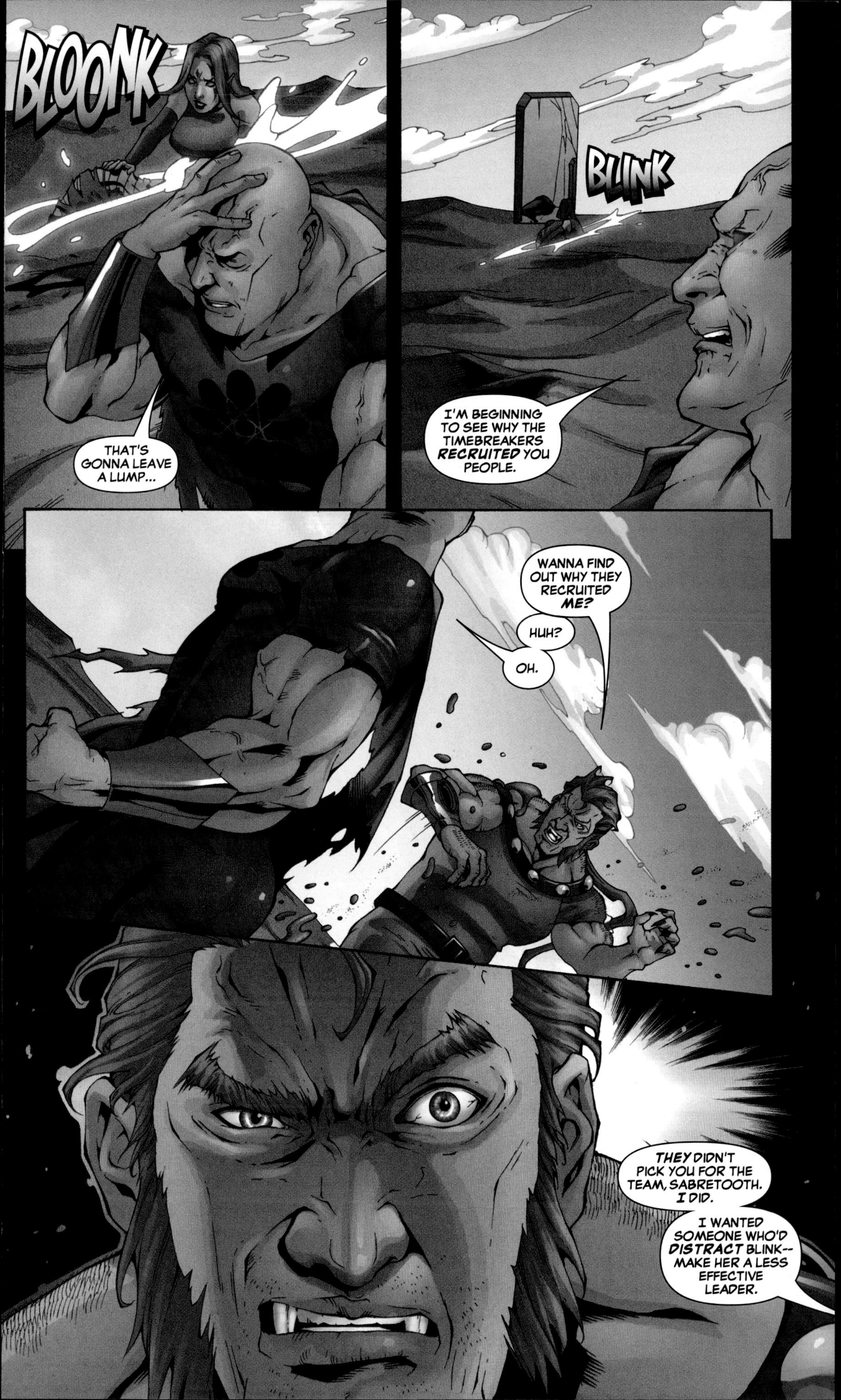
BLOONK
THAT'S GONNA LEAVE A LUMP...
BLINK
I'M BEGINNING TO SEE WHY THE TIMEBREAKERS RECRUITED YOU PEOPLE.
WANNA FIND OUT WHY THEY RECRUITED ME?
HUH?
OH.
THEY DIDN'T PICK YOU FOR THE TEAM, SABRETOOTH. I DID.
I WANTED SOMEONE WHO'D DISTRACT BLINK-- MAKE HER A LESS EFFECTIVE LEADER.

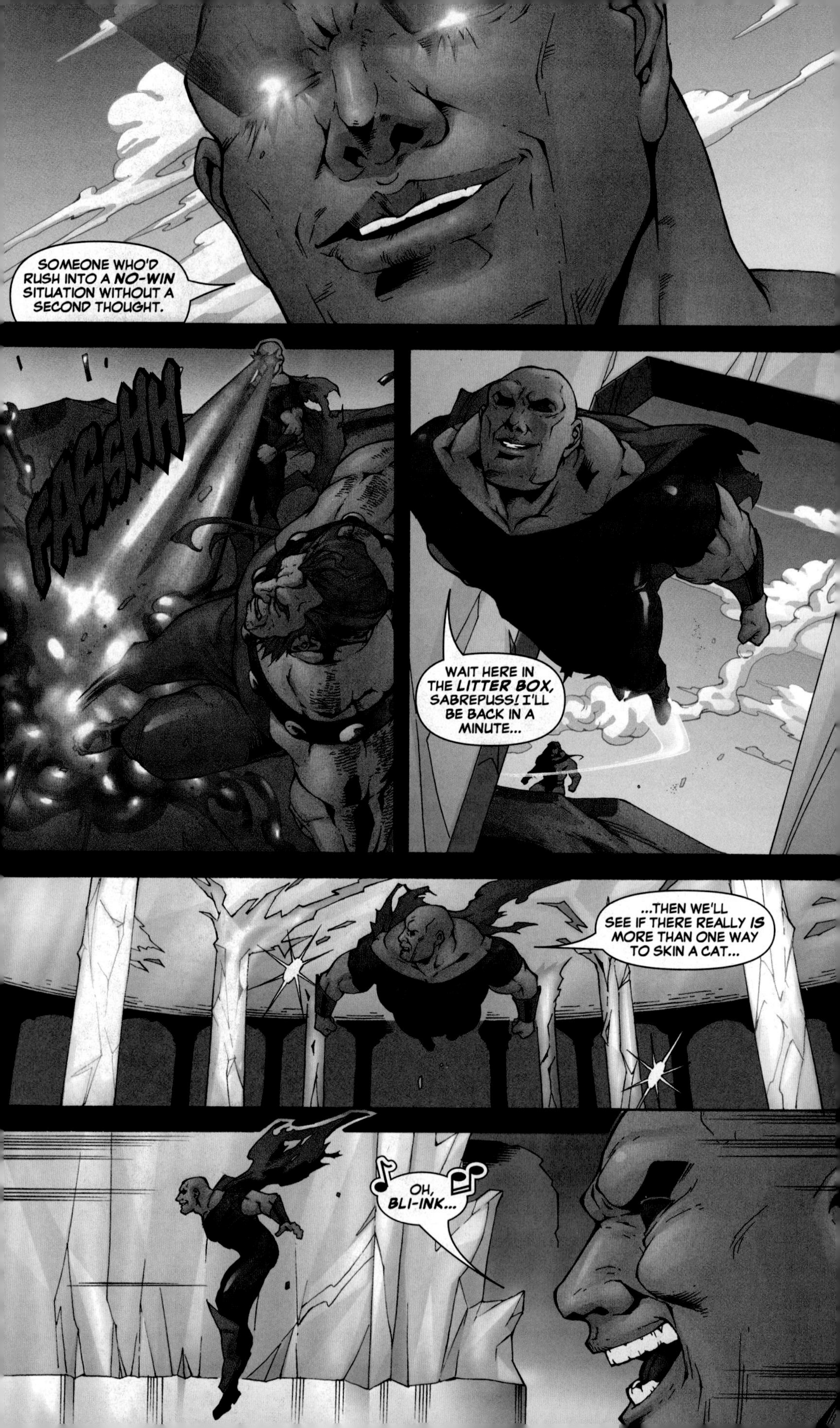
SOMEONE WHO'D RUSH INTO A NO-WIN SITUATION WITHOUT A SECOND THOUGHT.
FASSHH
WAIT HERE IN THE LITTER BOX, SABREPUSS! I'LL BE BACK IN A MINUTE...
...THEN WE'LL SEE IF THERE REALLY IS MORE THAN ONE WAY TO SKIN A CAT...
OH, BLI-INK...

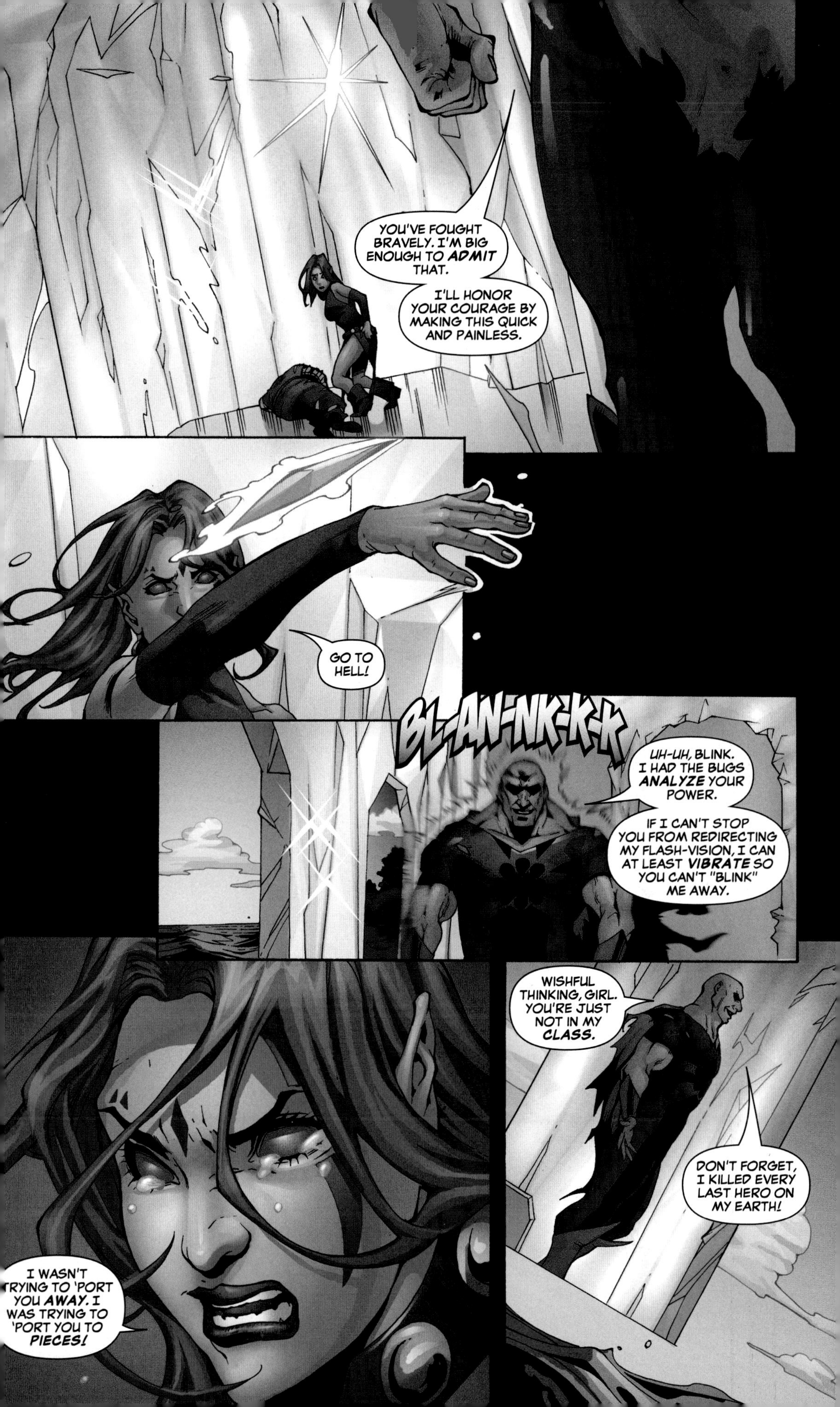

YOU'VE FOUGHT BRAVELY. I'M BIG ENOUGH TO ADMIT THAT.
I'LL HONOR YOUR COURAGE BY MAKING THIS QUICK AND PAINLESS.
GO TO HELL!
BL-AN-NK-K-K
UH-UH, BLINK. I HAD THE BUGS ANALYZE YOUR POWER.
IF I CAN'T STOP YOU FROM REDIRECTING MY FLASH-VISION, I CAN AT LEAST VIBRATE SO YOU CAN'T "BLINK" ME AWAY.
WISHFUL THINKING, GIRL. YOU'RE JUST NOT IN MY CLASS.
DON'T FORGET, I KILLED EVERY LAST HERO ON MY EARTH!
I WASN'T TRYING TO 'PORT YOU AWAY. I WAS TRYING TO 'PORT YOU TO PIECES!

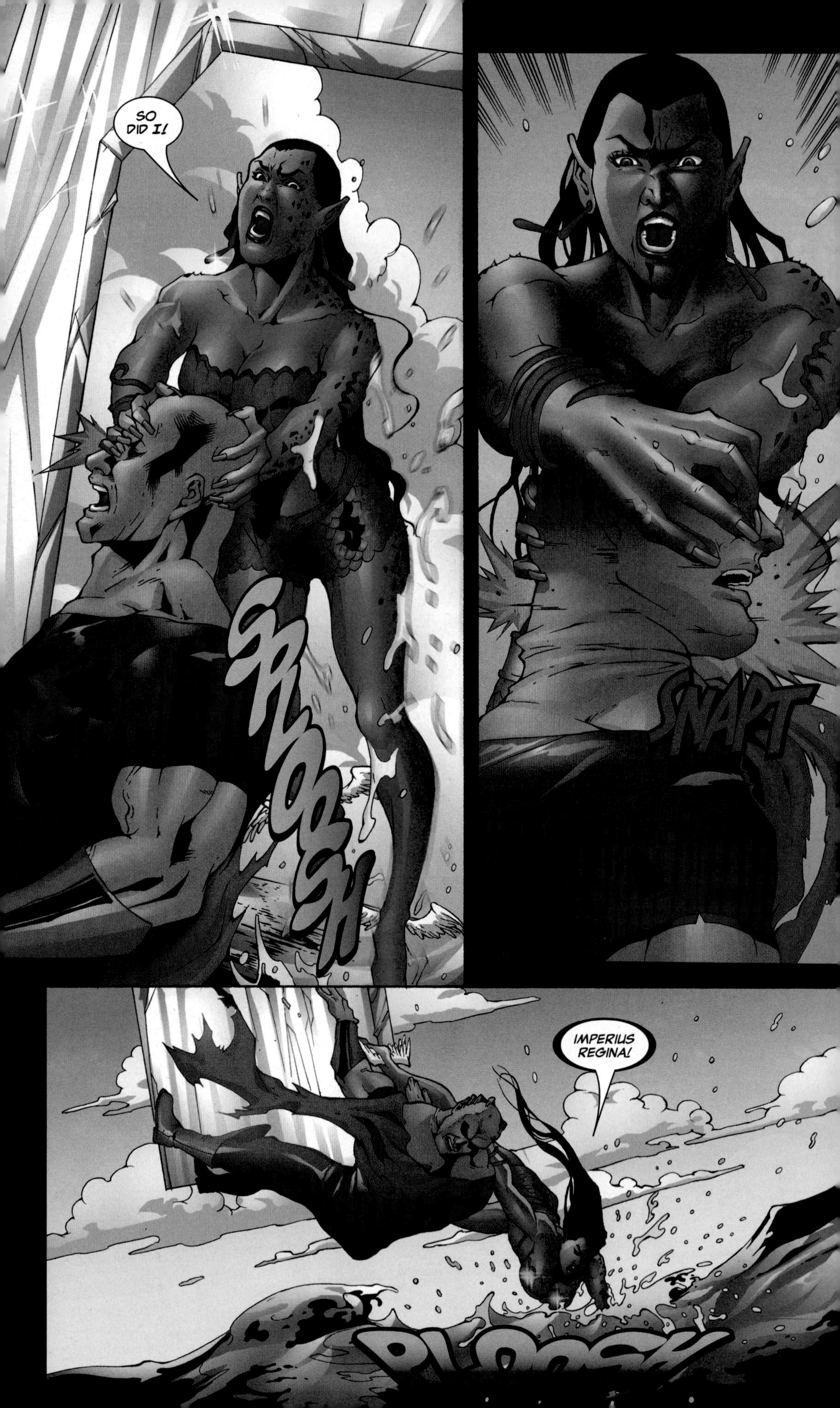
SO DID I!
SPLOOSH
SNAPT
IMPERIUS REGINA!
PLOOSH

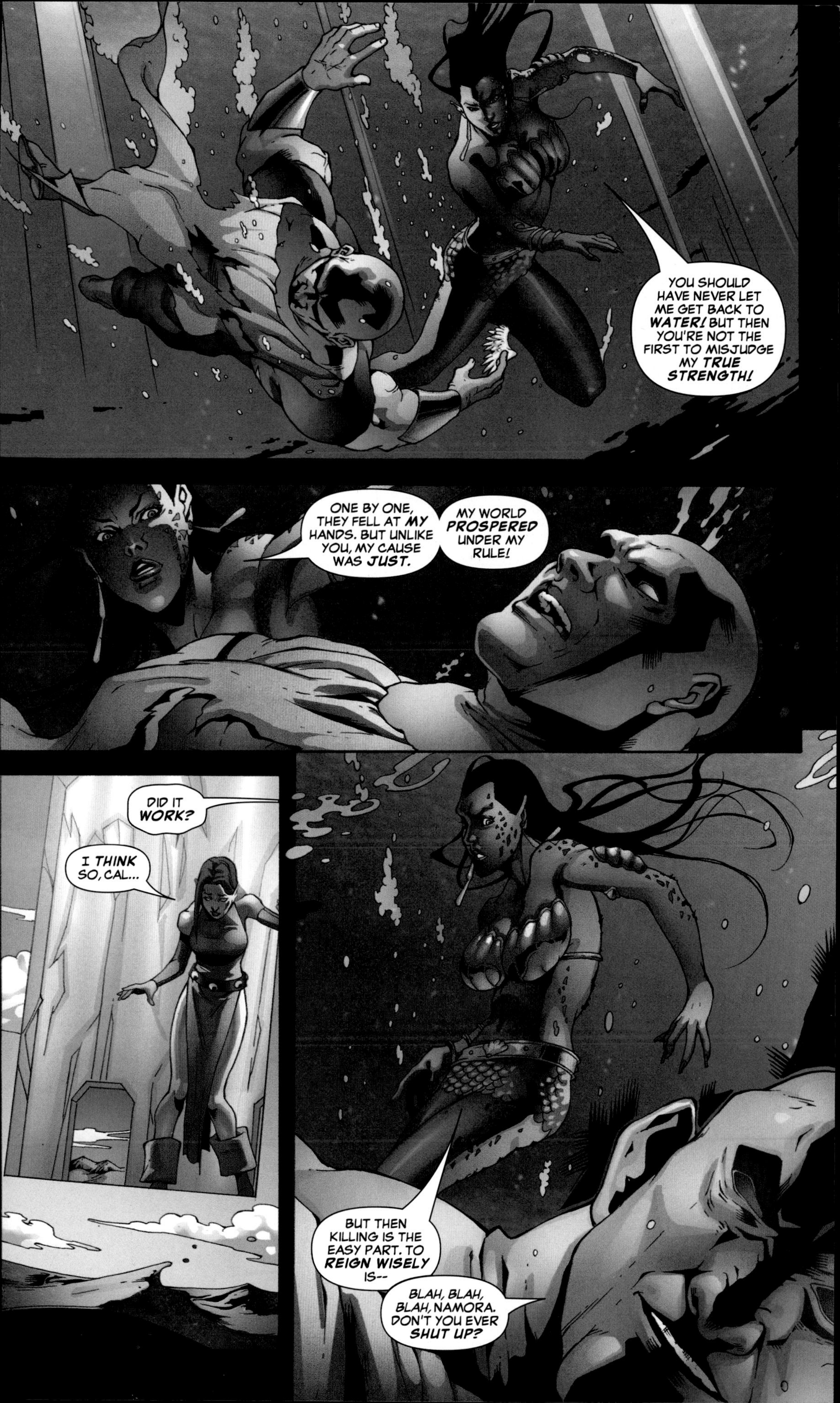
YOU SHOULD HAVE NEVER LET ME GET BACK TO WATER! BUT THEN YOU'RE NOT THE FIRST TO MISJUDGE MY TRUE STRENGTH!
ONE BY ONE, THEY FELL AT MY HANDS. BUT UNLIKE YOU, MY CAUSE WAS JUST.
MY WORLD PROSPERED UNDER MY RULE!
DID IT WORK?
I THINK SO, CAL...
BUT THEN KILLING IS THE EASY PART. TO REIGN WISELY IS--
BLAH, BLAH, BLAH, NAMORA. DON'T YOU EVER SHUT UP?

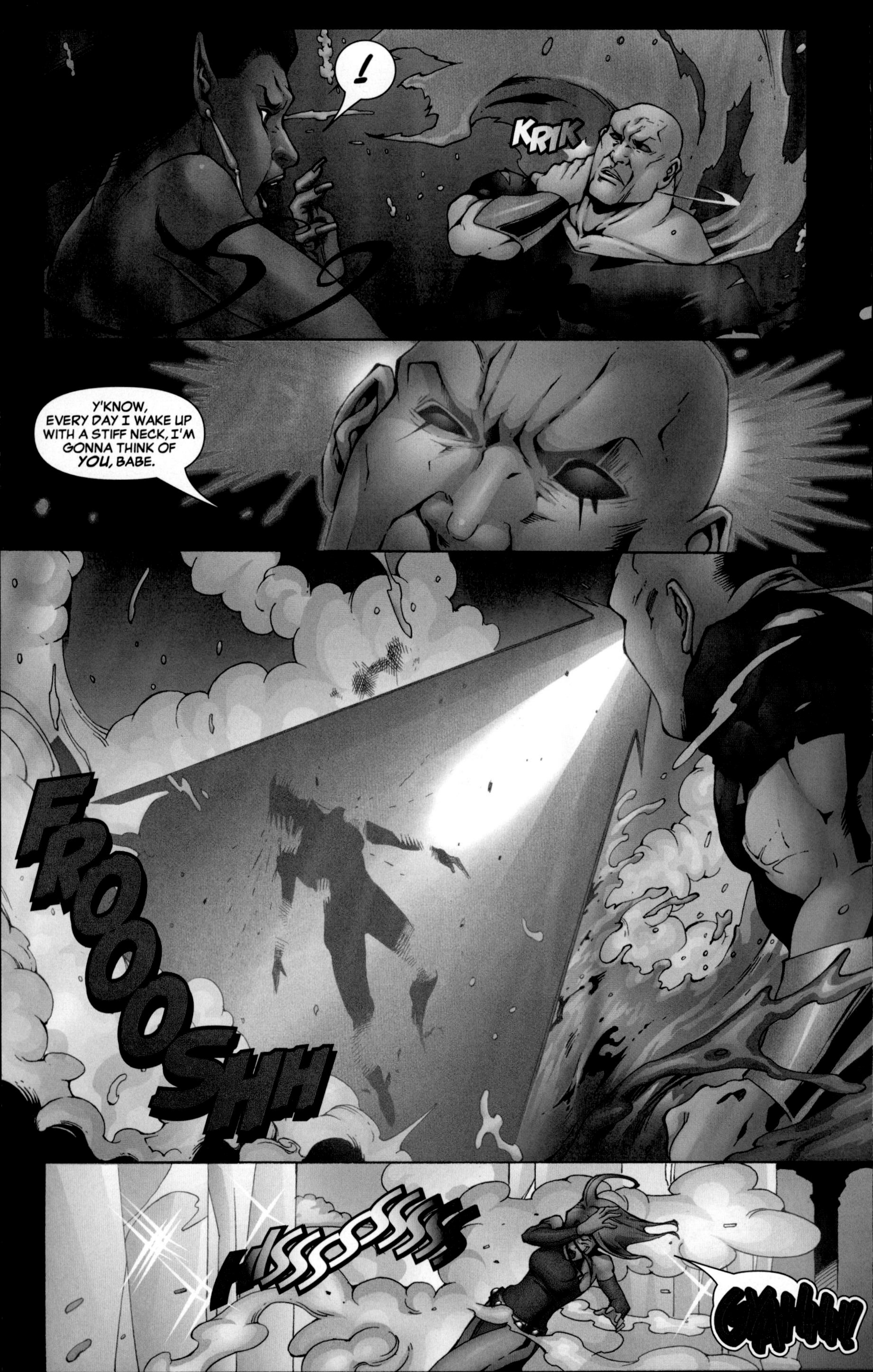
!
KRIK
Y'KNOW, EVERY DAY I WAKE UP WITH A STIFF NECK, I'M GONNA THINK OF YOU, BABE.
FROOOOSHH
HISSSSSS
GYAHHH!

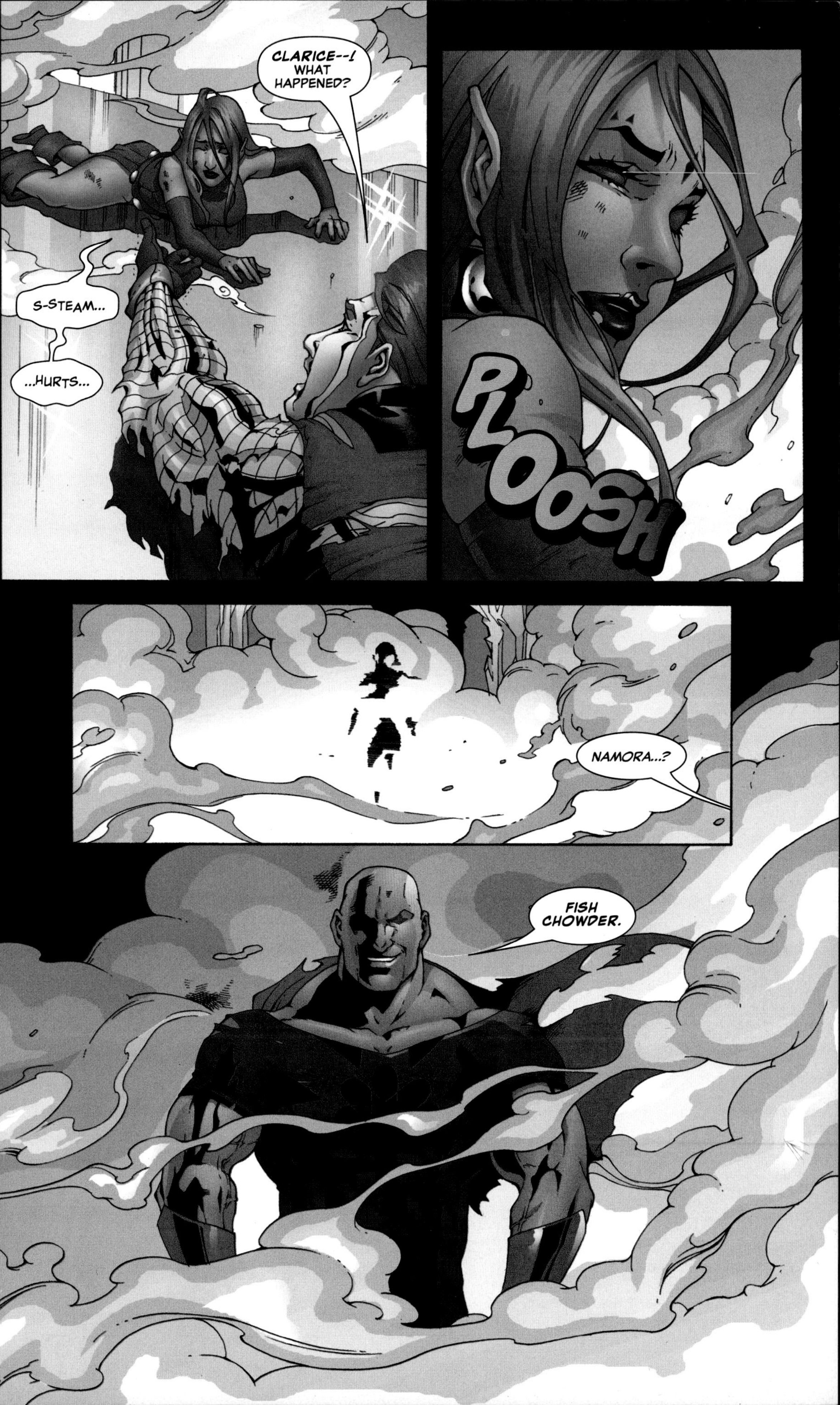

CLARICE--! WHAT HAPPENED?
S-STEAM...
...HURTS...
PLOOSH
NAMORA...?
FISH CHOWDER.

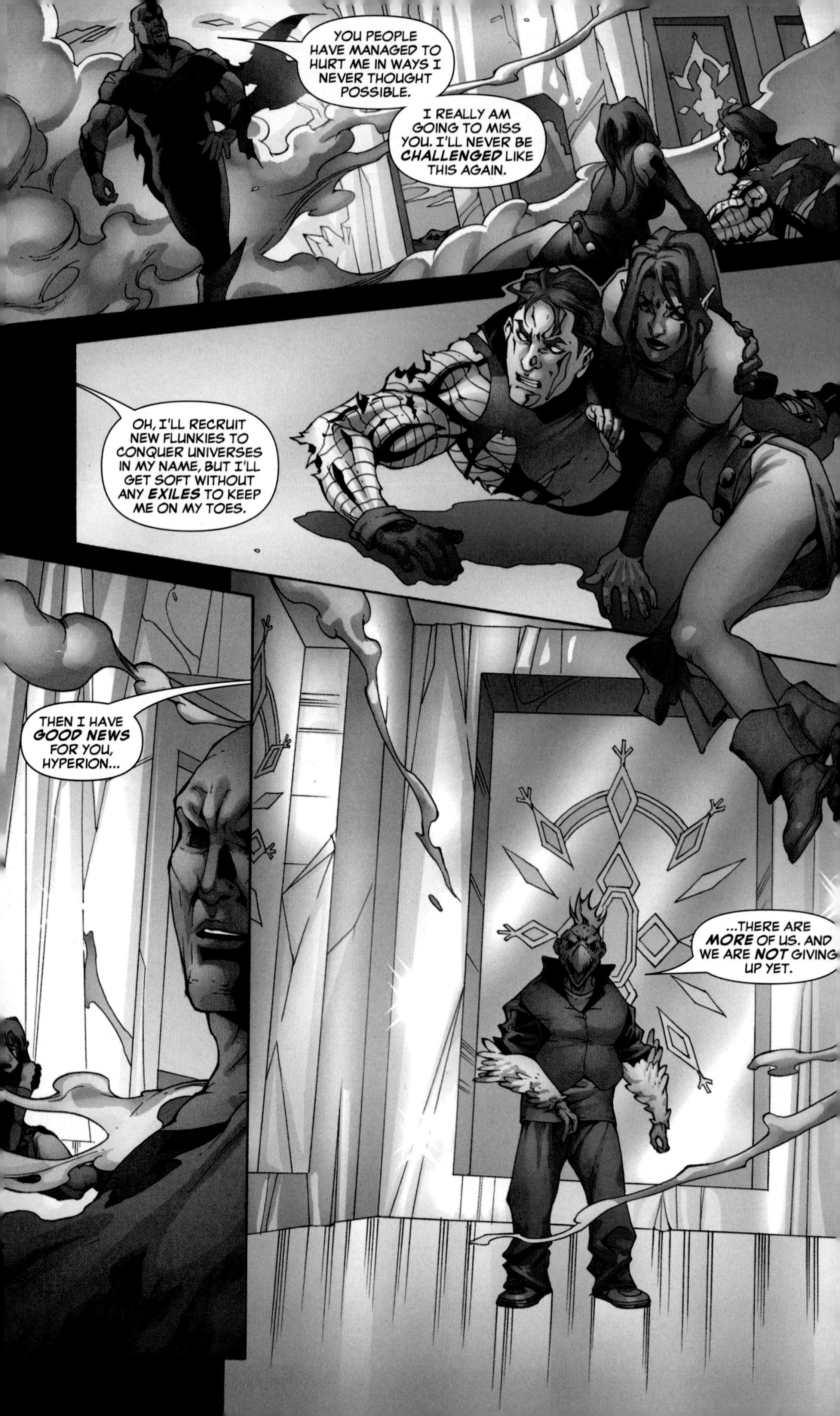
YOU PEOPLE HAVE MANAGED TO HURT ME IN WAYS I NEVER THOUGHT POSSIBLE.
I REALLY AM GOING TO MISS YOU. I'LL NEVER BE CHALLENGED LIKE THIS AGAIN.
OH, I'LL RECRUIT NEW FLUNKIES TO CONQUER UNIVERSES IN MY NAME, BUT I'LL GET SOFT WITHOUT ANY EXILES TO KEEP ME ON MY TOES.
THEN I HAVE GOOD NEWS FOR YOU, HYPERION...
...THERE ARE MORE OF US. AND WE ARE NOT GIVING UP YET.

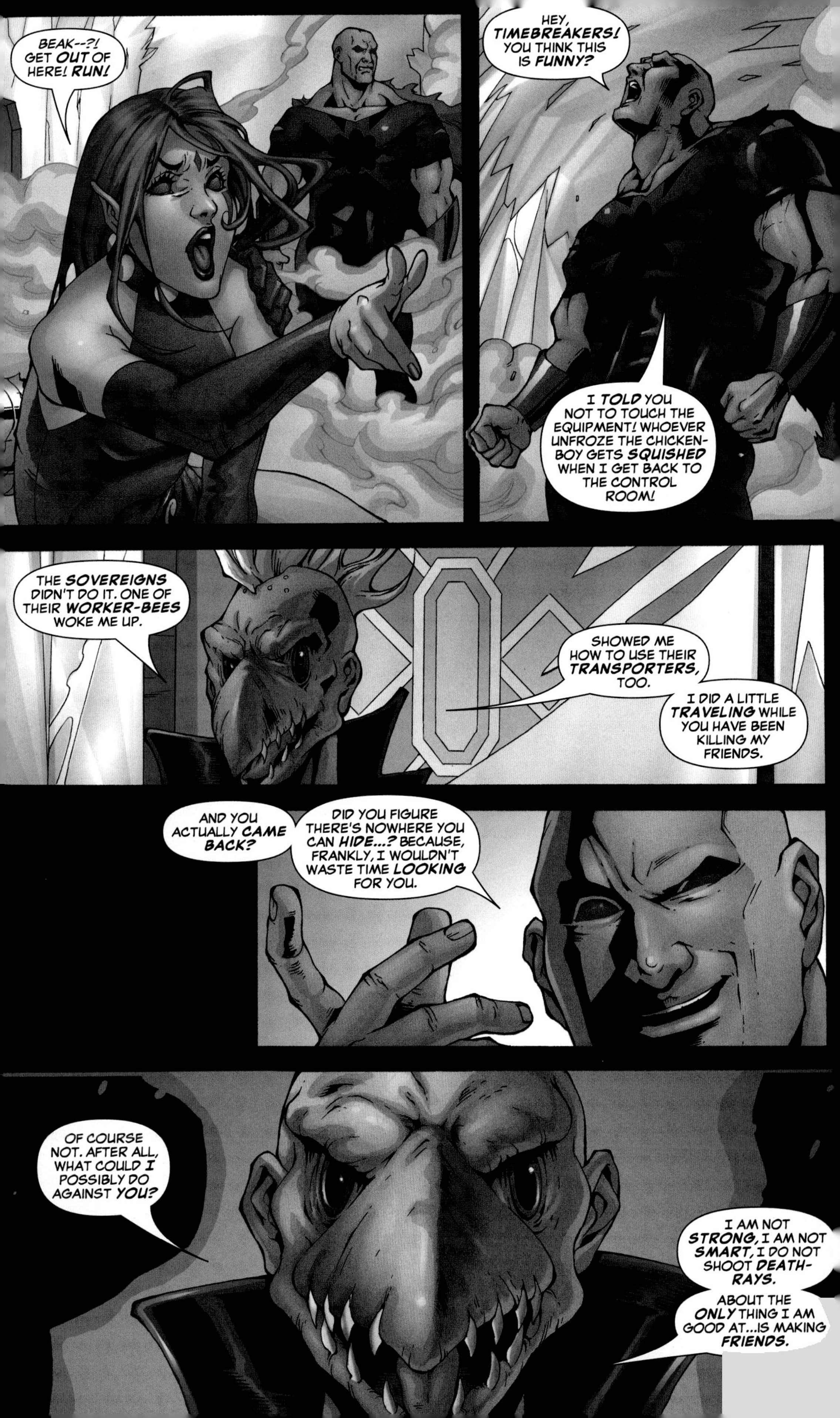
BEAK--?! GET OUT OF HERE! RUN!
HEY, TIMEBREAKERS! YOU THINK THIS IS FUNNY?
I TOLD YOU NOT TO TOUCH THE EQUIPMENT! WHOEVER UNFROZE THE CHICKEN-BOY GETS SQUISHED WHEN I GET BACK TO THE CONTROL ROOM!
THE SOVEREIGNS DIDN'T DO IT. ONE OF THEIR WORKER-BEES WOKE ME UP.
SHOWED ME HOW TO USE THEIR TRANSPORTERS, TOO.
I DID A LITTLE TRAVELING WHILE YOU HAVE BEEN KILLING MY FRIENDS.
AND YOU ACTUALLY CAME BACK?
DID YOU FIGURE THERE'S NOWHERE YOU CAN HIDE...? BECAUSE, FRANKLY, I WOULDN'T WASTE TIME LOOKING FOR YOU.
OF COURSE NOT. AFTER ALL, WHAT COULD I POSSIBLY DO AGAINST YOU?
I AM NOT STRONG, I AM NOT SMART, I DO NOT SHOOT DEATH-RAYS.
ABOUT THE ONLY THING I AM GOOD AT...IS MAKING FRIENDS.

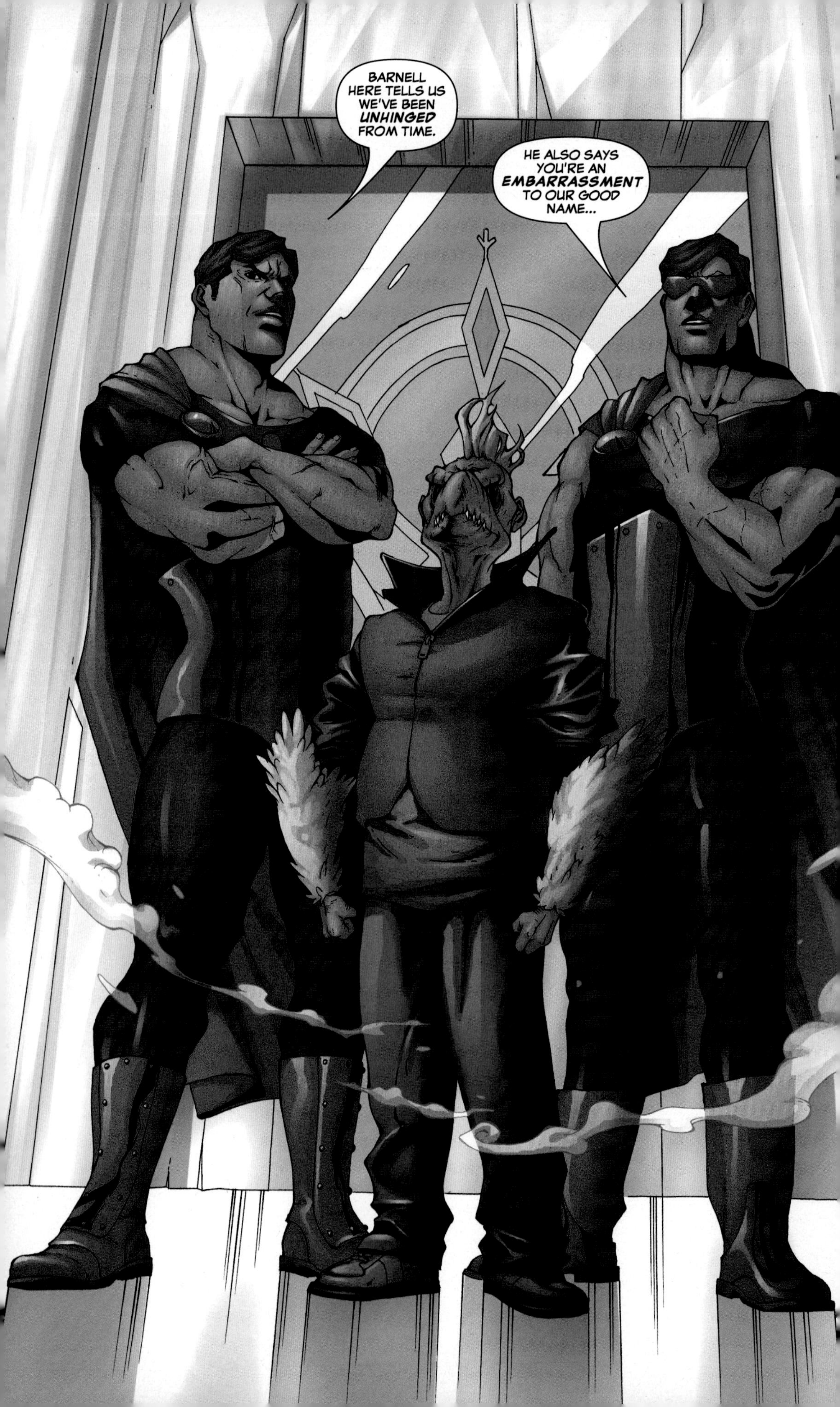
BARNELL HERE TELLS US WE'VE BEEN UNHINGED FROM TIME.
HE ALSO SAYS YOU'RE AN EMBARRASSMENT TO OUR GOOD NAME...

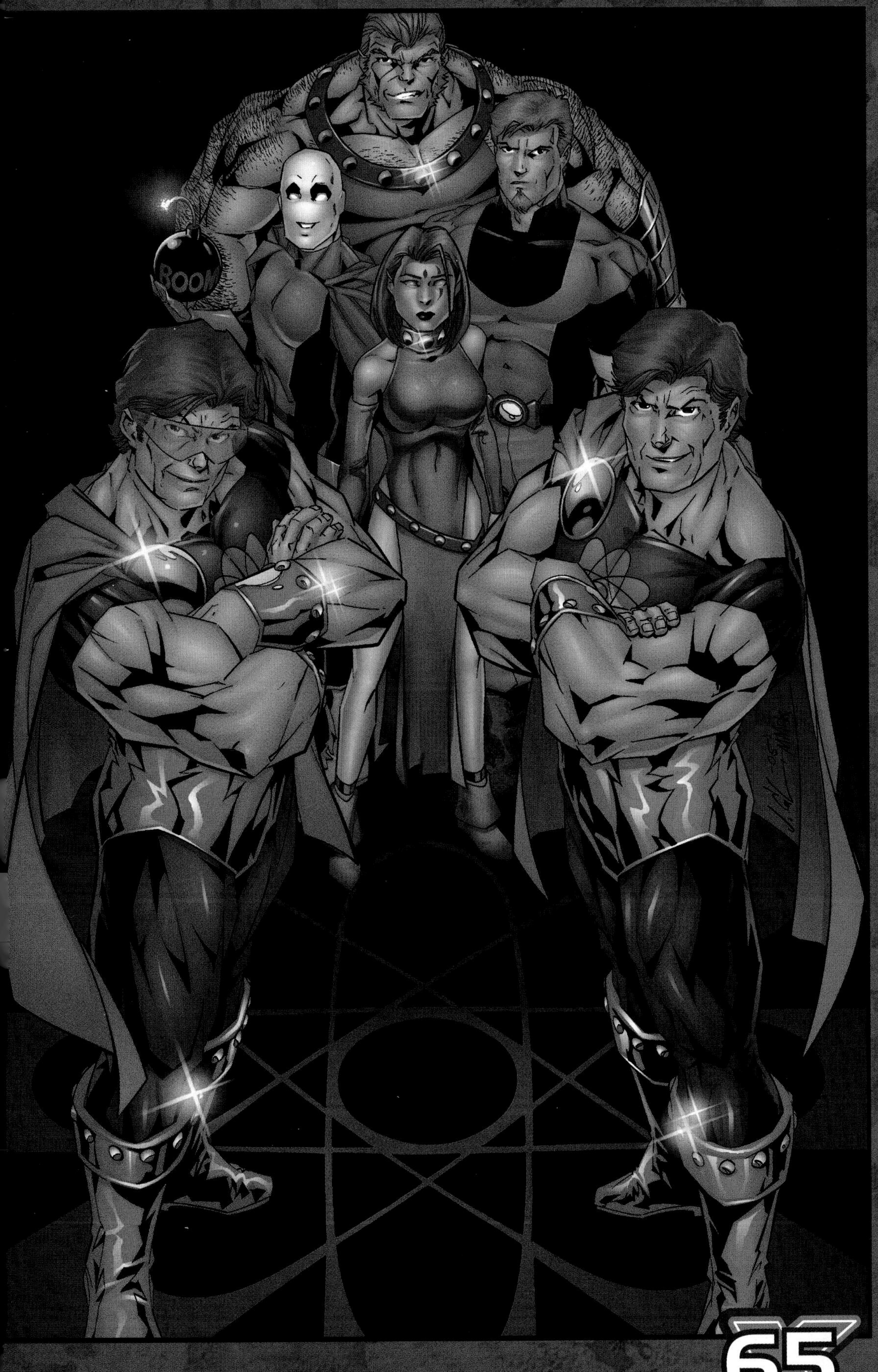
BOOM

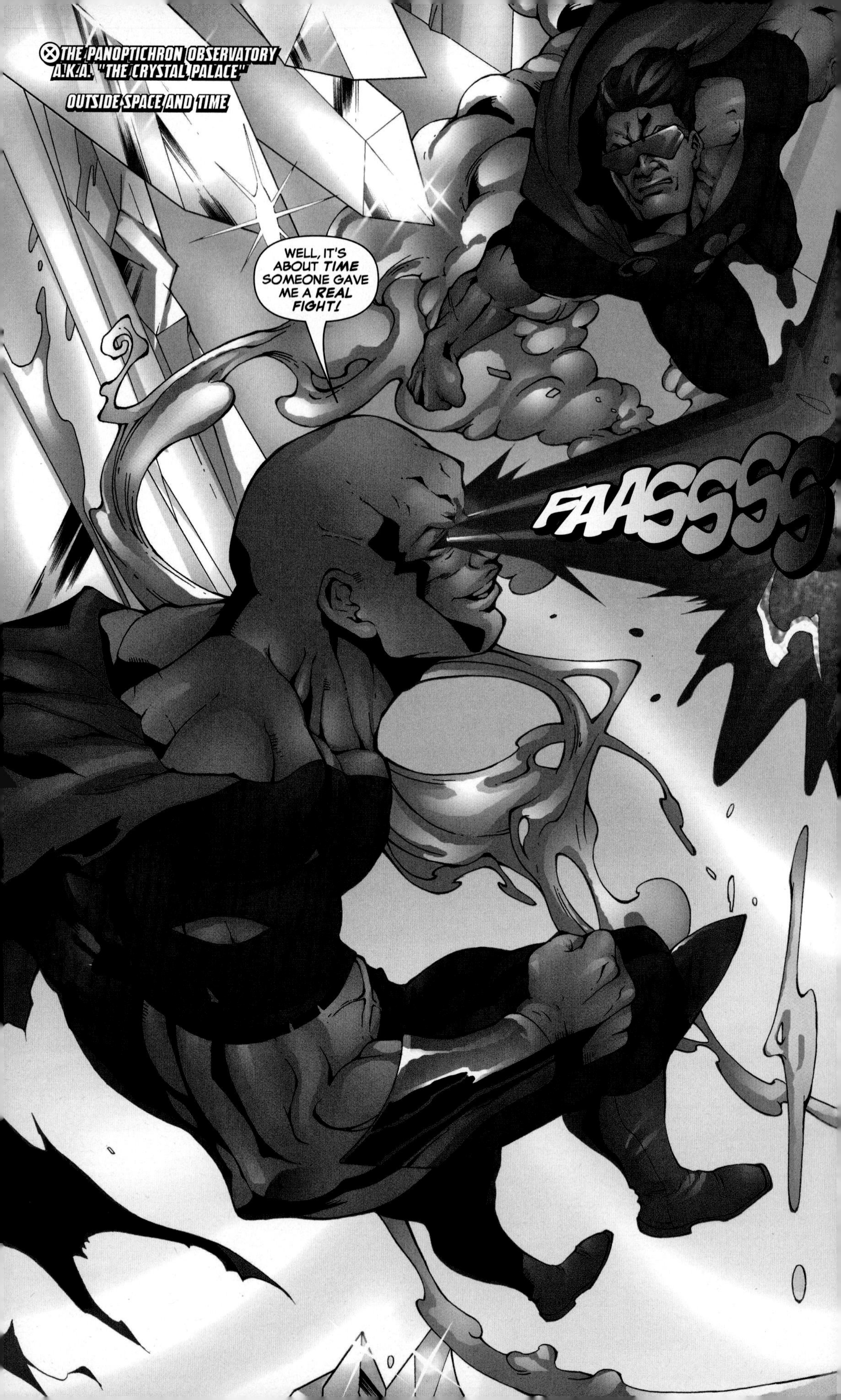
THE PANOPTICHRON OBSERVATORY A.K.A. "THE CRYSTAL PALACE"
OUTSIDE SPACE AND TIME
WELL, IT'S ABOUT TIME SOMEONE GAVE ME A REAL FIGHT!
FAASSSS

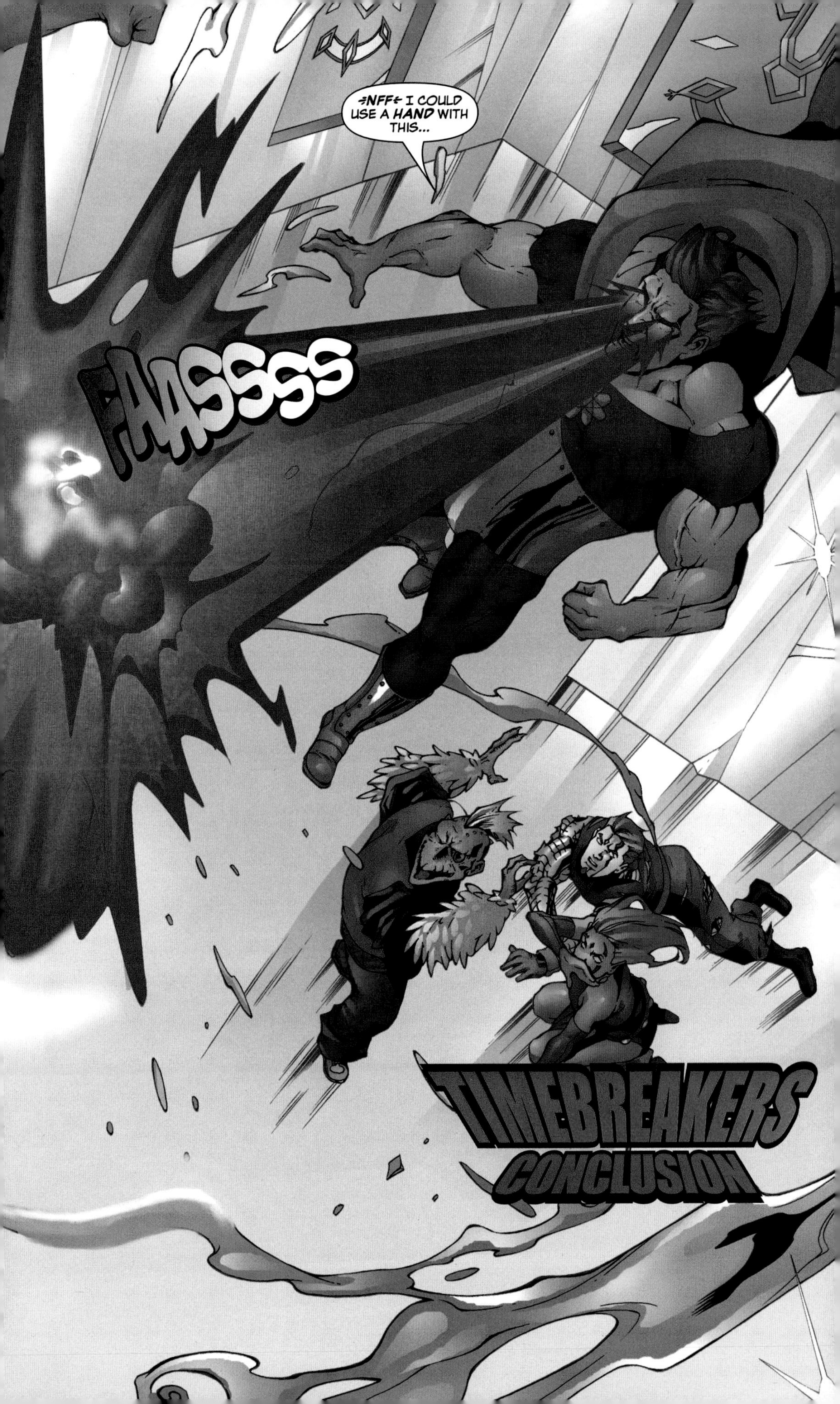
NFF I COULD USE A HAND WITH THIS...
FAASSSS
TIMEBREAKERS
CONCLUSION

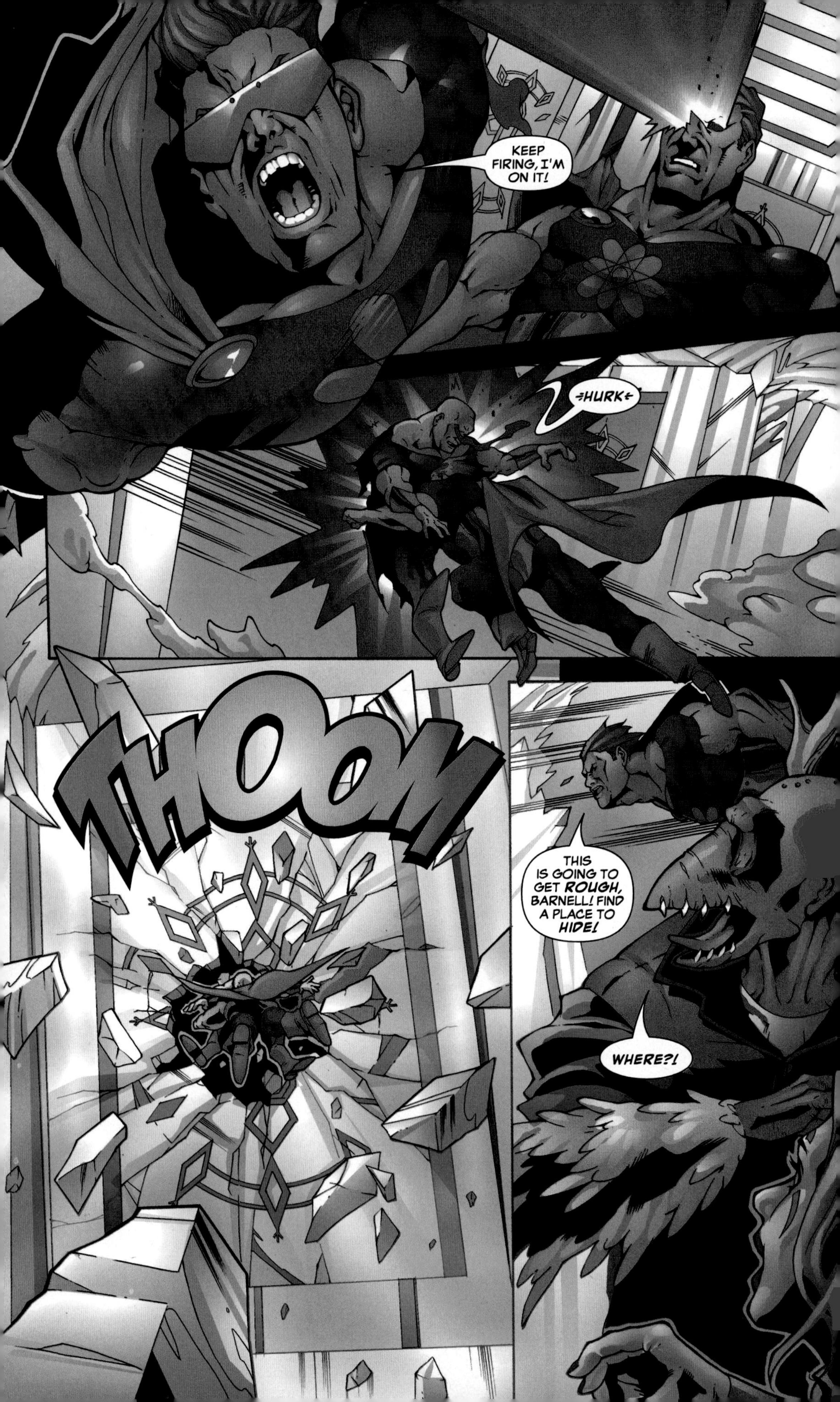
KEEP FIRING, I'M ON IT!
HURK
THOOM
THIS IS GOING TO GET ROUGH, BARNELL! FIND A PLACE TO HIDE!
WHERE?!

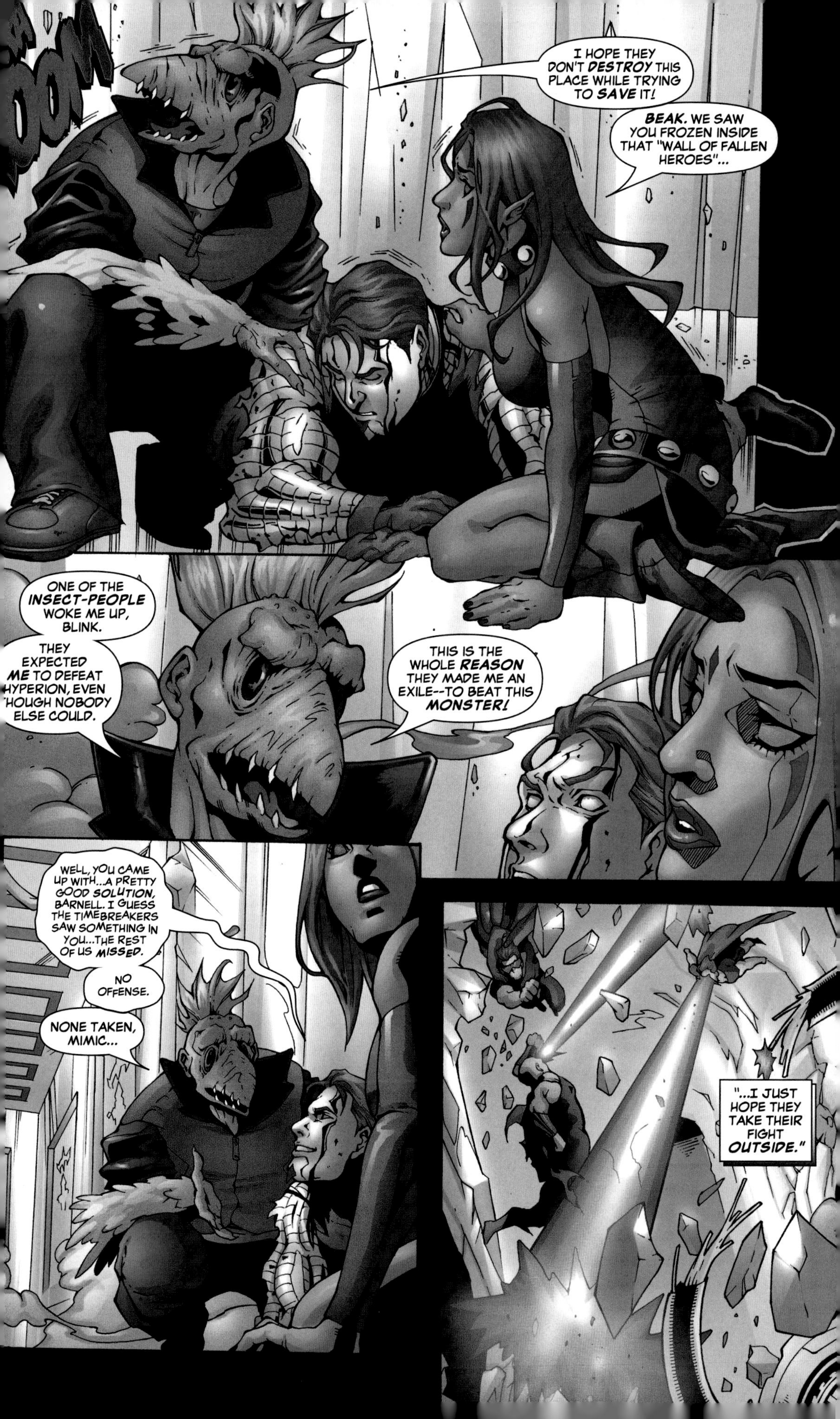

I HOPE THEY DON'T DESTROY THIS PLACE WHILE TRYING TO SAVE IT!
BEAK. WE SAW YOU FROZEN INSIDE THAT "WALL OF FALLEN HEROES"...
ONE OF THE INSECT-PEOPLE WOKE ME UP, BLINK.
THEY EXPECTED ME TO DEFEAT HYPERION, EVEN THOUGH NOBODY ELSE COULD.
THIS IS THE WHOLE REASON THEY MADE ME AN EXILE--TO BEAT THIS MONSTER!
WELL, YOU CAME UP WITH...A PRETTY GOOD SOLUTION, BARNELL. I GUESS THE TIMEBREAKERS SAW SOMETHING IN YOU...THE REST OF US MISSED.
NO OFFENSE.
NONE TAKEN, MIMIC...
"...I JUST HOPE THEY TAKE THEIR FIGHT OUTSIDE."

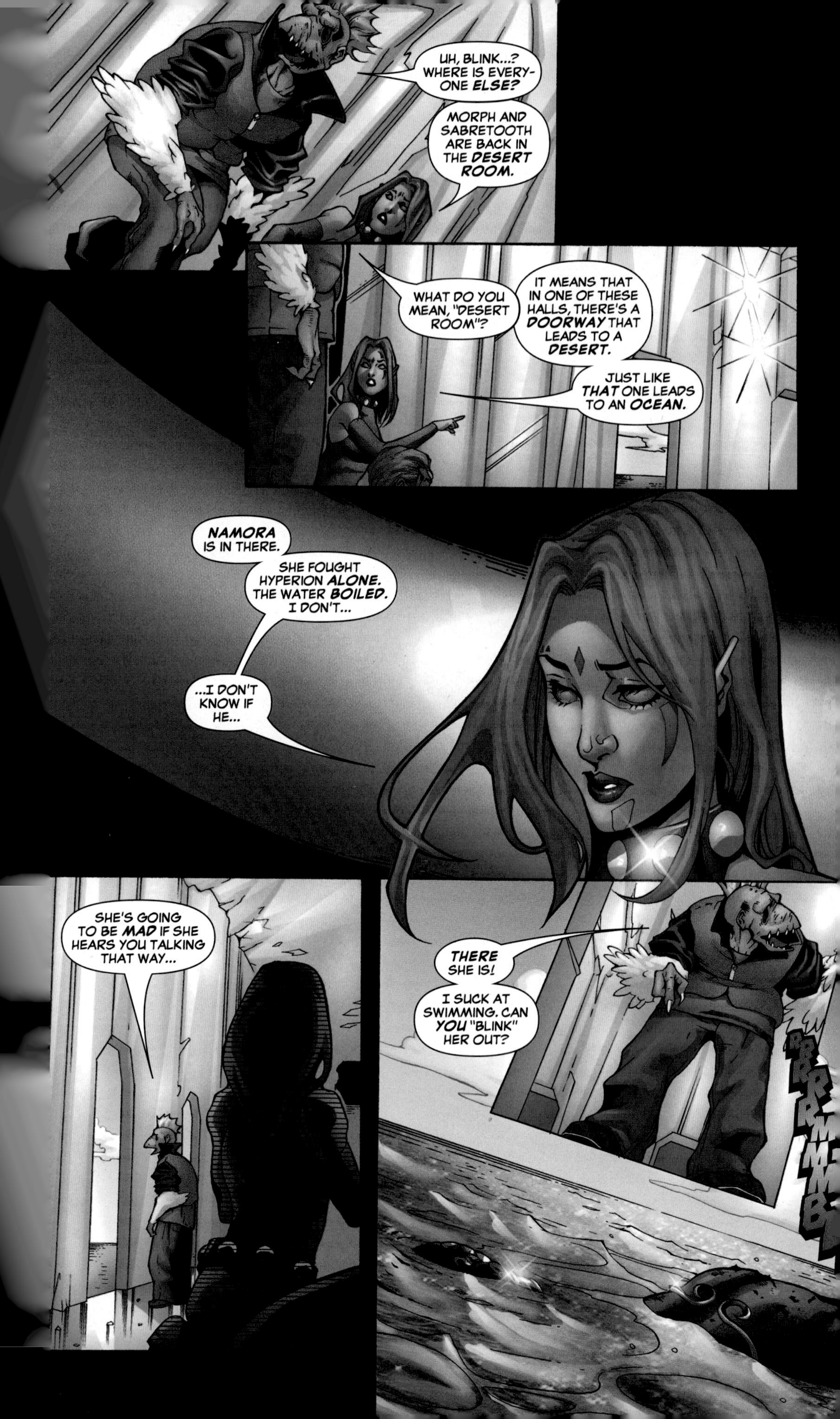
UH, BLINK...? WHERE IS EVERY-ONE ELSE?
MORPH AND SABRETOOTH ARE BACK IN THE DESERT ROOM.
WHAT DO YOU MEAN, "DESERT ROOM"?
IT MEANS THAT IN ONE OF THESE HALLS, THERE'S A DOORWAY THAT LEADS TO A DESERT.
JUST LIKE THAT ONE LEADS TO AN OCEAN.
NAMORA IS IN THERE.
SHE FOUGHT HYPERION ALONE. THE WATER BOILED. I DON'T...
...I DON'T KNOW IF HE...
SHE'S GOING TO BE MAD IF SHE HEARS YOU TALKING THAT WAY...
THERE SHE IS!
I SUCK AT SWIMMING. CAN YOU "BLINK" HER OUT?
RRRRRMMMB

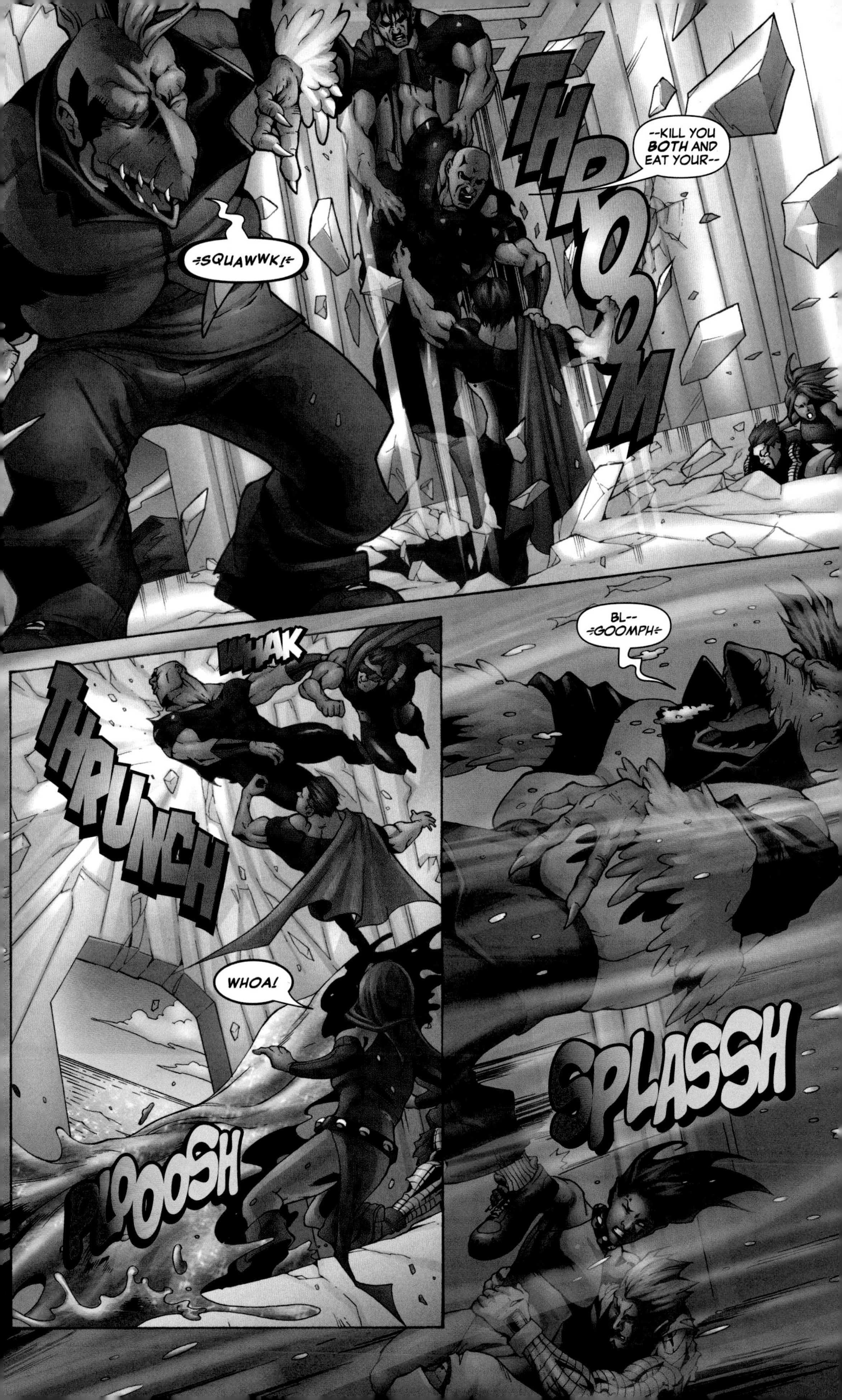

THDOOM
--KILL YOU BOTH AND EAT YOUR--
=SQUAWWK!=
WHAK
THRUNCH
WHOA!
PLOOOSH
BL-- =GOOMPH=
SPLASSH

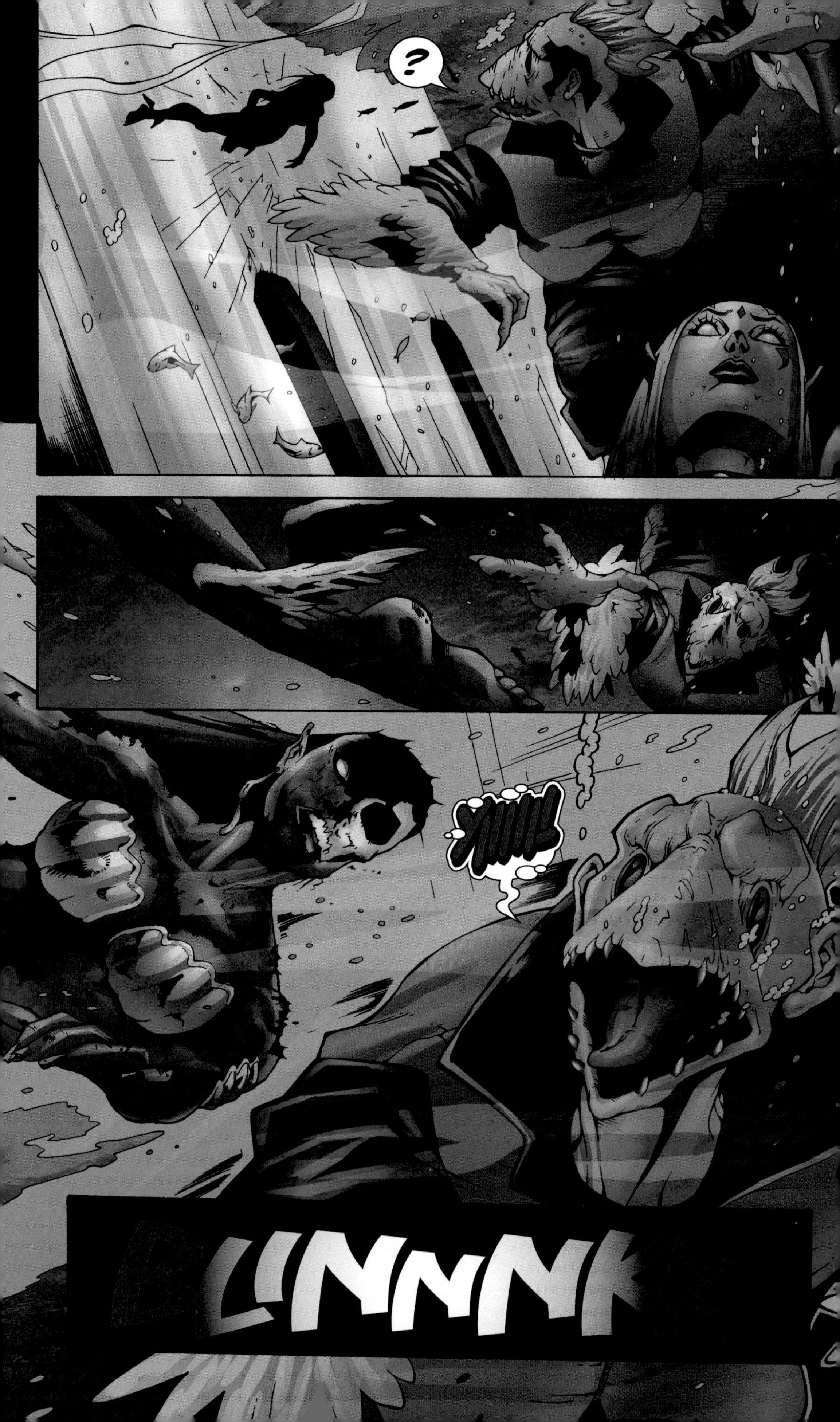
?
LINNNK

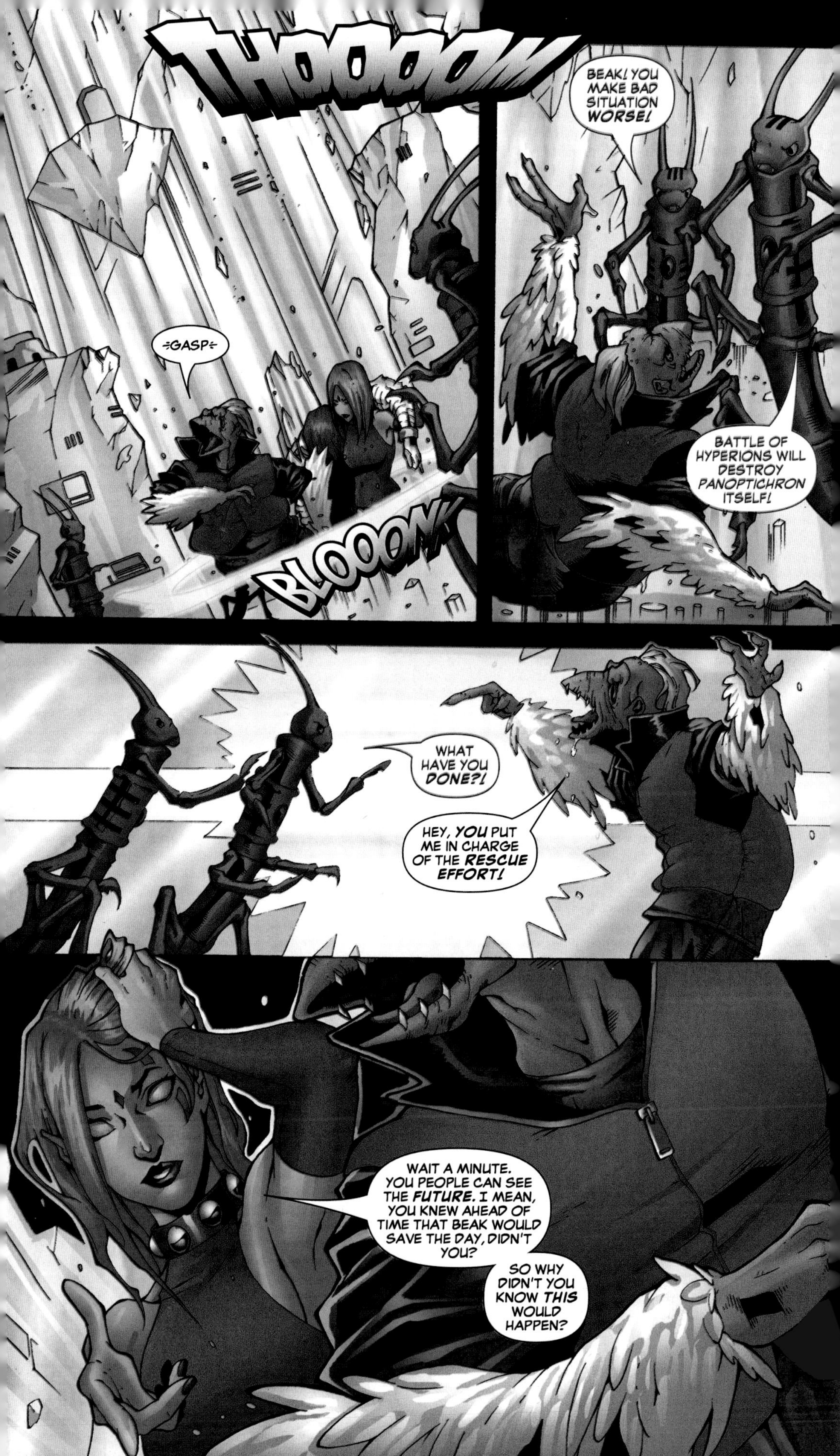
THOOOOOM
=GASP=
BLOOOOM
BEAK! YOU MAKE BAD SITUATION WORSE!
BATTLE OF HYPERIONS WILL DESTROY PANOPTICHRON ITSELF!
WHAT HAVE YOU DONE?!
HEY, YOU PUT ME IN CHARGE OF THE RESCUE EFFORT!
WAIT A MINUTE. YOU PEOPLE CAN SEE THE FUTURE. I MEAN, YOU KNEW AHEAD OF TIME THAT BEAK WOULD SAVE THE DAY, DIDN'T YOU?
SO WHY DIDN'T YOU KNOW THIS WOULD HAPPEN?

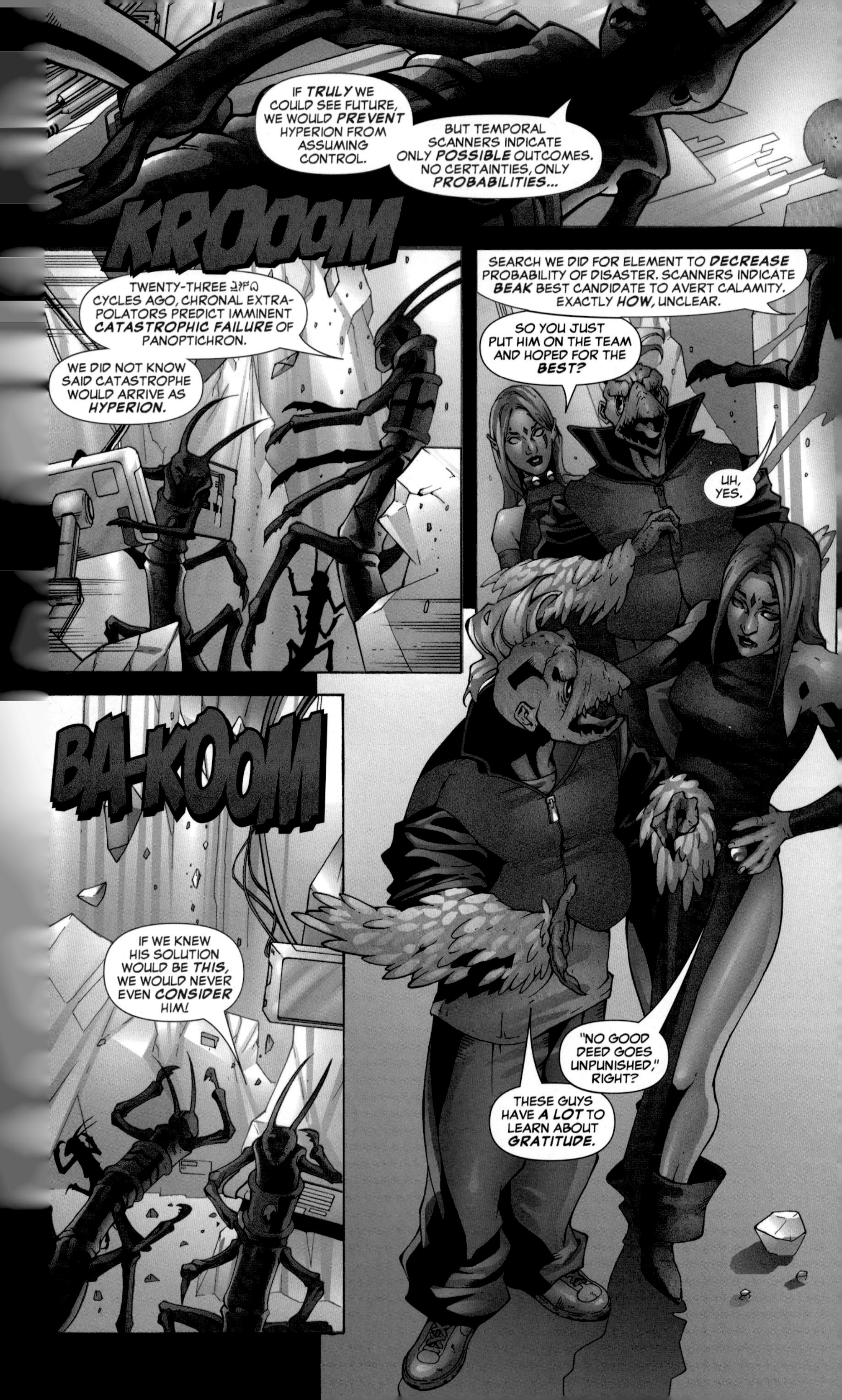

IF TRULY WE COULD SEE FUTURE, WE WOULD PREVENT HYPERION FROM ASSUMING CONTROL.
BUT TEMPORAL SCANNERS INDICATE ONLY POSSIBLE OUTCOMES. NO CERTAINTIES, ONLY PROBABILITIES...
KROOOM
TWENTY-THREE CYCLES AGO, CHRONAL EXTRAPOLATORS PREDICT IMMINENT CATASTROPHIC FAILURE OF PANOPTICHRON.
WE DID NOT KNOW SAID CATASTROPHE WOULD ARRIVE AS HYPERION.
SEARCH WE DID FOR ELEMENT TO DECREASE PROBABILITY OF DISASTER. SCANNERS INDICATE BEAK BEST CANDIDATE TO AVERT CALAMITY. EXACTLY HOW, UNCLEAR.
SO YOU JUST PUT HIM ON THE TEAM AND HOPED FOR THE BEST?
UH, YES.
BA-KOOM
IF WE KNEW HIS SOLUTION WOULD BE THIS, WE WOULD NEVER EVEN CONSIDER HIM!
"NO GOOD DEED GOES UNPUNISHED," RIGHT?
THESE GUYS HAVE A LOT TO LEARN ABOUT GRATITUDE.

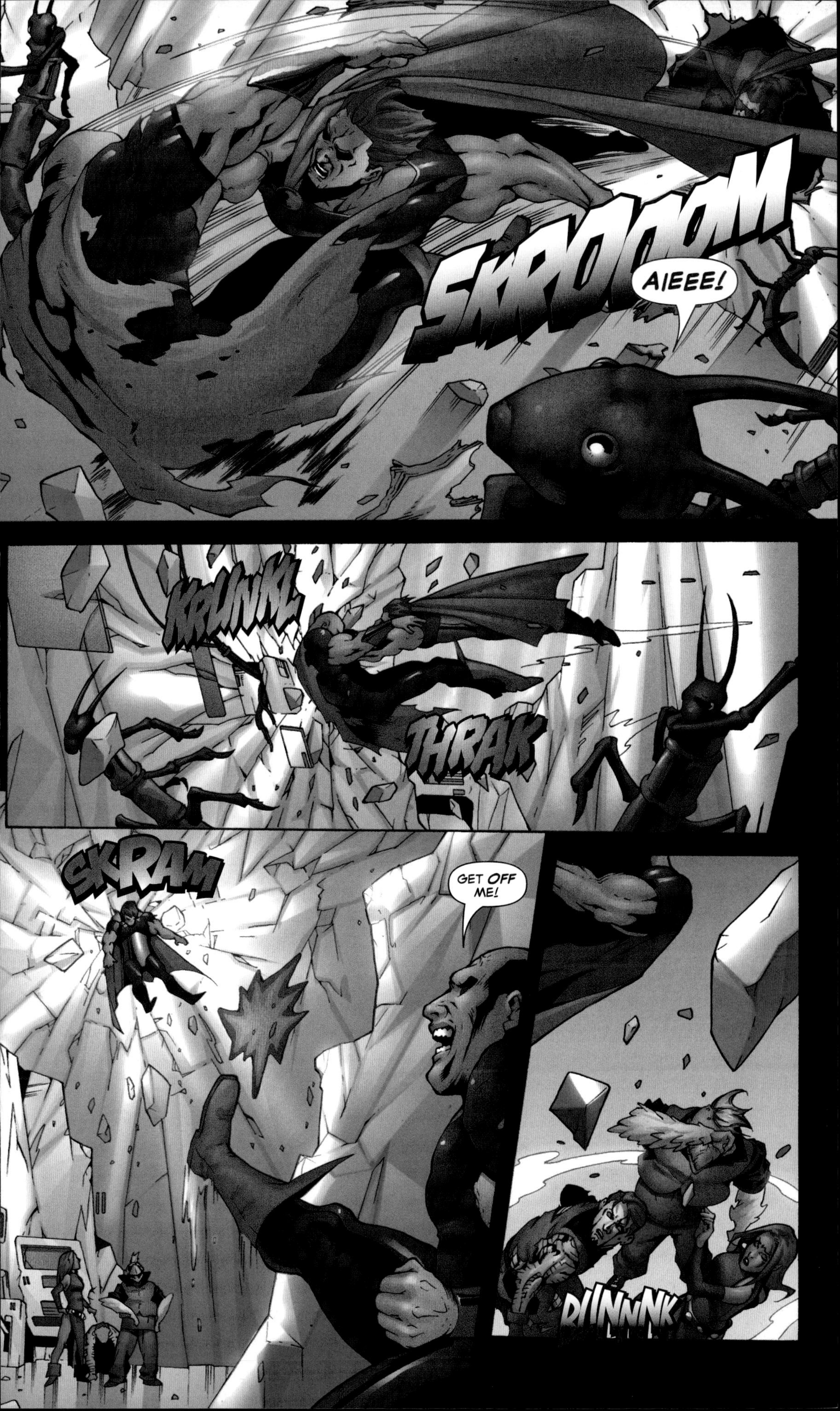

SKROOOOM
AIEEE!
KRUNKL
THRAK
SKRAM
GET OFF ME!
DUNNNK

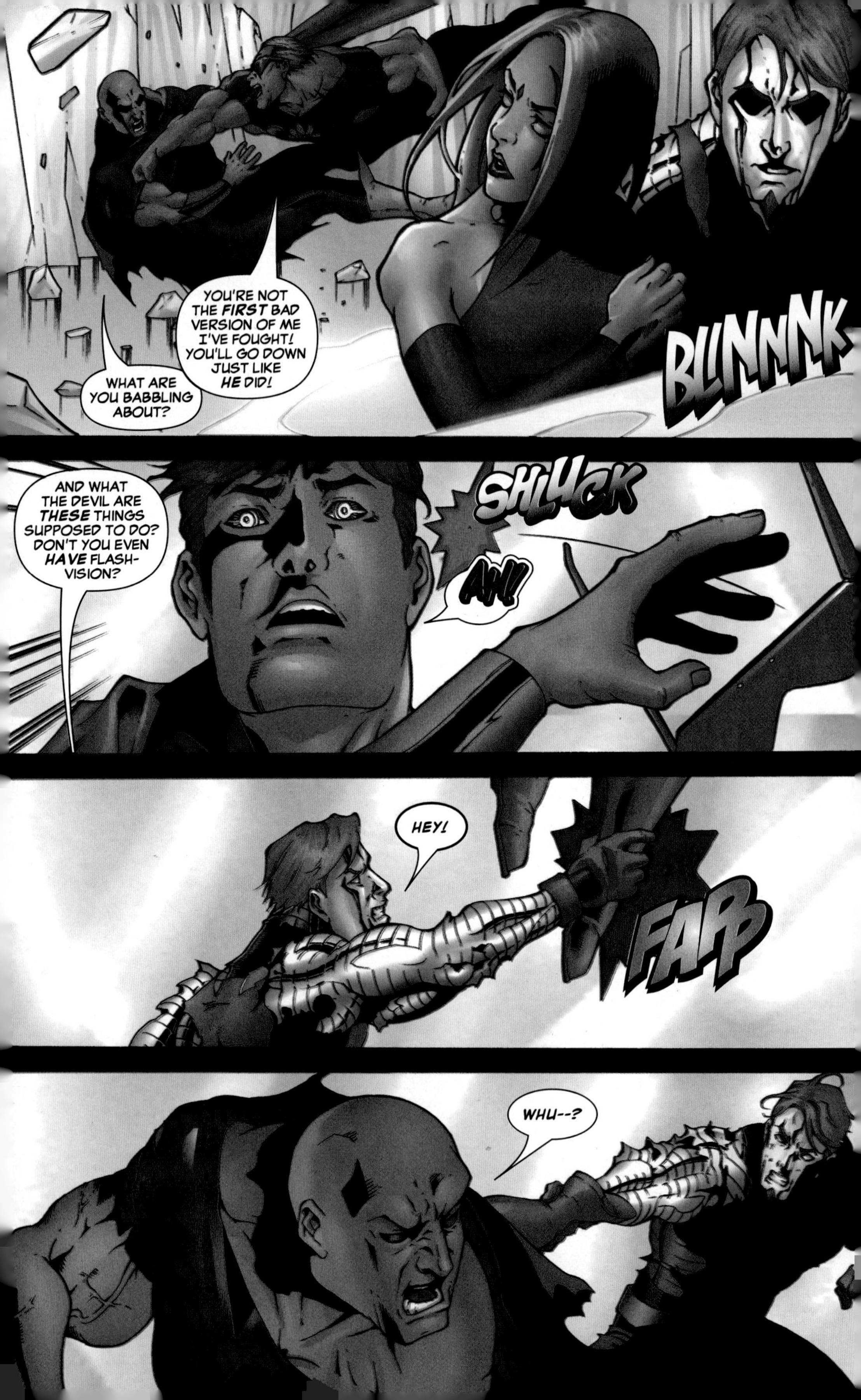

YOU'RE NOT THE FIRST BAD VERSION OF ME I'VE FOUGHT! YOU'LL GO DOWN JUST LIKE HE DID!
WHAT ARE YOU BABBLING ABOUT?
BLINNNK
AND WHAT THE DEVIL ARE THESE THINGS SUPPOSED TO DO? DON'T YOU EVEN HAVE FLASH-VISION?
SHLUCK
AH!
HEY!
FAP
WHU--?

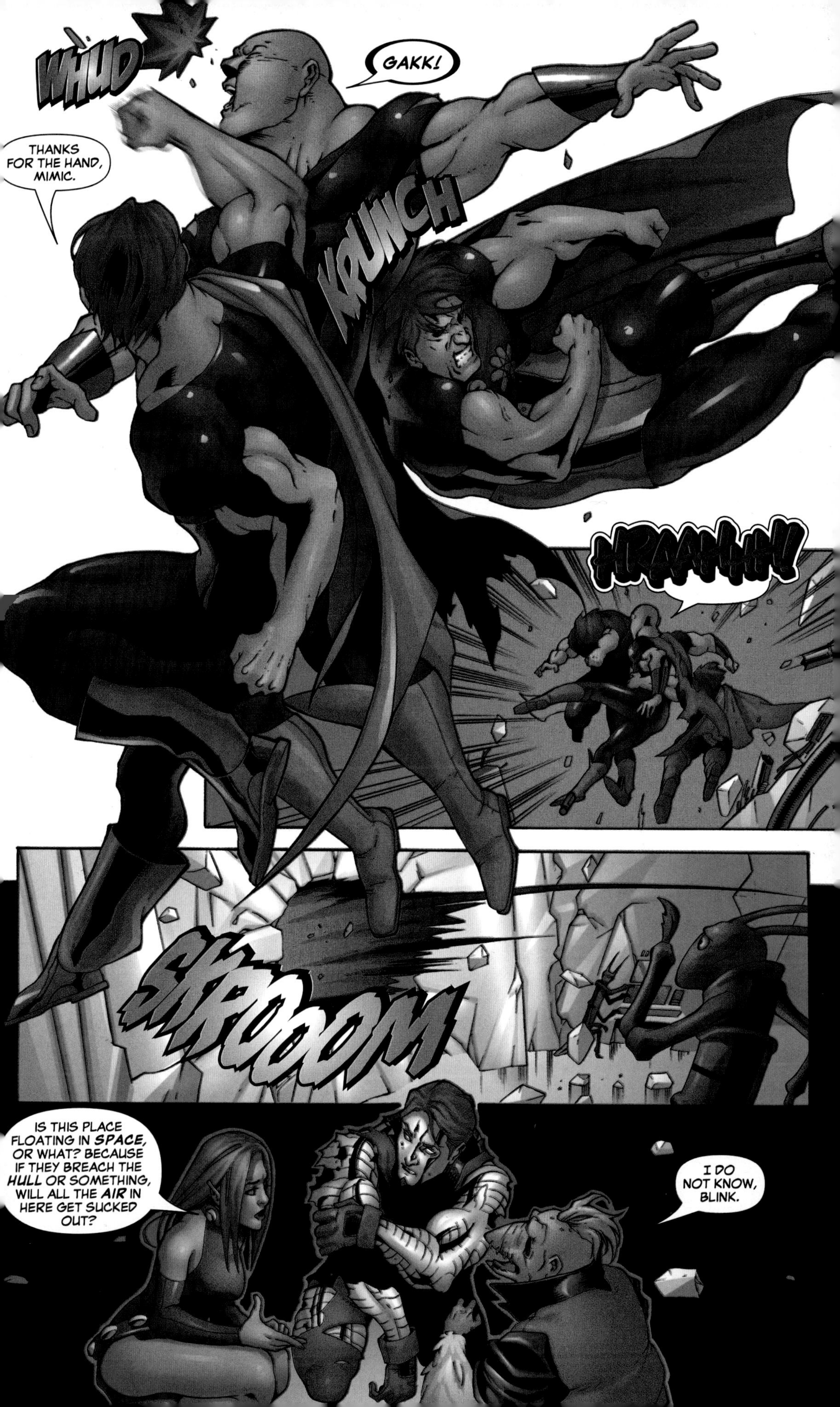
WHUD
GAKK!
THANKS FOR THE HAND, MIMIC.
KRUNCH
HRAAHHH!!
SKROOOM
IS THIS PLACE FLOATING IN SPACE, OR WHAT? BECAUSE IF THEY BREACH THE HULL OR SOMETHING, WILL ALL THE AIR IN HERE GET SUCKED OUT?
I DO NOT KNOW, BLINK.

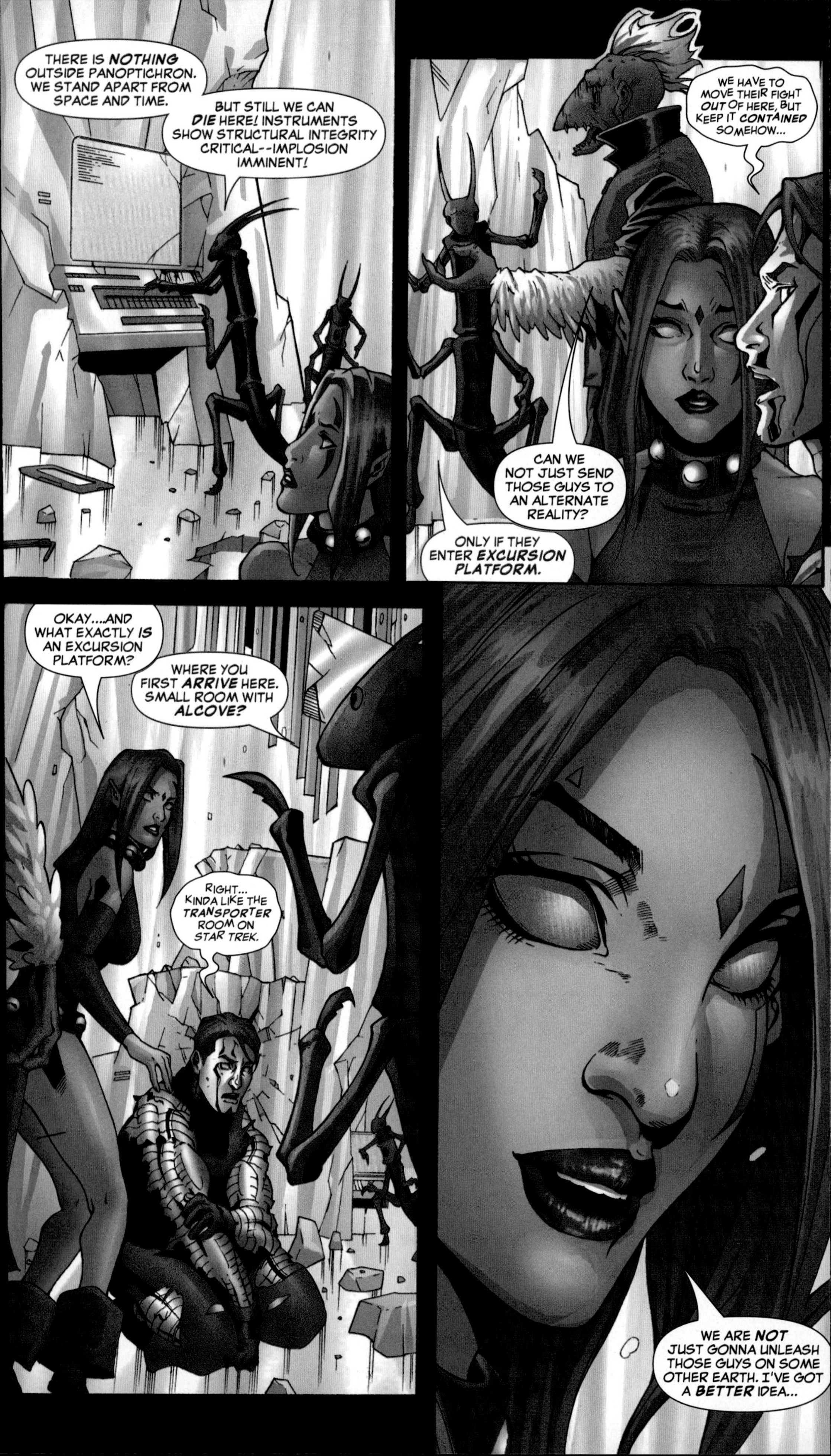
THERE IS NOTHING OUTSIDE PANOPTICHRON. WE STAND APART FROM SPACE AND TIME.
BUT STILL WE CAN DIE HERE! INSTRUMENTS SHOW STRUCTURAL INTEGRITY CRITICAL--IMPLOSION IMMINENT!
WE HAVE TO MOVE THEIR FIGHT OUT OF HERE, BUT KEEP IT CONTAINED SOMEHOW...
CAN WE NOT JUST SEND THOSE GUYS TO AN ALTERNATE REALITY?
ONLY IF THEY ENTER EXCURSION PLATFORM.
OKAY....AND WHAT EXACTLY IS AN EXCURSION PLATFORM?
WHERE YOU FIRST ARRIVE HERE. SMALL ROOM WITH ALCOVE?
RIGHT... KINDA LIKE THE TRANSPORTER ROOM ON STAR TREK.
WE ARE NOT JUST GONNA UNLEASH THOSE GUYS ON SOME OTHER EARTH. I'VE GOT A BETTER IDEA...

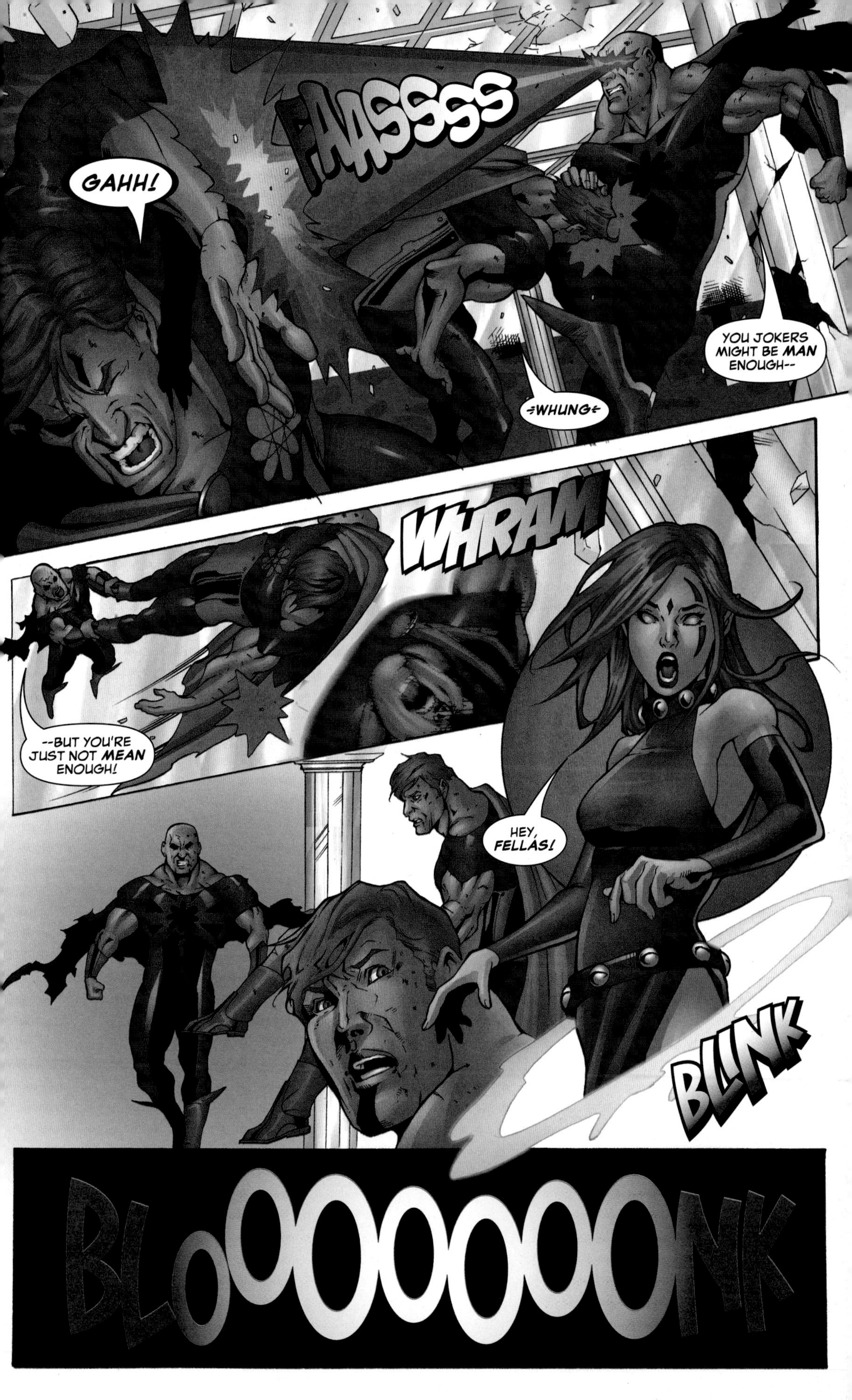
FAASSSS
GAHH!
YOU JOKERS MIGHT BE MAN ENOUGH--
WHUNG
WHRAM
--BUT YOU'RE JUST NOT MEAN ENOUGH!
HEY, FELLAS!
BLINK
BLOOOOOOONK

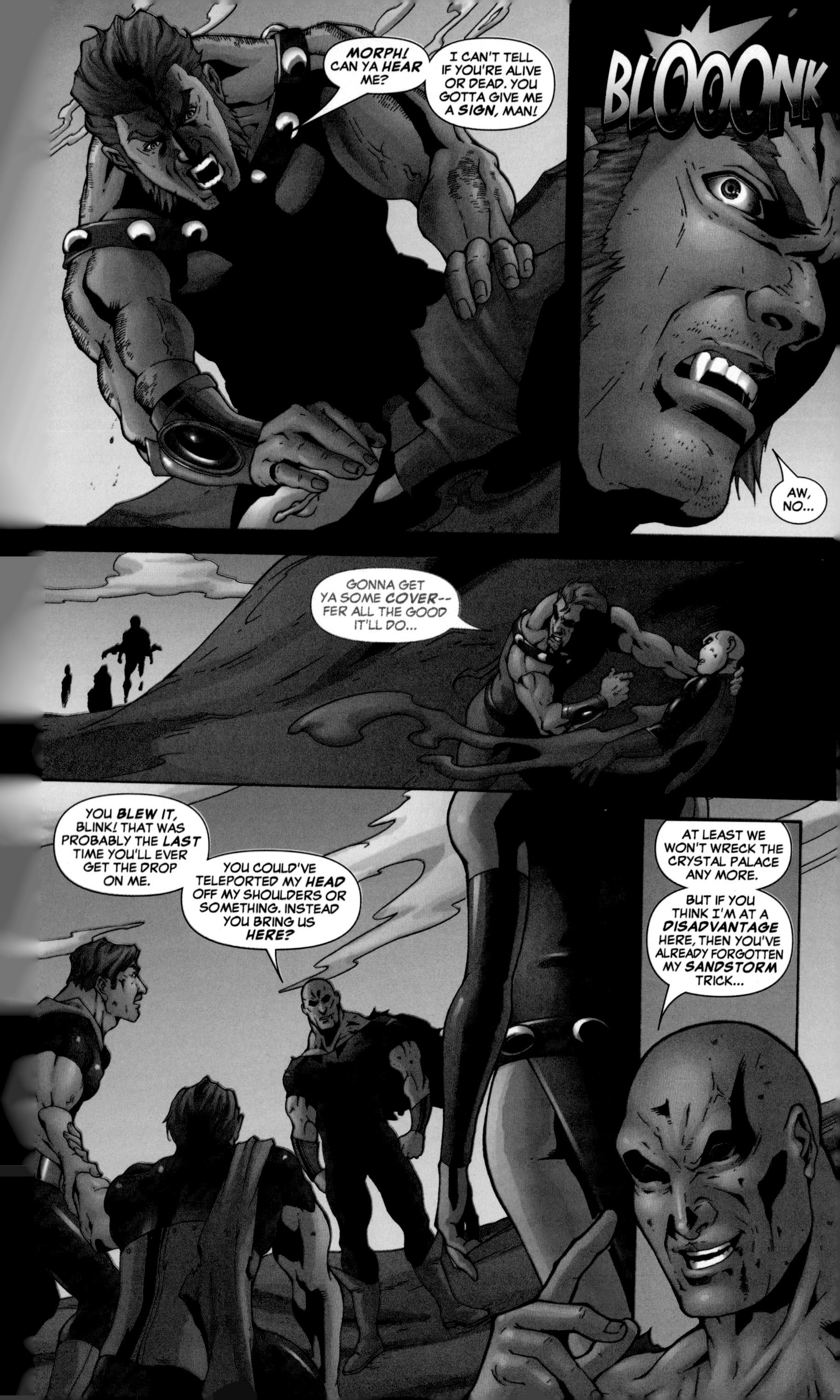
MORPH! CAN YA HEAR ME?
I CAN'T TELL IF YOU'RE ALIVE OR DEAD. YOU GOTTA GIVE ME A SIGN, MAN!
BLOOONK
AW, NO...
GONNA GET YA SOME COVER-- FER ALL THE GOOD IT'LL DO...
YOU BLEW IT, BLINK! THAT WAS PROBABLY THE LAST TIME YOU'LL EVER GET THE DROP ON ME.
YOU COULD'VE TELEPORTED MY HEAD OFF MY SHOULDERS OR SOMETHING. INSTEAD YOU BRING US HERE?
AT LEAST WE WON'T WRECK THE CRYSTAL PALACE ANY MORE.
BUT IF YOU THINK I'M AT A DISADVANTAGE HERE, THEN YOU'VE ALREADY FORGOTTEN MY SANDSTORM TRICK...

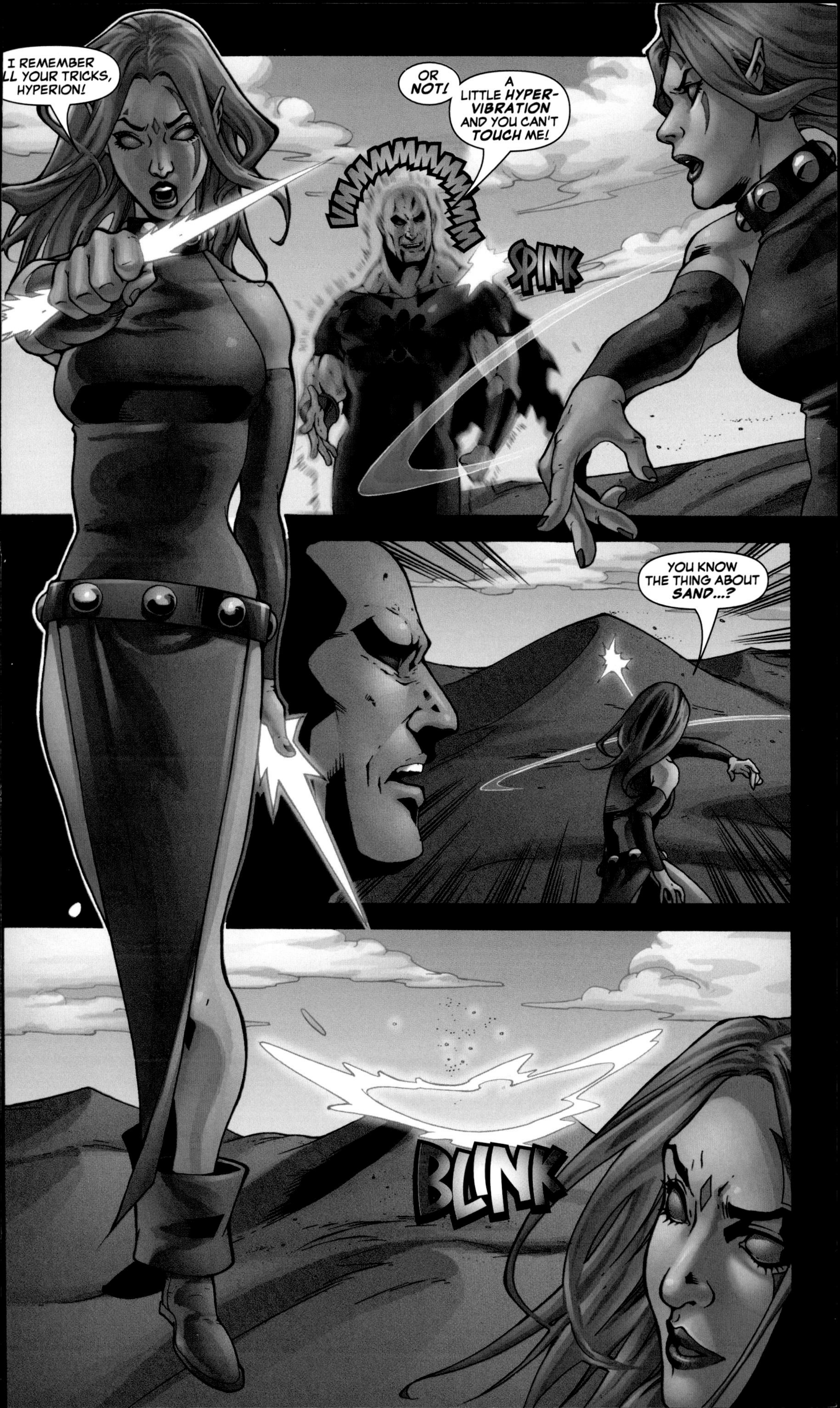
I REMEMBER
LL YOUR TRICKS, HYPERION!
OR NOT!
A LITTLE HYPER-VIBRATION AND YOU CAN'T TOUCH ME!
VMMMMMMMMM
SPINK
YOU KNOW THE THING ABOUT SAND...?
BLINK

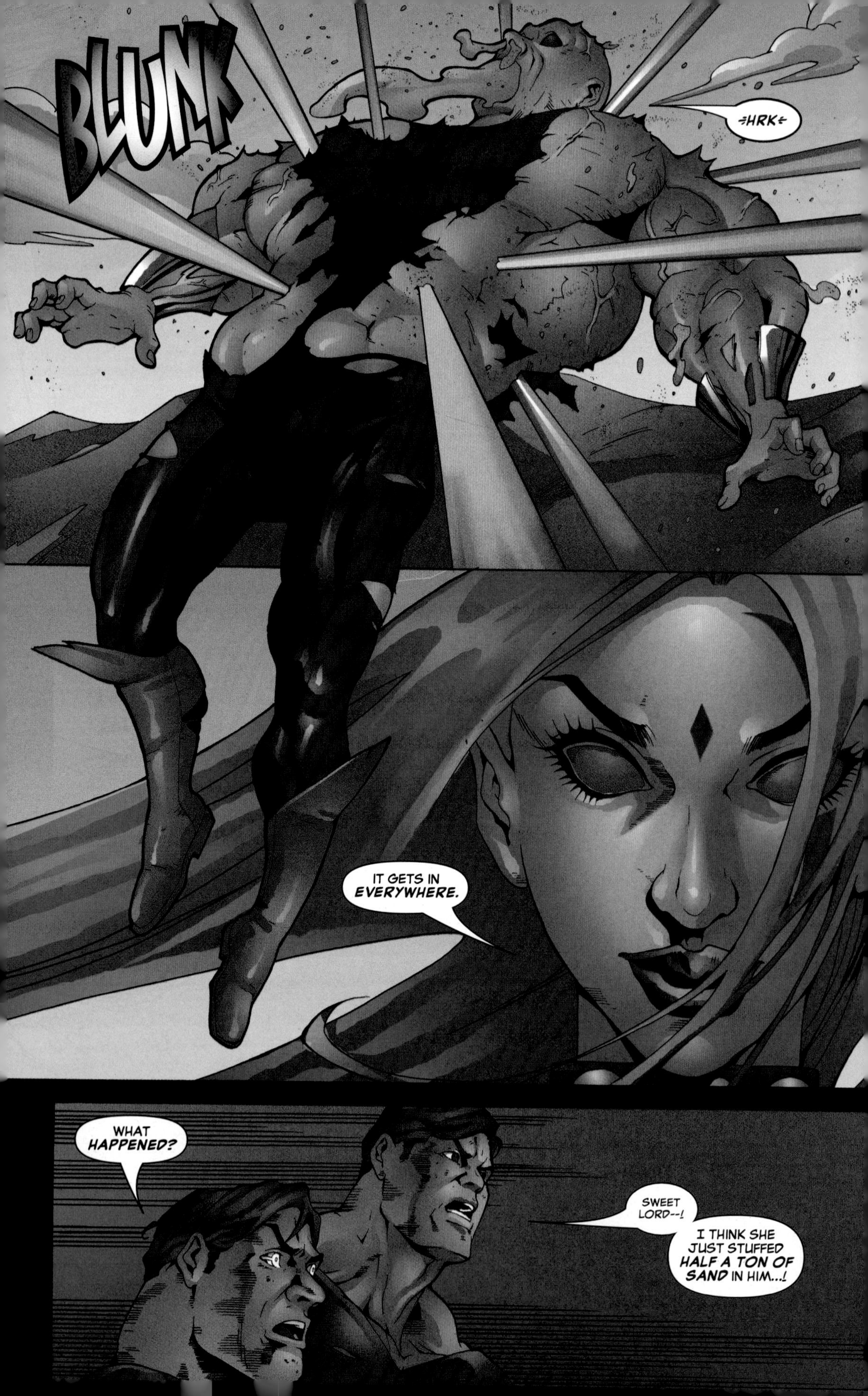
BLUNK
HRK
IT GETS IN EVERYWHERE.
WHAT HAPPENED?
SWEET LORD--!
I THINK SHE JUST STUFFED HALF A TON OF SAND IN HIM...!

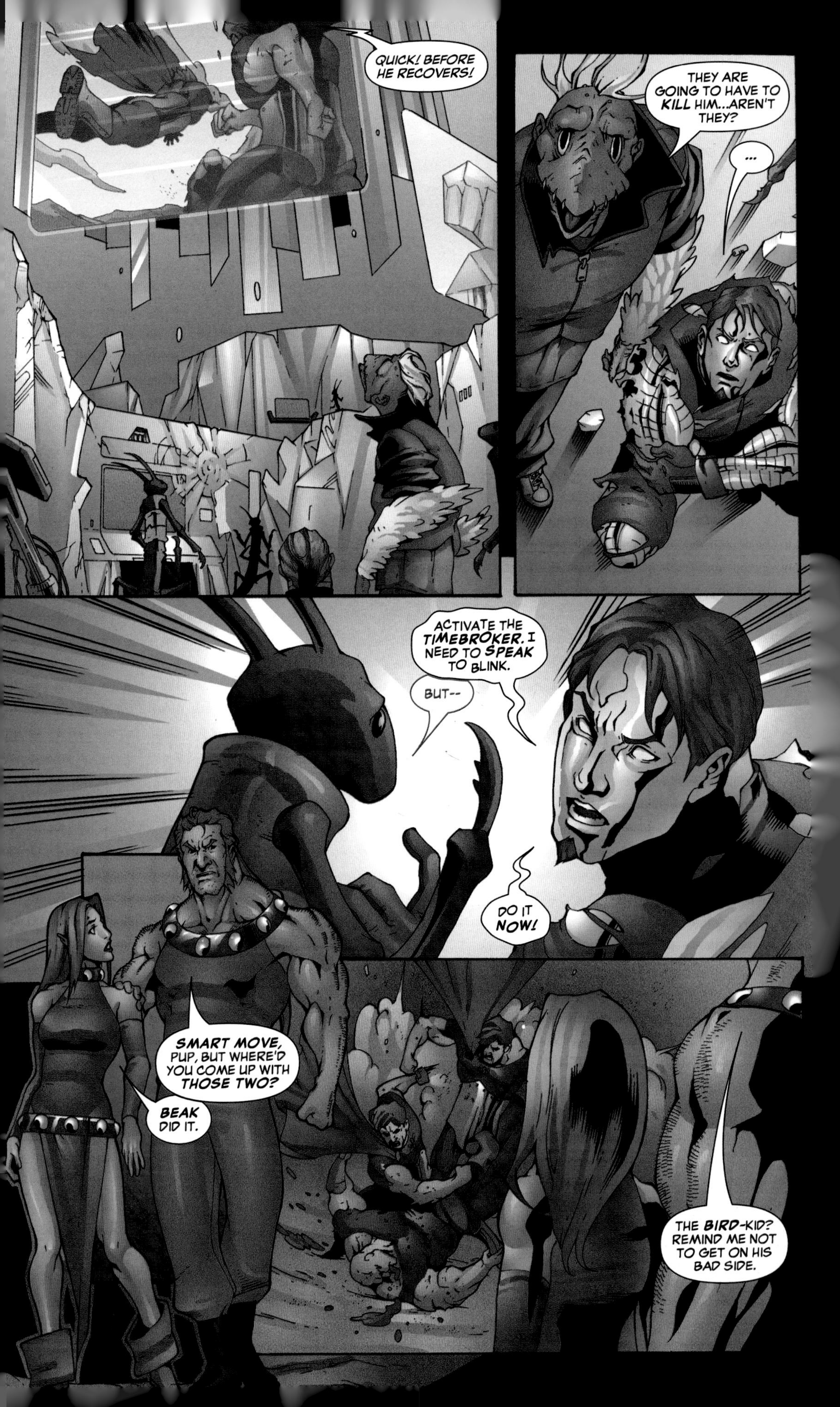
QUICK! BEFORE HE RECOVERS!
THEY ARE GOING TO HAVE TO KILL HIM...AREN'T THEY?
...
ACTIVATE THE TIMEBROKER. I NEED TO SPEAK TO BLINK.
BUT--
DO IT NOW!
SMART MOVE, PUP, BUT WHERE'D YOU COME UP WITH THOSE TWO?
BEAK DID IT.
THE BIRD-KID? REMIND ME NOT TO GET ON HIS BAD SIDE.

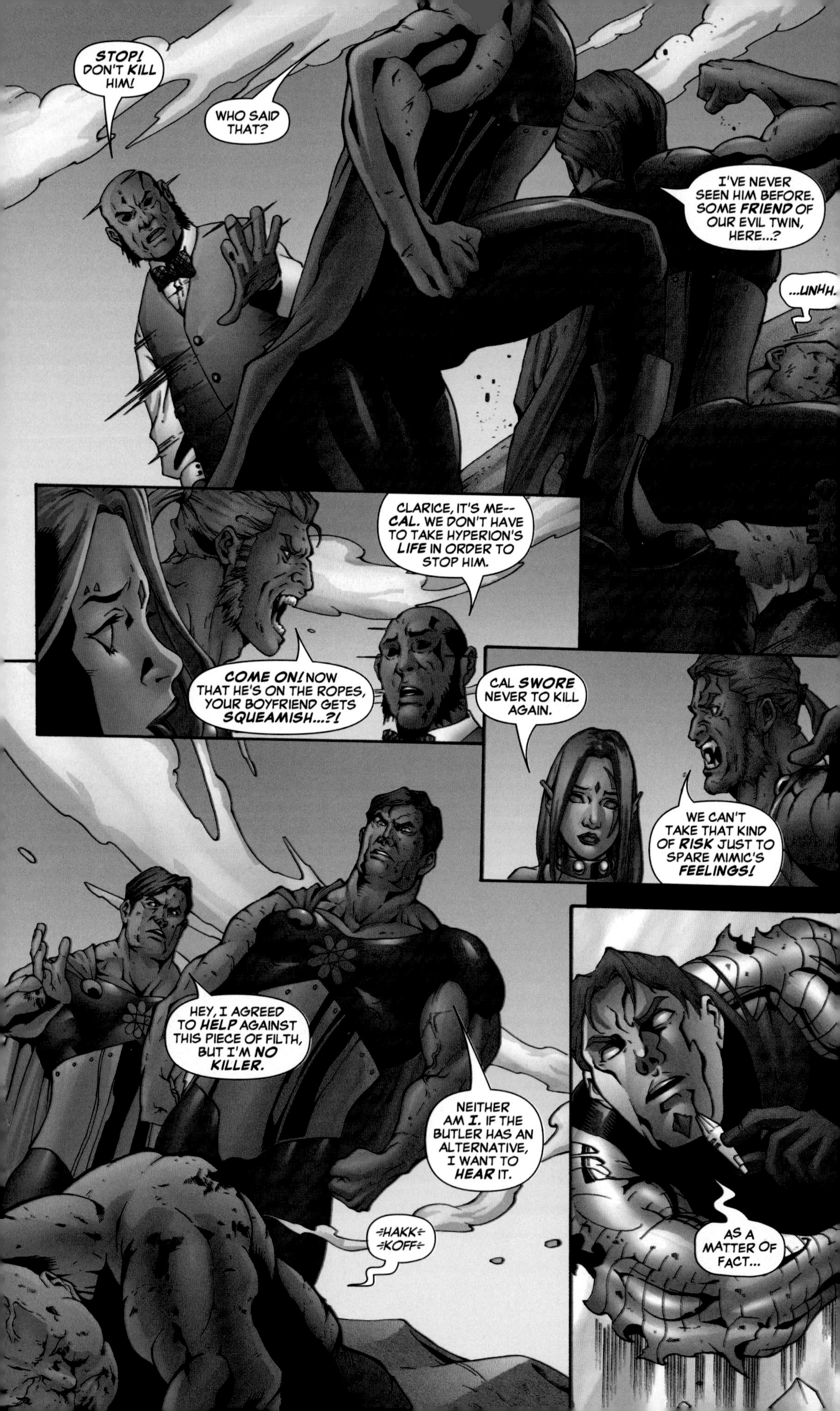

STOP! DON'T KILL HIM!
WHO SAID THAT?
I'VE NEVER SEEN HIM BEFORE. SOME FRIEND OF OUR EVIL TWIN, HERE...?
...UNHH.
CLARICE, IT'S ME--CAL. WE DON'T HAVE TO TAKE HYPERION'S LIFE IN ORDER TO STOP HIM.
COME ON! NOW THAT HE'S ON THE ROPES, YOUR BOYFRIEND GETS SQUEAMISH...?!
CAL SWORE NEVER TO KILL AGAIN.
WE CAN'T TAKE THAT KIND OF RISK JUST TO SPARE MIMIC'S FEELINGS!
HEY, I AGREED TO HELP AGAINST THIS PIECE OF FILTH, BUT I'M NO KILLER.
NEITHER AM I. IF THE BUTLER HAS AN ALTERNATIVE, I WANT TO HEAR IT.
HAKK KOFF
AS A MATTER OF FACT...

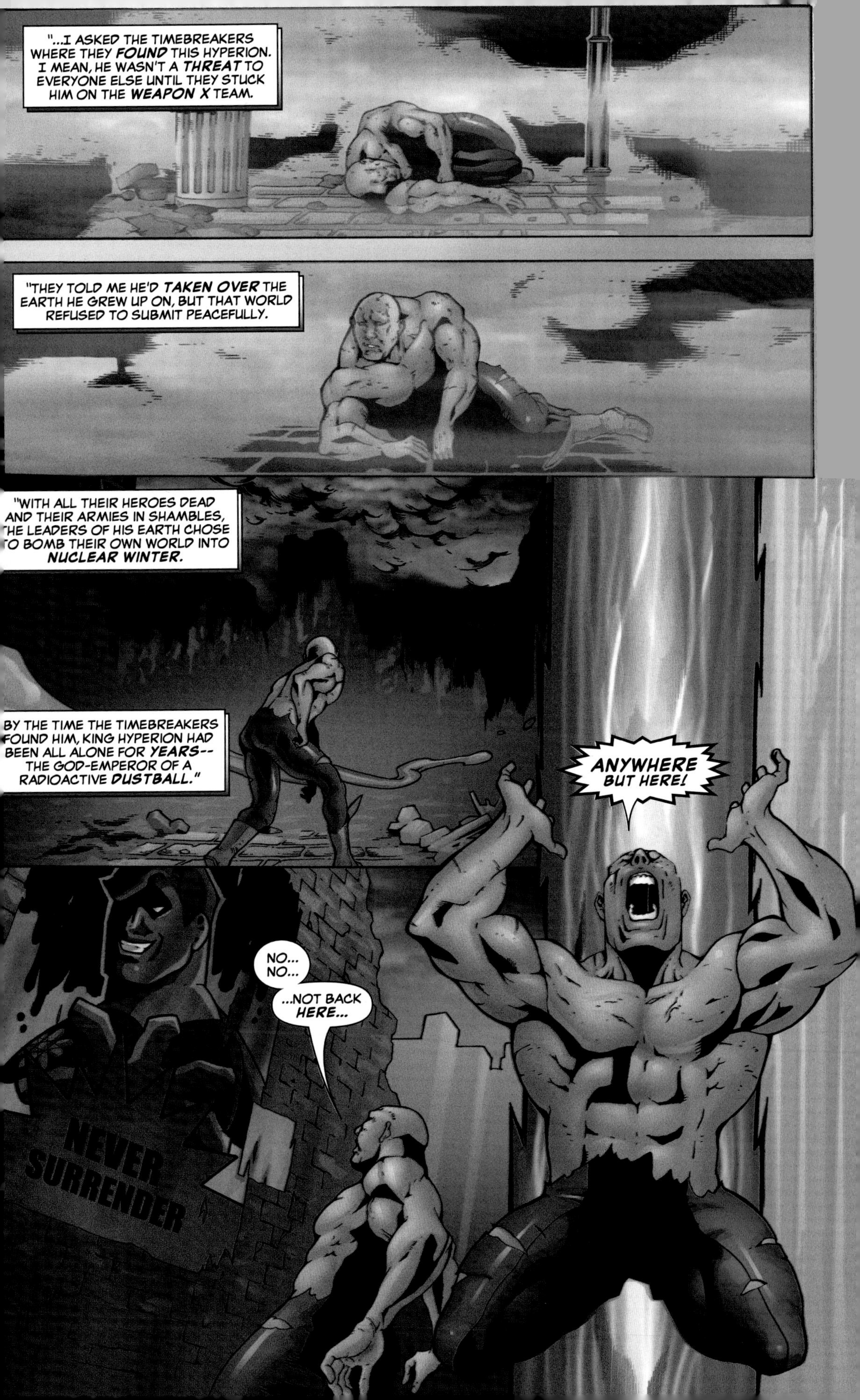
"...I ASKED THE TIMEBREAKERS WHERE THEY FOUND THIS HYPERION. I MEAN, HE WASN'T A THREAT TO EVERYONE ELSE UNTIL THEY STUCK HIM ON THE WEAPON X TEAM.
"THEY TOLD ME HE'D TAKEN OVER THE EARTH HE GREW UP ON, BUT THAT WORLD REFUSED TO SUBMIT PEACEFULLY.
"WITH ALL THEIR HEROES DEAD AND THEIR ARMIES IN SHAMBLES, THE LEADERS OF HIS EARTH CHOSE TO BOMB THEIR OWN WORLD INTO NUCLEAR WINTER.
BY THE TIME THE TIMEBREAKERS FOUND HIM, KING HYPERION HAD BEEN ALL ALONE FOR YEARS-- THE GOD-EMPEROR OF A RADIOACTIVE DUSTBALL."
ANYWHERE BUT HERE!
NO... NO...
...NOT BACK HERE...
NEVER SURRENDER

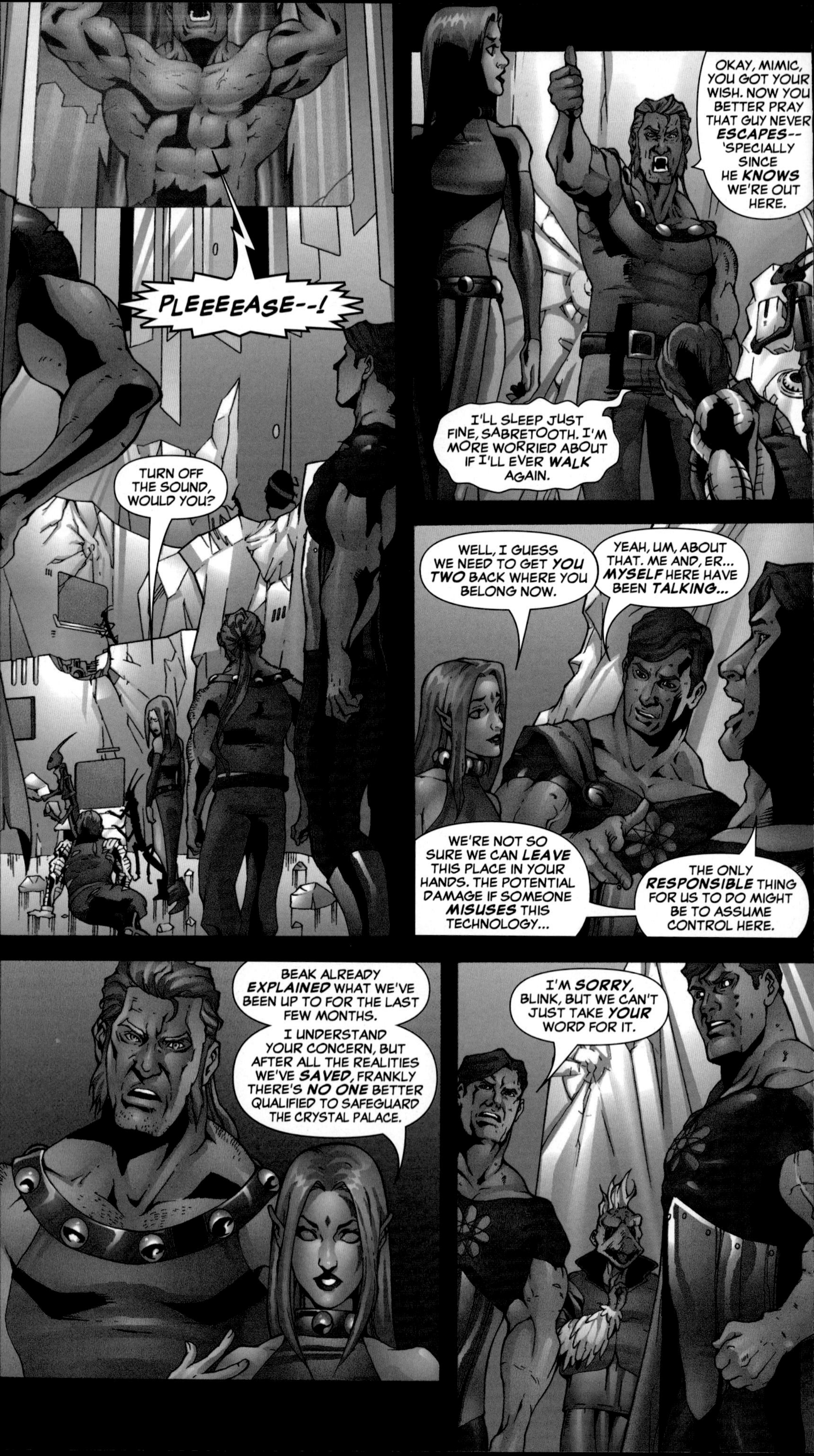
PLEEEEASE--!
TURN OFF THE SOUND, WOULD YOU?
OKAY, MIMIC, YOU GOT YOUR WISH. NOW YOU BETTER PRAY THAT GUY NEVER ESCAPES-- 'SPECIALLY SINCE HE KNOWS WE'RE OUT HERE.
I'LL SLEEP JUST FINE, SABRETOOTH. I'M MORE WORRIED ABOUT IF I'LL EVER WALK AGAIN.
WELL, I GUESS WE NEED TO GET YOU TWO BACK WHERE YOU BELONG NOW.
YEAH, UM, ABOUT THAT. ME AND, ER... MYSELF HERE HAVE BEEN TALKING...
WE'RE NOT SO SURE WE CAN LEAVE THIS PLACE IN YOUR HANDS. THE POTENTIAL DAMAGE IF SOMEONE MISUSES THIS TECHNOLOGY...
THE ONLY RESPONSIBLE THING FOR US TO DO MIGHT BE TO ASSUME CONTROL HERE.
BEAK ALREADY EXPLAINED WHAT WE'VE BEEN UP TO FOR THE LAST FEW MONTHS.
I UNDERSTAND YOUR CONCERN, BUT AFTER ALL THE REALITIES WE'VE SAVED, FRANKLY THERE'S NO ONE BETTER QUALIFIED TO SAFEGUARD THE CRYSTAL PALACE.
I'M SORRY, BLINK, BUT WE CAN'T JUST TAKE YOUR WORD FOR IT.

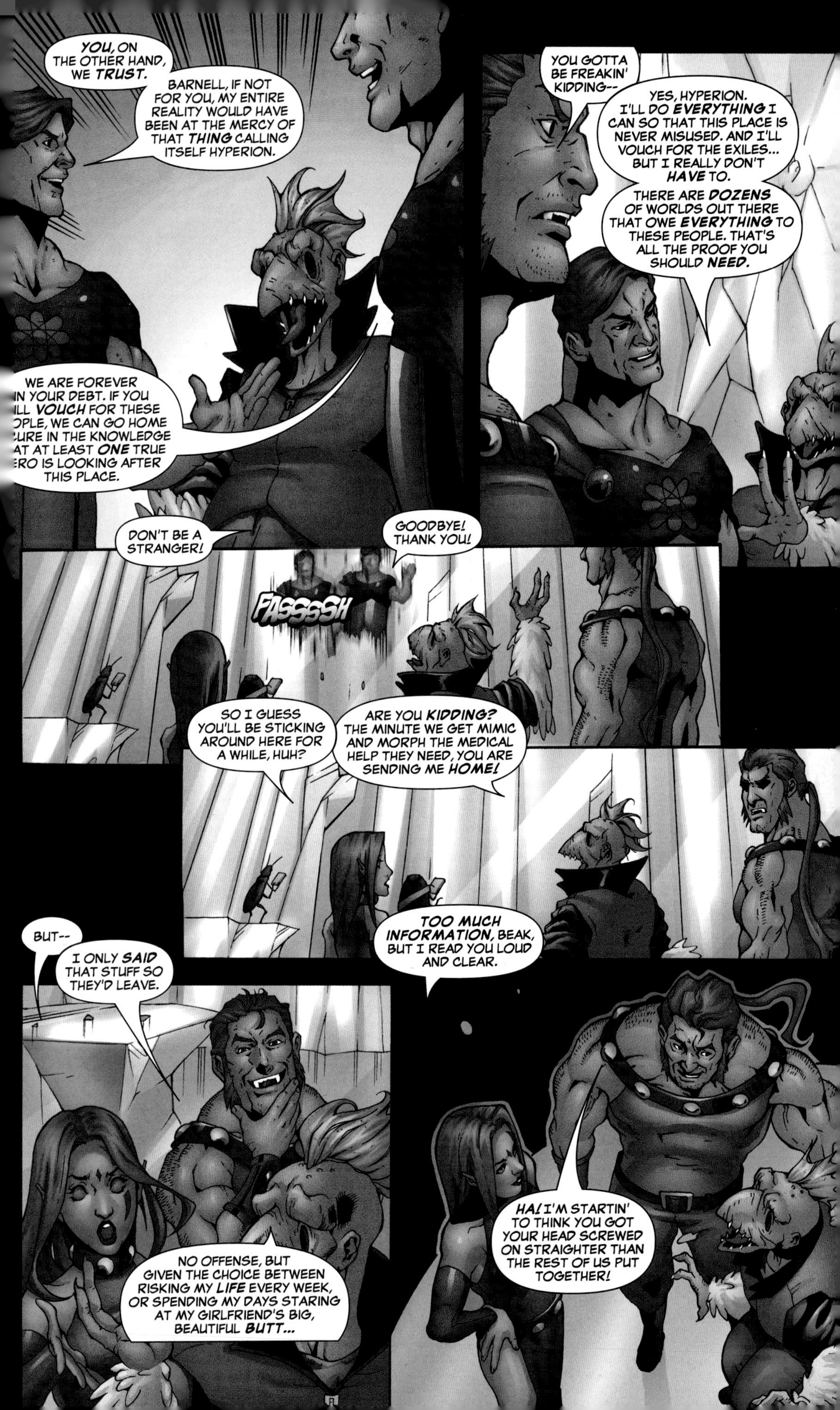

YOU, ON THE OTHER HAND, WE TRUST.
BARNELL, IF NOT FOR YOU, MY ENTIRE REALITY WOULD HAVE BEEN AT THE MERCY OF THAT THING CALLING ITSELF HYPERION.
WE ARE FOREVER IN YOUR DEBT. IF YOU WILL VOUCH FOR THESE PEOPLE, WE CAN GO HOME SECURE IN THE KNOWLEDGE THAT AT LEAST ONE TRUE HERO IS LOOKING AFTER THIS PLACE.
YOU GOTTA BE FREAKIN' KIDDING--
YES, HYPERION. I'LL DO EVERYTHING I CAN SO THAT THIS PLACE IS NEVER MISUSED. AND I'LL VOUCH FOR THE EXILES... BUT I REALLY DON'T HAVE TO.
THERE ARE DOZENS OF WORLDS OUT THERE THAT OWE EVERYTHING TO THESE PEOPLE. THAT'S ALL THE PROOF YOU SHOULD NEED.
DON'T BE A STRANGER!
GOODBYE! THANK YOU!
FASSSSH
SO I GUESS YOU'LL BE STICKING AROUND HERE FOR A WHILE, HUH?
ARE YOU KIDDING? THE MINUTE WE GET MIMIC AND MORPH THE MEDICAL HELP THEY NEED, YOU ARE SENDING ME HOME!
BUT--
I ONLY SAID THAT STUFF SO THEY'D LEAVE.
NO OFFENSE, BUT GIVEN THE CHOICE BETWEEN RISKING MY LIFE EVERY WEEK, OR SPENDING MY DAYS STARING AT MY GIRLFRIEND'S BIG, BEAUTIFUL BUTT...
TOO MUCH INFORMATION, BEAK, BUT I READ YOU LOUD AND CLEAR.
HA! I'M STARTIN' TO THINK YOU GOT YOUR HEAD SCREWED ON STRAIGHTER THAN THE REST OF US PUT TOGETHER!

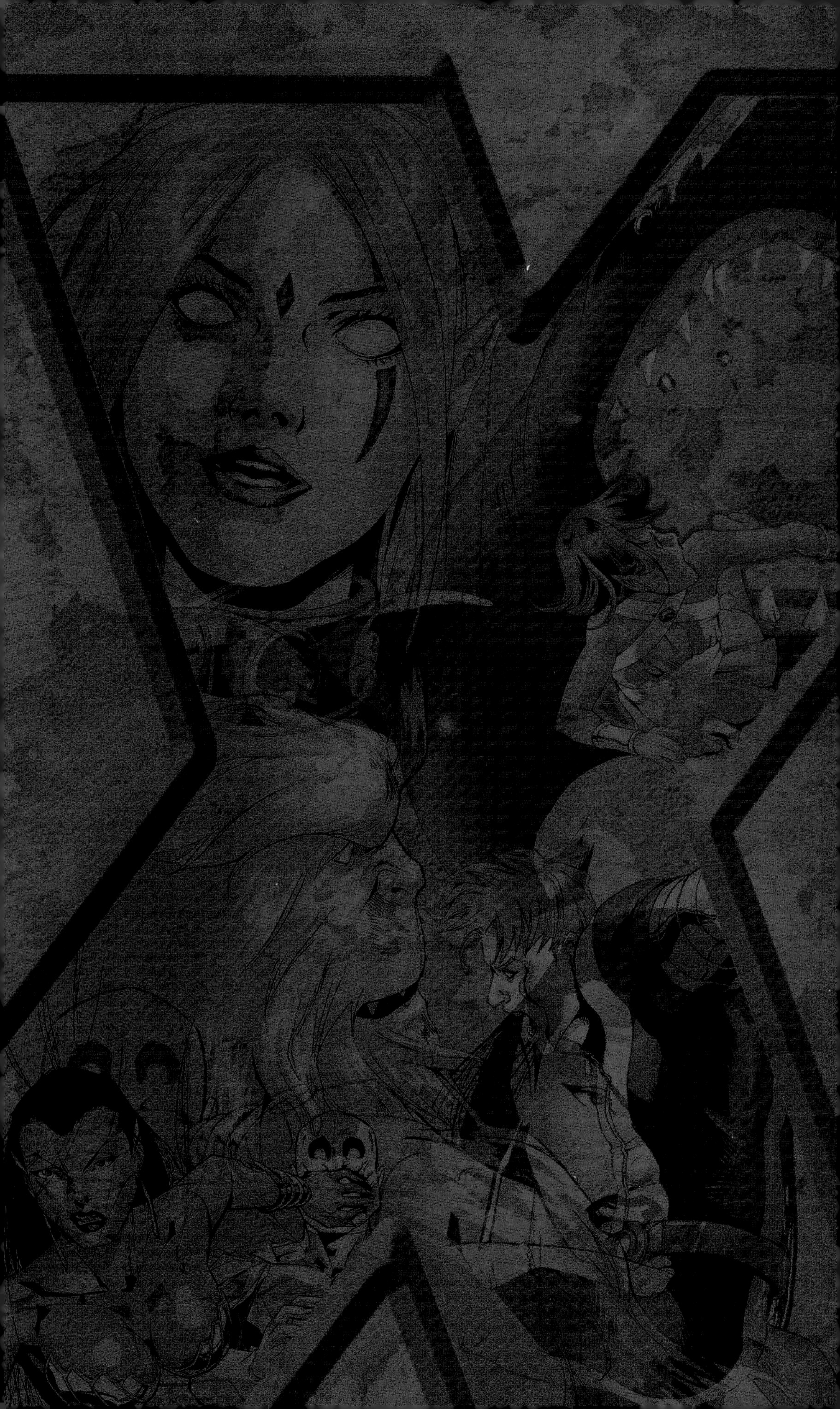

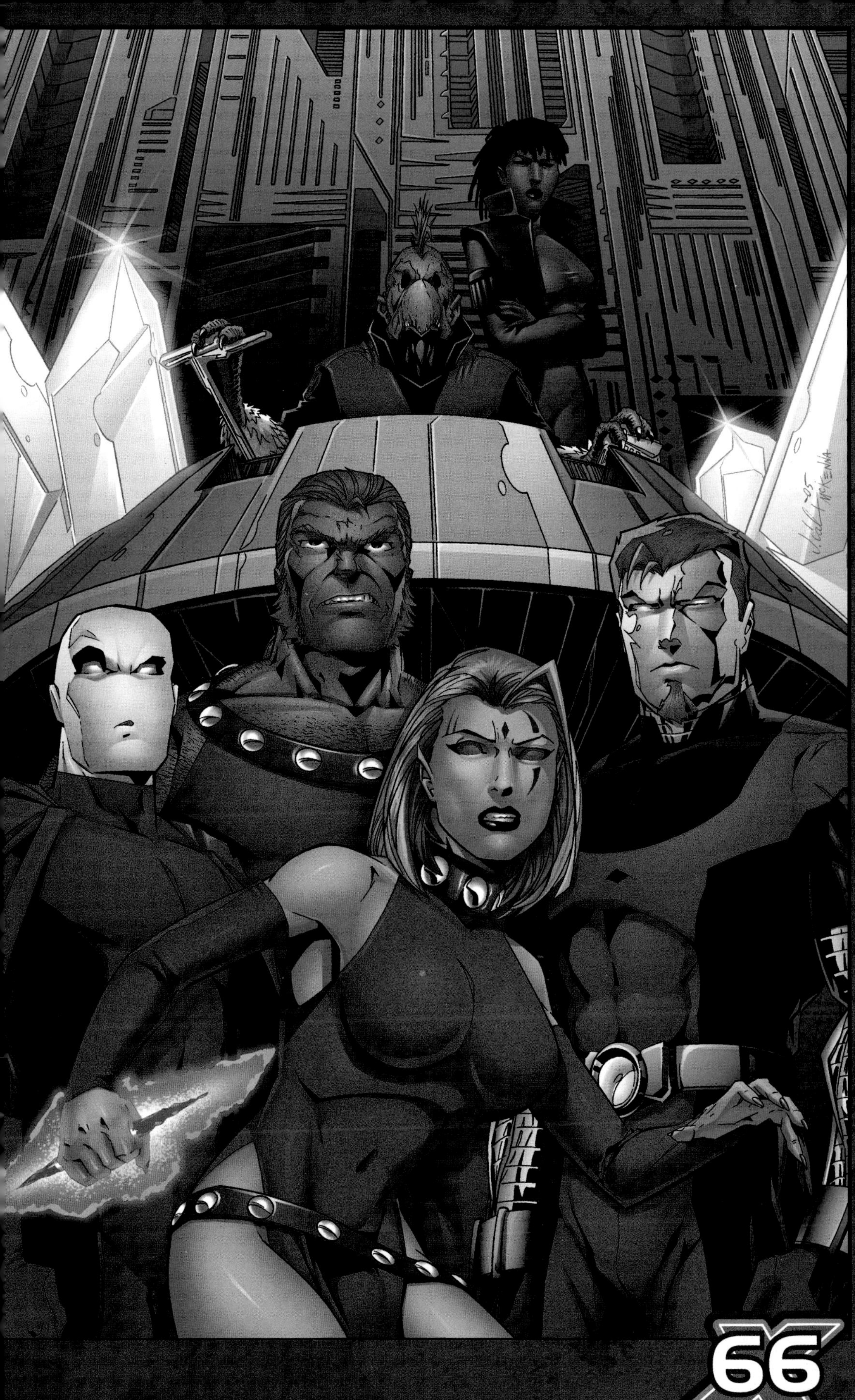

66

THE STASIS GALLERY, OUTSIDE SPACE AND TIME...
BRACE YOURSELF, HEATHER. YOU ARE IN FOR A SHOCK...
DESTROY ALL MONSTERS
PART I OF III

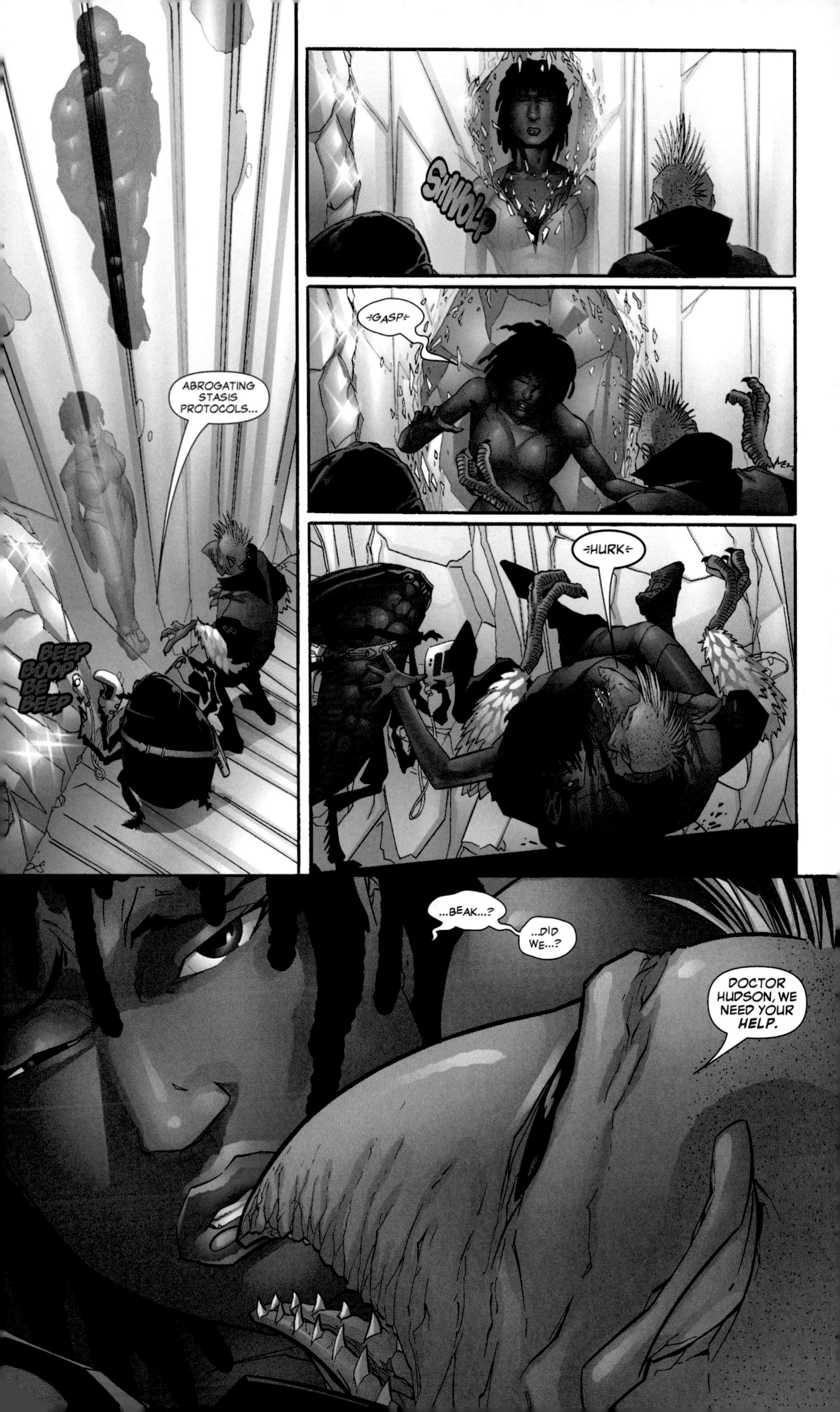
ABROGATING STASIS PROTOCOLS...
BEEP BOOP BE BEEP
SHWOLP
GASP
HURK
...BEAK...?
...DID WE...?
DOCTOR HUDSON, WE NEED YOUR HELP.

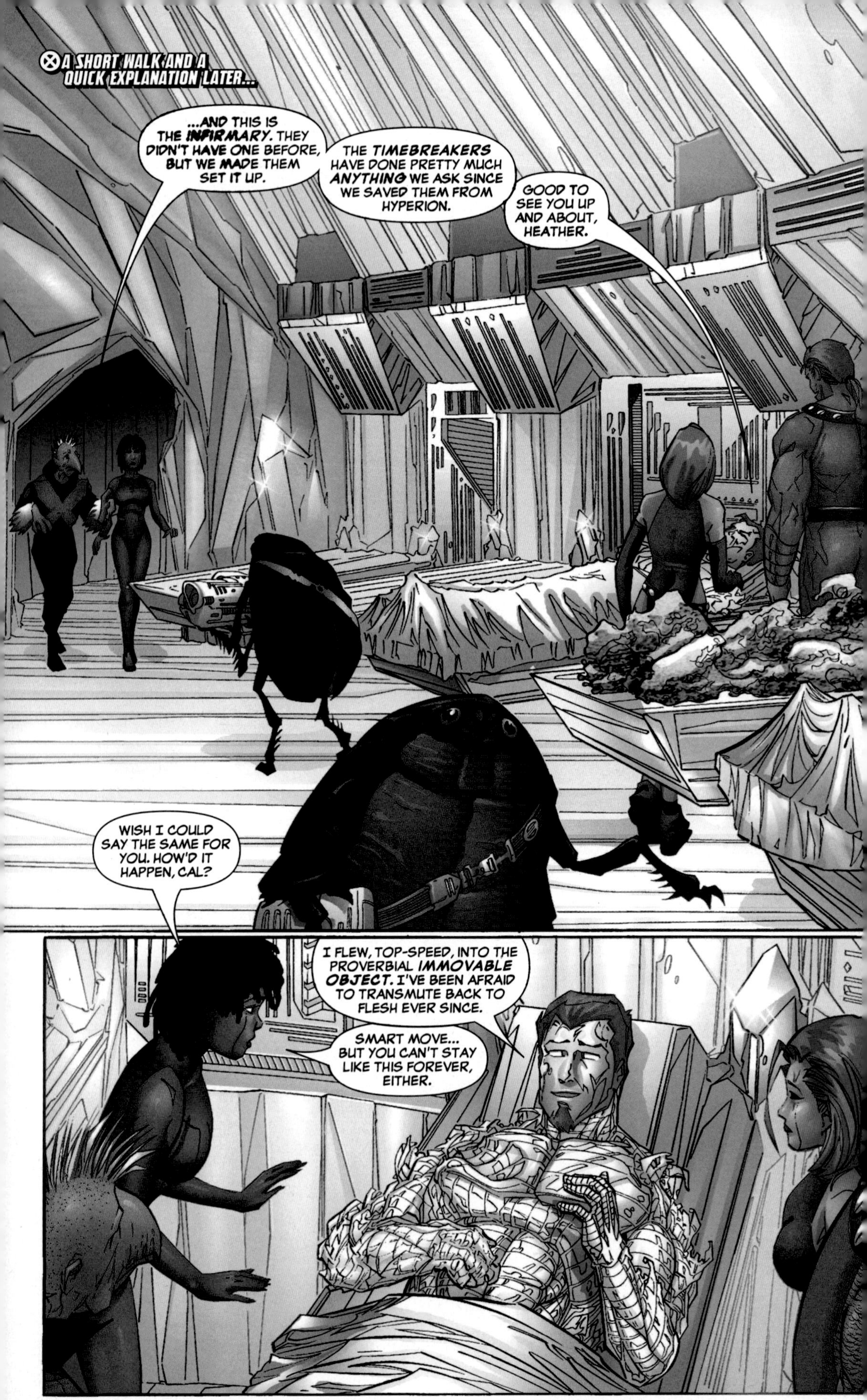
A SHORT WALK AND A QUICK EXPLANATION LATER...
...AND THIS IS THE INFIRMARY. THEY DIDN'T HAVE ONE BEFORE, BUT WE MADE THEM SET IT UP.
THE TIMEBREAKERS HAVE DONE PRETTY MUCH ANYTHING WE ASK SINCE WE SAVED THEM FROM HYPERION.
GOOD TO SEE YOU UP AND ABOUT, HEATHER.
WISH I COULD SAY THE SAME FOR YOU. HOW'D IT HAPPEN, CAL?
I FLEW, TOP-SPEED, INTO THE PROVERBIAL IMMOVABLE OBJECT. I'VE BEEN AFRAID TO TRANSMUTE BACK TO FLESH EVER SINCE.
SMART MOVE... BUT YOU CAN'T STAY LIKE THIS FOREVER, EITHER.

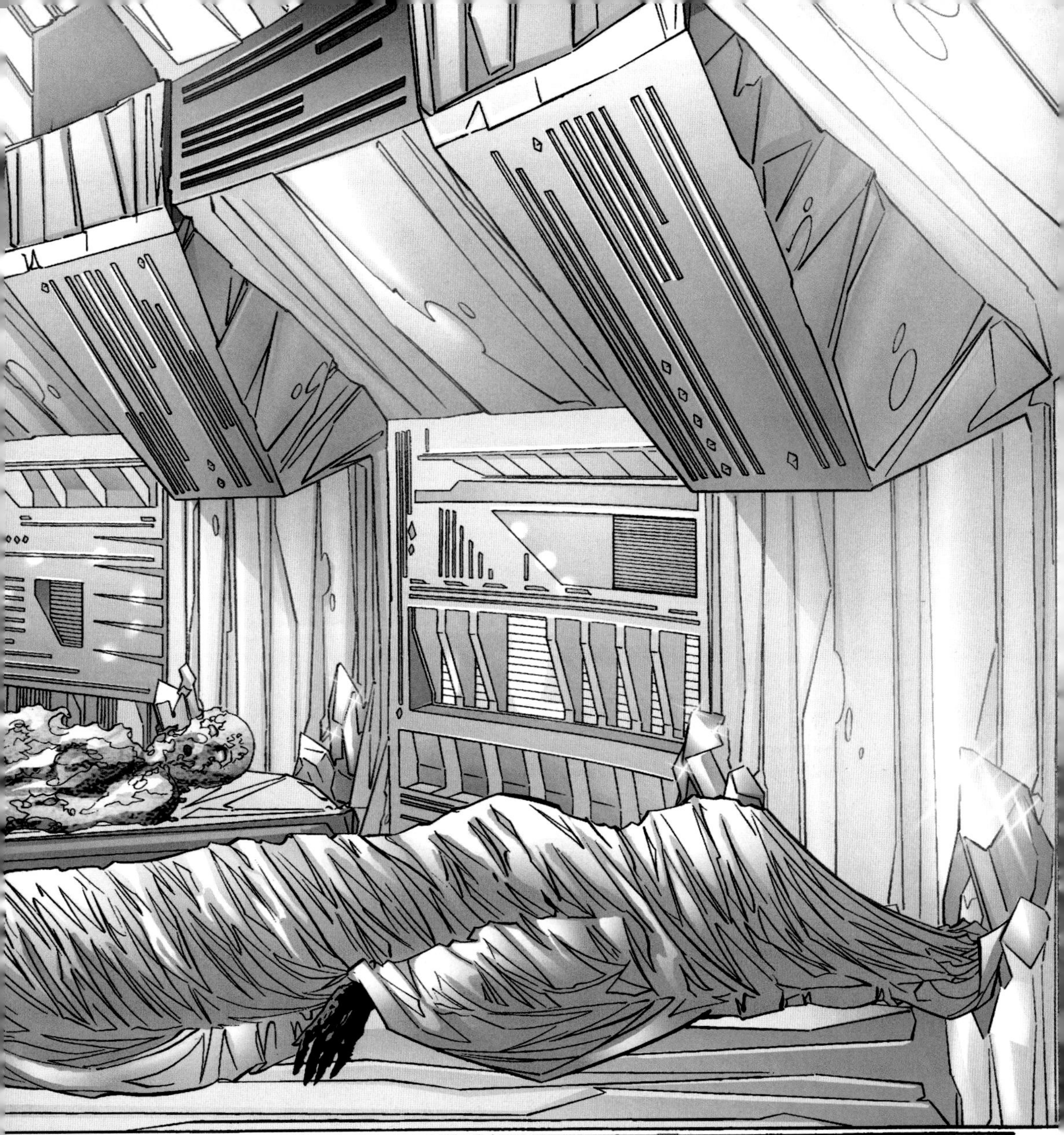

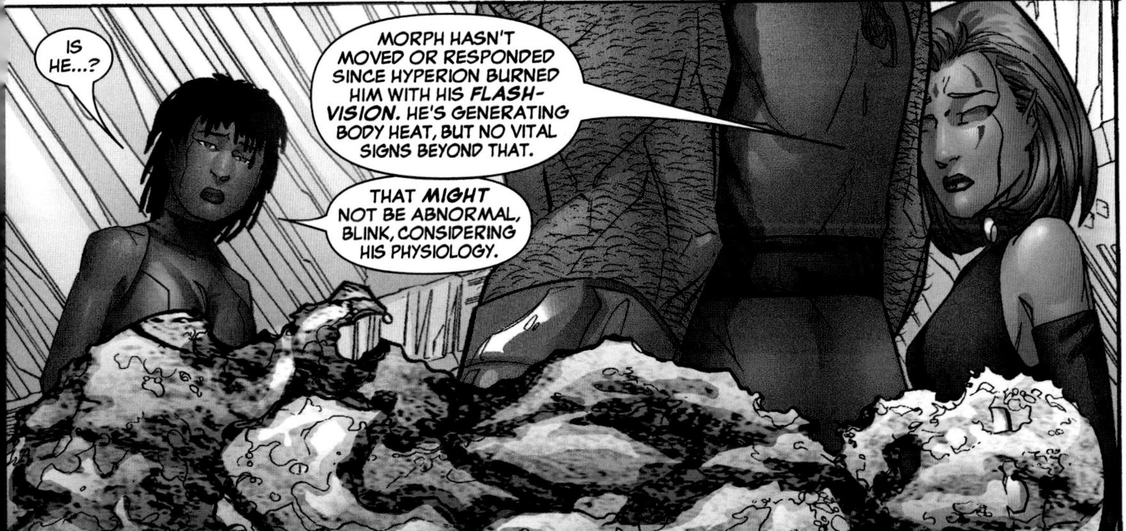
IS HE...?
MORPH HASN'T MOVED OR RESPONDED SINCE HYPERION BURNED HIM WITH HIS FLASH-VISION. HE'S GENERATING BODY HEAT, BUT NO VITAL SIGNS BEYOND THAT.
THAT MIGHT NOT BE ABNORMAL, BLINK, CONSIDERING HIS PHYSIOLOGY.

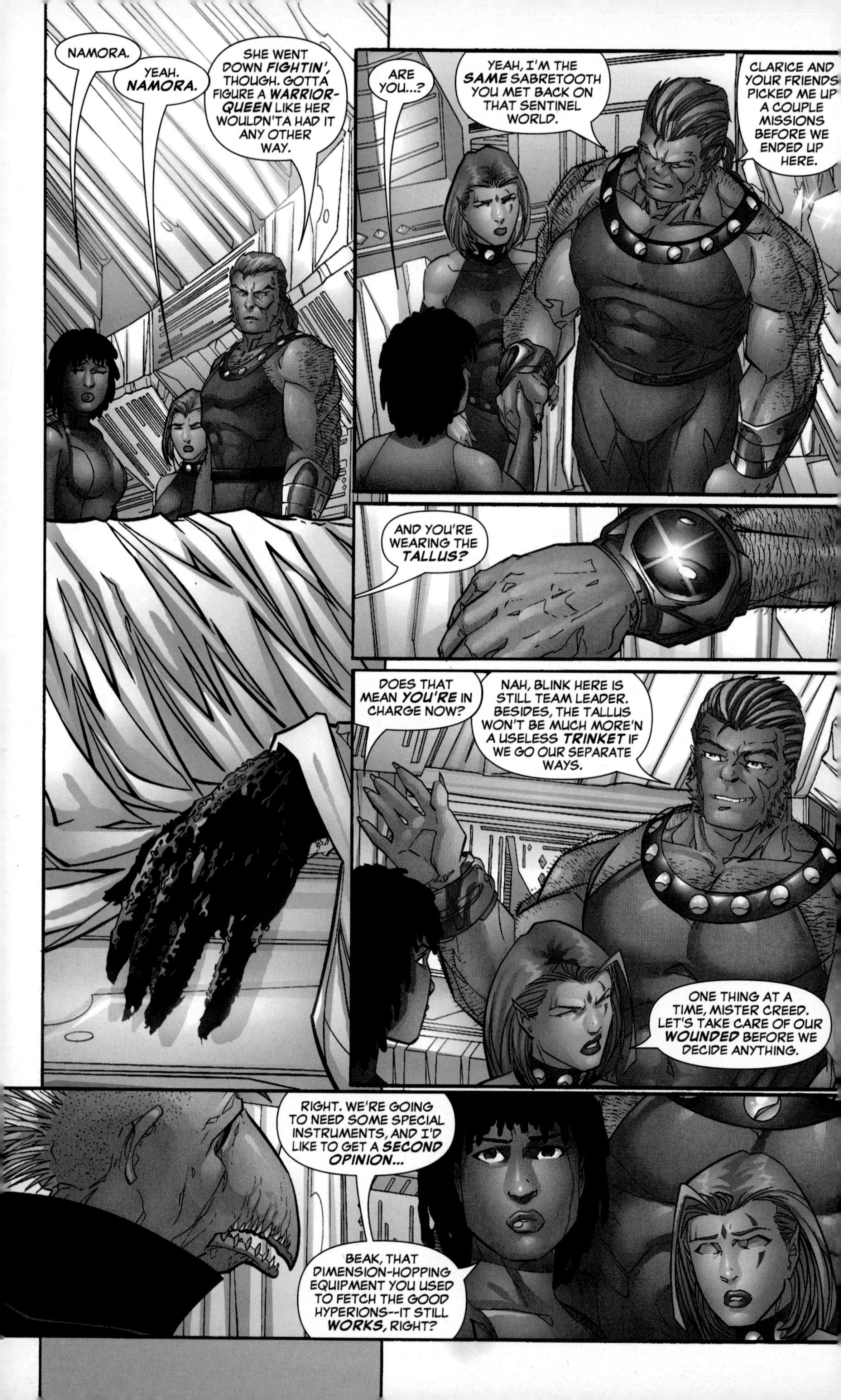
NAMORA.
YEAH. NAMORA.
SHE WENT DOWN FIGHTIN', THOUGH. GOTTA FIGURE A WARRIOR-QUEEN LIKE HER WOULDN'TA HAD IT ANY OTHER WAY.
ARE YOU...?
YEAH, I'M THE SAME SABRETOOTH YOU MET BACK ON THAT SENTINEL WORLD.
CLARICE AND YOUR FRIENDS PICKED ME UP A COUPLE MISSIONS BEFORE WE ENDED UP HERE.
AND YOU'RE WEARING THE TALLUS?
DOES THAT MEAN YOU'RE IN CHARGE NOW?
NAH, BLINK HERE IS STILL TEAM LEADER. BESIDES, THE TALLUS WON'T BE MUCH MORE'N A USELESS TRINKET IF WE GO OUR SEPARATE WAYS.
ONE THING AT A TIME, MISTER CREED. LET'S TAKE CARE OF OUR WOUNDED BEFORE WE DECIDE ANYTHING.
RIGHT. WE'RE GOING TO NEED SOME SPECIAL INSTRUMENTS, AND I'D LIKE TO GET A SECOND OPINION...
BEAK, THAT DIMENSION-HOPPING EQUIPMENT YOU USED TO FETCH THE GOOD HYPERIONS--IT STILL WORKS, RIGHT?

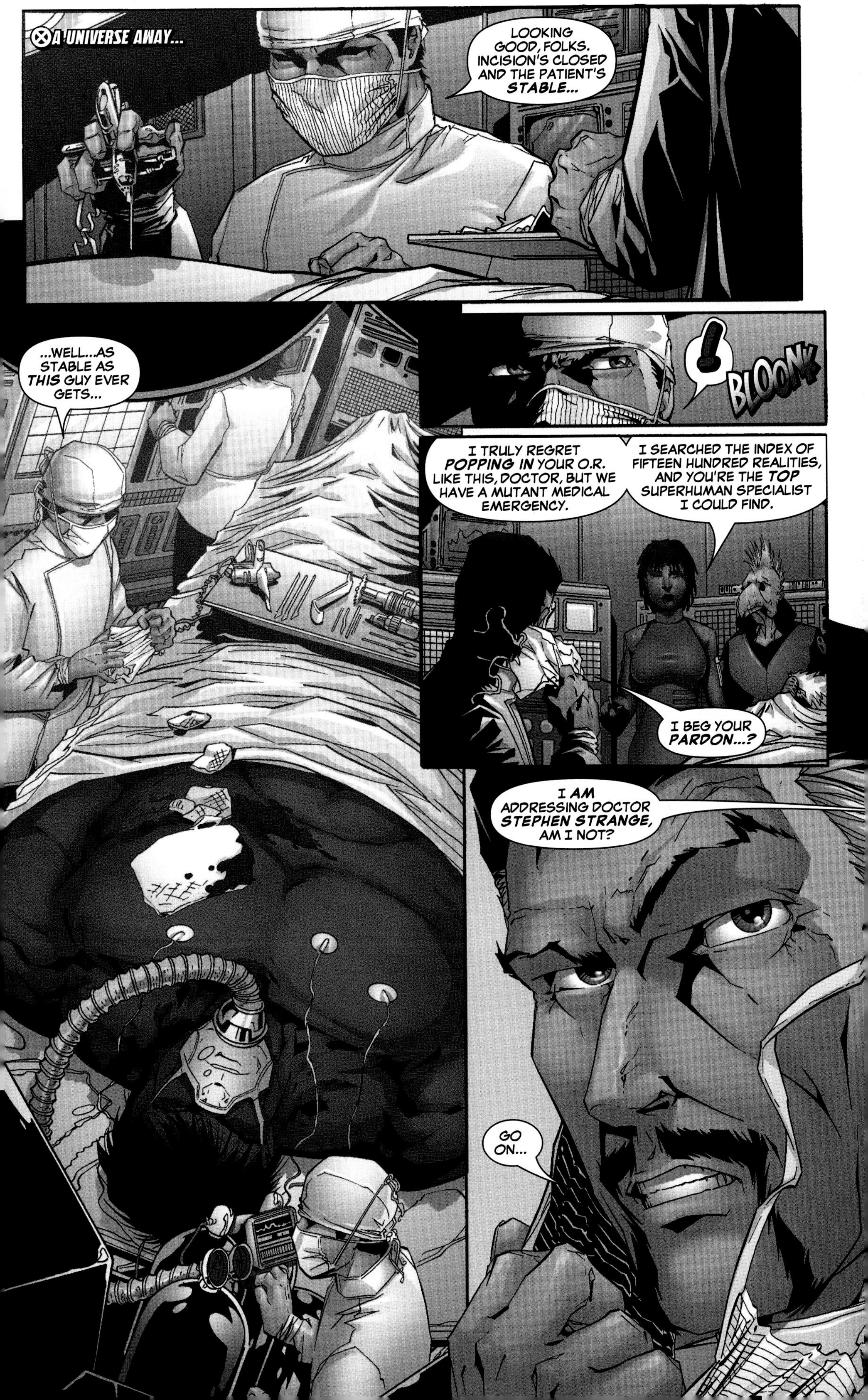
A UNIVERSE AWAY...
LOOKING GOOD, FOLKS. INCISION'S CLOSED AND THE PATIENT'S STABLE...
...WELL...AS STABLE AS THIS GUY EVER GETS...
!
BLOONK
I TRULY REGRET POPPING IN YOUR O.R. LIKE THIS, DOCTOR, BUT WE HAVE A MUTANT MEDICAL EMERGENCY.
I SEARCHED THE INDEX OF FIFTEEN HUNDRED REALITIES, AND YOU'RE THE TOP SUPERHUMAN SPECIALIST I COULD FIND.
I BEG YOUR PARDON...?
I AM ADDRESSING DOCTOR STEPHEN STRANGE, AM I NOT?
GO ON...

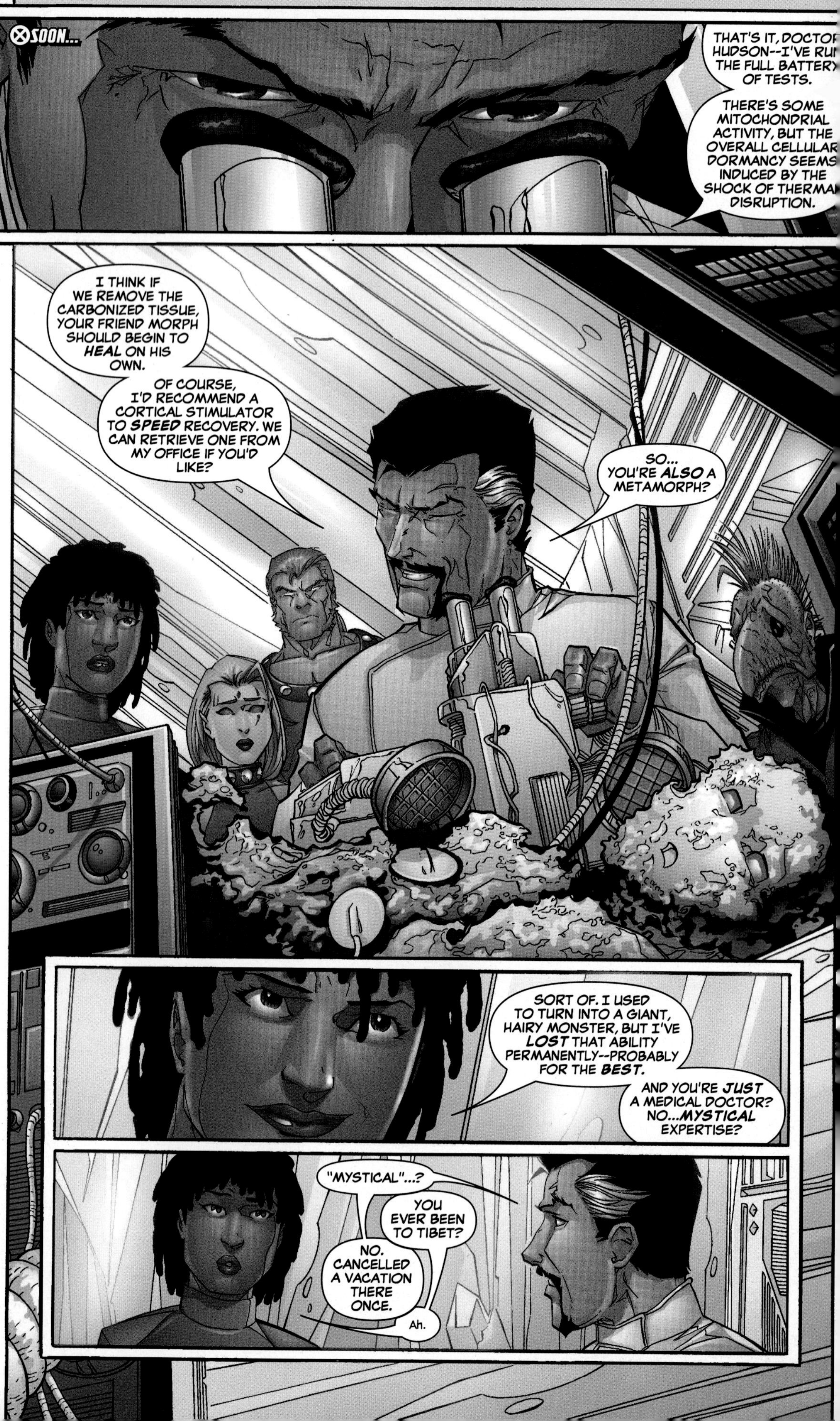
SOON...
THAT'S IT, DOCTOR HUDSON--I'VE RUN THE FULL BATTERY OF TESTS.
THERE'S SOME MITOCHONDRIAL ACTIVITY, BUT THE OVERALL CELLULAR DORMANCY SEEMS INDUCED BY THE SHOCK OF THERMAL DISRUPTION.
I THINK IF WE REMOVE THE CARBONIZED TISSUE, YOUR FRIEND MORPH SHOULD BEGIN TO HEAL ON HIS OWN.
OF COURSE, I'D RECOMMEND A CORTICAL STIMULATOR TO SPEED RECOVERY. WE CAN RETRIEVE ONE FROM MY OFFICE IF YOU'D LIKE?
SO... YOU'RE ALSO A METAMORPH?
SORT OF. I USED TO TURN INTO A GIANT, HAIRY MONSTER, BUT I'VE LOST THAT ABILITY PERMANENTLY--PROBABLY FOR THE BEST.
AND YOU'RE JUST A MEDICAL DOCTOR? NO...MYSTICAL EXPERTISE?
"MYSTICAL"...?
YOU EVER BEEN TO TIBET?
NO. CANCELLED A VACATION THERE ONCE.
Ah.

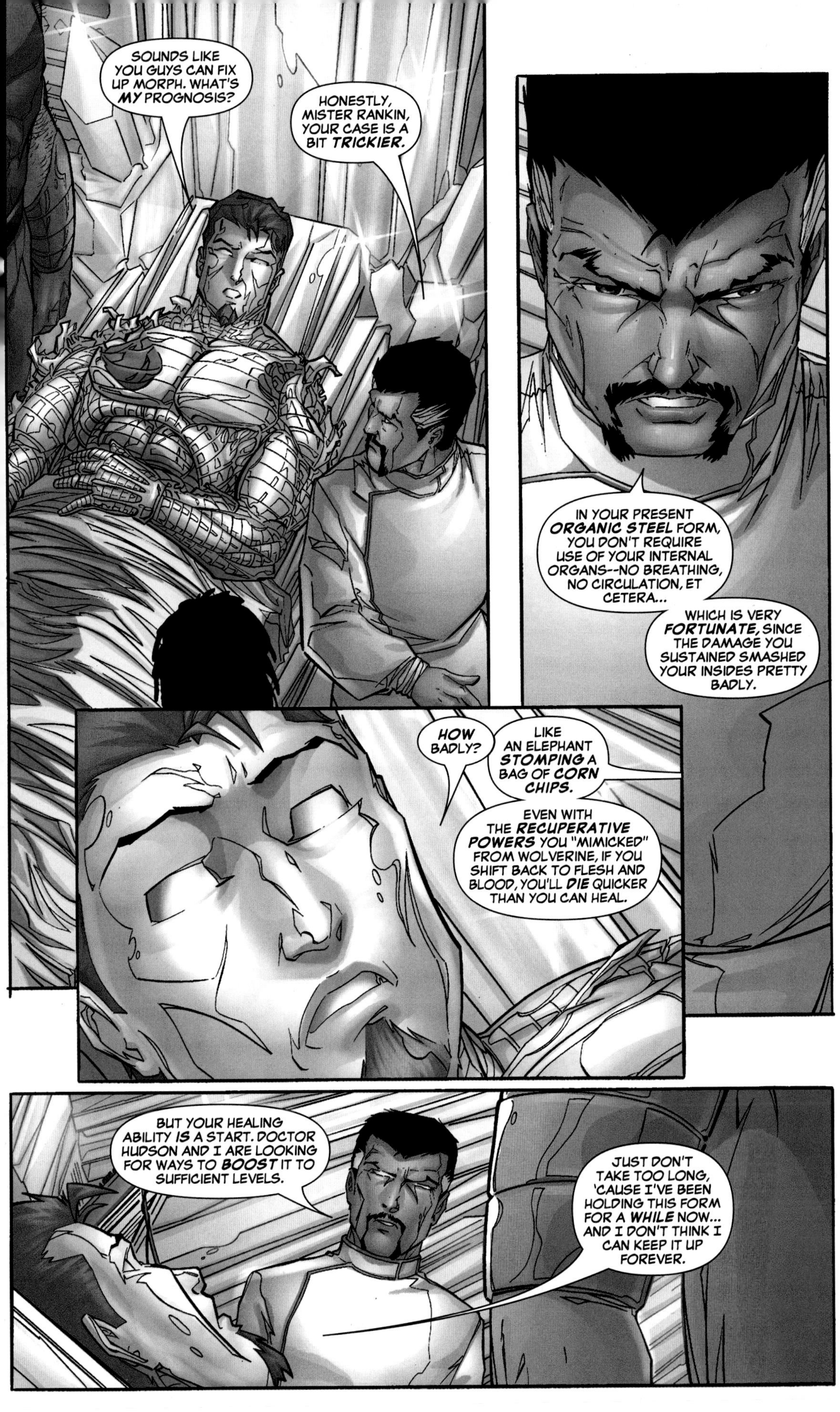
SOUNDS LIKE YOU GUYS CAN FIX UP MORPH. WHAT'S MY PROGNOSIS?
HONESTLY, MISTER RANKIN, YOUR CASE IS A BIT TRICKIER.
IN YOUR PRESENT ORGANIC STEEL FORM, YOU DON'T REQUIRE USE OF YOUR INTERNAL ORGANS--NO BREATHING, NO CIRCULATION, ET CETERA...
WHICH IS VERY FORTUNATE, SINCE THE DAMAGE YOU SUSTAINED SMASHED YOUR INSIDES PRETTY BADLY.
HOW BADLY?
LIKE AN ELEPHANT STOMPING A BAG OF CORN CHIPS.
EVEN WITH THE RECUPERATIVE POWERS YOU "MIMICKED" FROM WOLVERINE, IF YOU SHIFT BACK TO FLESH AND BLOOD, YOU'LL DIE QUICKER THAN YOU CAN HEAL.
BUT YOUR HEALING ABILITY IS A START. DOCTOR HUDSON AND I ARE LOOKING FOR WAYS TO BOOST IT TO SUFFICIENT LEVELS.
JUST DON'T TAKE TOO LONG, 'CAUSE I'VE BEEN HOLDING THIS FORM FOR A WHILE NOW... AND I DON'T THINK I CAN KEEP IT UP FOREVER.

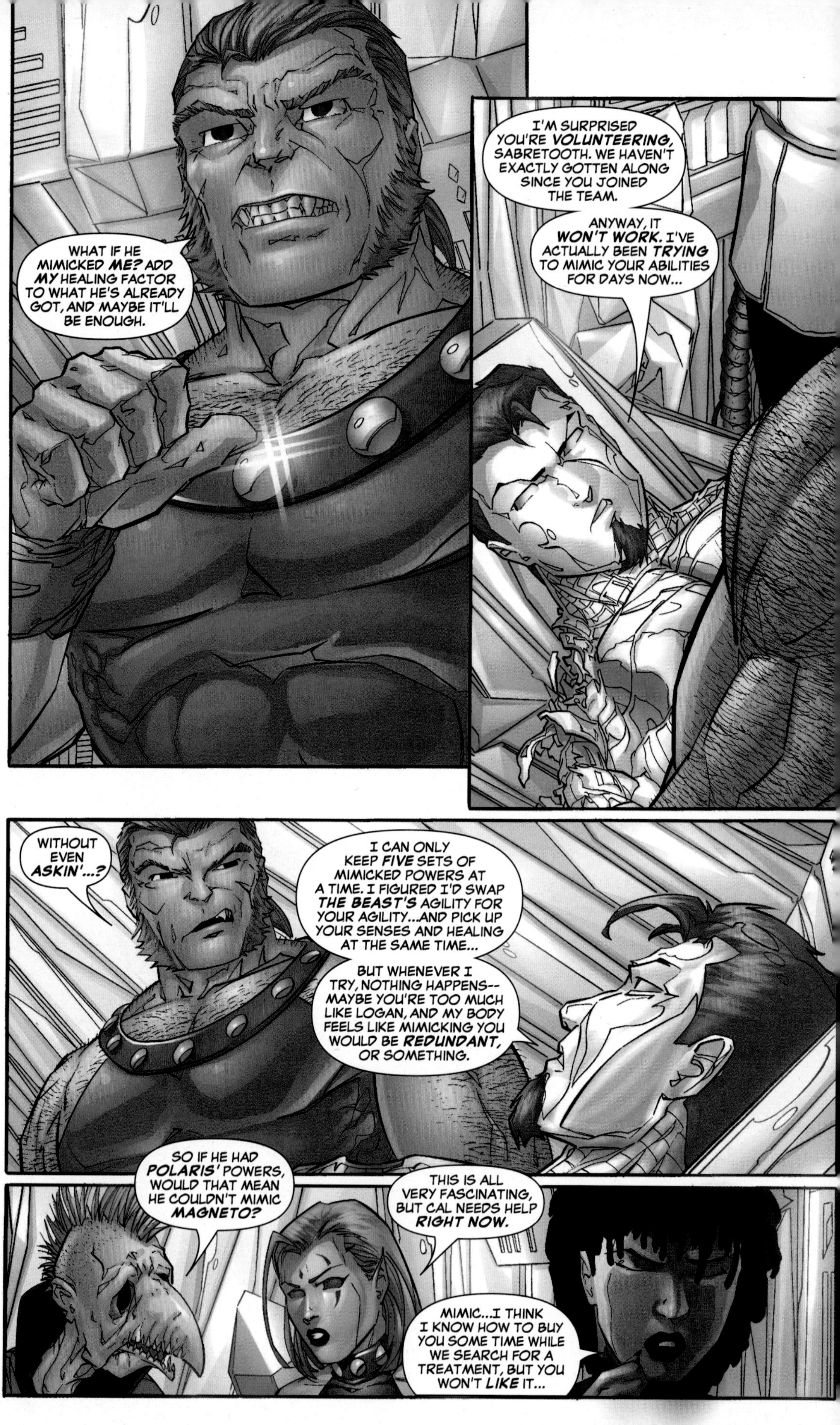
WHAT IF HE MIMICKED ME? ADD MY HEALING FACTOR TO WHAT HE'S ALREADY GOT, AND MAYBE IT'LL BE ENOUGH.
I'M SURPRISED YOU'RE VOLUNTEERING, SABRETOOTH. WE HAVEN'T EXACTLY GOTTEN ALONG SINCE YOU JOINED THE TEAM.
ANYWAY, IT WON'T WORK. I'VE ACTUALLY BEEN TRYING TO MIMIC YOUR ABILITIES FOR DAYS NOW...
WITHOUT EVEN ASKIN'...?
I CAN ONLY KEEP FIVE SETS OF MIMICKED POWERS AT A TIME. I FIGURED I'D SWAP THE BEAST'S AGILITY FOR YOUR AGILITY...AND PICK UP YOUR SENSES AND HEALING AT THE SAME TIME...
BUT WHENEVER I TRY, NOTHING HAPPENS--MAYBE YOU'RE TOO MUCH LIKE LOGAN, AND MY BODY FEELS LIKE MIMICKING YOU WOULD BE REDUNDANT, OR SOMETHING.
SO IF HE HAD POLARIS' POWERS, WOULD THAT MEAN HE COULDN'T MIMIC MAGNETO?
THIS IS ALL VERY FASCINATING, BUT CAL NEEDS HELP RIGHT NOW.
MIMIC...I THINK I KNOW HOW TO BUY YOU SOME TIME WHILE WE SEARCH FOR A TREATMENT, BUT YOU WON'T LIKE IT...

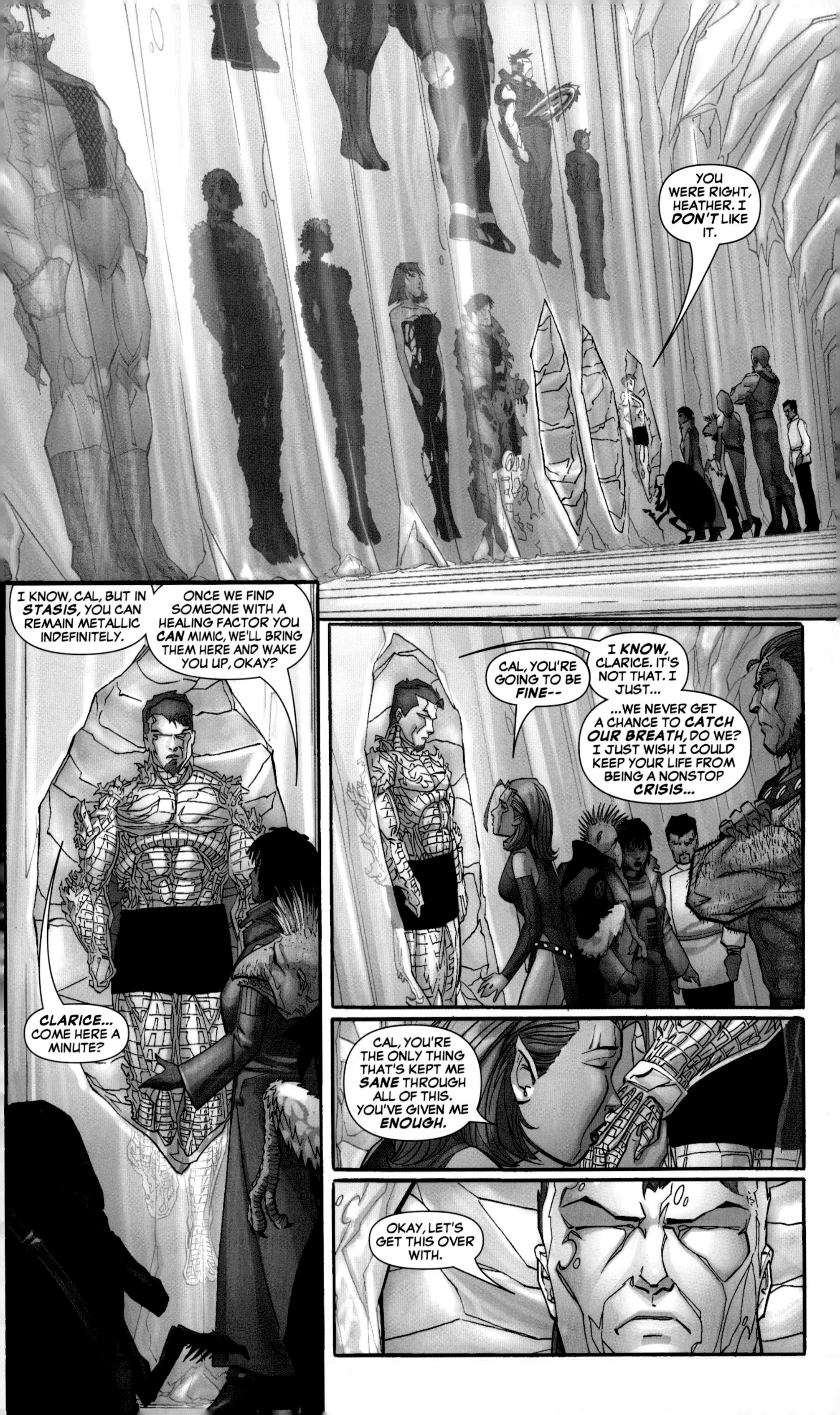
YOU WERE RIGHT, HEATHER. I DON'T LIKE IT.
I KNOW, CAL, BUT IN STASIS, YOU CAN REMAIN METALLIC INDEFINITELY.
ONCE WE FIND SOMEONE WITH A HEALING FACTOR YOU CAN MIMIC, WE'LL BRING THEM HERE AND WAKE YOU UP, OKAY?
CLARICE... COME HERE A MINUTE?
CAL, YOU'RE GOING TO BE FINE--
I KNOW, CLARICE. IT'S NOT THAT. I JUST...
...WE NEVER GET A CHANCE TO CATCH OUR BREATH, DO WE? I JUST WISH I COULD KEEP YOUR LIFE FROM BEING A NONSTOP CRISIS...
CAL, YOU'RE THE ONLY THING THAT'S KEPT ME SANE THROUGH ALL OF THIS. YOU'VE GIVEN ME ENOUGH.
OKAY, LET'S GET THIS OVER WITH.

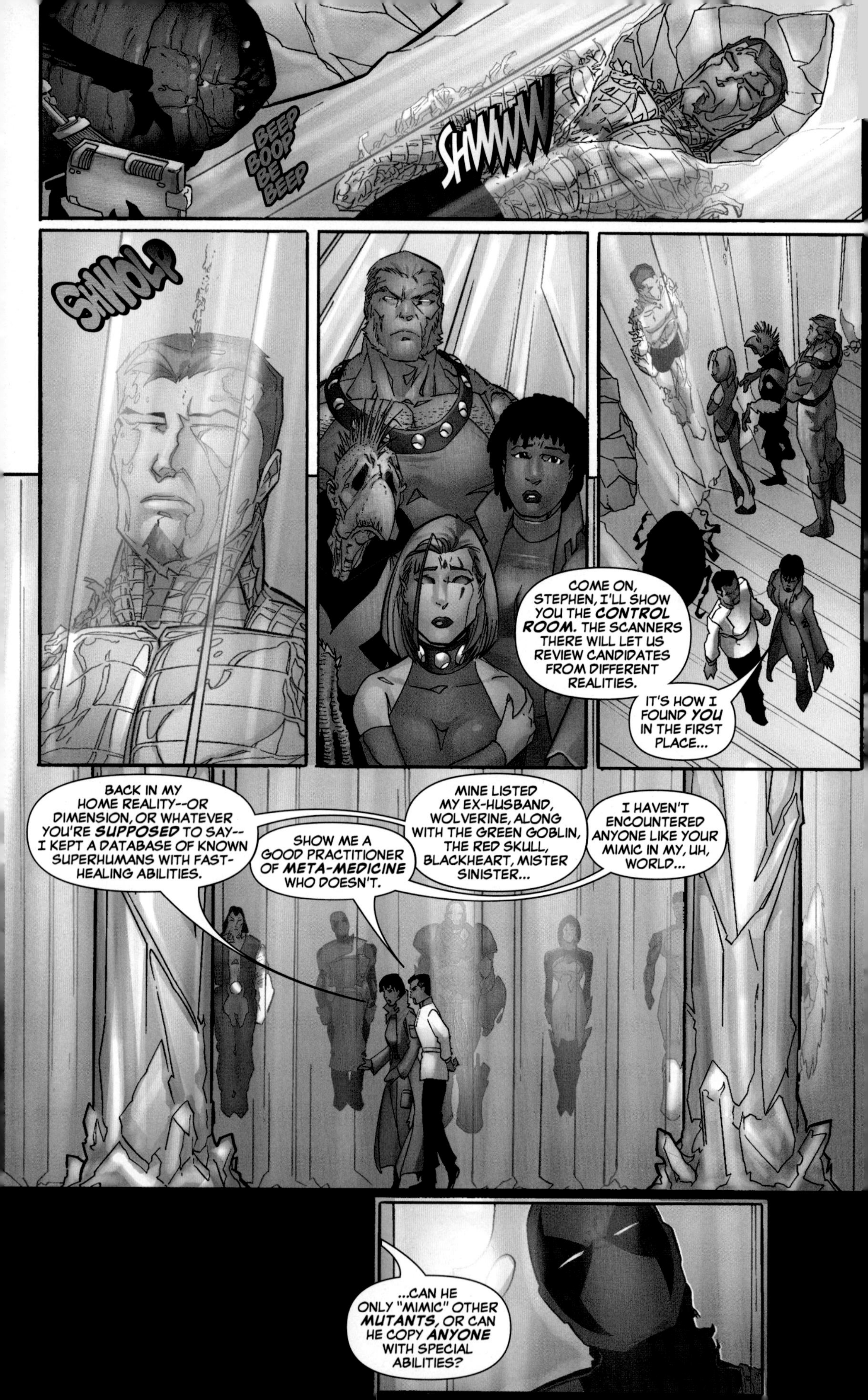

BEEP BOOP BE BEEP
SHWWW
SHWOLP
COME ON, STEPHEN, I'LL SHOW YOU THE CONTROL ROOM. THE SCANNERS THERE WILL LET US REVIEW CANDIDATES FROM DIFFERENT REALITIES.
IT'S HOW I FOUND YOU IN THE FIRST PLACE...
BACK IN MY HOME REALITY--OR DIMENSION, OR WHATEVER YOU'RE SUPPOSED TO SAY--I KEPT A DATABASE OF KNOWN SUPERHUMANS WITH FAST-HEALING ABILITIES.
SHOW ME A GOOD PRACTITIONER OF META-MEDICINE WHO DOESN'T.
MINE LISTED MY EX-HUSBAND, WOLVERINE, ALONG WITH THE GREEN GOBLIN, THE RED SKULL, BLACKHEART, MISTER SINISTER...
I HAVEN'T ENCOUNTERED ANYONE LIKE YOUR MIMIC IN MY, UH, WORLD...
...CAN HE ONLY "MIMIC" OTHER MUTANTS, OR CAN HE COPY ANYONE WITH SPECIAL ABILITIES?

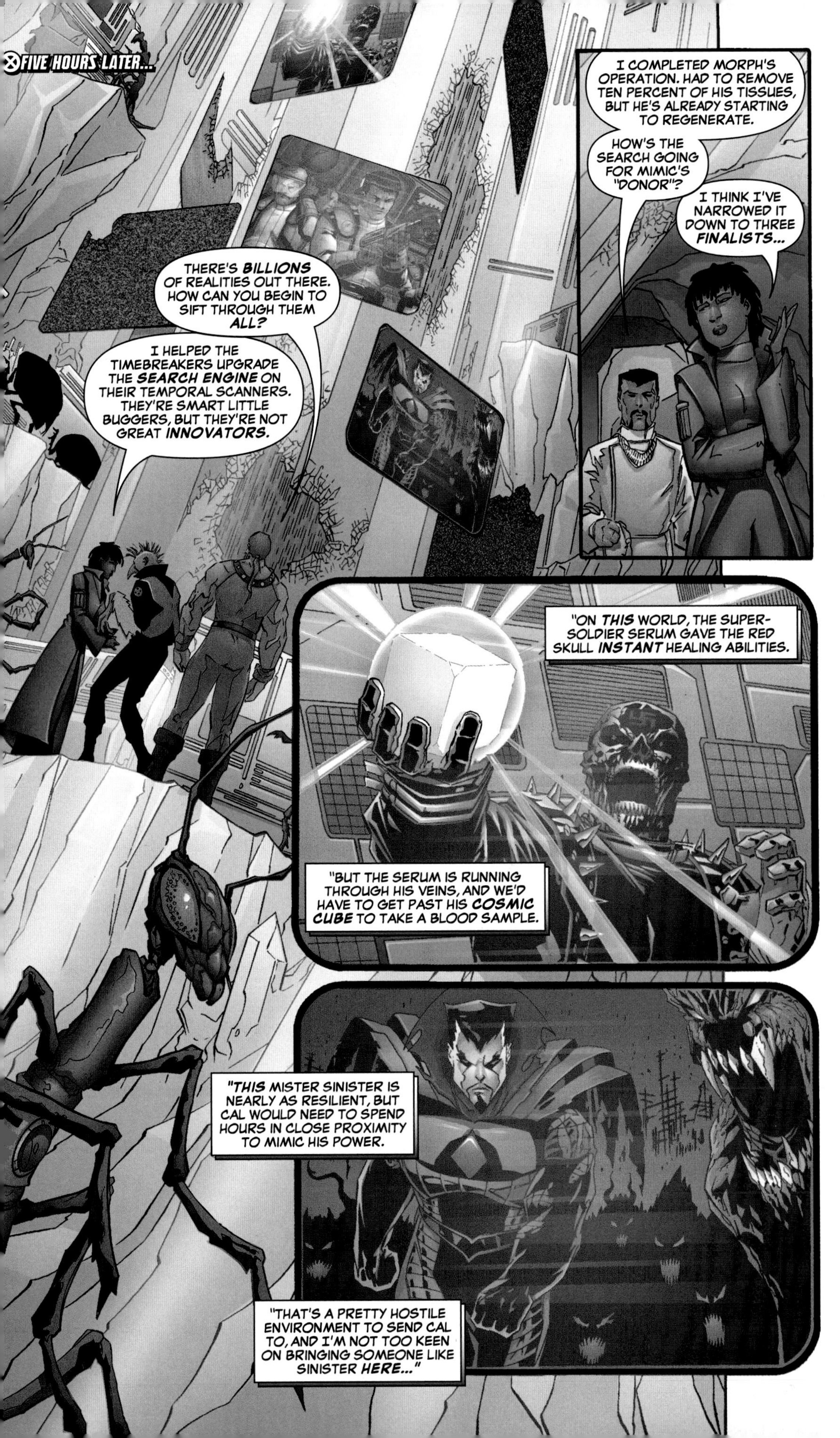
FIVE HOURS LATER...
I COMPLETED MORPH'S OPERATION. HAD TO REMOVE TEN PERCENT OF HIS TISSUES, BUT HE'S ALREADY STARTING TO REGENERATE.
HOW'S THE SEARCH GOING FOR MIMIC'S "DONOR"?
I THINK I'VE NARROWED IT DOWN TO THREE FINALISTS...
THERE'S BILLIONS OF REALITIES OUT THERE. HOW CAN YOU BEGIN TO SIFT THROUGH THEM ALL?
I HELPED THE TIMEBREAKERS UPGRADE THE SEARCH ENGINE ON THEIR TEMPORAL SCANNERS. THEY'RE SMART LITTLE BUGGERS, BUT THEY'RE NOT GREAT INNOVATORS.
"ON THIS WORLD, THE SUPER-SOLDIER SERUM GAVE THE RED SKULL INSTANT HEALING ABILITIES.
"BUT THE SERUM IS RUNNING THROUGH HIS VEINS, AND WE'D HAVE TO GET PAST HIS COSMIC CUBE TO TAKE A BLOOD SAMPLE.
"THIS MISTER SINISTER IS NEARLY AS RESILIENT, BUT CAL WOULD NEED TO SPEND HOURS IN CLOSE PROXIMITY TO MIMIC HIS POWER.
"THAT'S A PRETTY HOSTILE ENVIRONMENT TO SEND CAL TO, AND I'M NOT TOO KEEN ON BRINGING SOMEONE LIKE SINISTER HERE..."

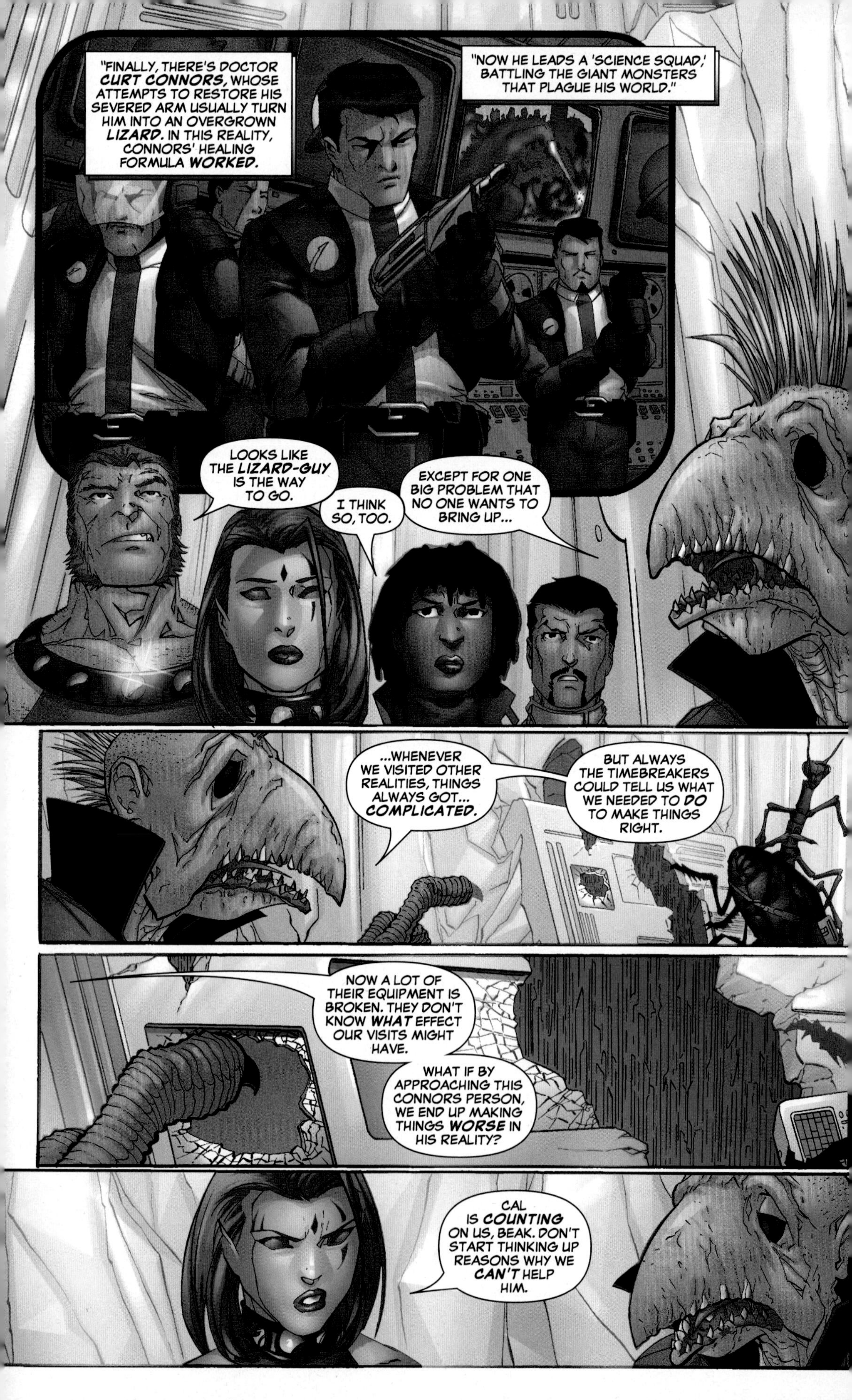
"FINALLY, THERE'S DOCTOR CURT CONNORS, WHOSE ATTEMPTS TO RESTORE HIS SEVERED ARM USUALLY TURN HIM INTO AN OVERGROWN LIZARD. IN THIS REALITY, CONNORS' HEALING FORMULA WORKED.
"NOW HE LEADS A 'SCIENCE SQUAD,' BATTLING THE GIANT MONSTERS THAT PLAGUE HIS WORLD."
LOOKS LIKE THE LIZARD-GUY IS THE WAY TO GO.
I THINK SO, TOO.
EXCEPT FOR ONE BIG PROBLEM THAT NO ONE WANTS TO BRING UP...
...WHENEVER WE VISITED OTHER REALITIES, THINGS ALWAYS GOT... COMPLICATED.
BUT ALWAYS THE TIMEBREAKERS COULD TELL US WHAT WE NEEDED TO DO TO MAKE THINGS RIGHT.
NOW A LOT OF THEIR EQUIPMENT IS BROKEN. THEY DON'T KNOW WHAT EFFECT OUR VISITS MIGHT HAVE.
WHAT IF BY APPROACHING THIS CONNORS PERSON, WE END UP MAKING THINGS WORSE IN HIS REALITY?
CAL IS COUNTING ON US, BEAK. DON'T START THINKING UP REASONS WHY WE CAN'T HELP HIM.

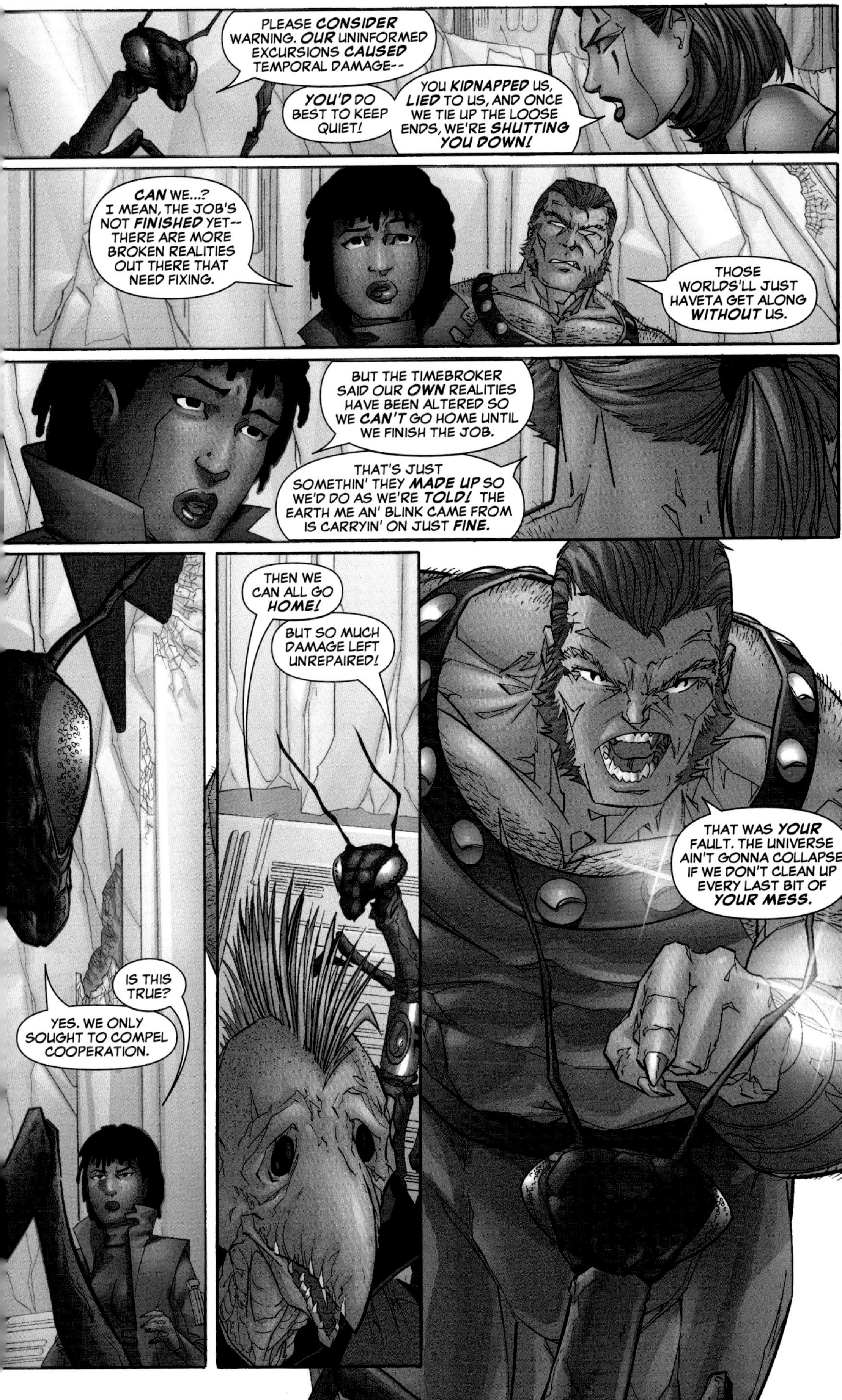
PLEASE CONSIDER WARNING. OUR UNINFORMED EXCURSIONS CAUSED TEMPORAL DAMAGE--
YOU'D DO BEST TO KEEP QUIET!
YOU KIDNAPPED US, LIED TO US, AND ONCE WE TIE UP THE LOOSE ENDS, WE'RE SHUTTING YOU DOWN!
CAN WE...? I MEAN, THE JOB'S NOT FINISHED YET-- THERE ARE MORE BROKEN REALITIES OUT THERE THAT NEED FIXING.
THOSE WORLDS'LL JUST HAVETA GET ALONG WITHOUT US.
BUT THE TIMEBROKER SAID OUR OWN REALITIES HAVE BEEN ALTERED SO WE CAN'T GO HOME UNTIL WE FINISH THE JOB.
THAT'S JUST SOMETHIN' THEY MADE UP SO WE'D DO AS WE'RE TOLD! THE EARTH ME AN' BLINK CAME FROM IS CARRYIN' ON JUST FINE.
IS THIS TRUE?
YES. WE ONLY SOUGHT TO COMPEL COOPERATION.
THEN WE CAN ALL GO HOME!
BUT SO MUCH DAMAGE LEFT UNREPAIRED!
THAT WAS YOUR FAULT. THE UNIVERSE AIN'T GONNA COLLAPSE IF WE DON'T CLEAN UP EVERY LAST BIT OF YOUR MESS.

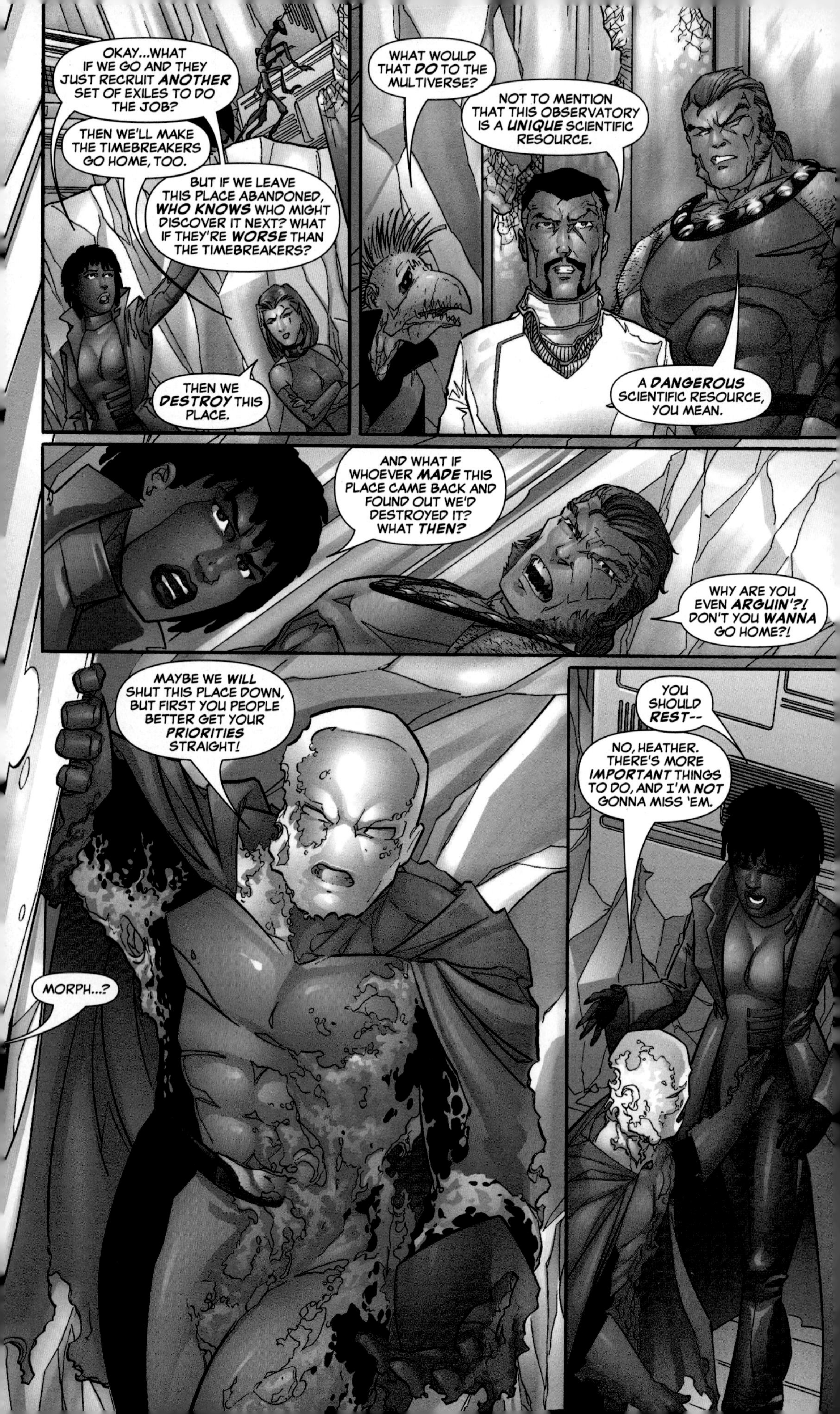
OKAY...WHAT IF WE GO AND THEY JUST RECRUIT ANOTHER SET OF EXILES TO DO THE JOB?
THEN WE'LL MAKE THE TIMEBREAKERS GO HOME, TOO.
BUT IF WE LEAVE THIS PLACE ABANDONED, WHO KNOWS WHO MIGHT DISCOVER IT NEXT? WHAT IF THEY'RE WORSE THAN THE TIMEBREAKERS?
THEN WE DESTROY THIS PLACE.
WHAT WOULD THAT DO TO THE MULTIVERSE?
NOT TO MENTION THAT THIS OBSERVATORY IS A UNIQUE SCIENTIFIC RESOURCE.
A DANGEROUS SCIENTIFIC RESOURCE, YOU MEAN.
AND WHAT IF WHOEVER MADE THIS PLACE CAME BACK AND FOUND OUT WE'D DESTROYED IT? WHAT THEN?
WHY ARE YOU EVEN ARGUIN'?! DON'T YOU WANNA GO HOME?!
MAYBE WE WILL SHUT THIS PLACE DOWN, BUT FIRST YOU PEOPLE BETTER GET YOUR PRIORITIES STRAIGHT!
MORPH...?
YOU SHOULD REST--
NO, HEATHER. THERE'S MORE IMPORTANT THINGS TO DO, AND I'M NOT GONNA MISS 'EM.

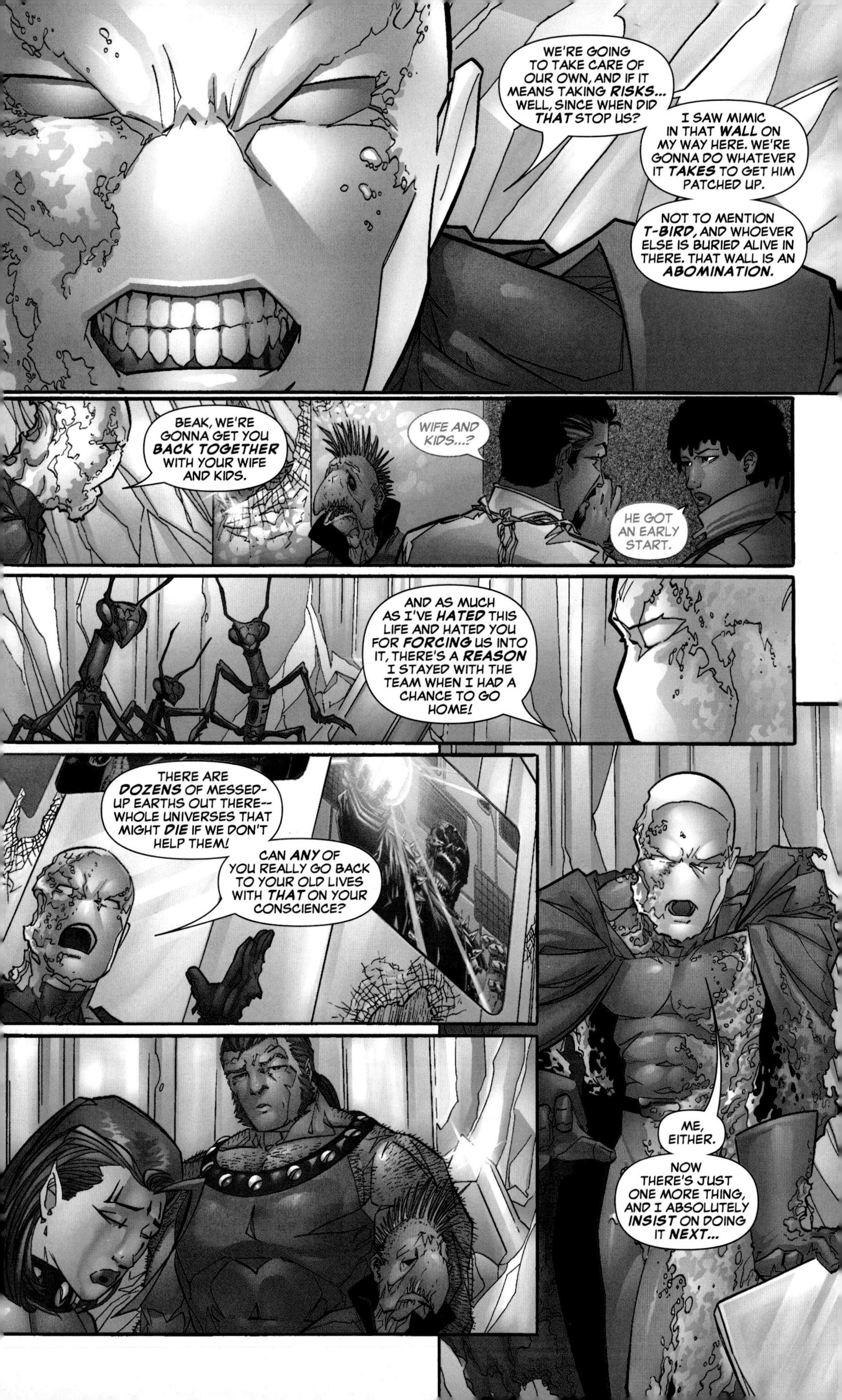
WE'RE GOING TO TAKE CARE OF OUR OWN, AND IF IT MEANS TAKING RISKS... WELL, SINCE WHEN DID THAT STOP US?
I SAW MIMIC IN THAT WALL ON MY WAY HERE. WE'RE GONNA DO WHATEVER IT TAKES TO GET HIM PATCHED UP.
NOT TO MENTION T-BIRD, AND WHOEVER ELSE IS BURIED ALIVE IN THERE. THAT WALL IS AN ABOMINATION.
BEAK, WE'RE GONNA GET YOU BACK TOGETHER WITH YOUR WIFE AND KIDS.
WIFE AND KIDS...?
HE GOT AN EARLY START.
AND AS MUCH AS I'VE HATED THIS LIFE AND HATED YOU FOR FORCING US INTO IT, THERE'S A REASON I STAYED WITH THE TEAM WHEN I HAD A CHANCE TO GO HOME!
THERE ARE DOZENS OF MESSED-UP EARTHS OUT THERE-- WHOLE UNIVERSES THAT MIGHT DIE IF WE DON'T HELP THEM!
CAN ANY OF YOU REALLY GO BACK TO YOUR OLD LIVES WITH THAT ON YOUR CONSCIENCE?
ME, EITHER.
NOW THERE'S JUST ONE MORE THING, AND I ABSOLUTELY INSIST ON DOING IT NEXT...

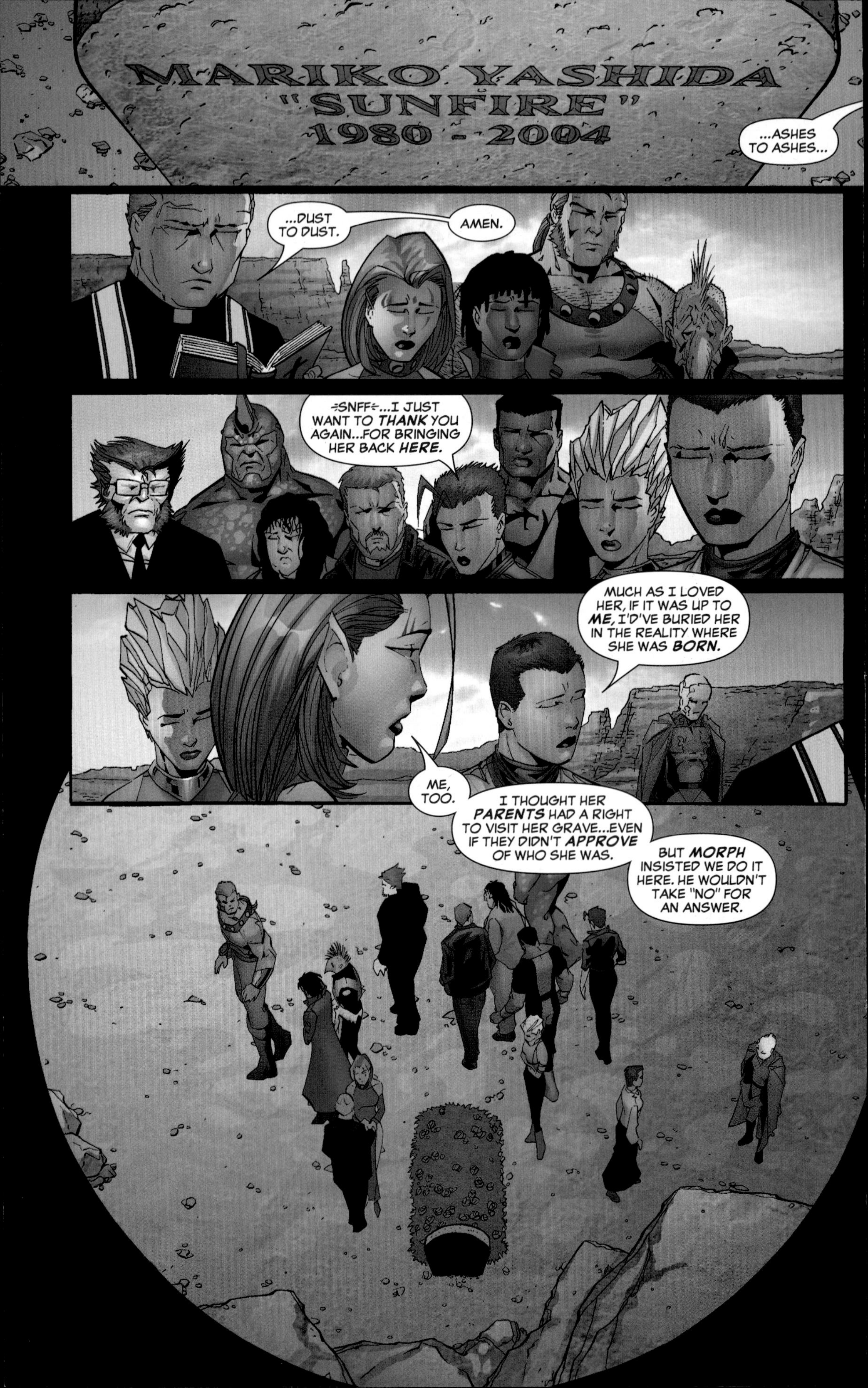
MARIKO YASHIDA "SUNFIRE" 1980 - 2004
...ASHES TO ASHES...
...DUST TO DUST.
AMEN.
=SNFF=...I JUST WANT TO THANK YOU AGAIN...FOR BRINGING HER BACK HERE.
MUCH AS I LOVED HER, IF IT WAS UP TO ME, I'D'VE BURIED HER IN THE REALITY WHERE SHE WAS BORN.
ME, TOO.
I THOUGHT HER PARENTS HAD A RIGHT TO VISIT HER GRAVE...EVEN IF THEY DIDN'T APPROVE OF WHO SHE WAS.
BUT MORPH INSISTED WE DO IT HERE. HE WOULDN'T TAKE "NO" FOR AN ANSWER.

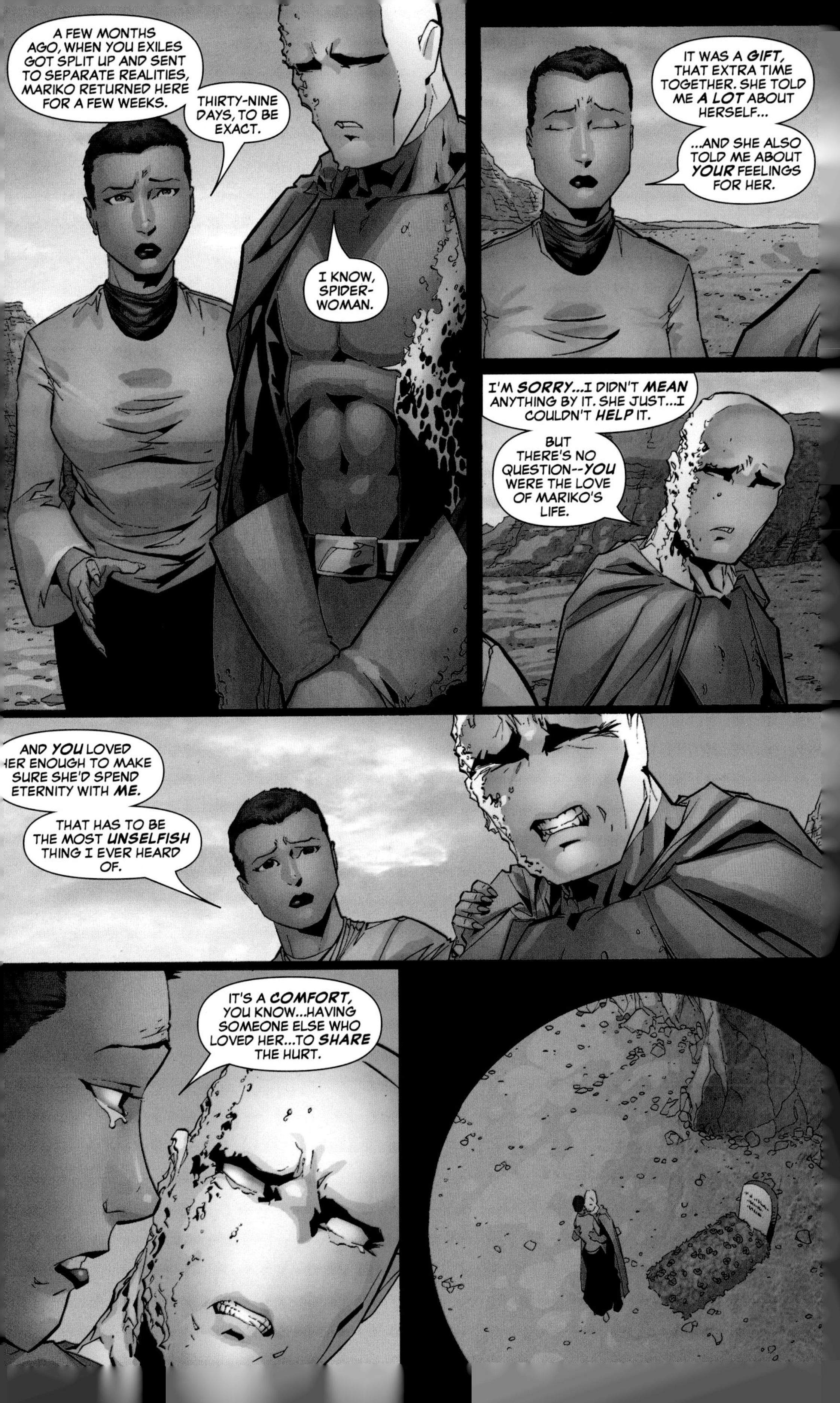
A FEW MONTHS AGO, WHEN YOU EXILES GOT SPLIT UP AND SENT TO SEPARATE REALITIES, MARIKO RETURNED HERE FOR A FEW WEEKS.
THIRTY-NINE DAYS, TO BE EXACT.
I KNOW, SPIDER-WOMAN.
IT WAS A GIFT, THAT EXTRA TIME TOGETHER. SHE TOLD ME A LOT ABOUT HERSELF...
...AND SHE ALSO TOLD ME ABOUT YOUR FEELINGS FOR HER.
I'M SORRY...I DIDN'T MEAN ANYTHING BY IT. SHE JUST...I COULDN'T HELP IT.
BUT THERE'S NO QUESTION--YOU WERE THE LOVE OF MARIKO'S LIFE.
AND YOU LOVED HER ENOUGH TO MAKE SURE SHE'D SPEND ETERNITY WITH ME.
THAT HAS TO BE THE MOST UNSELFISH THING I EVER HEARD OF.
IT'S A COMFORT, YOU KNOW...HAVING SOMEONE ELSE WHO LOVED HER...TO SHARE THE HURT.

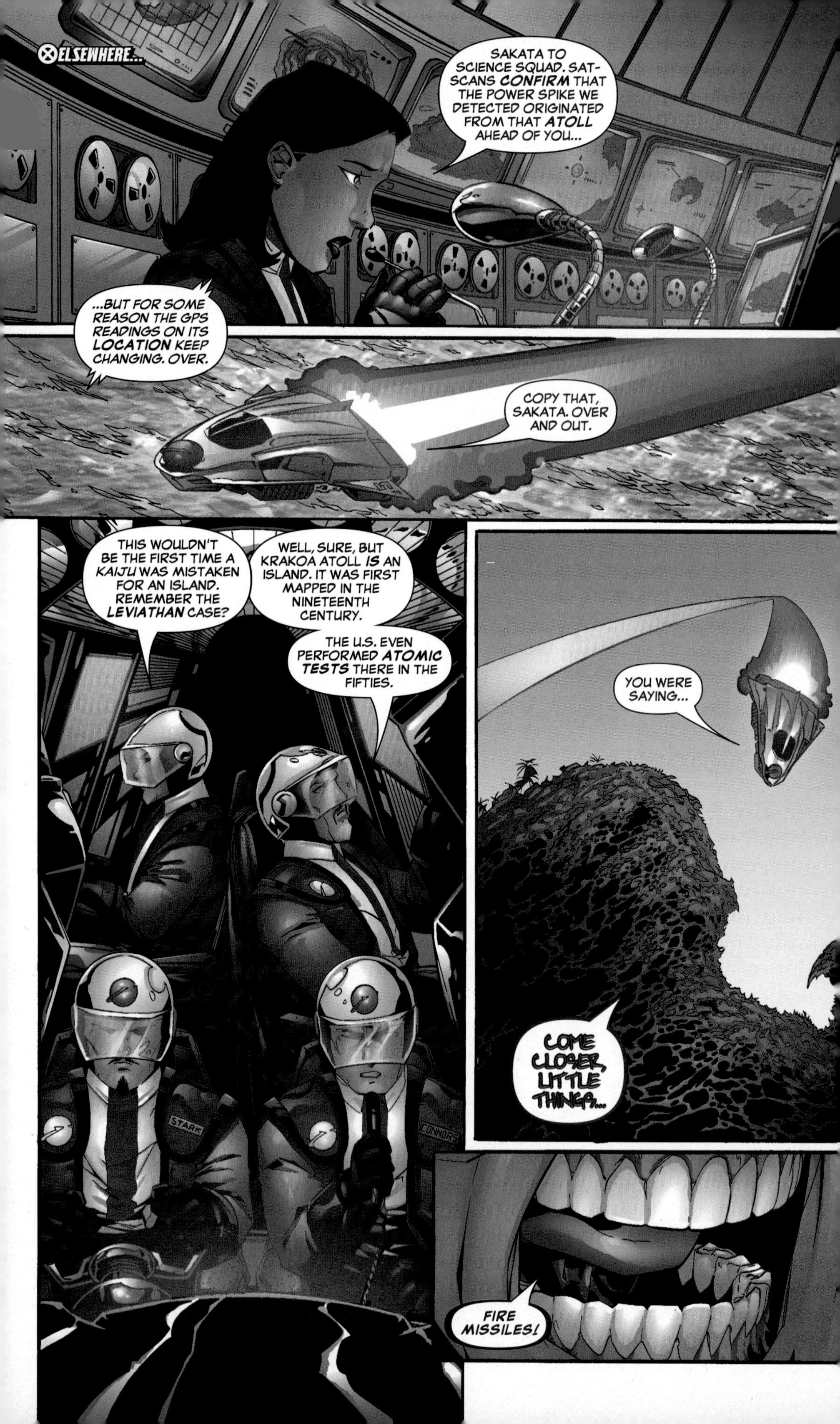
ELSEWHERE...
SAKATA TO SCIENCE SQUAD. SAT-SCANS CONFIRM THAT THE POWER SPIKE WE DETECTED ORIGINATED FROM THAT ATOLL AHEAD OF YOU...
...BUT FOR SOME REASON THE GPS READINGS ON ITS LOCATION KEEP CHANGING. OVER.
COPY THAT, SAKATA. OVER AND OUT.
THIS WOULDN'T BE THE FIRST TIME A KAIJU WAS MISTAKEN FOR AN ISLAND. REMEMBER THE LEVIATHAN CASE?
WELL, SURE, BUT KRAKOA ATOLL IS AN ISLAND. IT WAS FIRST MAPPED IN THE NINETEENTH CENTURY.
THE U.S. EVEN PERFORMED ATOMIC TESTS THERE IN THE FIFTIES.
STARK
CONNORS
YOU WERE SAYING...
COME CLOSER, LITTLE THINGS...
FIRE MISSILES!

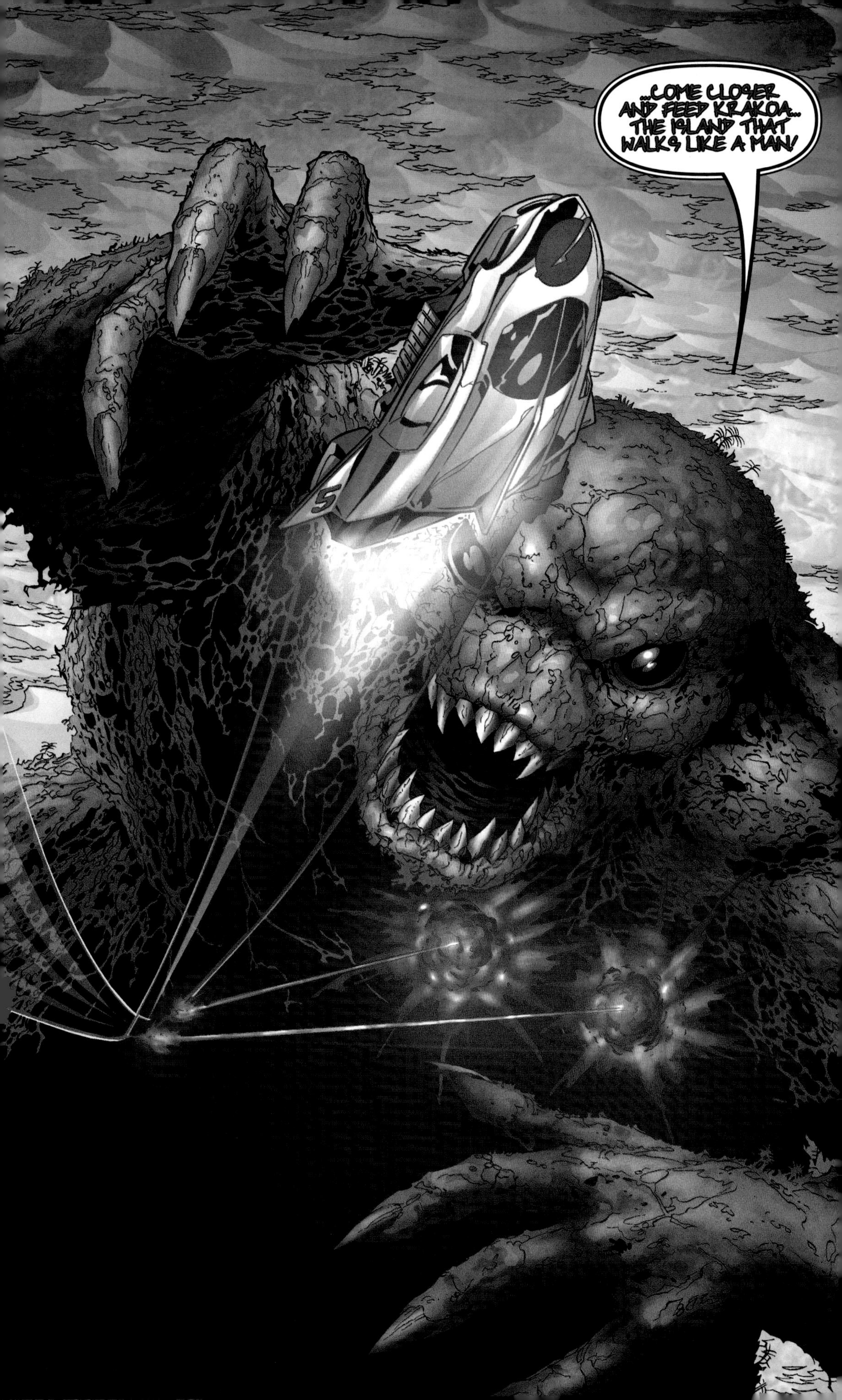
...COME CLOSER AND FEED KRAKOA... THE ISLAND THAT WALKS LIKE A MAN!

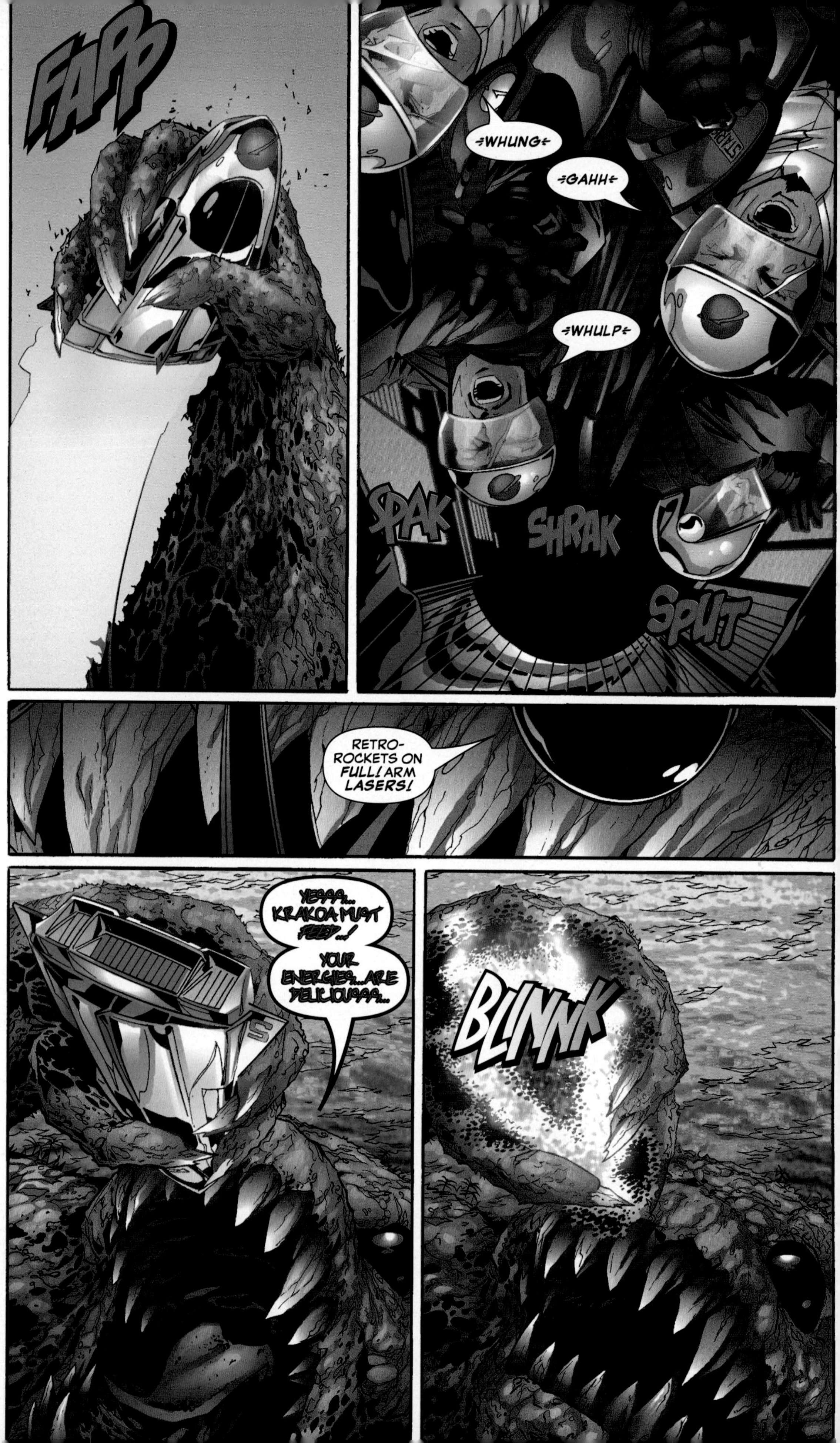
FAPP
WHUNG
GAHH
WHULP
SPAK
SHRAK
SPUT
RETRO-ROCKETS ON FULL! ARM LASERS!
YESSS... KRAKOA MUST FEED...!
YOUR ENERGIES...ARE DELICIOUSSS...
BLINNK

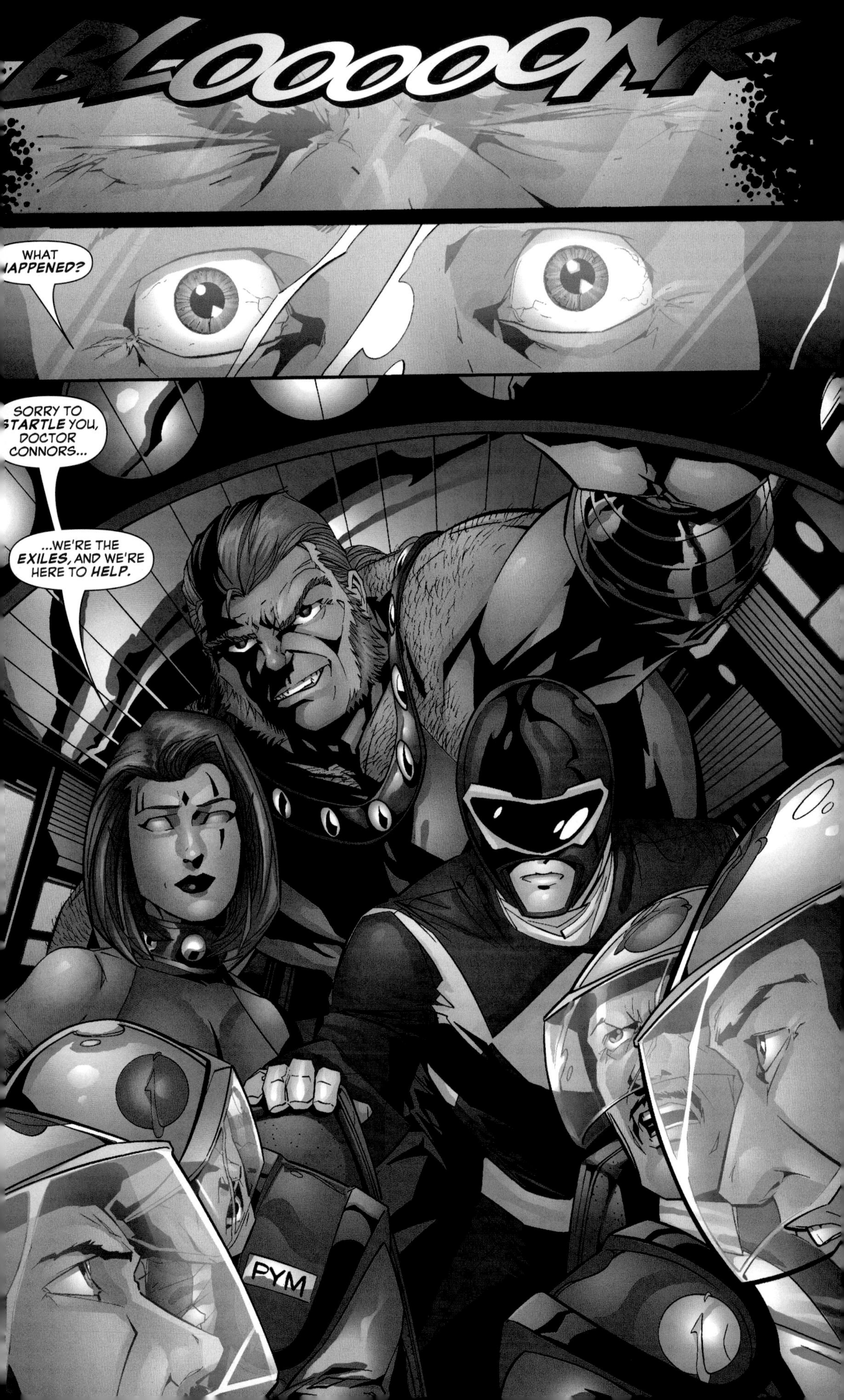
BLOOOOONK
WHAT HAPPENED?
SORRY TO STARTLE YOU, DOCTOR CONNORS...
...WE'RE THE EXILES, AND WE'RE HERE TO HELP.
PYM

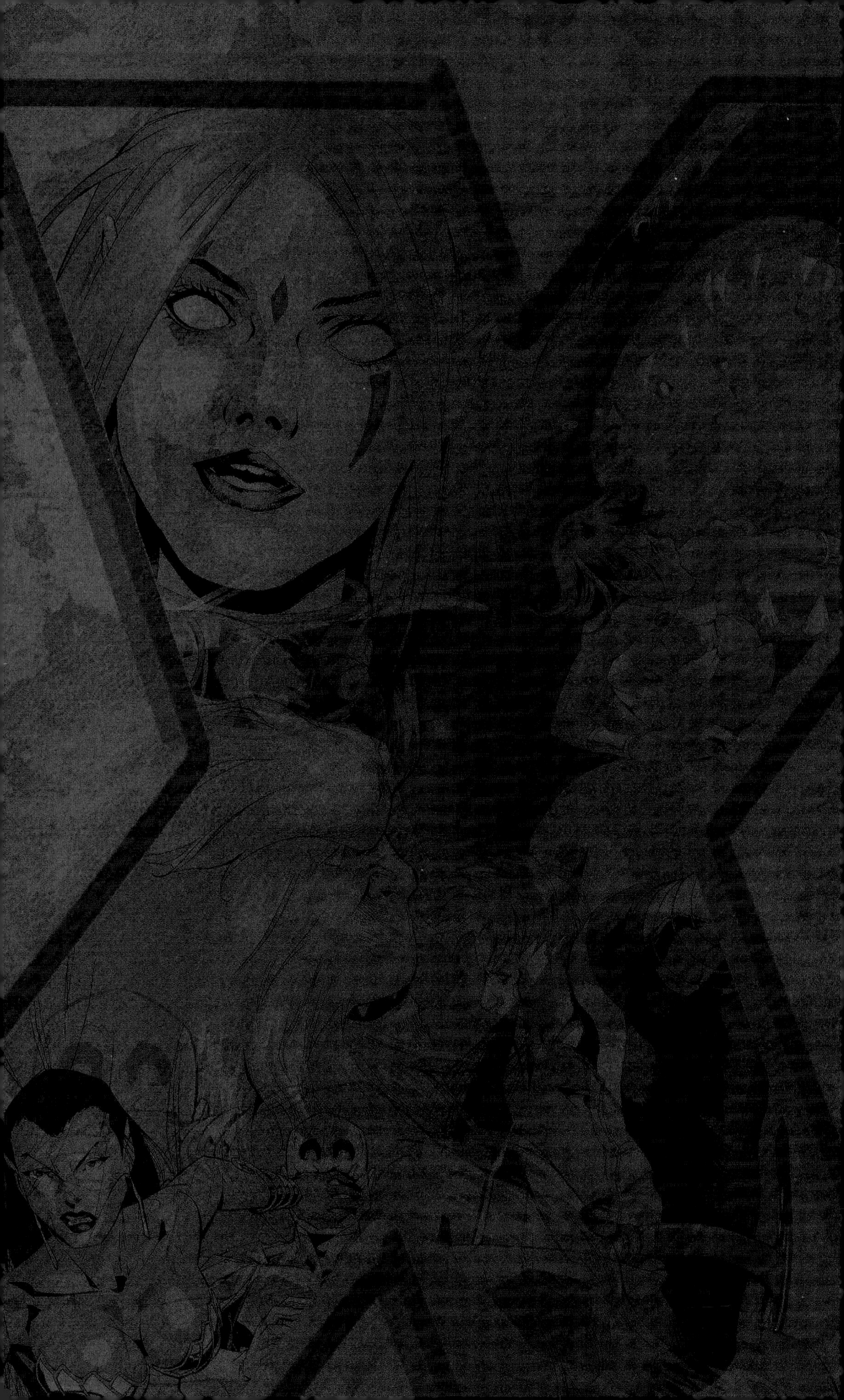

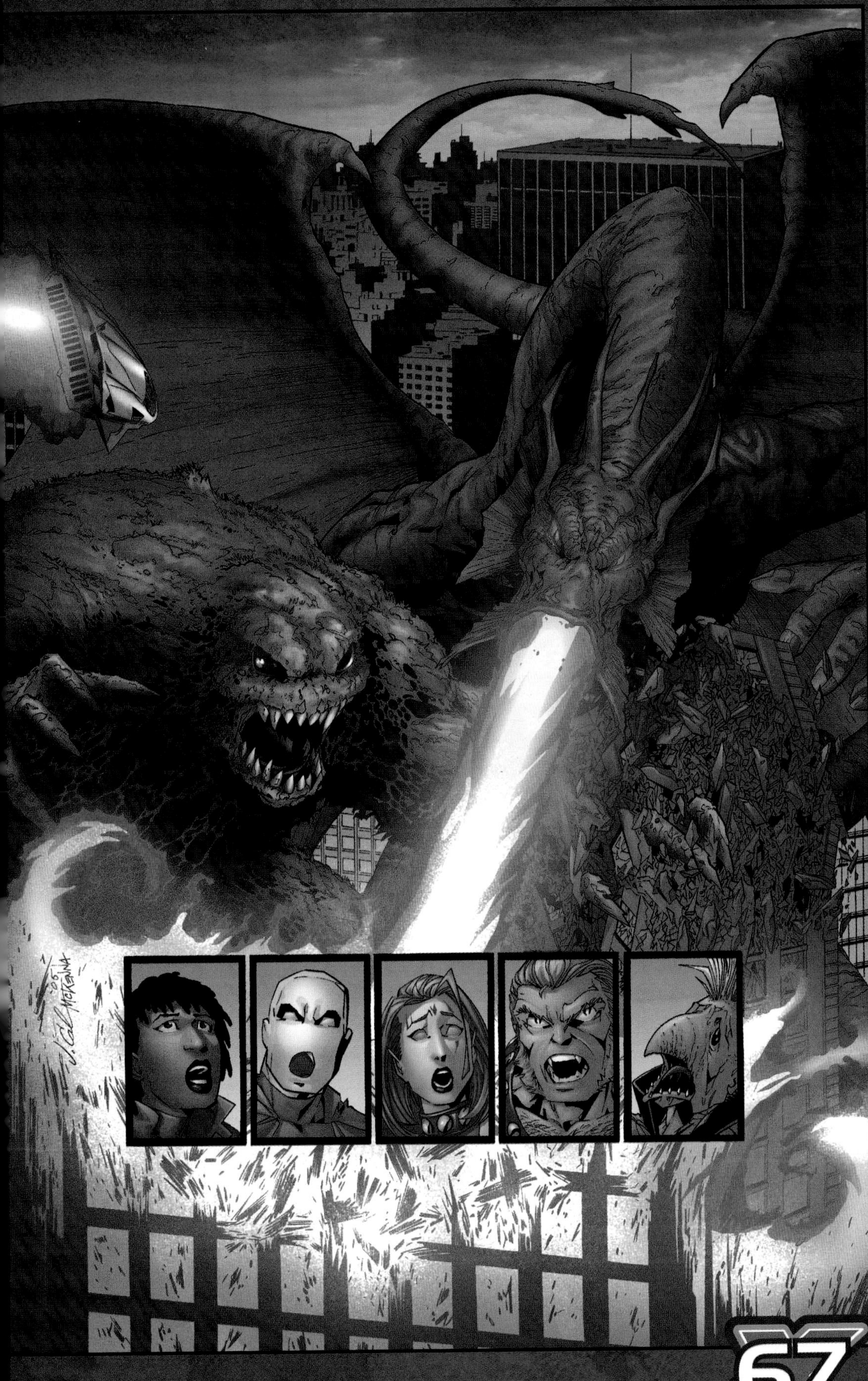

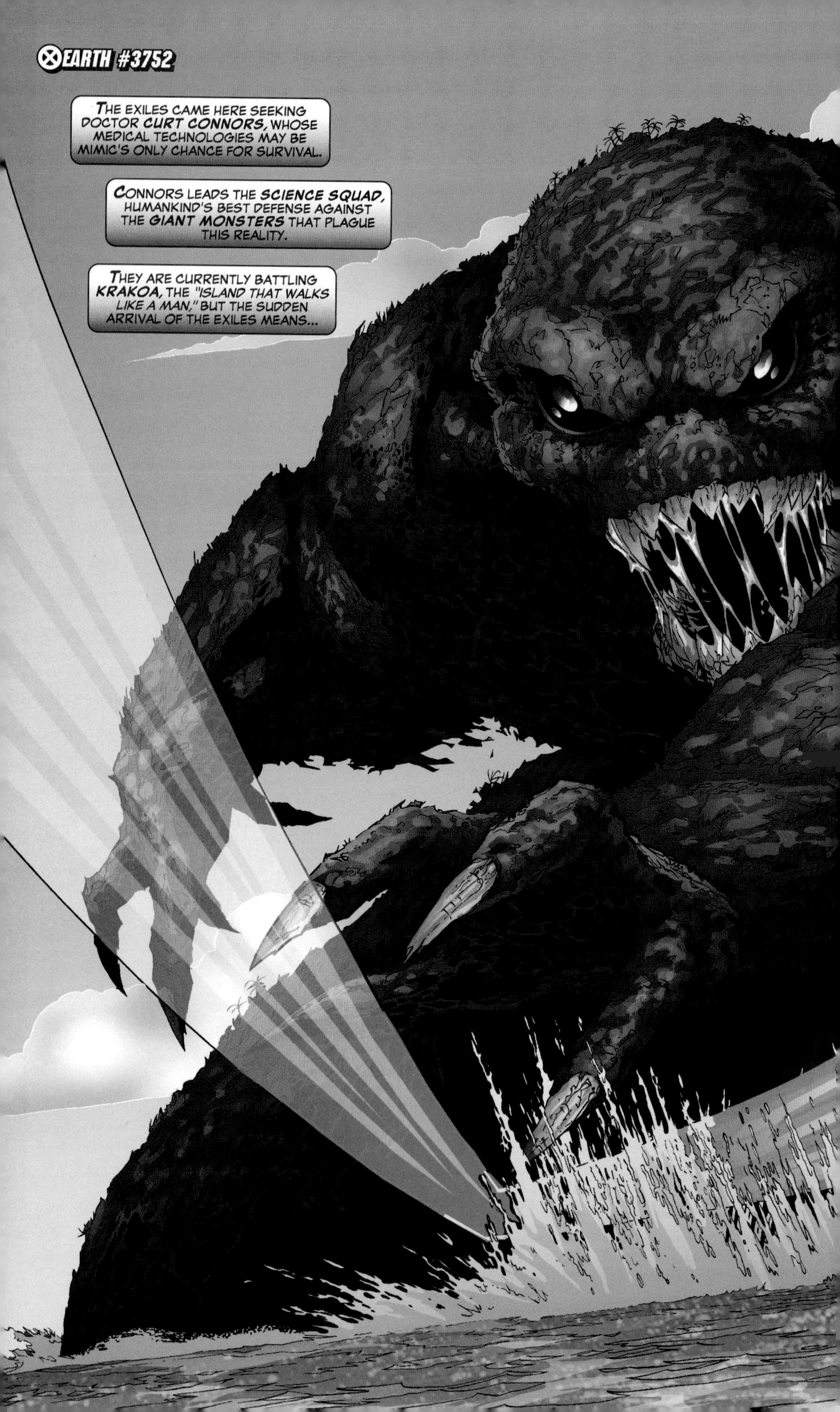
EARTH #3752
THE EXILES CAME HERE SEEKING DOCTOR CURT CONNORS, WHOSE MEDICAL TECHNOLOGIES MAY BE MIMIC'S ONLY CHANCE FOR SURVIVAL.
CONNORS LEADS THE SCIENCE SQUAD, HUMANKIND'S BEST DEFENSE AGAINST THE GIANT MONSTERS THAT PLAGUE THIS REALITY.
THEY ARE CURRENTLY BATTLING KRAKOA, THE "ISLAND THAT WALKS LIKE A MAN," BUT THE SUDDEN ARRIVAL OF THE EXILES MEANS...

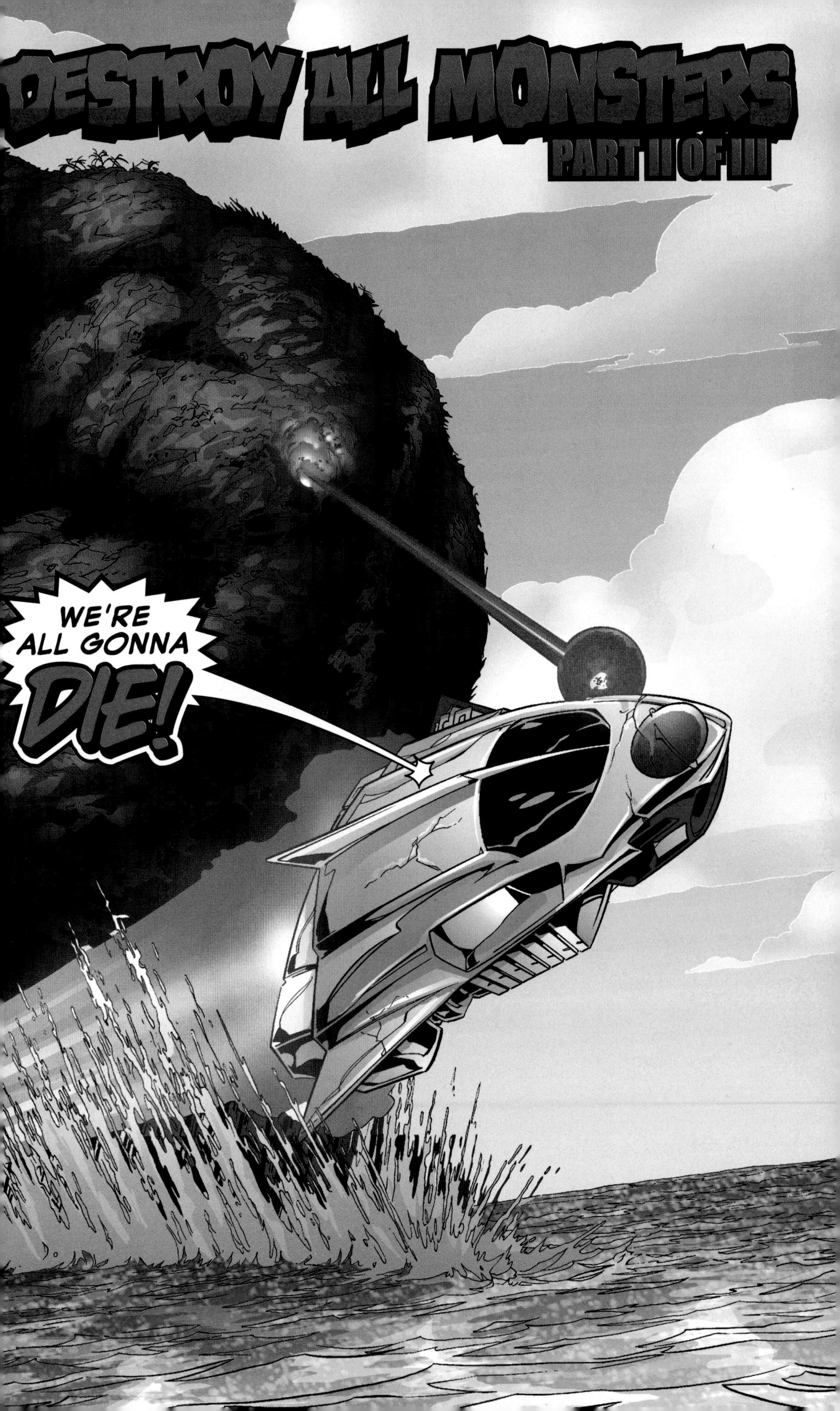
DESTROY ALL MONSTERS
PART II OF III
WE'RE ALL GONNA DIE!

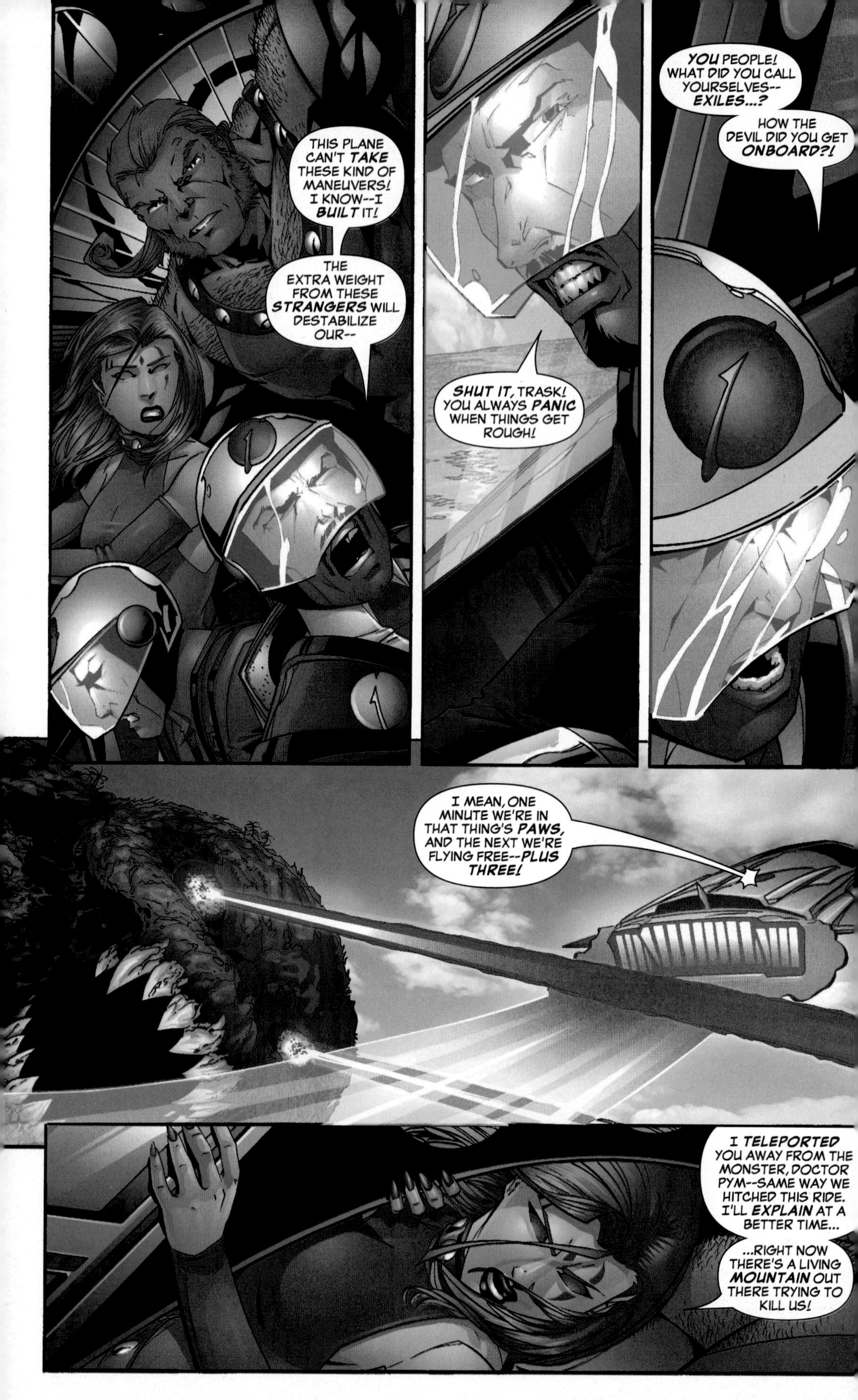
THIS PLANE CAN'T TAKE THESE KIND OF MANEUVERS! I KNOW--I BUILT IT!
THE EXTRA WEIGHT FROM THESE STRANGERS WILL DESTABILIZE OUR--
SHUT IT, TRASK! YOU ALWAYS PANIC WHEN THINGS GET ROUGH!
YOU PEOPLE! WHAT DID YOU CALL YOURSELVES-- EXILES...?
HOW THE DEVIL DID YOU GET ONBOARD?!
I MEAN, ONE MINUTE WE'RE IN THAT THING'S PAWS, AND THE NEXT WE'RE FLYING FREE--PLUS THREE!
I TELEPORTED YOU AWAY FROM THE MONSTER, DOCTOR PYM--SAME WAY WE HITCHED THIS RIDE. I'LL EXPLAIN AT A BETTER TIME...
...RIGHT NOW THERE'S A LIVING MOUNTAIN OUT THERE TRYING TO KILL US!

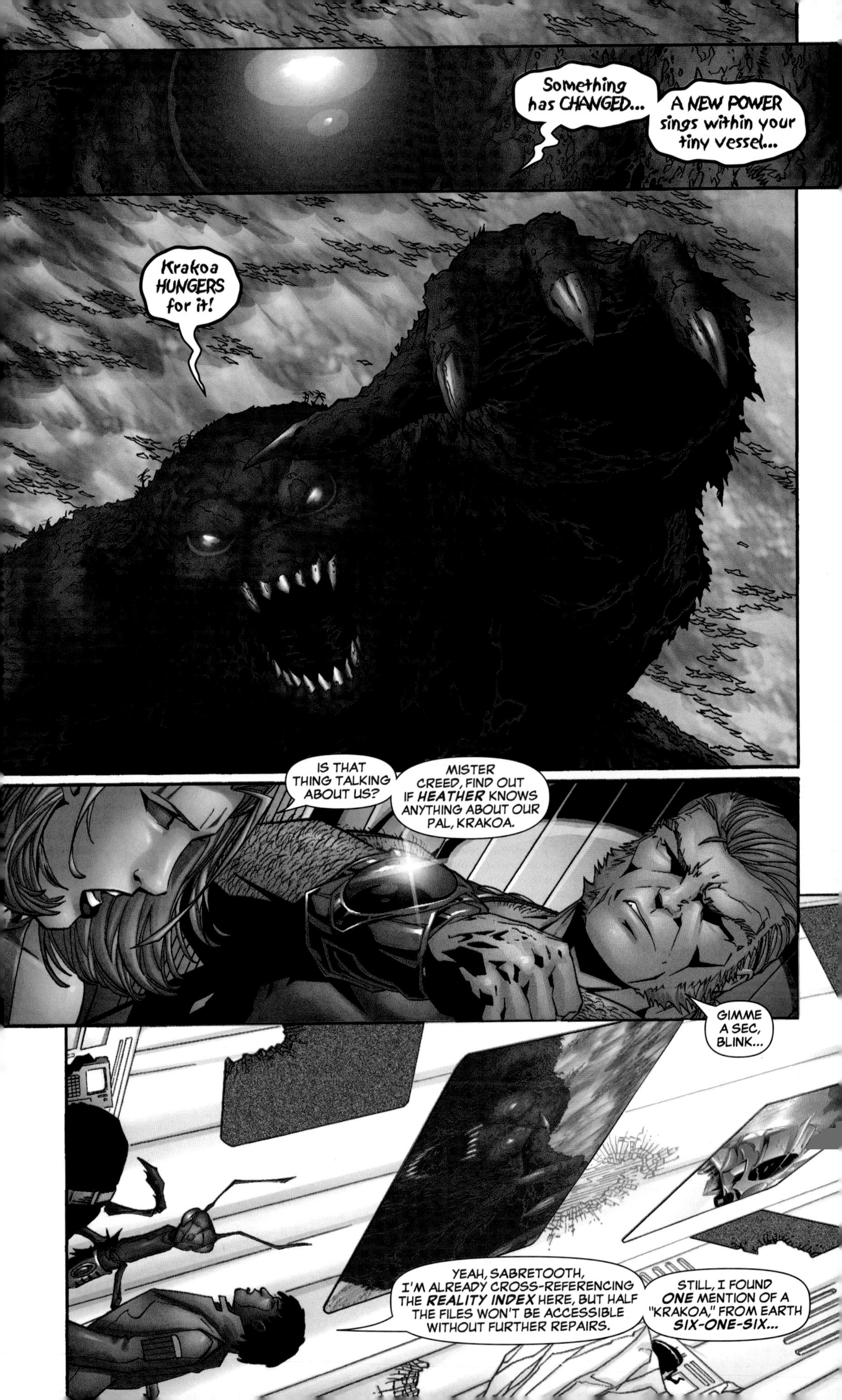
Something has CHANGED...
A NEW POWER sings within your tiny vessel...
Krakoa HUNGERS for it!
IS THAT THING TALKING ABOUT US?
MISTER CREED, FIND OUT IF HEATHER KNOWS ANYTHING ABOUT OUR PAL, KRAKOA.
GIMME A SEC, BLINK...
YEAH, SABRETOOTH, I'M ALREADY CROSS-REFERENCING THE REALITY INDEX HERE, BUT HALF THE FILES WON'T BE ACCESSIBLE WITHOUT FURTHER REPAIRS.
STILL, I FOUND ONE MENTION OF A "KRAKOA," FROM EARTH SIX-ONE-SIX...

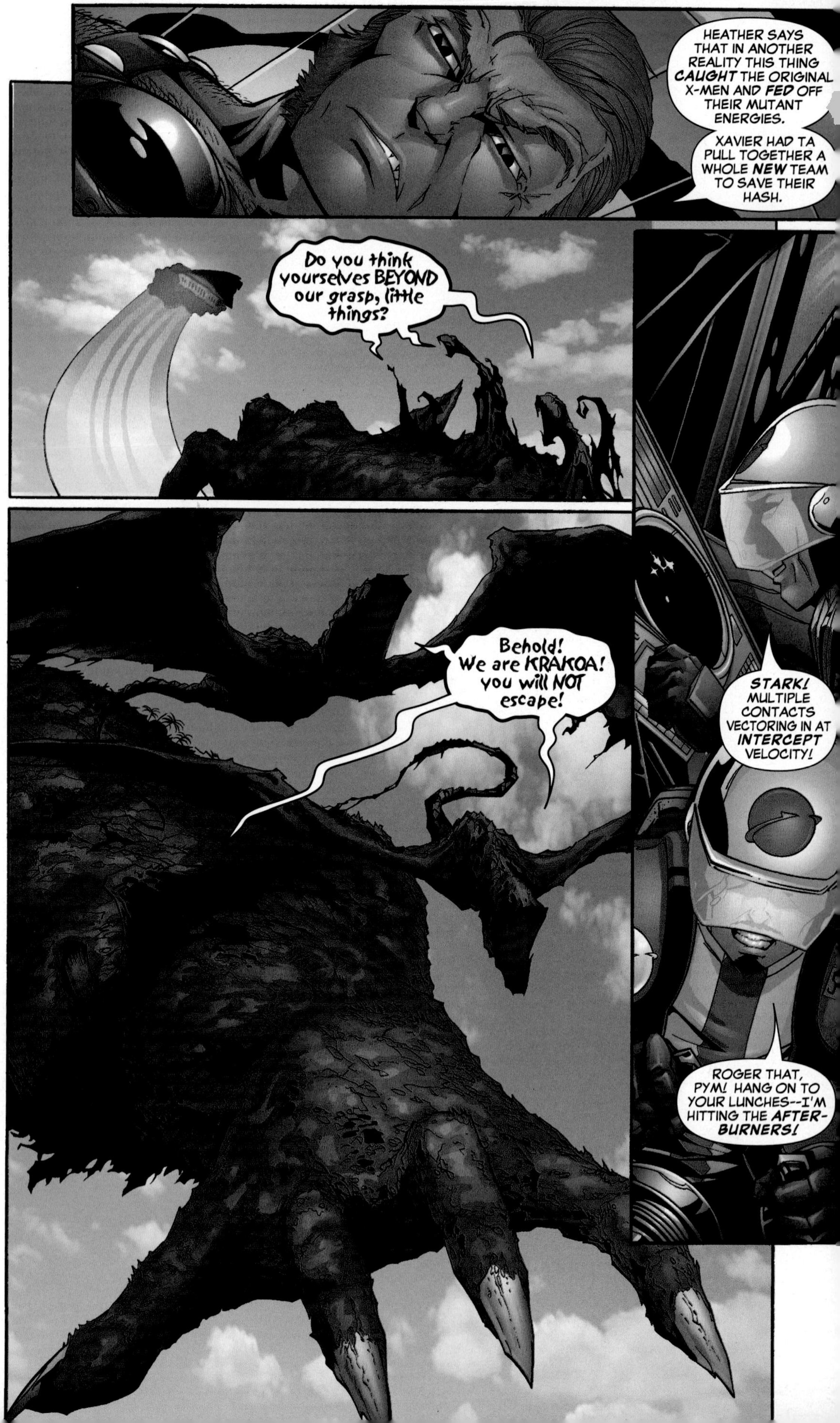
HEATHER SAYS THAT IN ANOTHER REALITY THIS THING CAUGHT THE ORIGINAL X-MEN AND FED OFF THEIR MUTANT ENERGIES.
XAVIER HAD TA PULL TOGETHER A WHOLE NEW TEAM TO SAVE THEIR HASH.
Do you think yourselves BEYOND our grasp, little things?
Behold! We are KRAKOA! you will NOT escape!
STARK! MULTIPLE CONTACTS VECTORING IN AT INTERCEPT VELOCITY!
ROGER THAT, PYM! HANG ON TO YOUR LUNCHES--I'M HITTING THE AFTER-BURNERS!

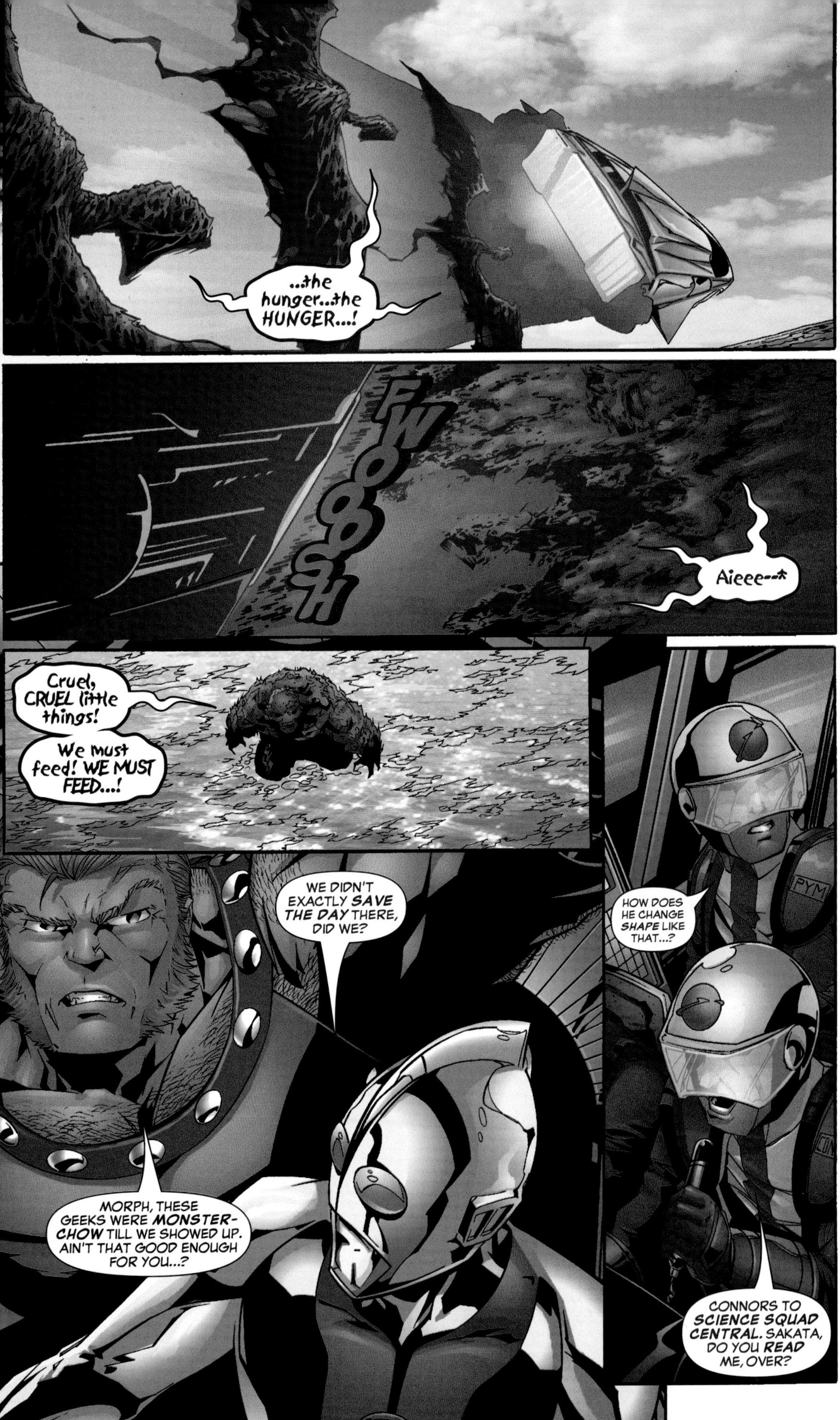
...the hunger...the HUNGER...!
FWOOOSH
Aieee--*
Cruel, CRUEL little things!
We must feed! WE MUST FEED...!
WE DIDN'T EXACTLY SAVE THE DAY THERE, DID WE?
MORPH, THESE GEEKS WERE MONSTER-CHOW TILL WE SHOWED UP. AIN'T THAT GOOD ENOUGH FOR YOU...?
HOW DOES HE CHANGE SHAPE LIKE THAT...?
PYM
CONNORS TO SCIENCE SQUAD CENTRAL. SAKATA, DO YOU READ ME, OVER?

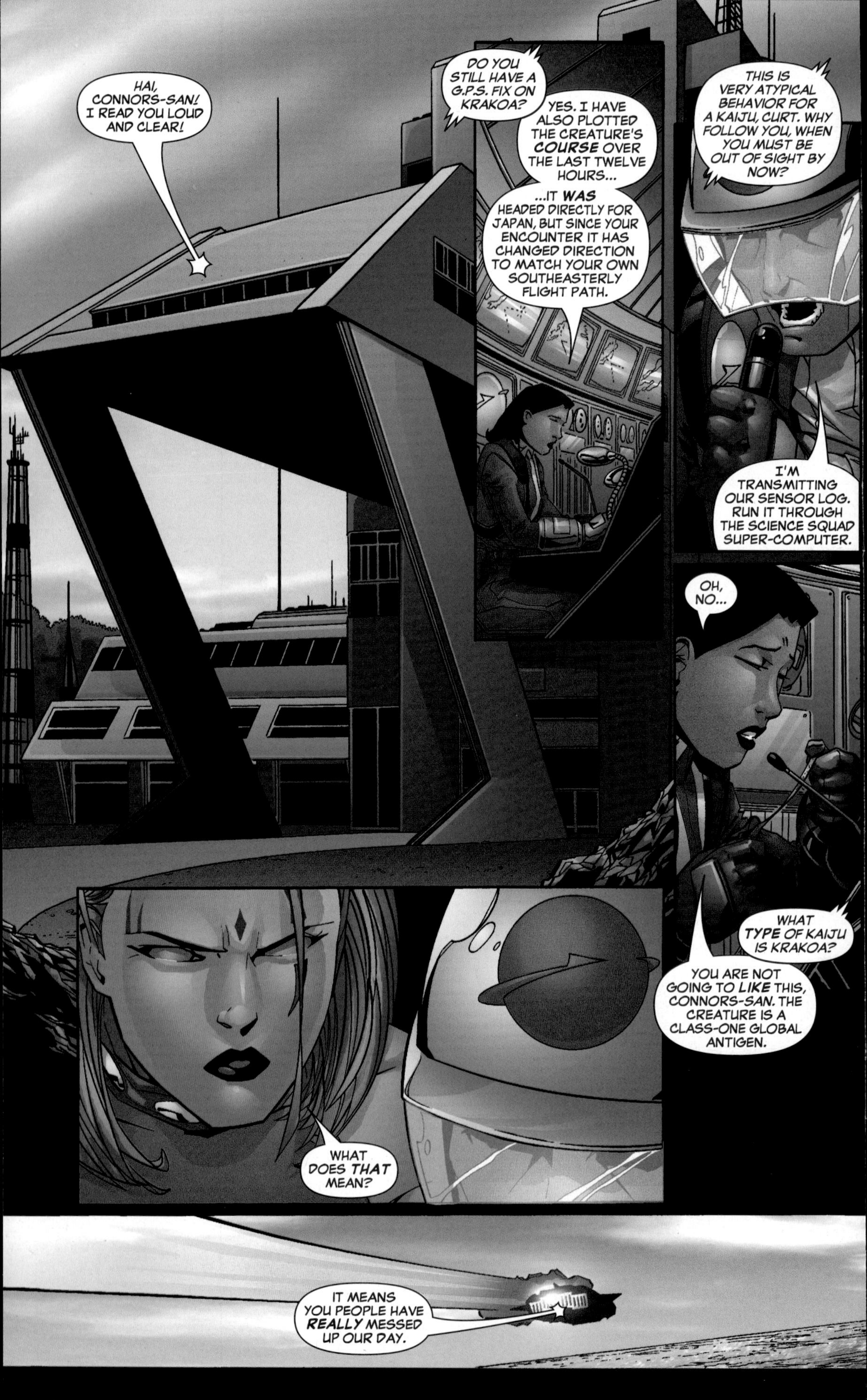
HAI, CONNORS-SAN! I READ YOU LOUD AND CLEAR!
DO YOU STILL HAVE A G.P.S. FIX ON KRAKOA?
YES. I HAVE ALSO PLOTTED THE CREATURE'S **COURSE** OVER THE LAST TWELVE HOURS...
...IT **WAS** HEADED DIRECTLY FOR JAPAN, BUT SINCE YOUR ENCOUNTER IT HAS CHANGED DIRECTION TO MATCH YOUR OWN SOUTHEASTERLY FLIGHT PATH.
THIS IS VERY ATYPICAL BEHAVIOR FOR A KAIJU, CURT. WHY FOLLOW YOU, WHEN YOU MUST BE OUT OF SIGHT BY NOW?
I'M TRANSMITTING OUR SENSOR LOG. RUN IT THROUGH THE SCIENCE SQUAD SUPER-COMPUTER.
OH, NO...
WHAT **TYPE** OF KAIJU IS KRAKOA?
YOU ARE NOT GOING TO **LIKE** THIS, CONNORS-SAN. THE CREATURE IS A CLASS-ONE GLOBAL ANTIGEN.
WHAT DOES **THAT** MEAN?
IT MEANS YOU PEOPLE HAVE **REALLY** MESSED UP OUR DAY.

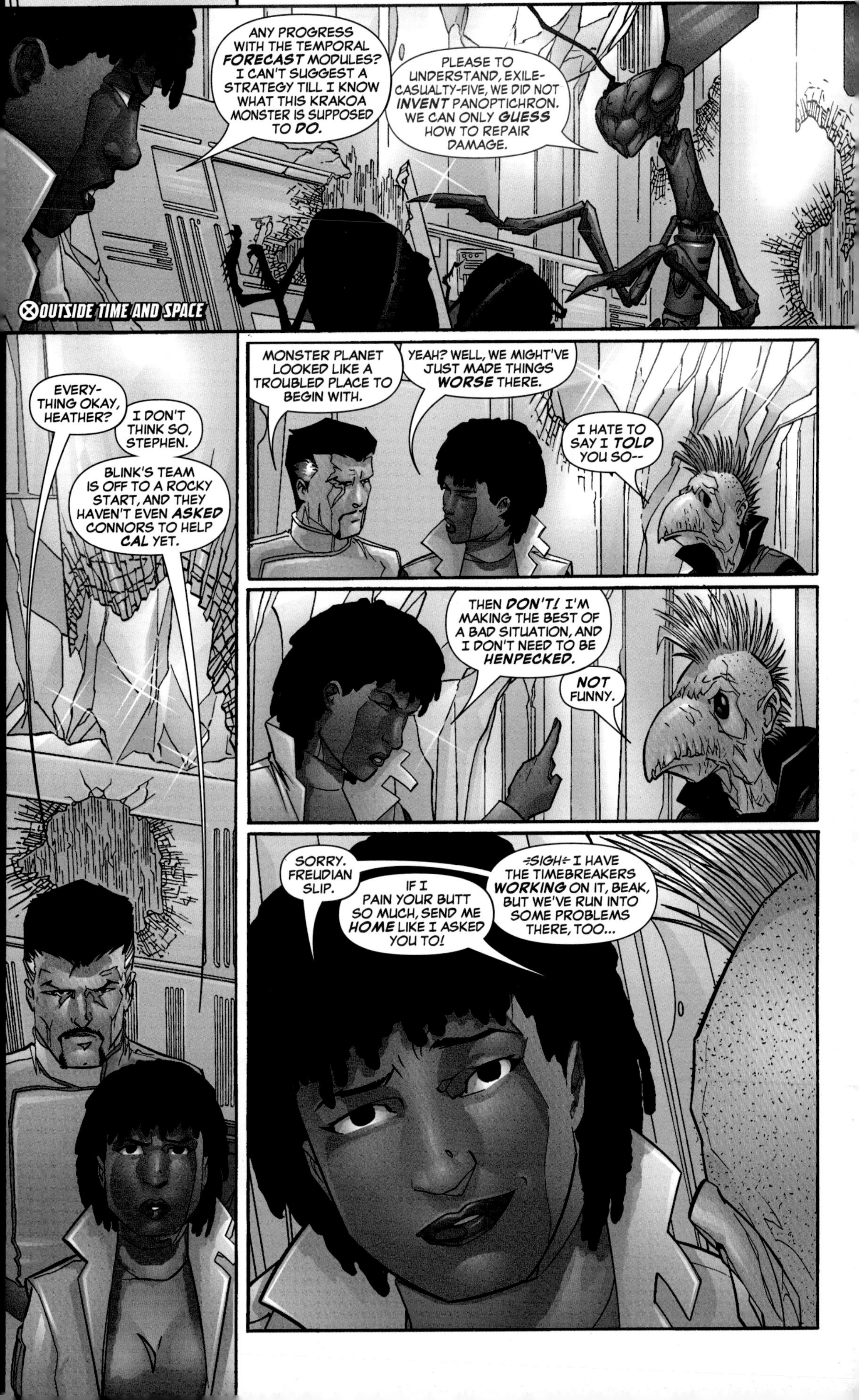
OUTSIDE TIME AND SPACE
ANY PROGRESS WITH THE TEMPORAL FORECAST MODULES? I CAN'T SUGGEST A STRATEGY TILL I KNOW WHAT THIS KRAKOA MONSTER IS SUPPOSED TO DO.
PLEASE TO UNDERSTAND, EXILE-CASUALTY-FIVE, WE DID NOT INVENT PANOPTICHRON. WE CAN ONLY GUESS HOW TO REPAIR DAMAGE.
EVERY-THING OKAY, HEATHER?
I DON'T THINK SO, STEPHEN.
BLINK'S TEAM IS OFF TO A ROCKY START, AND THEY HAVEN'T EVEN ASKED CONNORS TO HELP CAL YET.
MONSTER PLANET LOOKED LIKE A TROUBLED PLACE TO BEGIN WITH.
YEAH? WELL, WE MIGHT'VE JUST MADE THINGS WORSE THERE.
I HATE TO SAY I TOLD YOU SO--
THEN DON'T! I'M MAKING THE BEST OF A BAD SITUATION, AND I DON'T NEED TO BE HENPECKED.
NOT FUNNY.
SORRY. FREUDIAN SLIP.
=SIGH= I HAVE THE TIMEBREAKERS WORKING ON IT, BEAK, BUT WE'VE RUN INTO SOME PROBLEMS THERE, TOO...
IF I PAIN YOUR BUTT SO MUCH, SEND ME HOME LIKE I ASKED YOU TO!

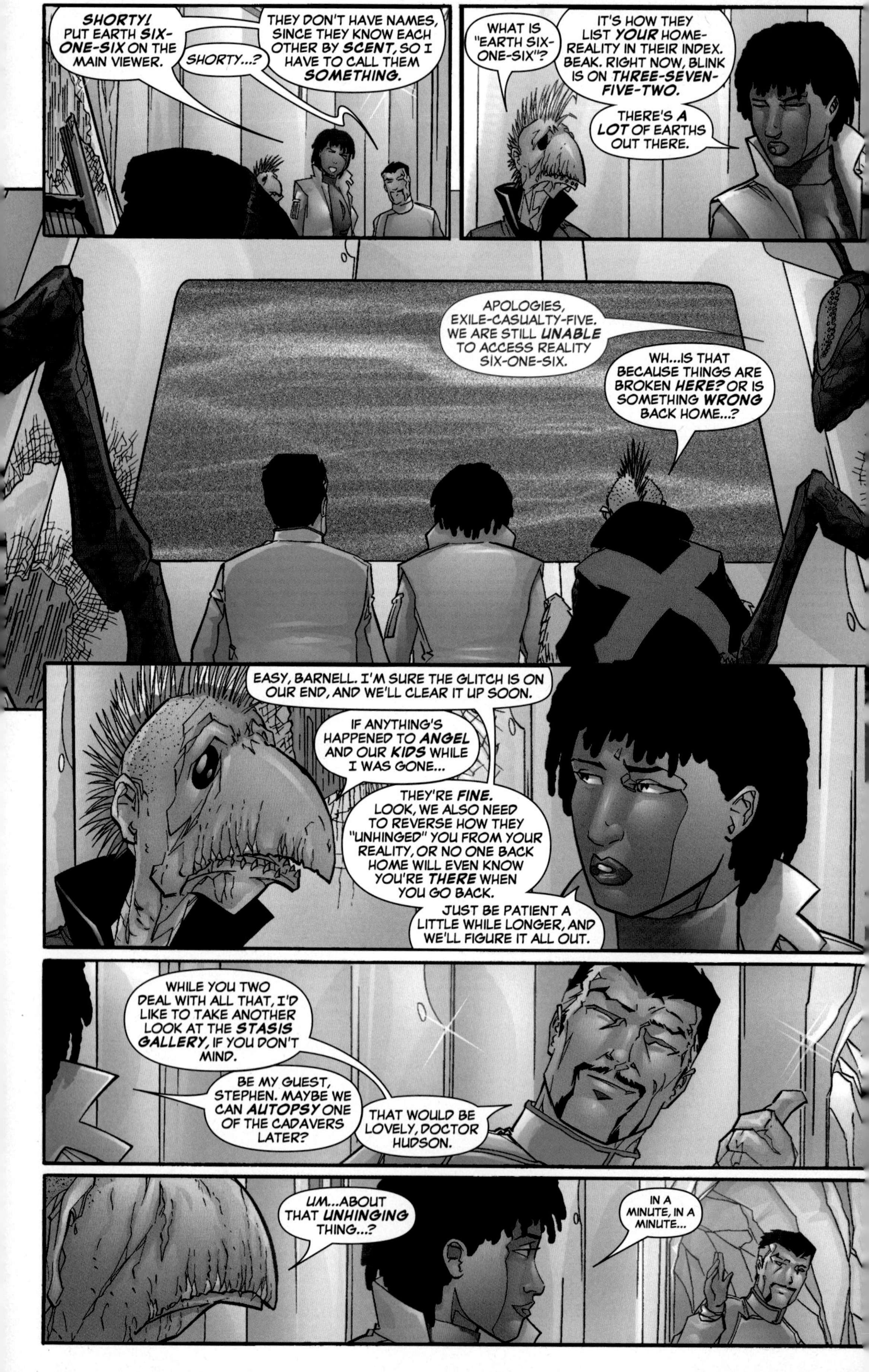
SHORTY! PUT EARTH SIX-ONE-SIX ON THE MAIN VIEWER.
SHORTY...?
THEY DON'T HAVE NAMES, SINCE THEY KNOW EACH OTHER BY SCENT, SO I HAVE TO CALL THEM SOMETHING.
WHAT IS "EARTH SIX-ONE-SIX"?
IT'S HOW THEY LIST YOUR HOME-REALITY IN THEIR INDEX. BEAK. RIGHT NOW, BLINK IS ON THREE-SEVEN-FIVE-TWO.
THERE'S A LOT OF EARTHS OUT THERE.
APOLOGIES, EXILE-CASUALTY-FIVE. WE ARE STILL UNABLE TO ACCESS REALITY SIX-ONE-SIX.
WH...IS THAT BECAUSE THINGS ARE BROKEN HERE? OR IS SOMETHING WRONG BACK HOME...?
EASY, BARNELL. I'M SURE THE GLITCH IS ON OUR END, AND WE'LL CLEAR IT UP SOON.
IF ANYTHING'S HAPPENED TO ANGEL AND OUR KIDS WHILE I WAS GONE...
THEY'RE FINE. LOOK, WE ALSO NEED TO REVERSE HOW THEY "UNHINGED" YOU FROM YOUR REALITY, OR NO ONE BACK HOME WILL EVEN KNOW YOU'RE THERE WHEN YOU GO BACK.
JUST BE PATIENT A LITTLE WHILE LONGER, AND WE'LL FIGURE IT ALL OUT.
WHILE YOU TWO DEAL WITH ALL THAT, I'D LIKE TO TAKE ANOTHER LOOK AT THE STASIS GALLERY, IF YOU DON'T MIND.
BE MY GUEST, STEPHEN. MAYBE WE CAN AUTOPSY ONE OF THE CADAVERS LATER?
THAT WOULD BE LOVELY, DOCTOR HUDSON.
UM...ABOUT THAT UNHINGING THING...?
IN A MINUTE, IN A MINUTE...

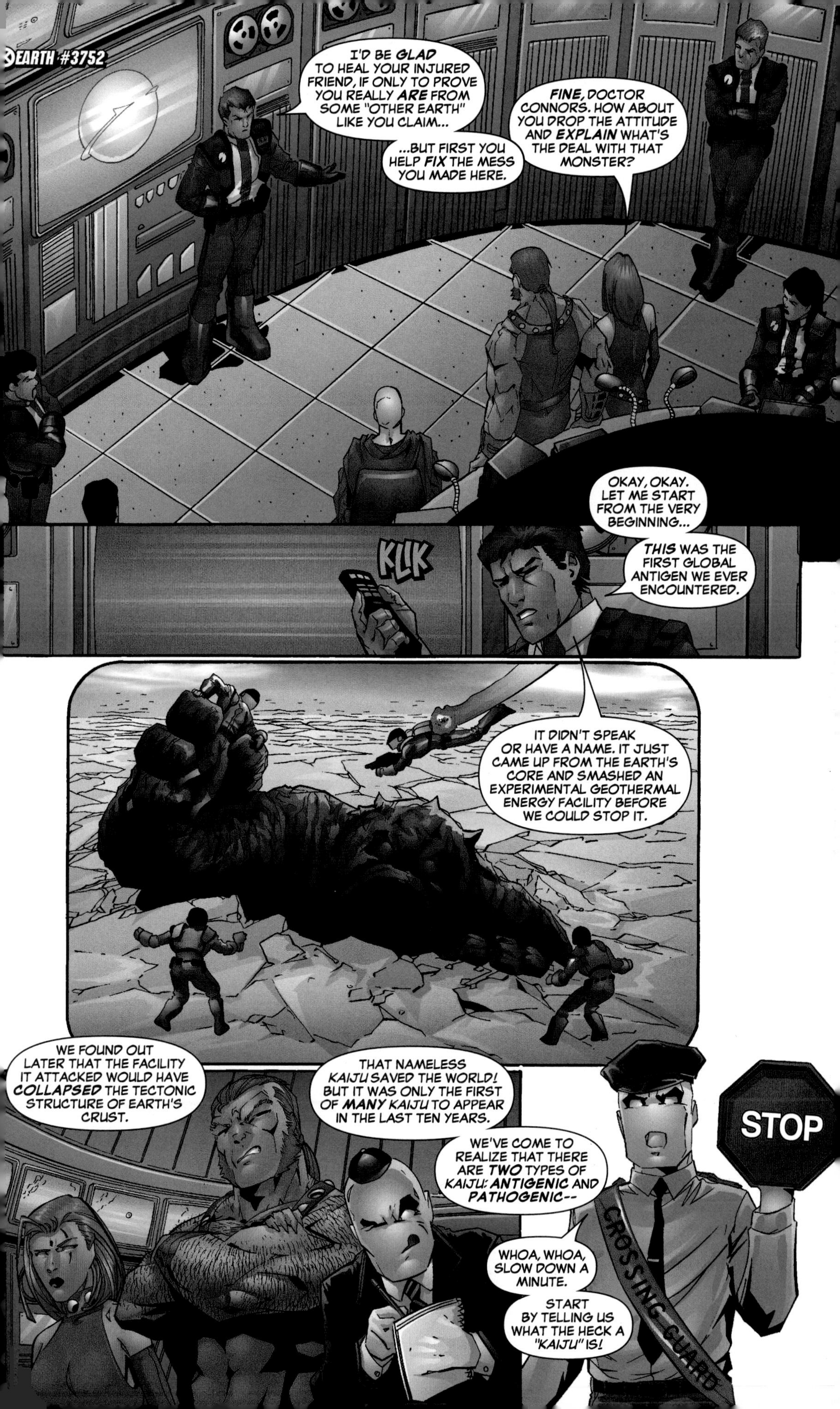
EARTH #3752
I'D BE GLAD TO HEAL YOUR INJURED FRIEND, IF ONLY TO PROVE YOU REALLY ARE FROM SOME "OTHER EARTH" LIKE YOU CLAIM...
...BUT FIRST YOU HELP FIX THE MESS YOU MADE HERE.
FINE, DOCTOR CONNORS. HOW ABOUT YOU DROP THE ATTITUDE AND EXPLAIN WHAT'S THE DEAL WITH THAT MONSTER?
OKAY, OKAY. LET ME START FROM THE VERY BEGINNING...
KLIK
THIS WAS THE FIRST GLOBAL ANTIGEN WE EVER ENCOUNTERED.
IT DIDN'T SPEAK OR HAVE A NAME. IT JUST CAME UP FROM THE EARTH'S CORE AND SMASHED AN EXPERIMENTAL GEOTHERMAL ENERGY FACILITY BEFORE WE COULD STOP IT.
WE FOUND OUT LATER THAT THE FACILITY IT ATTACKED WOULD HAVE COLLAPSED THE TECTONIC STRUCTURE OF EARTH'S CRUST.
THAT NAMELESS KAIJU SAVED THE WORLD! BUT IT WAS ONLY THE FIRST OF MANY KAIJU TO APPEAR IN THE LAST TEN YEARS.
WE'VE COME TO REALIZE THAT THERE ARE TWO TYPES OF KAIJU: ANTIGENIC AND PATHOGENIC--
STOP
CROSSING GUARD
WHOA, WHOA, SLOW DOWN A MINUTE.
START BY TELLING US WHAT THE HECK A "KAIJU" IS!

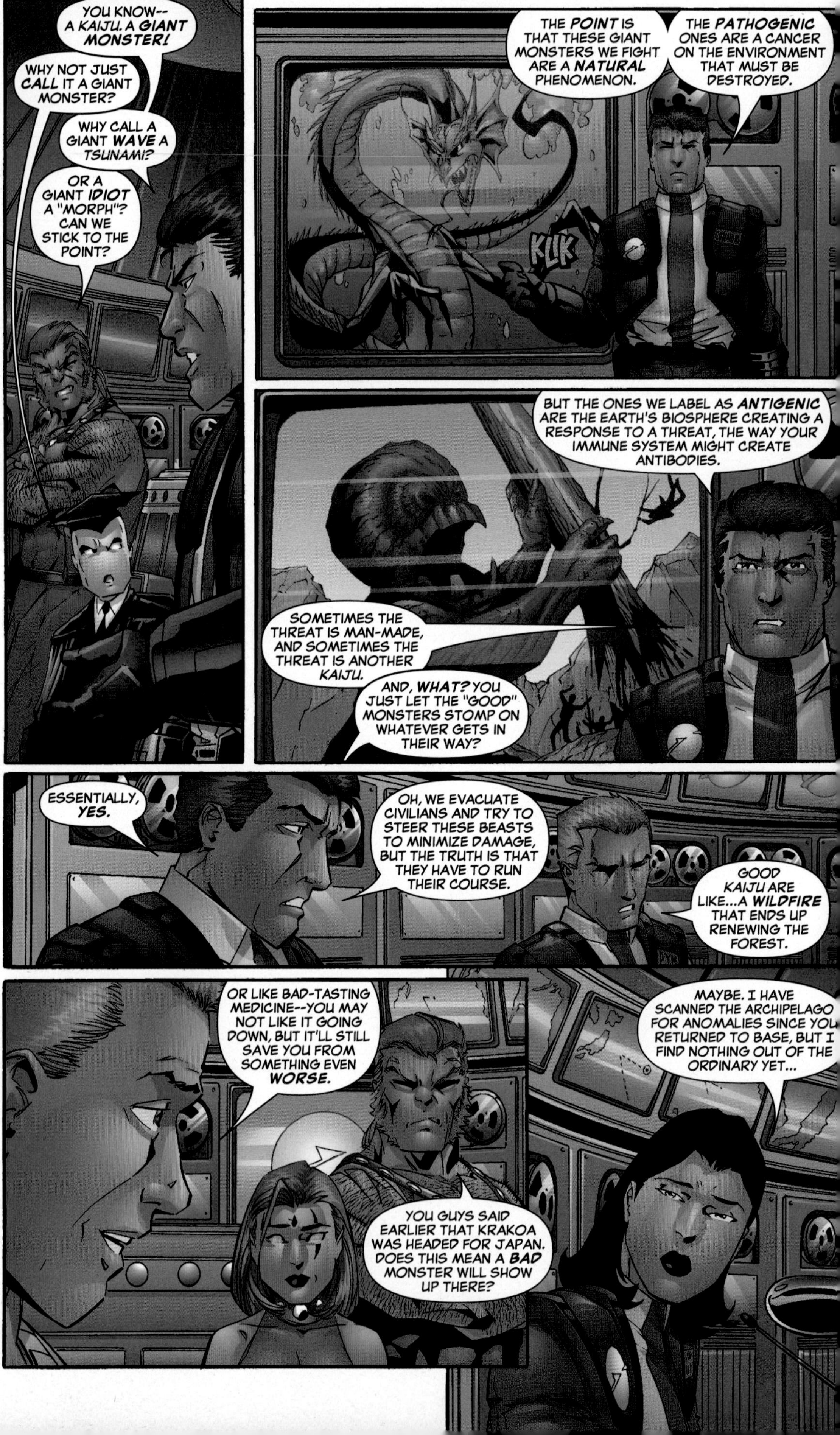
YOU KNOW-- A KAIJU. A GIANT MONSTER!
WHY NOT JUST CALL IT A GIANT MONSTER?
WHY CALL A GIANT WAVE A TSUNAMI?
OR A GIANT IDIOT A "MORPH"? CAN WE STICK TO THE POINT?
THE POINT IS THAT THESE GIANT MONSTERS WE FIGHT ARE A NATURAL PHENOMENON.
THE PATHOGENIC ONES ARE A CANCER ON THE ENVIRONMENT THAT MUST BE DESTROYED.
KLIK
BUT THE ONES WE LABEL AS ANTIGENIC ARE THE EARTH'S BIOSPHERE CREATING A RESPONSE TO A THREAT, THE WAY YOUR IMMUNE SYSTEM MIGHT CREATE ANTIBODIES.
SOMETIMES THE THREAT IS MAN-MADE, AND SOMETIMES THE THREAT IS ANOTHER KAIJU.
AND, WHAT? YOU JUST LET THE "GOOD" MONSTERS STOMP ON WHATEVER GETS IN THEIR WAY?
ESSENTIALLY, YES.
OH, WE EVACUATE CIVILIANS AND TRY TO STEER THESE BEASTS TO MINIMIZE DAMAGE, BUT THE TRUTH IS THAT THEY HAVE TO RUN THEIR COURSE.
GOOD KAIJU ARE LIKE...A WILDFIRE THAT ENDS UP RENEWING THE FOREST.
OR LIKE BAD-TASTING MEDICINE--YOU MAY NOT LIKE IT GOING DOWN, BUT IT'LL STILL SAVE YOU FROM SOMETHING EVEN WORSE.
MAYBE. I HAVE SCANNED THE ARCHIPELAGO FOR ANOMALIES SINCE YOU RETURNED TO BASE, BUT I FIND NOTHING OUT OF THE ORDINARY YET...
YOU GUYS SAID EARLIER THAT KRAKOA WAS HEADED FOR JAPAN. DOES THIS MEAN A BAD MONSTER WILL SHOW UP THERE?

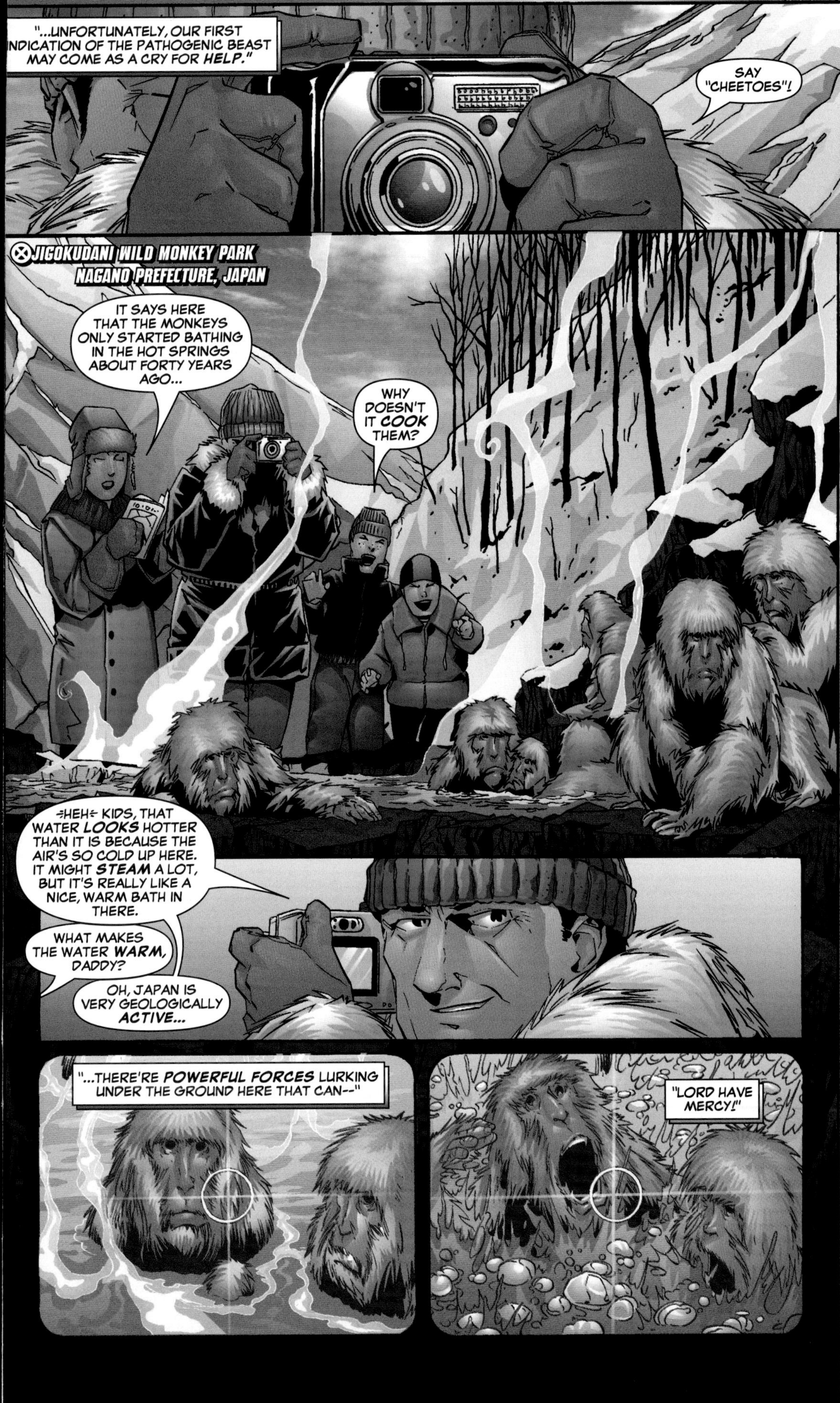
"...UNFORTUNATELY, OUR FIRST INDICATION OF THE PATHOGENIC BEAST MAY COME AS A CRY FOR HELP."
SAY "CHEETOES"!
JIGOKUDANI WILD MONKEY PARK
NAGANO PREFECTURE, JAPAN
IT SAYS HERE THAT THE MONKEYS ONLY STARTED BATHING IN THE HOT SPRINGS ABOUT FORTY YEARS AGO...
WHY DOESN'T IT COOK THEM?
HEH KIDS, THAT WATER LOOKS HOTTER THAN IT IS BECAUSE THE AIR'S SO COLD UP HERE. IT MIGHT STEAM A LOT, BUT IT'S REALLY LIKE A NICE, WARM BATH IN THERE.
WHAT MAKES THE WATER WARM, DADDY?
OH, JAPAN IS VERY GEOLOGICALLY ACTIVE...
"...THERE'RE POWERFUL FORCES LURKING UNDER THE GROUND HERE THAT CAN--"
"LORD HAVE MERCY!"

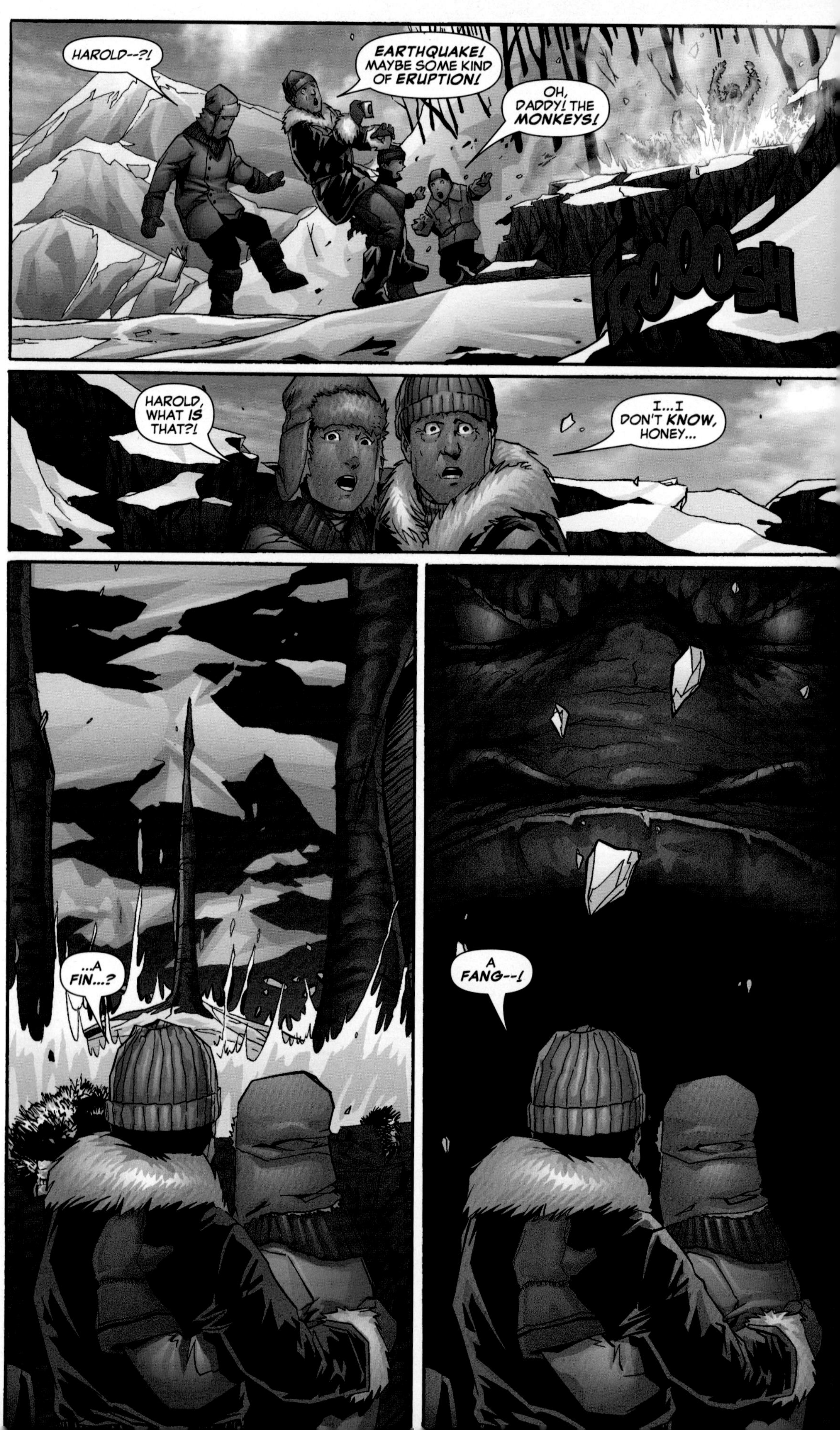
HAROLD--?!
EARTHQUAKE! MAYBE SOME KIND OF ERUPTION!
OH, DADDY! THE MONKEYS!
FROOOSH
HAROLD, WHAT IS THAT?!
I...I DON'T KNOW, HONEY...
...A FIN...?
A FANG--!

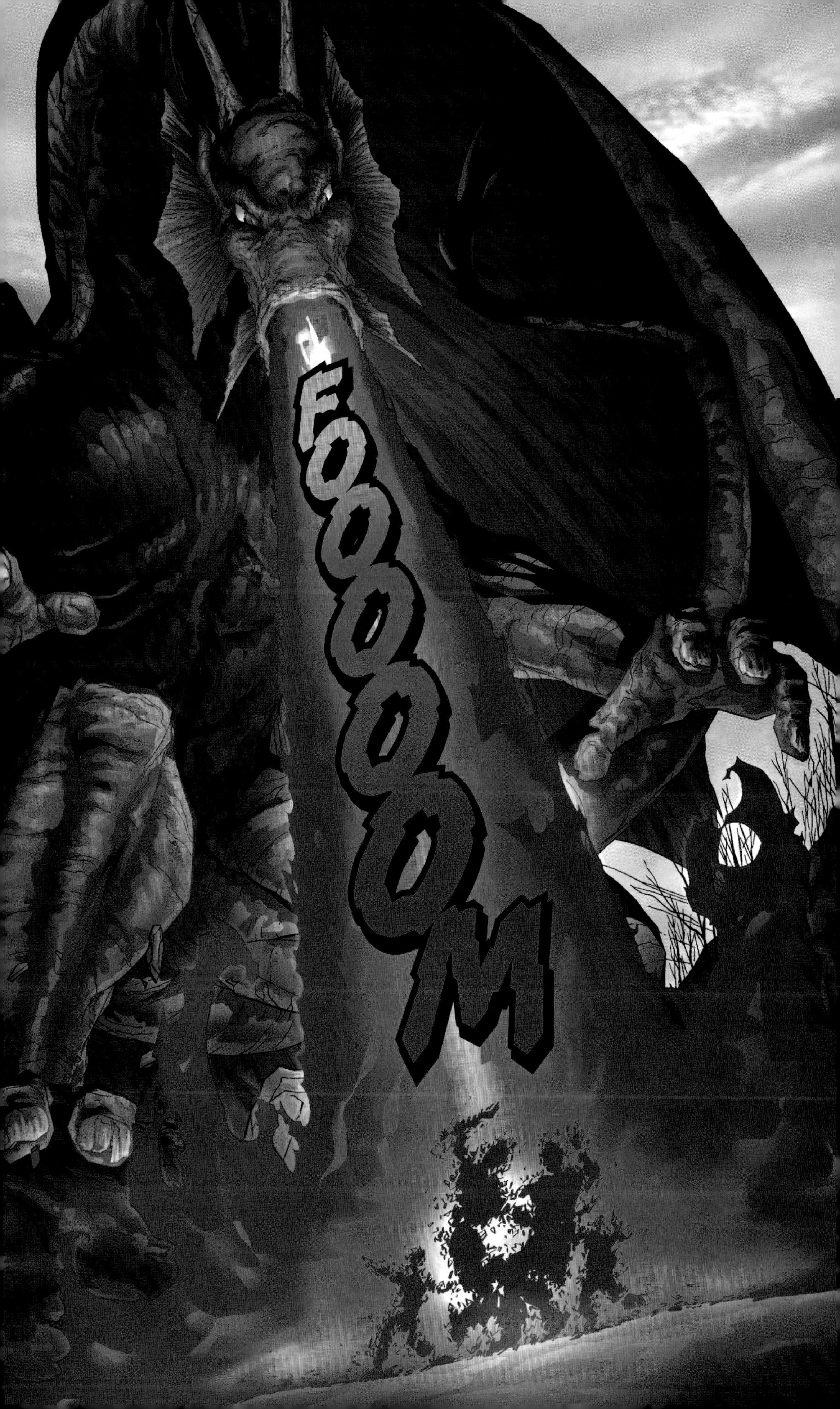
FOOOOOOM

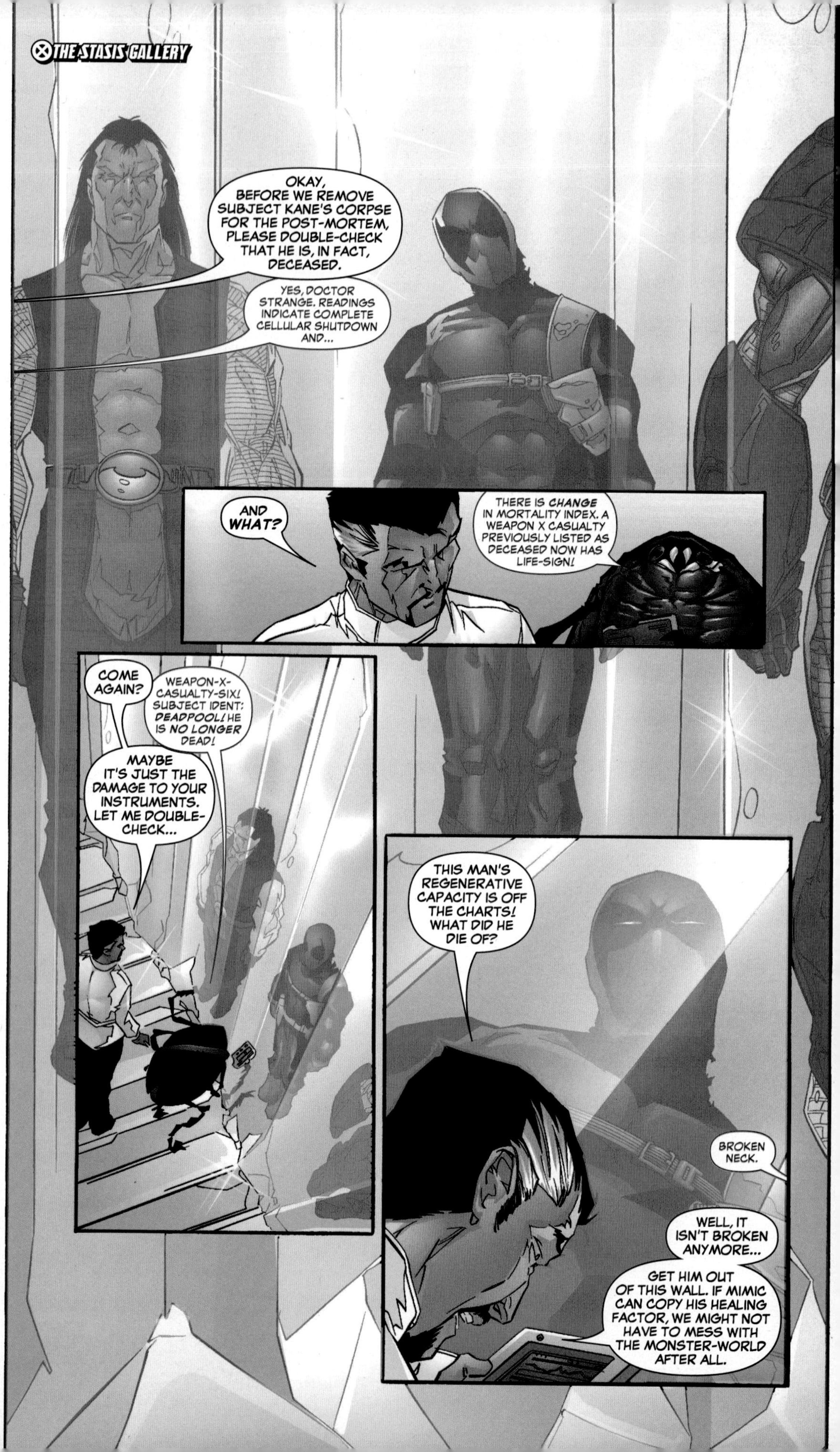
OKAY, BEFORE WE REMOVE SUBJECT KANE'S CORPSE FOR THE POST-MORTEM, PLEASE DOUBLE-CHECK THAT HE IS, IN FACT, DECEASED.
YES, DOCTOR STRANGE. READINGS INDICATE COMPLETE CELLULAR SHUTDOWN AND...
AND WHAT?
THERE IS CHANGE IN MORTALITY INDEX. A WEAPON X CASUALTY PREVIOUSLY LISTED AS DECEASED NOW HAS LIFE-SIGN!
COME AGAIN?
WEAPON-X-CASUALTY-SIX! SUBJECT IDENT: DEADPOOL! HE IS NO LONGER DEAD!
MAYBE IT'S JUST THE DAMAGE TO YOUR INSTRUMENTS. LET ME DOUBLE-CHECK...
THIS MAN'S REGENERATIVE CAPACITY IS OFF THE CHARTS! WHAT DID HE DIE OF?
BROKEN NECK.
WELL, IT ISN'T BROKEN ANYMORE...
GET HIM OUT OF THIS WALL. IF MIMIC CAN COPY HIS HEALING FACTOR, WE MIGHT NOT HAVE TO MESS WITH THE MONSTER-WORLD AFTER ALL.

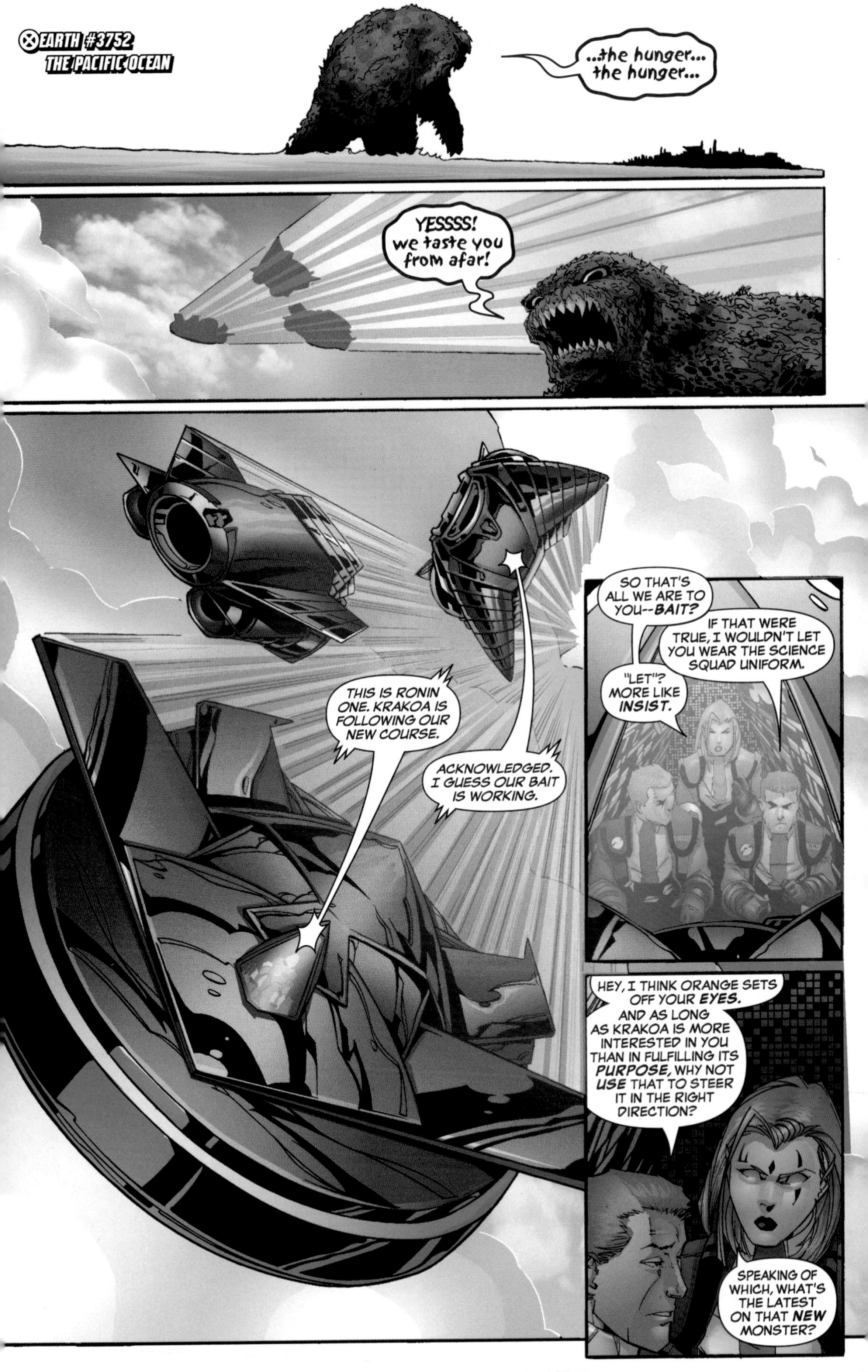
EARTH #3752
THE PACIFIC OCEAN
...the hunger... the hunger...
YESSSS! we taste you from afar!
THIS IS RONIN ONE. KRAKOA IS FOLLOWING OUR NEW COURSE.
ACKNOWLEDGED. I GUESS OUR BAIT IS WORKING.
SO THAT'S ALL WE ARE TO YOU--BAIT?
IF THAT WERE TRUE, I WOULDN'T LET YOU WEAR THE SCIENCE SQUAD UNIFORM.
"LET"? MORE LIKE INSIST.
HEY, I THINK ORANGE SETS OFF YOUR EYES.
AND AS LONG AS KRAKOA IS MORE INTERESTED IN YOU THAN IN FULFILLING ITS PURPOSE, WHY NOT USE THAT TO STEER IT IN THE RIGHT DIRECTION?
SPEAKING OF WHICH, WHAT'S THE LATEST ON THAT NEW MONSTER?

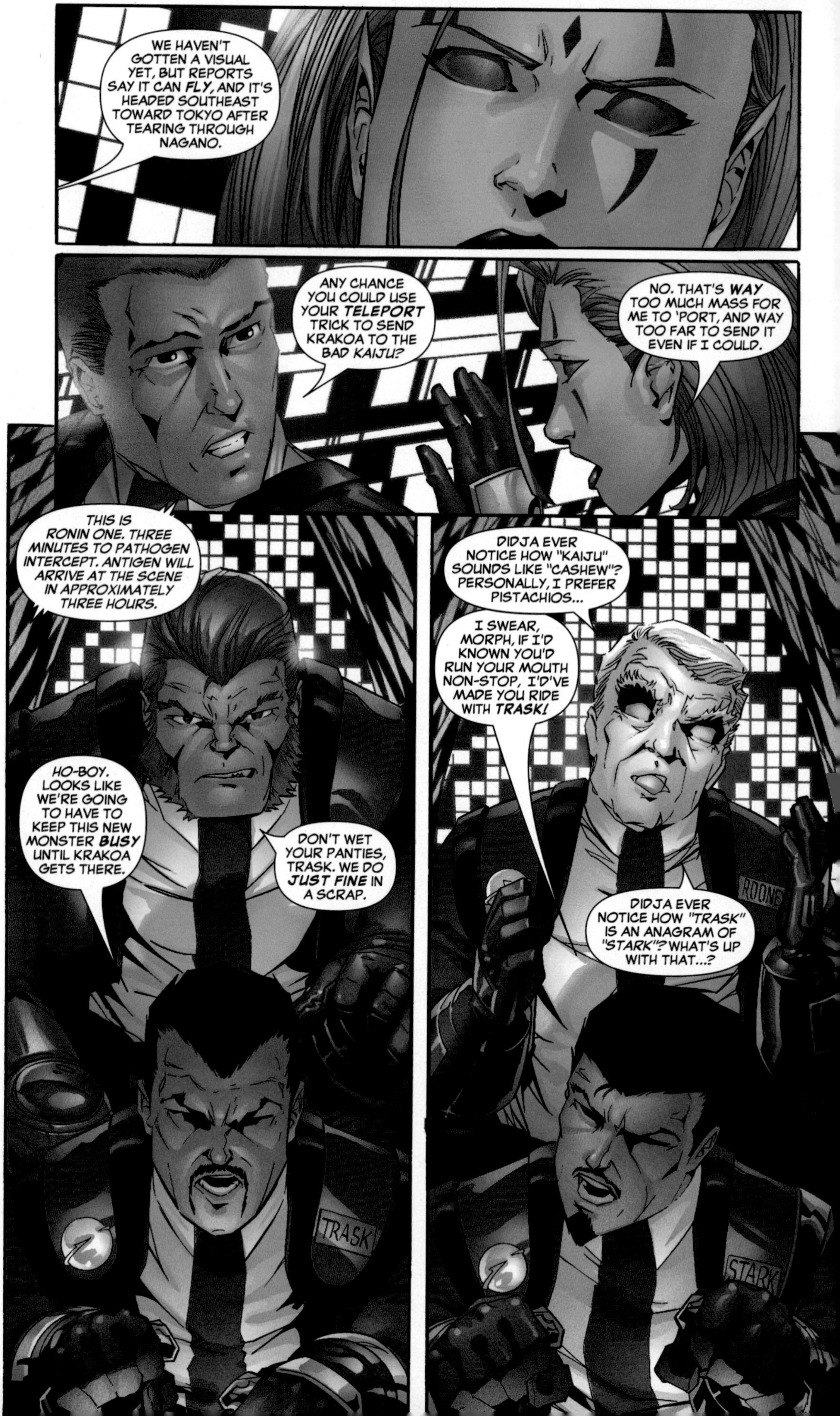
WE HAVEN'T GOTTEN A VISUAL YET, BUT REPORTS SAY IT CAN FLY, AND IT'S HEADED SOUTHEAST TOWARD TOKYO AFTER TEARING THROUGH NAGANO.
ANY CHANCE YOU COULD USE YOUR TELEPORT TRICK TO SEND KRAKOA TO THE BAD KAIJU?
NO. THAT'S WAY TOO MUCH MASS FOR ME TO 'PORT, AND WAY TOO FAR TO SEND IT EVEN IF I COULD.
THIS IS RONIN ONE. THREE MINUTES TO PATHOGEN INTERCEPT. ANTIGEN WILL ARRIVE AT THE SCENE IN APPROXIMATELY THREE HOURS.
HO-BOY. LOOKS LIKE WE'RE GOING TO HAVE TO KEEP THIS NEW MONSTER BUSY UNTIL KRAKOA GETS THERE.
DON'T WET YOUR PANTIES, TRASK. WE DO JUST FINE IN A SCRAP.
TRASK
DIDJA EVER NOTICE HOW "KAIJU" SOUNDS LIKE "CASHEW"? PERSONALLY, I PREFER PISTACHIOS...
I SWEAR, MORPH, IF I'D KNOWN YOU'D RUN YOUR MOUTH NON-STOP, I'D'VE MADE YOU RIDE WITH TRASK!
ROONE
DIDJA EVER NOTICE HOW "TRASK" IS AN ANAGRAM OF "STARK"? WHAT'S UP WITH THAT...?
STARK

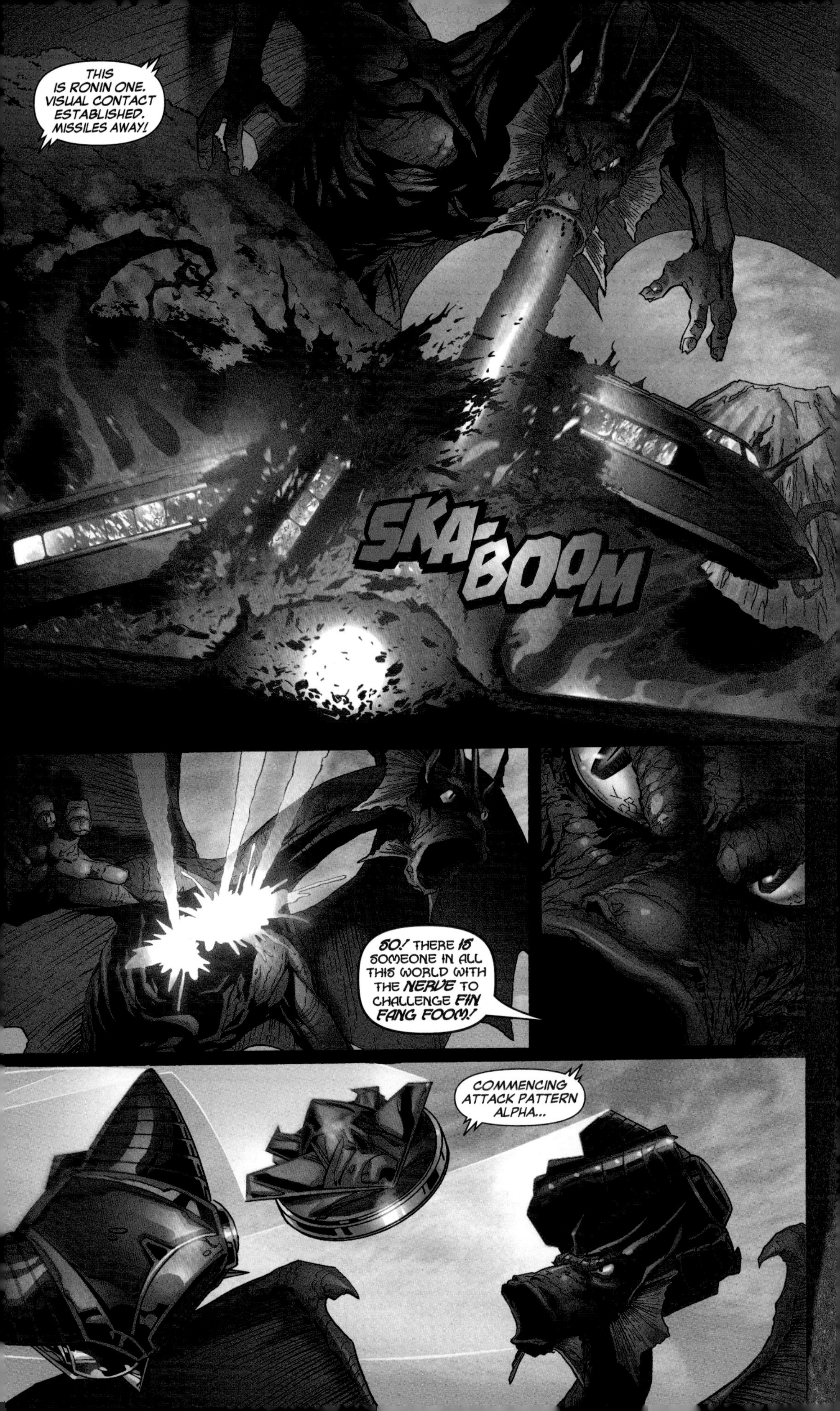
THIS IS RONIN ONE. VISUAL CONTACT ESTABLISHED. MISSILES AWAY!
SKA-BOOM
SO! THERE IS SOMEONE IN ALL THIS WORLD WITH THE NERVE TO CHALLENGE FIN FANG FOOM!
COMMENCING ATTACK PATTERN ALPHA...

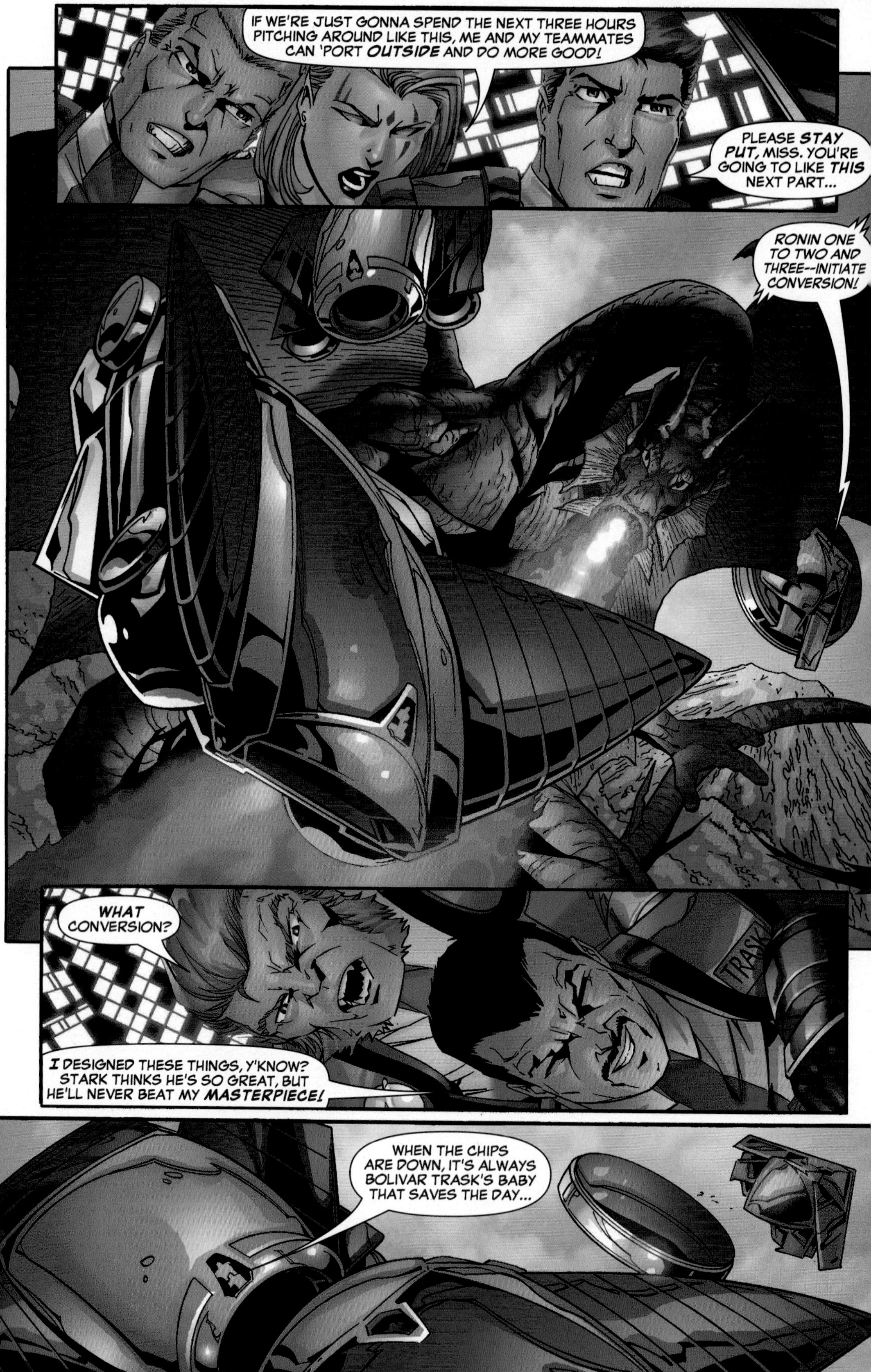
IF WE'RE JUST GONNA SPEND THE NEXT THREE HOURS PITCHING AROUND LIKE THIS, ME AND MY TEAMMATES CAN 'PORT OUTSIDE AND DO MORE GOOD!
PLEASE STAY PUT, MISS. YOU'RE GOING TO LIKE THIS NEXT PART...
RONIN ONE TO TWO AND THREE--INITIATE CONVERSION!
WHAT CONVERSION?
TRASK
I DESIGNED THESE THINGS, Y'KNOW? STARK THINKS HE'S SO GREAT, BUT HE'LL NEVER BEAT MY MASTERPIECE!
WHEN THE CHIPS ARE DOWN, IT'S ALWAYS BOLIVAR TRASK'S BABY THAT SAVES THE DAY...

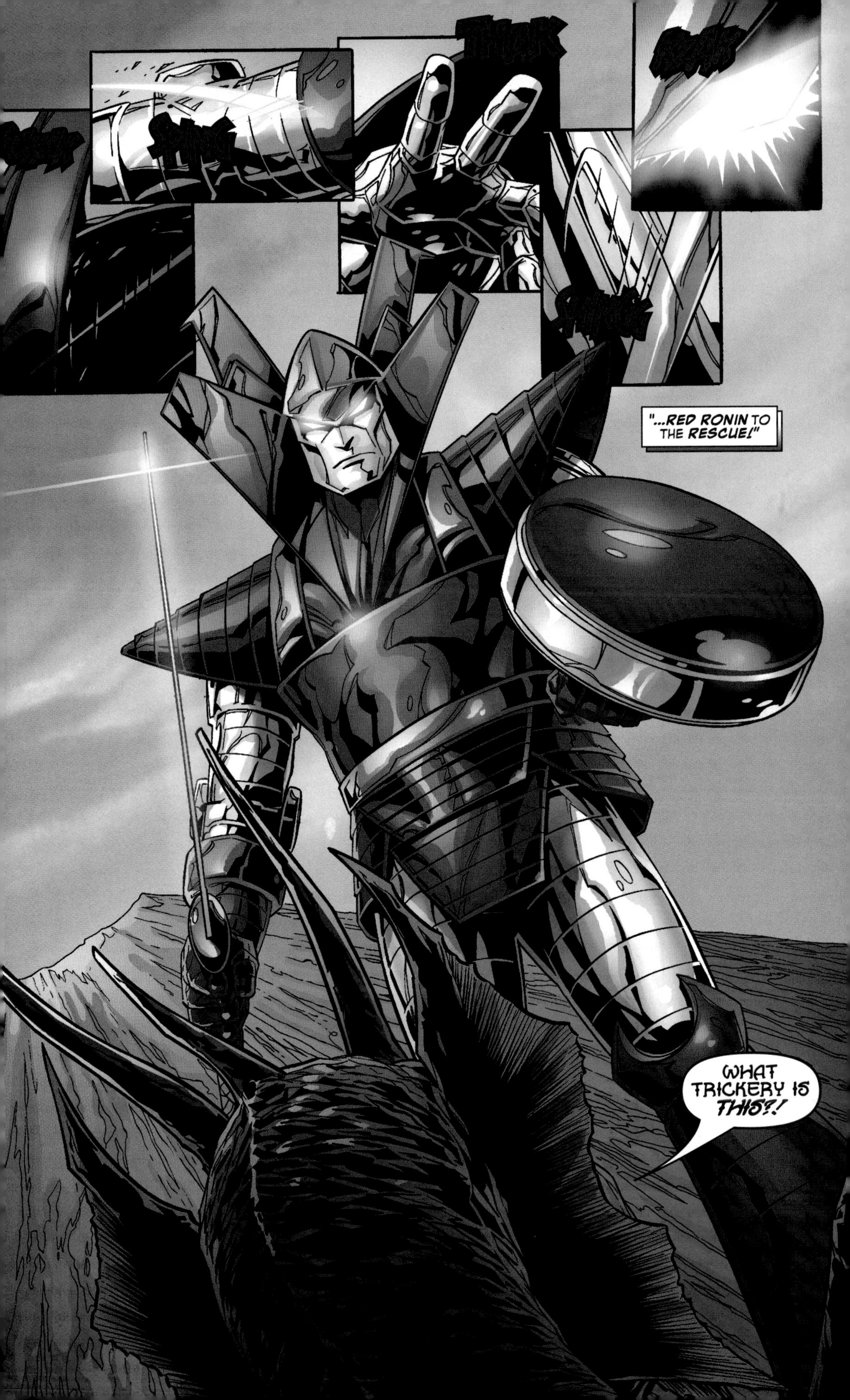

SPING
THUNK
"...RED RONIN TO THE RESCUE!"
WHAT TRICKERY IS THIS?!

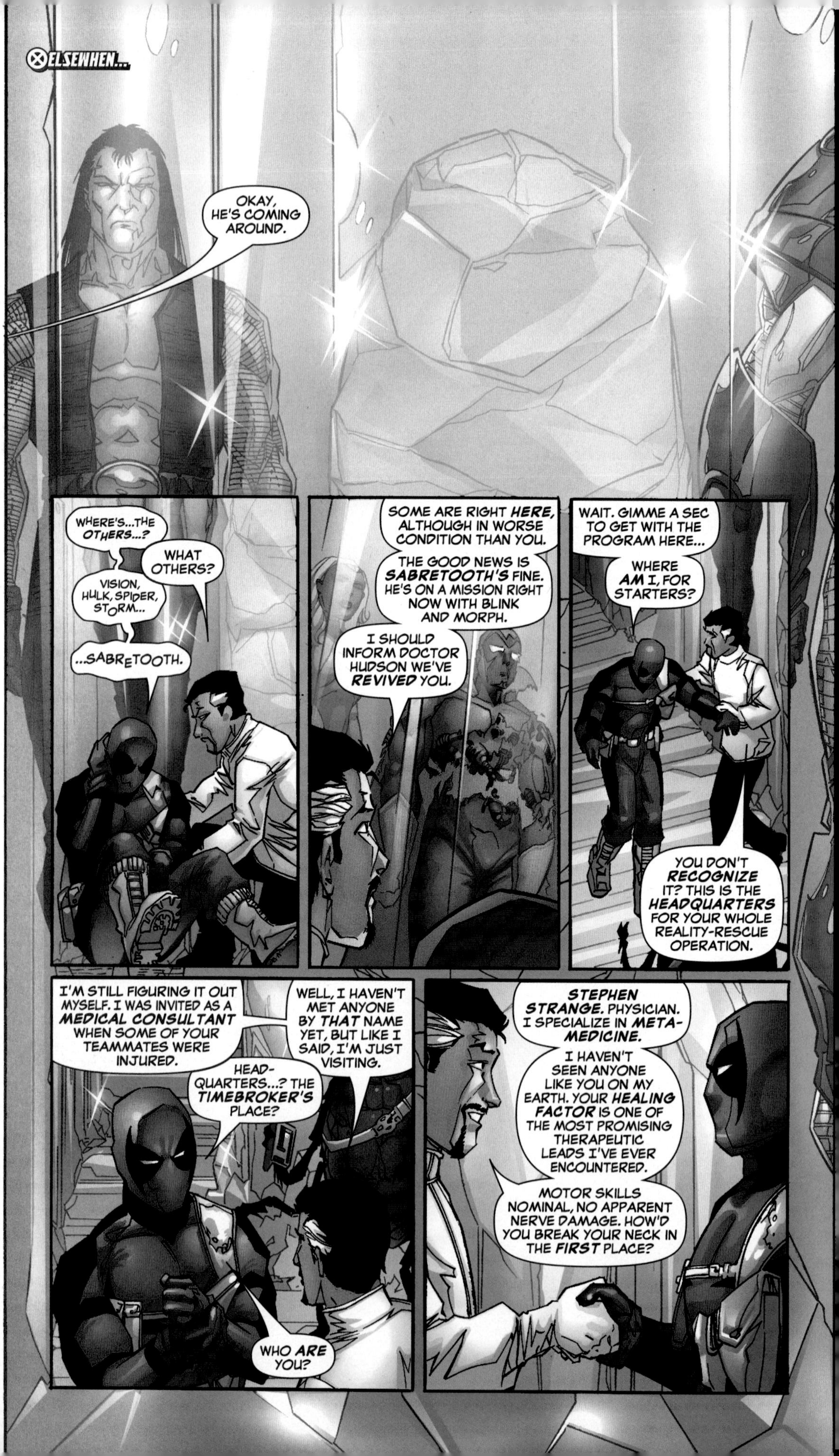

ELSEWHEN...
OKAY, HE'S COMING AROUND.
WHERE'S...THE OTHERS...?
WHAT OTHERS?
VISION, HULK, SPIDER, STORM...
...SABRETOOTH.
SOME ARE RIGHT HERE, ALTHOUGH IN WORSE CONDITION THAN YOU.
THE GOOD NEWS IS SABRETOOTH'S FINE. HE'S ON A MISSION RIGHT NOW WITH BLINK AND MORPH.
I SHOULD INFORM DOCTOR HUDSON WE'VE REVIVED YOU.
WAIT. GIMME A SEC TO GET WITH THE PROGRAM HERE...
WHERE AM I, FOR STARTERS?
YOU DON'T RECOGNIZE IT? THIS IS THE HEADQUARTERS FOR YOUR WHOLE REALITY-RESCUE OPERATION.
HEAD-QUARTERS...? THE TIMEBROKER'S PLACE?
WHO ARE YOU?
I'M STILL FIGURING IT OUT MYSELF. I WAS INVITED AS A MEDICAL CONSULTANT WHEN SOME OF YOUR TEAMMATES WERE INJURED.
WELL, I HAVEN'T MET ANYONE BY THAT NAME YET, BUT LIKE I SAID, I'M JUST VISITING.
STEPHEN STRANGE. PHYSICIAN. I SPECIALIZE IN META-MEDICINE.
I HAVEN'T SEEN ANYONE LIKE YOU ON MY EARTH. YOUR HEALING FACTOR IS ONE OF THE MOST PROMISING THERAPEUTIC LEADS I'VE EVER ENCOUNTERED.
MOTOR SKILLS NOMINAL, NO APPARENT NERVE DAMAGE. HOW'D YOU BREAK YOUR NECK IN THE FIRST PLACE?

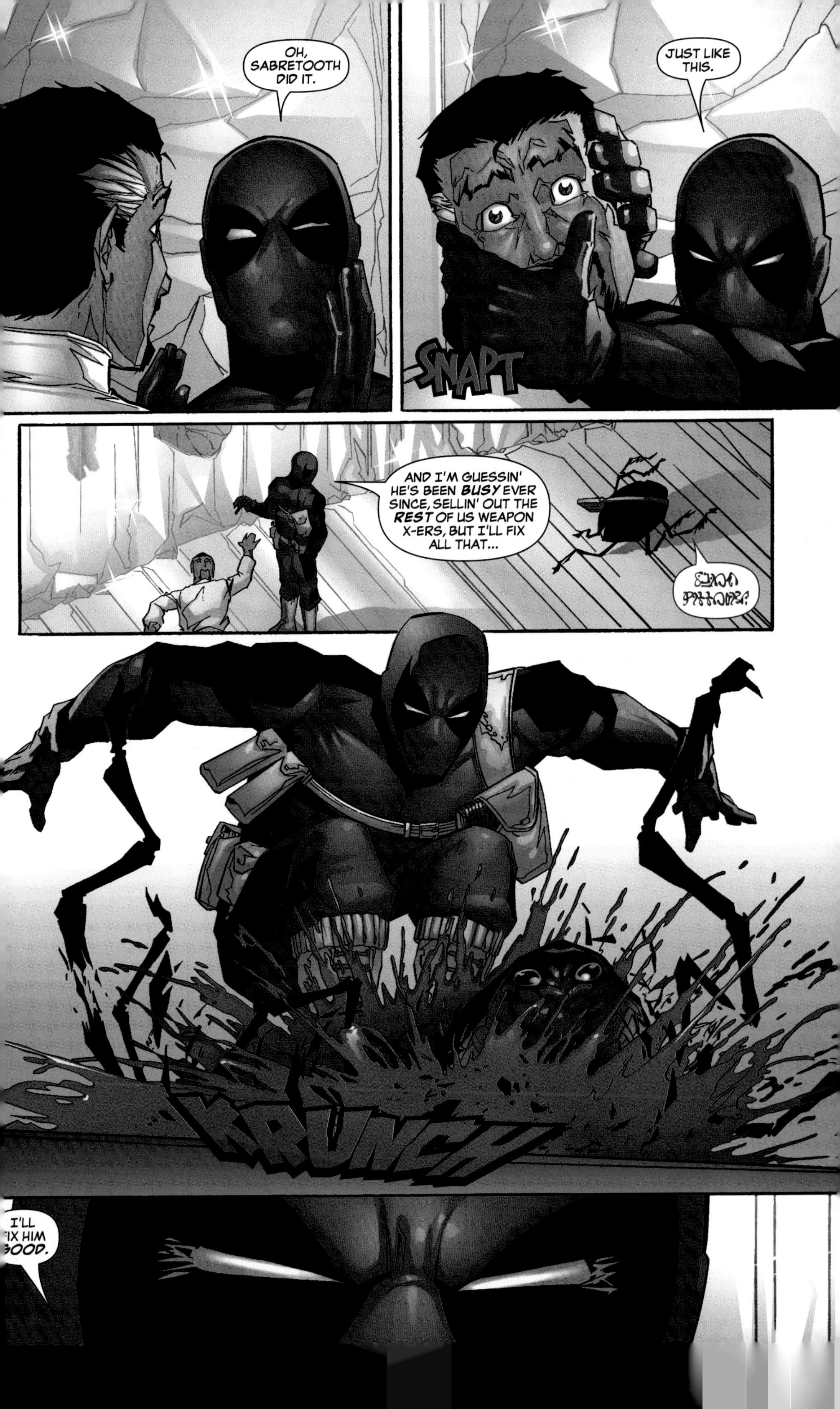
OH, SABRETOOTH DID IT.
JUST LIKE THIS.
SNAPT
AND I'M GUESSIN' HE'S BEEN BUSY EVER SINCE, SELLIN' OUT THE REST OF US WEAPON X-ERS, BUT I'LL FIX ALL THAT...
KRUNCH
I'LL FIX HIM GOOD.

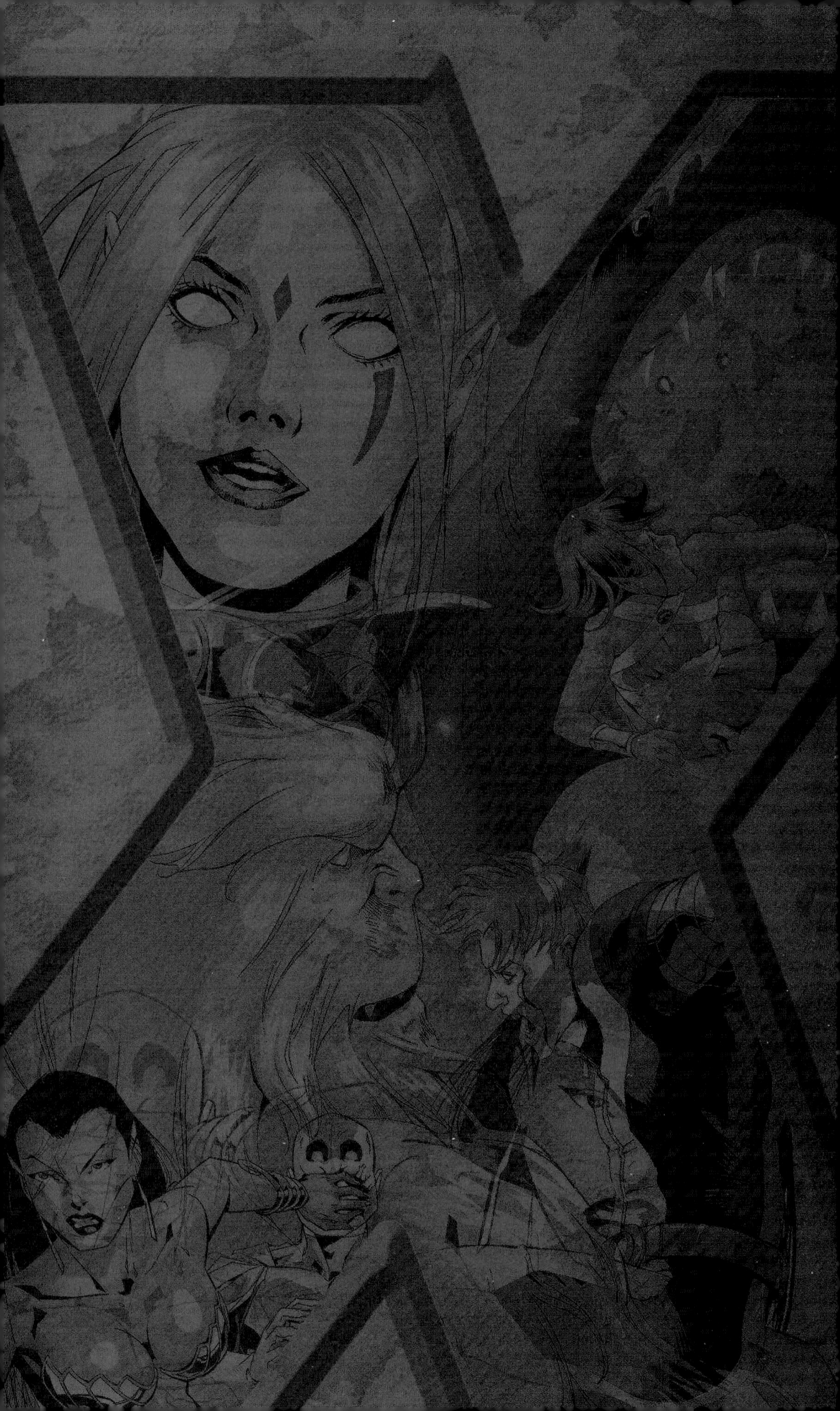

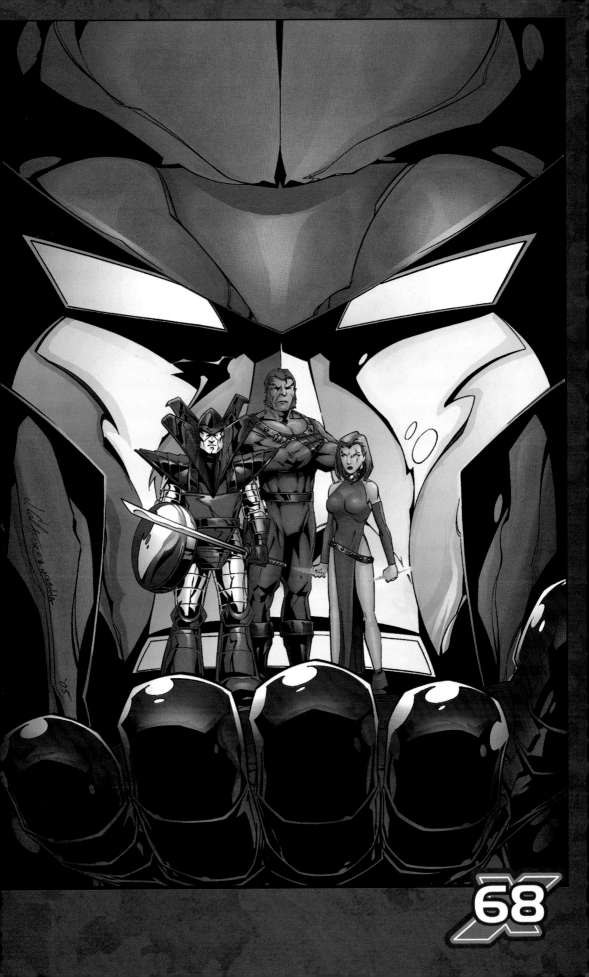

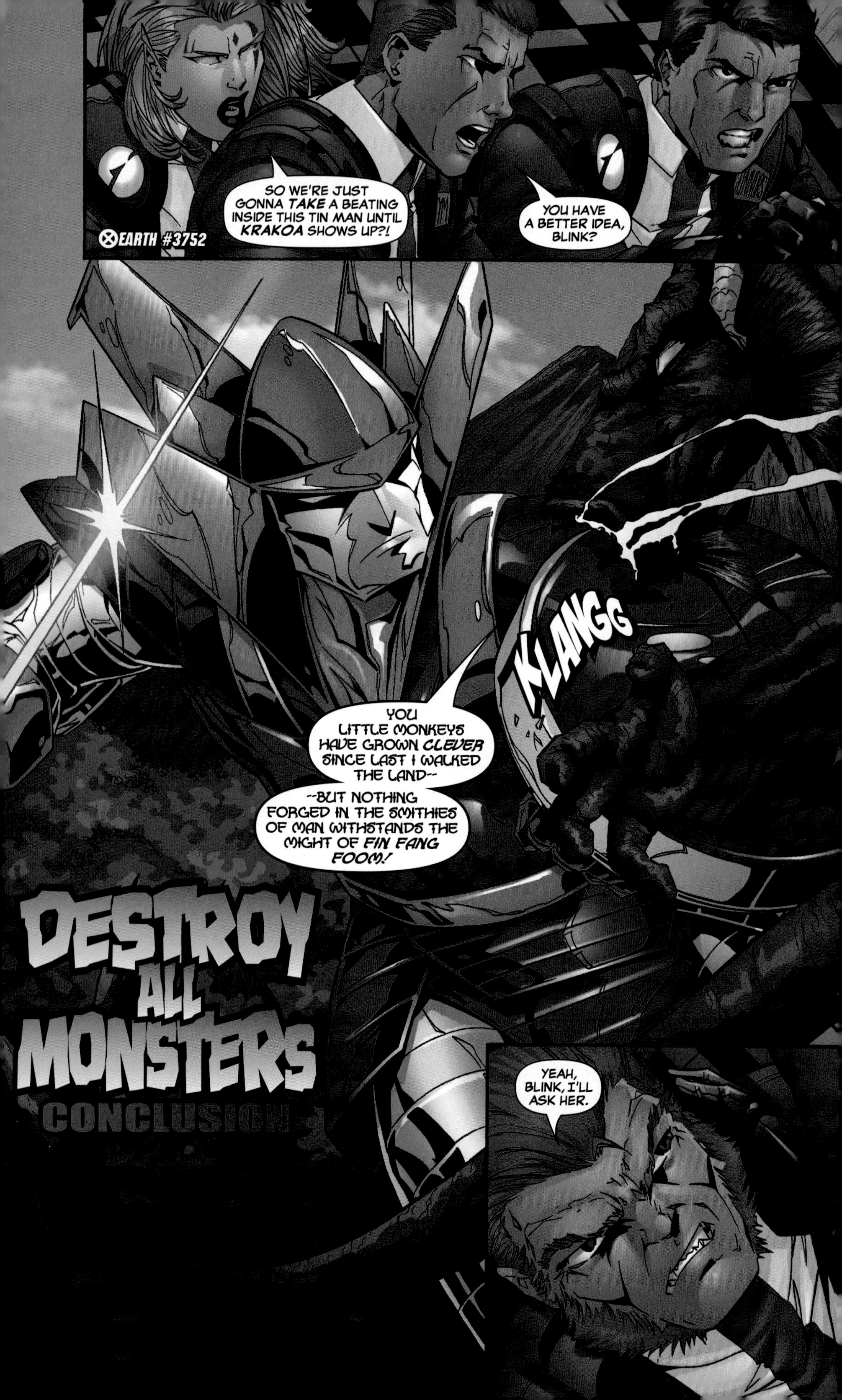
EARTH #3752
SO WE'RE JUST GONNA TAKE A BEATING INSIDE THIS TIN MAN UNTIL KRAKOA SHOWS UP?!
YOU HAVE A BETTER IDEA, BLINK?
KLANGG
YOU LITTLE MONKEYS HAVE GROWN CLEVER SINCE LAST I WALKED THE LAND--
--BUT NOTHING FORGED IN THE SMITHIES OF MAN WITHSTANDS THE MIGHT OF FIN FANG FOOM!
DESTROY ALL MONSTERS
CONCLUSION
YEAH, BLINK, I'LL ASK HER.

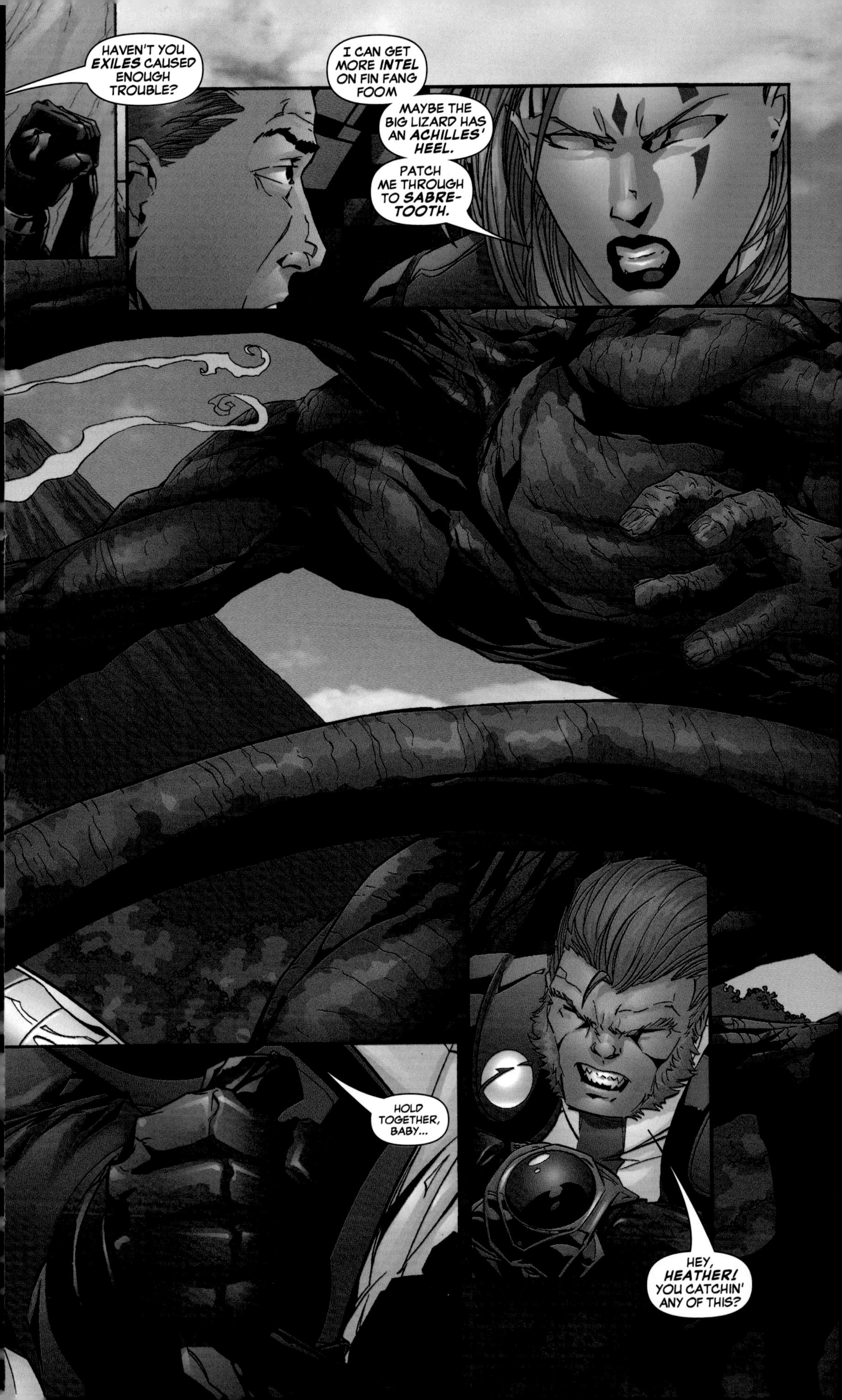
HAVEN'T YOU EXILES CAUSED ENOUGH TROUBLE?
I CAN GET MORE INTEL ON FIN FANG FOOM
MAYBE THE BIG LIZARD HAS AN ACHILLES' HEEL.
PATCH ME THROUGH TO SABRE-TOOTH.
HOLD TOGETHER, BABY...
HEY, HEATHER! YOU CATCHIN' ANY OF THIS?

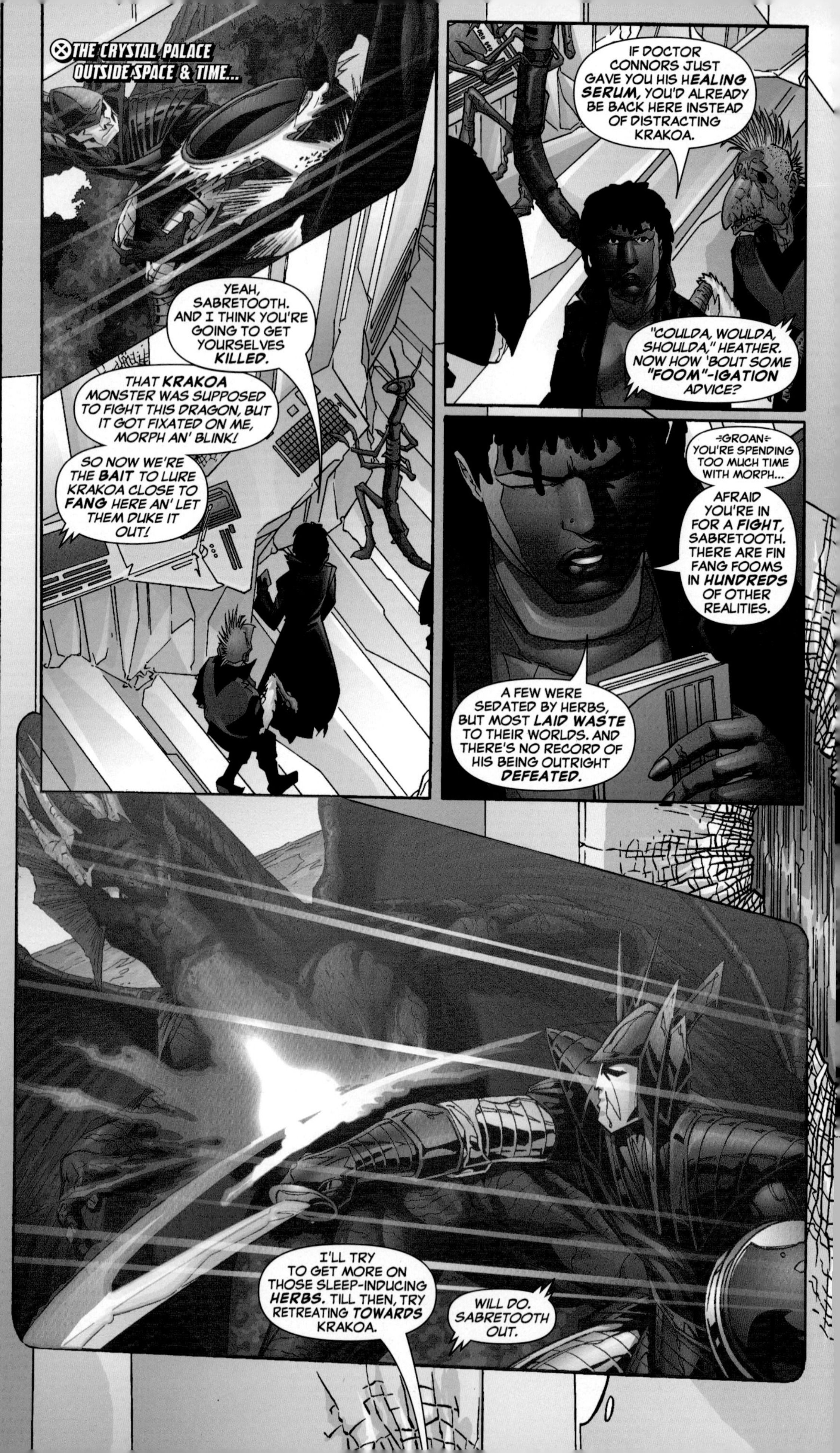
THE CRYSTAL PALACE OUTSIDE SPACE & TIME...
YEAH, SABRETOOTH. AND I THINK YOU'RE GOING TO GET YOURSELVES KILLED.
THAT KRAKOA MONSTER WAS SUPPOSED TO FIGHT THIS DRAGON, BUT IT GOT FIXATED ON ME, MORPH AN' BLINK!
SO NOW WE'RE THE BAIT TO LURE KRAKOA CLOSE TO FANG HERE AN' LET THEM DUKE IT OUT!
IF DOCTOR CONNORS JUST GAVE YOU HIS HEALING SERUM, YOU'D ALREADY BE BACK HERE INSTEAD OF DISTRACTING KRAKOA.
"COULDA, WOULDA, SHOULDA," HEATHER. NOW HOW 'BOUT SOME "FOOM"-IGATION ADVICE?
=GROAN= YOU'RE SPENDING TOO MUCH TIME WITH MORPH...
AFRAID YOU'RE IN FOR A FIGHT, SABRETOOTH. THERE ARE FIN FANG FOOMS IN HUNDREDS OF OTHER REALITIES.
A FEW WERE SEDATED BY HERBS, BUT MOST LAID WASTE TO THEIR WORLDS. AND THERE'S NO RECORD OF HIS BEING OUTRIGHT DEFEATED.
I'LL TRY TO GET MORE ON THOSE SLEEP-INDUCING HERBS. TILL THEN, TRY RETREATING TOWARDS KRAKOA.
WILL DO. SABRETOOTH OUT.

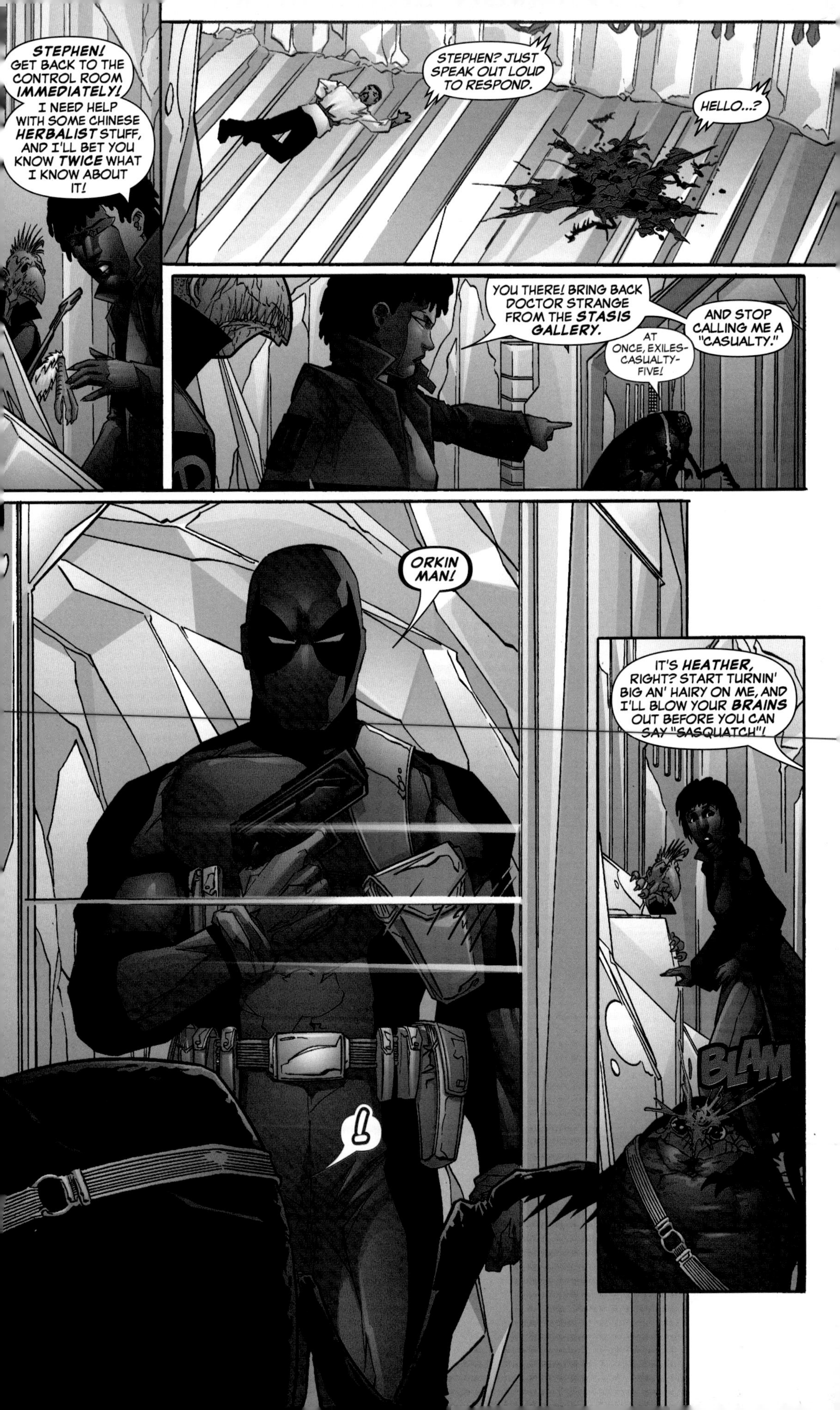

STEPHEN! GET BACK TO THE CONTROL ROOM IMMEDIATELY! I NEED HELP WITH SOME CHINESE HERBALIST STUFF, AND I'LL BET YOU KNOW TWICE WHAT I KNOW ABOUT IT!
STEPHEN? JUST SPEAK OUT LOUD TO RESPOND.
HELLO...?
YOU THERE! BRING BACK DOCTOR STRANGE FROM THE STASIS GALLERY.
AT ONCE, EXILES-CASUALTY-FIVE!
AND STOP CALLING ME A "CASUALTY."
ORKIN MAN!
IT'S HEATHER, RIGHT? START TURNIN' BIG AN' HAIRY ON ME, AND I'LL BLOW YOUR BRAINS OUT BEFORE YOU CAN SAY "SASQUATCH"!
BLAM
!

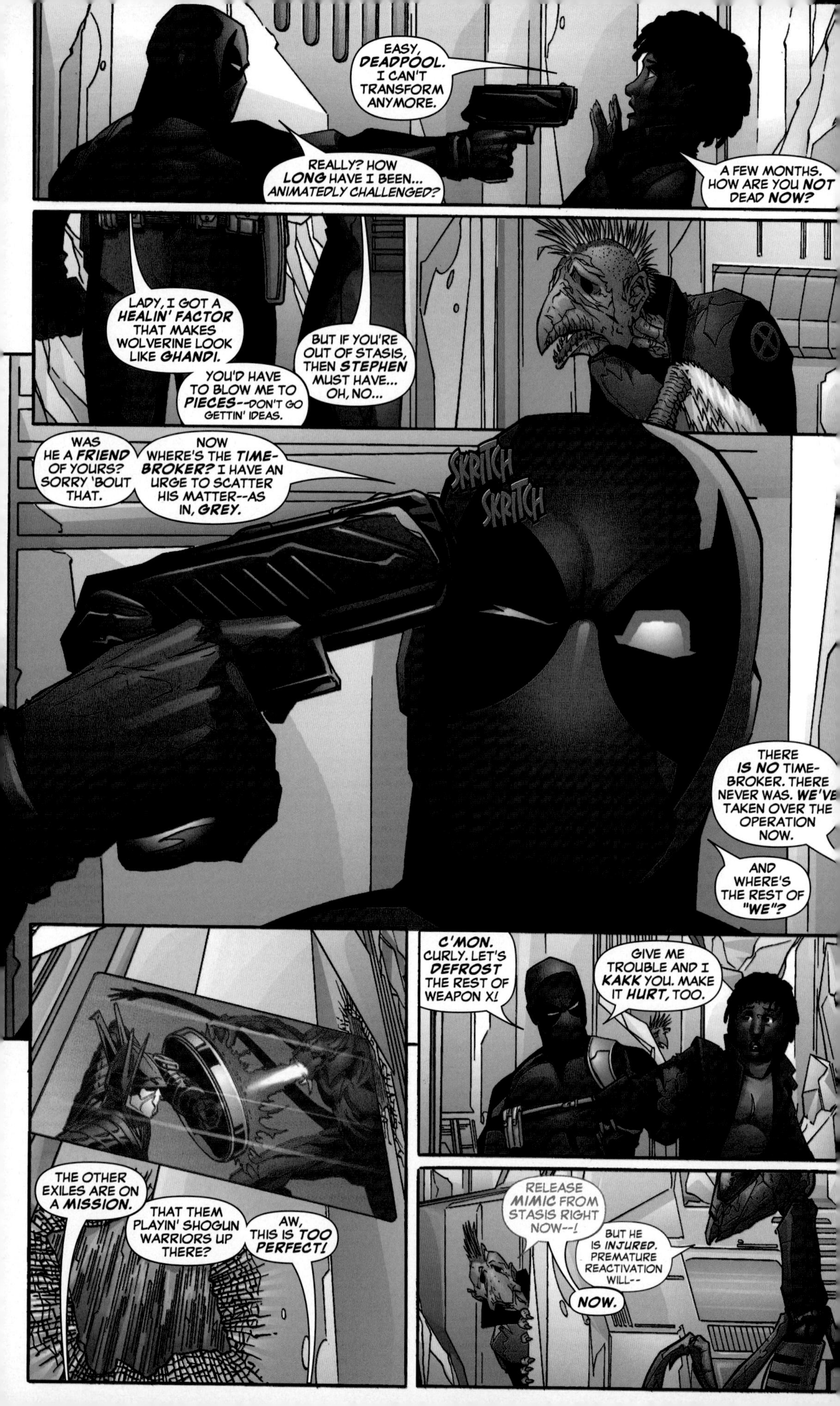

EASY, DEADPOOL. I CAN'T TRANSFORM ANYMORE.
REALLY? HOW LONG HAVE I BEEN... ANIMATEDLY CHALLENGED?
A FEW MONTHS. HOW ARE YOU NOT DEAD NOW?
LADY, I GOT A HEALIN' FACTOR THAT MAKES WOLVERINE LOOK LIKE GHANDI.
YOU'D HAVE TO BLOW ME TO PIECES--DON'T GO GETTIN' IDEAS.
BUT IF YOU'RE OUT OF STASIS, THEN STEPHEN MUST HAVE... OH, NO...
WAS HE A FRIEND OF YOURS? SORRY 'BOUT THAT.
NOW WHERE'S THE TIME-BROKER? I HAVE AN URGE TO SCATTER HIS MATTER--AS IN, GREY.
SKRITCH
SKRITCH
THERE IS NO TIME-BROKER. THERE NEVER WAS. WE'VE TAKEN OVER THE OPERATION NOW.
AND WHERE'S THE REST OF "WE"?
THE OTHER EXILES ARE ON A MISSION.
THAT THEM PLAYIN' SHOGUN WARRIORS UP THERE?
AW, THIS IS TOO PERFECT!
C'MON. CURLY. LET'S DEFROST THE REST OF WEAPON X!
GIVE ME TROUBLE AND I KAKK YOU. MAKE IT HURT, TOO.
RELEASE MIMIC FROM STASIS RIGHT NOW--!
BUT HE IS INJURED. PREMATURE REACTIVATION WILL--
NOW.

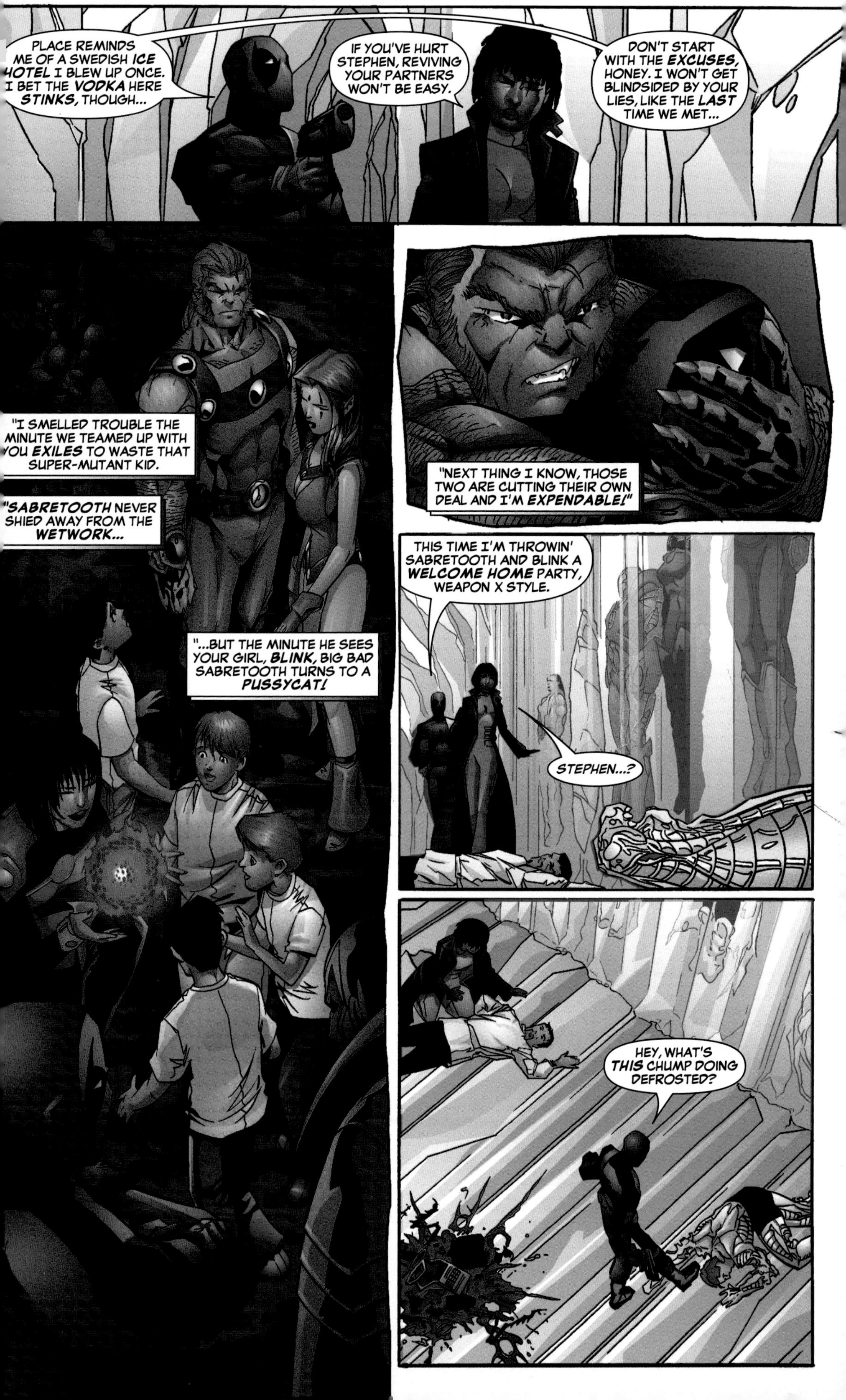
PLACE REMINDS ME OF A SWEDISH ICE HOTEL I BLEW UP ONCE. I BET THE VODKA HERE STINKS, THOUGH...
IF YOU'VE HURT STEPHEN, REVIVING YOUR PARTNERS WON'T BE EASY.
DON'T START WITH THE EXCUSES, HONEY. I WON'T GET BLINDSIDED BY YOUR LIES, LIKE THE LAST TIME WE MET...
"I SMELLED TROUBLE THE MINUTE WE TEAMED UP WITH YOU EXILES TO WASTE THAT SUPER-MUTANT KID.
"SABRETOOTH NEVER SHIED AWAY FROM THE WETWORK...
"...BUT THE MINUTE HE SEES YOUR GIRL, BLINK, BIG BAD SABRETOOTH TURNS TO A PUSSYCAT!
"NEXT THING I KNOW, THOSE TWO ARE CUTTING THEIR OWN DEAL AND I'M EXPENDABLE!"
THIS TIME I'M THROWIN' SABRETOOTH AND BLINK A WELCOME HOME PARTY, WEAPON X STYLE.
STEPHEN...?
HEY, WHAT'S THIS CHUMP DOING DEFROSTED?

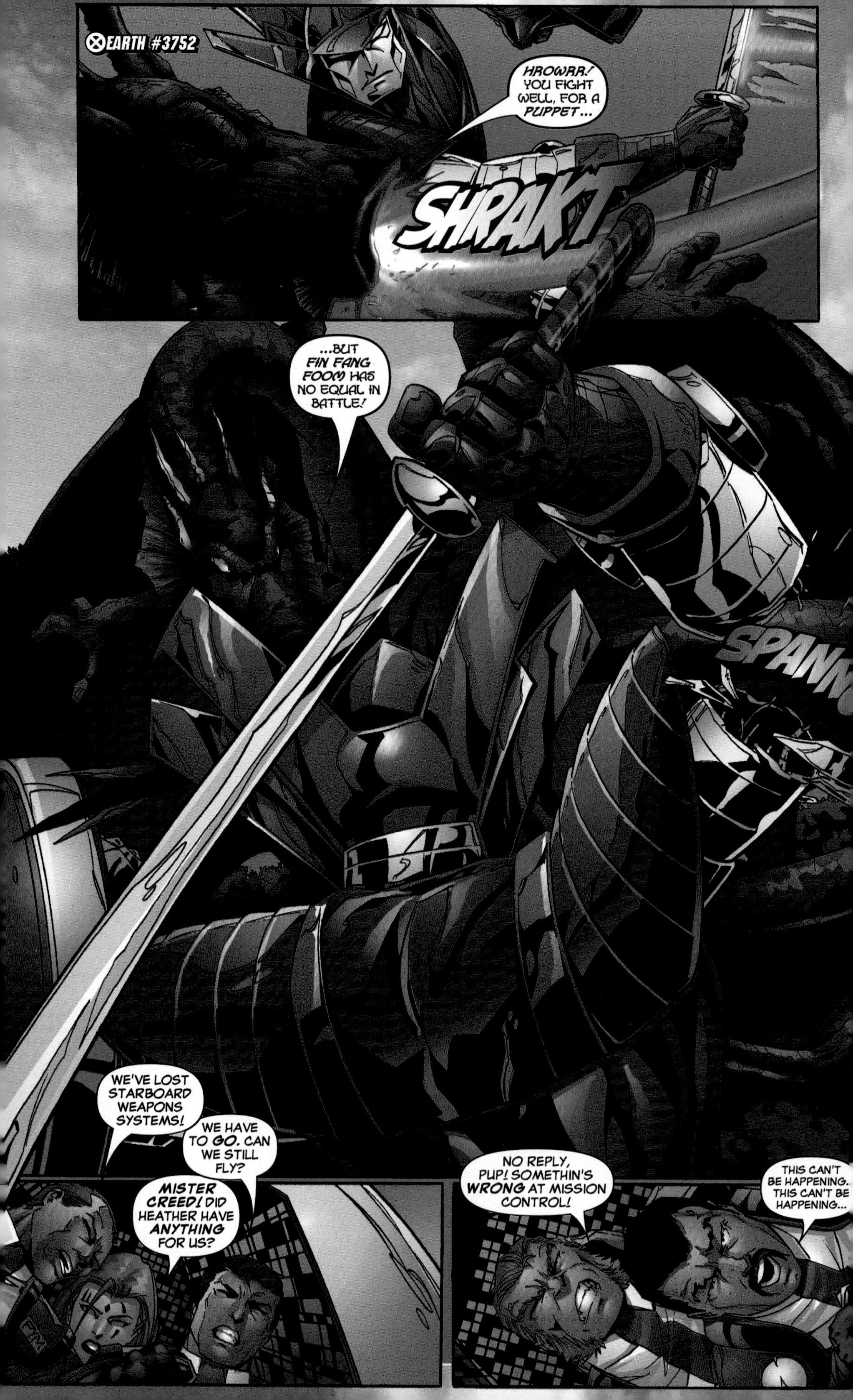
EARTH #3752
HROWRR! YOU FIGHT WELL, FOR A PUPPET...
SHRAKT
...BUT FIN FANG FOOM HAS NO EQUAL IN BATTLE!
SPANN
WE'VE LOST STARBOARD WEAPONS SYSTEMS!
WE HAVE TO GO. CAN WE STILL FLY?
MISTER CREED! DID HEATHER HAVE ANYTHING FOR US?
NO REPLY, PUP! SOMETHIN'S WRONG AT MISSION CONTROL!
THIS CAN'T BE HAPPENING. THIS CAN'T BE HAPPENING...

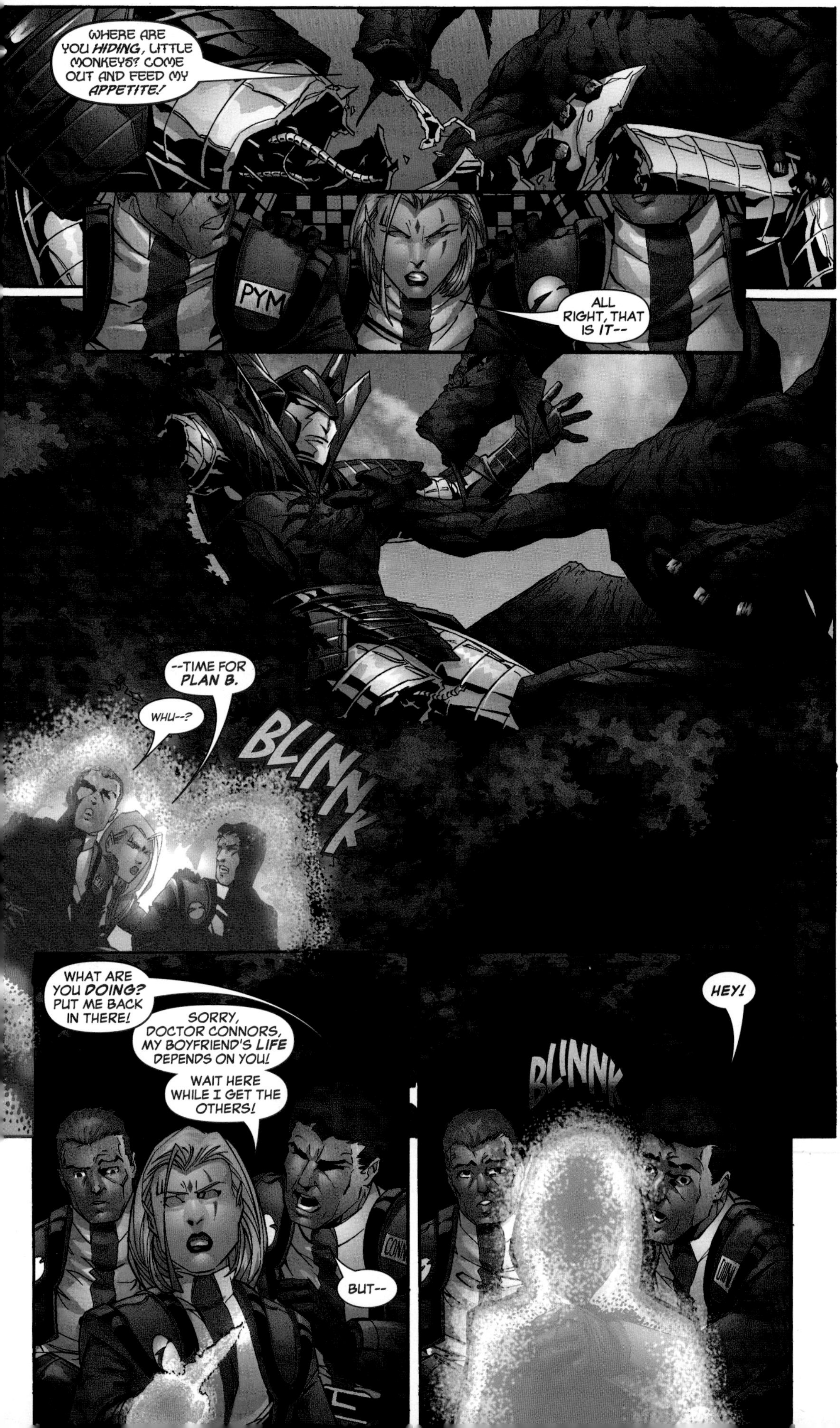
WHERE ARE YOU HIDING, LITTLE MONKEYS? COME OUT AND FEED MY APPETITE!
PYM
ALL RIGHT, THAT IS IT--
--TIME FOR PLAN B.
WHU--?
BLINNK
WHAT ARE YOU DOING? PUT ME BACK IN THERE!
SORRY, DOCTOR CONNORS, MY BOYFRIEND'S LIFE DEPENDS ON YOU!
WAIT HERE WHILE I GET THE OTHERS!
BUT--
HEY!
BLINNK

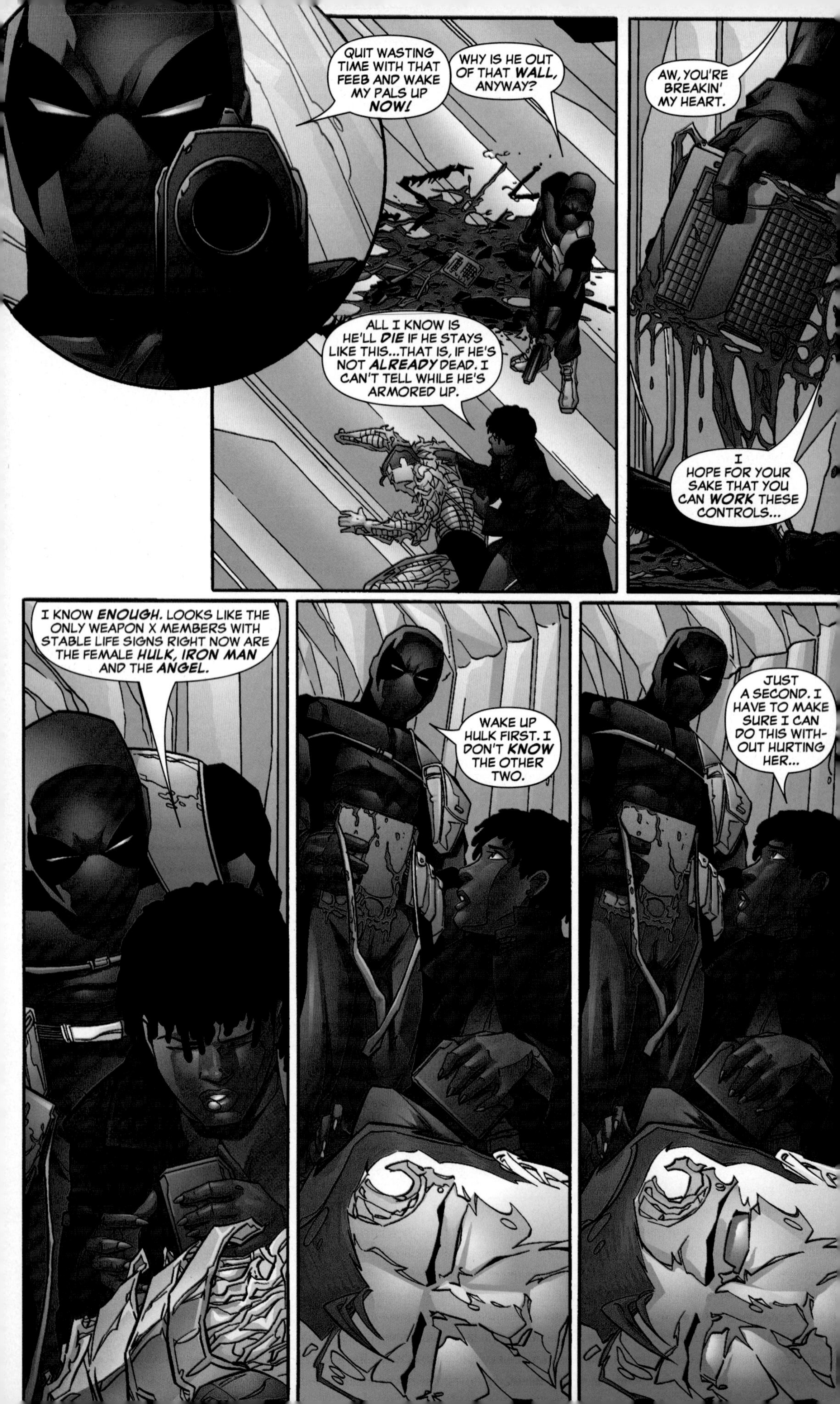

QUIT WASTING TIME WITH THAT FEEB AND WAKE MY PALS UP NOW!
WHY IS HE OUT OF THAT WALL, ANYWAY?
ALL I KNOW IS HE'LL DIE IF HE STAYS LIKE THIS...THAT IS, IF HE'S NOT ALREADY DEAD. I CAN'T TELL WHILE HE'S ARMORED UP.
AW, YOU'RE BREAKIN' MY HEART.
I HOPE FOR YOUR SAKE THAT YOU CAN WORK THESE CONTROLS...
I KNOW ENOUGH. LOOKS LIKE THE ONLY WEAPON X MEMBERS WITH STABLE LIFE SIGNS RIGHT NOW ARE THE FEMALE HULK, IRON MAN AND THE ANGEL.
WAKE UP HULK FIRST. I DON'T KNOW THE OTHER TWO.
JUST A SECOND. I HAVE TO MAKE SURE I CAN DO THIS WITHOUT HURTING HER...

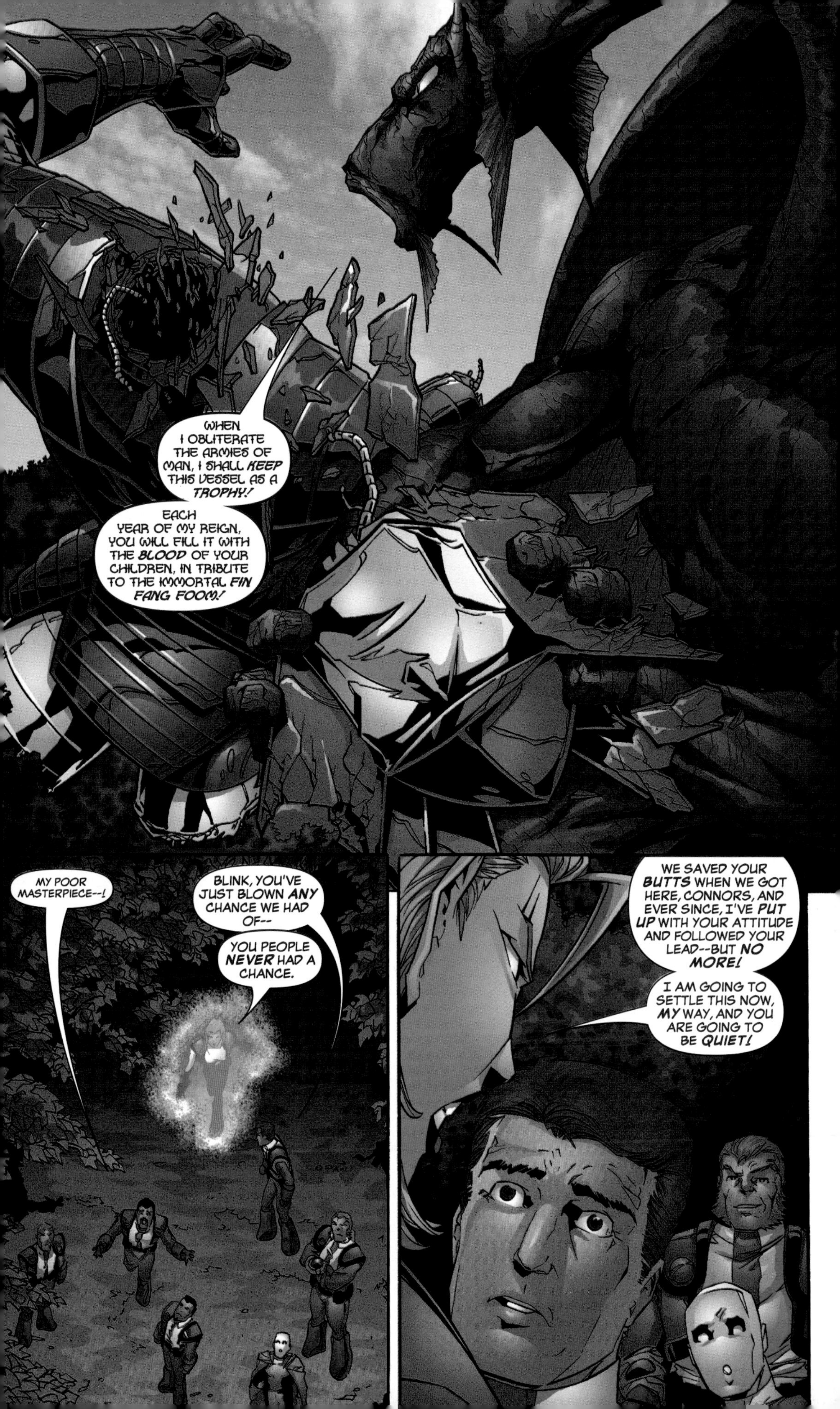
WHEN I OBLITERATE THE ARMIES OF MAN, I SHALL *KEEP* THIS VESSEL AS A *TROPHY!*
EACH YEAR OF MY REIGN, YOU WILL FILL IT WITH THE *BLOOD* OF YOUR CHILDREN, IN TRIBUTE TO THE IMMORTAL *FIN FANG FOOM!*
MY POOR MASTERPIECE--!
BLINK, YOU'VE JUST BLOWN *ANY* CHANCE WE HAD OF--
YOU PEOPLE *NEVER* HAD A CHANCE.
WE SAVED YOUR *BUTTS* WHEN WE GOT HERE, CONNORS, AND EVER SINCE, I'VE *PUT UP* WITH YOUR ATTITUDE AND FOLLOWED YOUR LEAD--BUT *NO MORE!*
I AM GOING TO SETTLE THIS NOW, *MY* WAY, AND YOU ARE GOING TO BE *QUIET!*

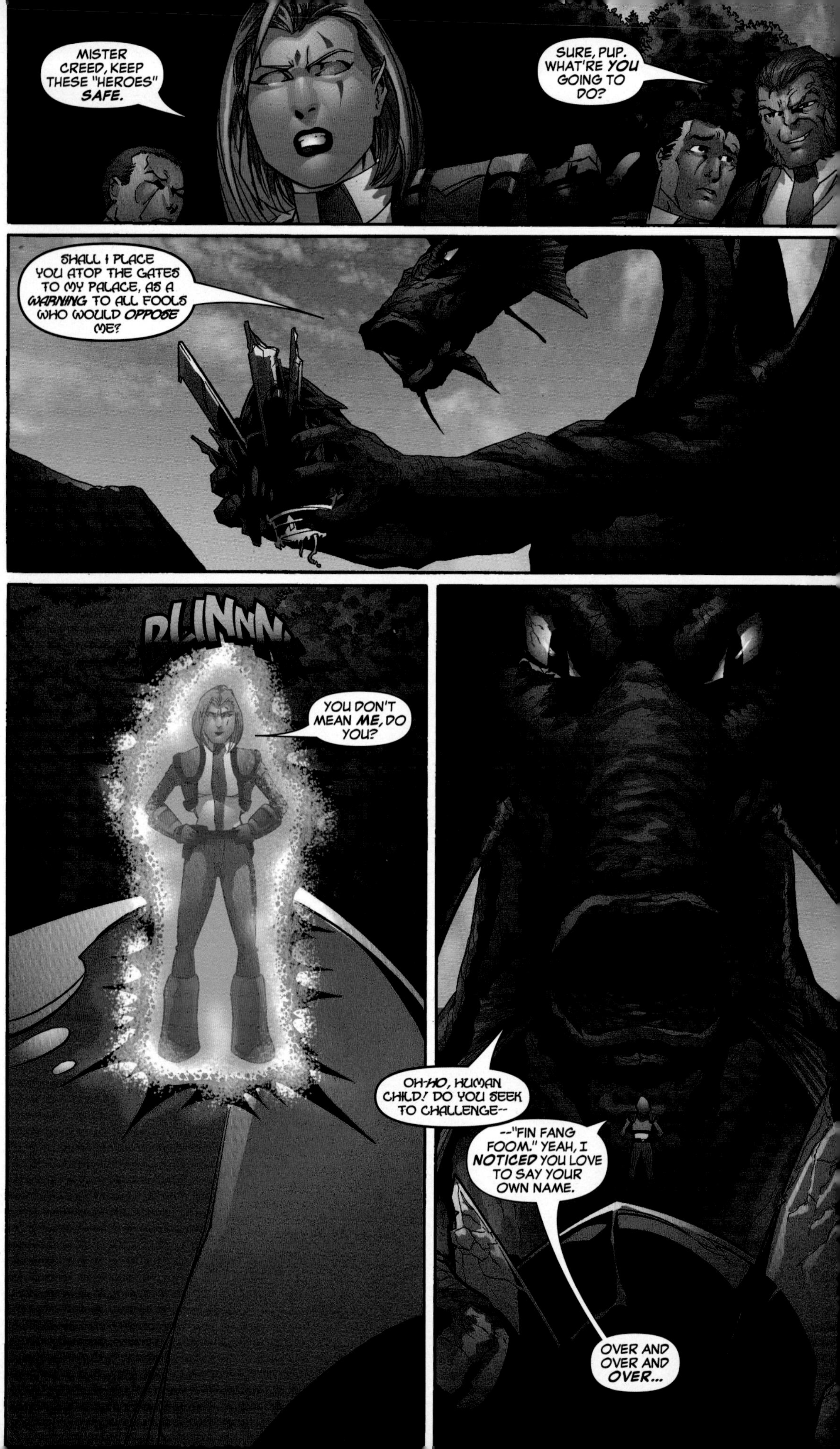

MISTER CREED, KEEP THESE "HEROES" SAFE.
SURE, PUP. WHAT'RE YOU GOING TO DO?
SHALL I PLACE YOU ATOP THE GATES TO MY PALACE, AS A WARNING TO ALL FOOLS WHO WOULD OPPOSE ME?
YOU DON'T MEAN ME, DO YOU?
OH-HO, HUMAN CHILD! DO YOU SEEK TO CHALLENGE--
--"FIN FANG FOOM." YEAH, I NOTICED YOU LOVE TO SAY YOUR OWN NAME.
OVER AND OVER AND OVER...

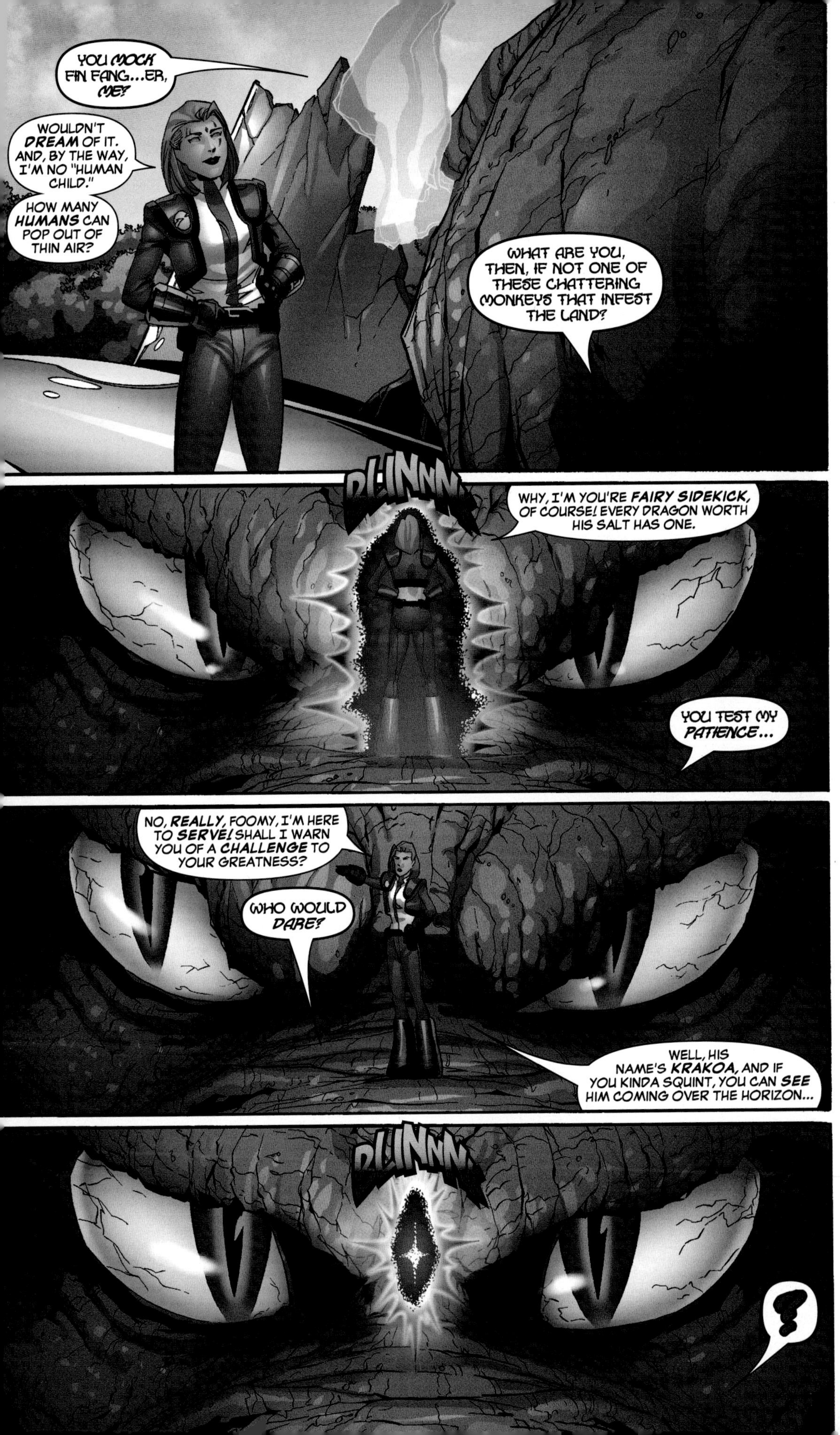

YOU MOCK FIN FANG...ER, ME?
WOULDN'T DREAM OF IT. AND, BY THE WAY, I'M NO "HUMAN CHILD."
HOW MANY HUMANS CAN POP OUT OF THIN AIR?
WHAT ARE YOU, THEN, IF NOT ONE OF THESE CHATTERING MONKEYS THAT INFEST THE LAND?
BLINNN
WHY, I'M YOU'RE FAIRY SIDEKICK, OF COURSE! EVERY DRAGON WORTH HIS SALT HAS ONE.
YOU TEST MY PATIENCE...
NO, REALLY, FOOMY, I'M HERE TO SERVE! SHALL I WARN YOU OF A CHALLENGE TO YOUR GREATNESS?
WHO WOULD DARE?
WELL, HIS NAME'S KRAKOA, AND IF YOU KINDA SQUINT, YOU CAN SEE HIM COMING OVER THE HORIZON...
BLINNN
?

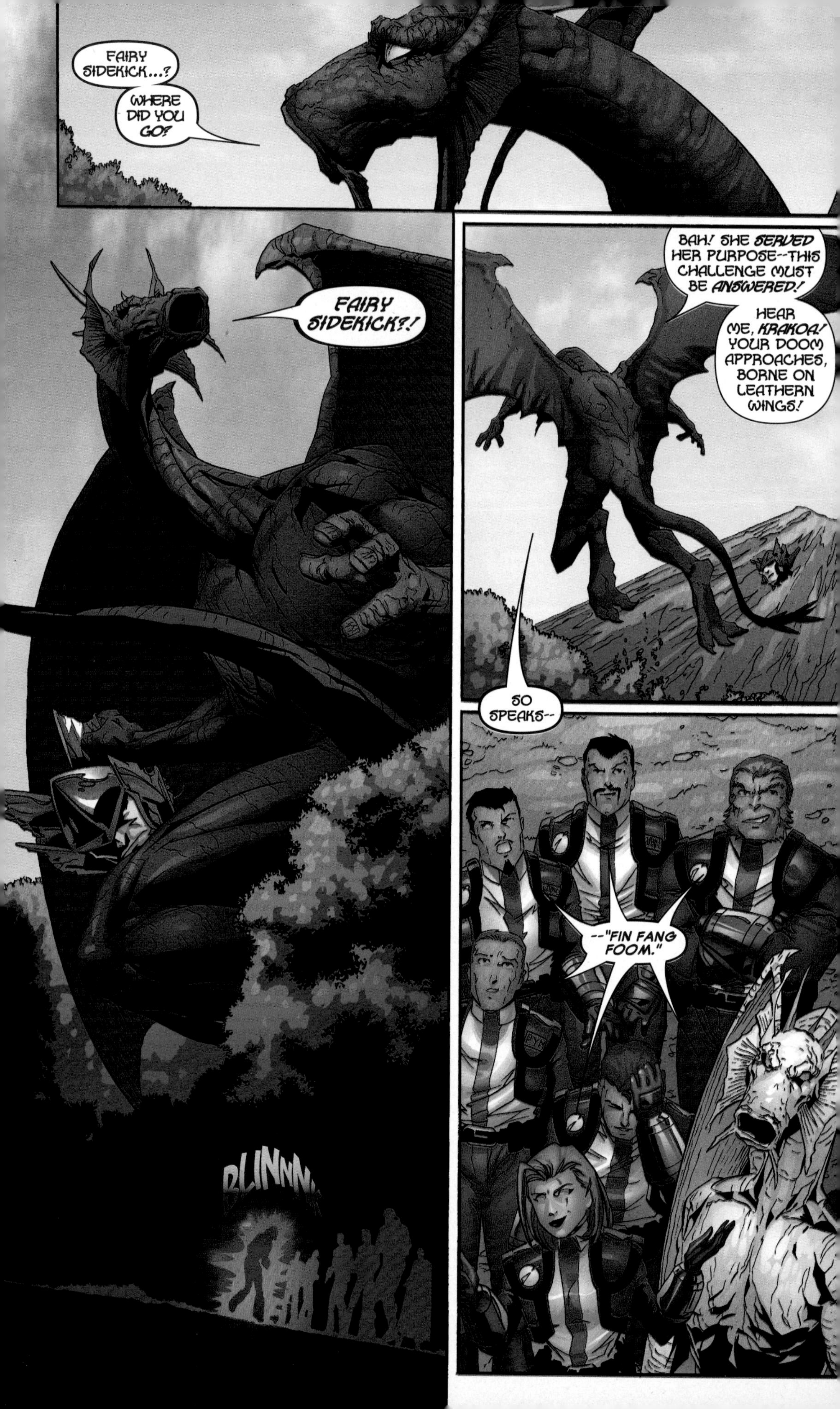

FAIRY SIDEKICK...?
WHERE DID YOU GO?
FAIRY SIDEKICK?!
BAH! SHE SERVED HER PURPOSE--THIS CHALLENGE MUST BE ANSWERED!
HEAR ME, KRAKOA! YOUR DOOM APPROACHES, BORNE ON LEATHERN WINGS!
SO SPEAKS--
--"FIN FANG FOOM."

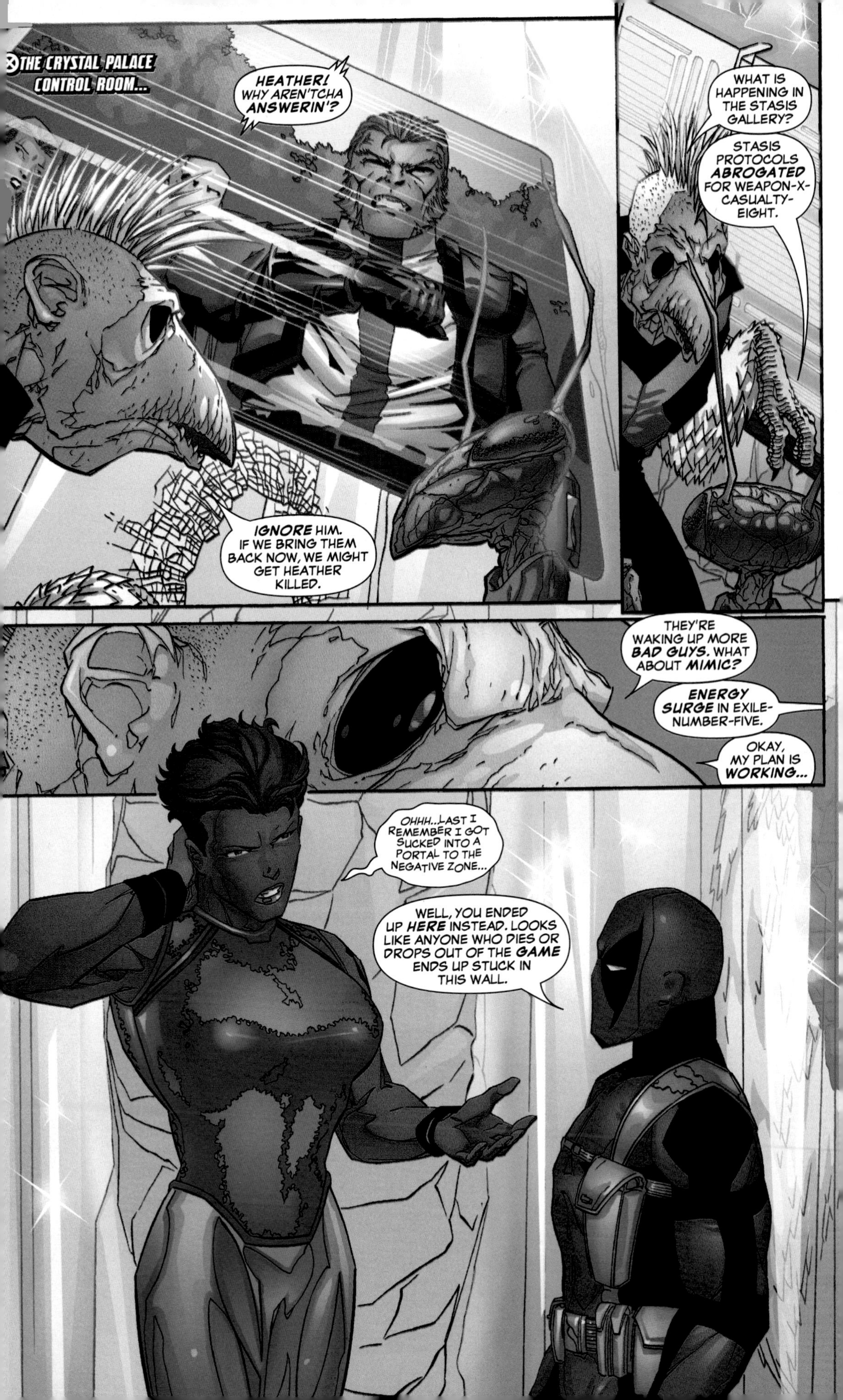
THE CRYSTAL PALACE CONTROL ROOM...
HEATHER! WHY AREN'TCHA ANSWERIN'?
IGNORE HIM. IF WE BRING THEM BACK NOW, WE MIGHT GET HEATHER KILLED.
WHAT IS HAPPENING IN THE STASIS GALLERY?
STASIS PROTOCOLS ABROGATED FOR WEAPON-X-CASUALTY-EIGHT.
THEY'RE WAKING UP MORE BAD GUYS. WHAT ABOUT MIMIC?
ENERGY SURGE IN EXILE-NUMBER-FIVE.
OKAY, MY PLAN IS WORKING...
OHHH...LAST I REMEMBER I GOT SUCKED INTO A PORTAL TO THE NEGATIVE ZONE...
WELL, YOU ENDED UP HERE INSTEAD. LOOKS LIKE ANYONE WHO DIES OR DROPS OUT OF THE GAME ENDS UP STUCK IN THIS WALL.

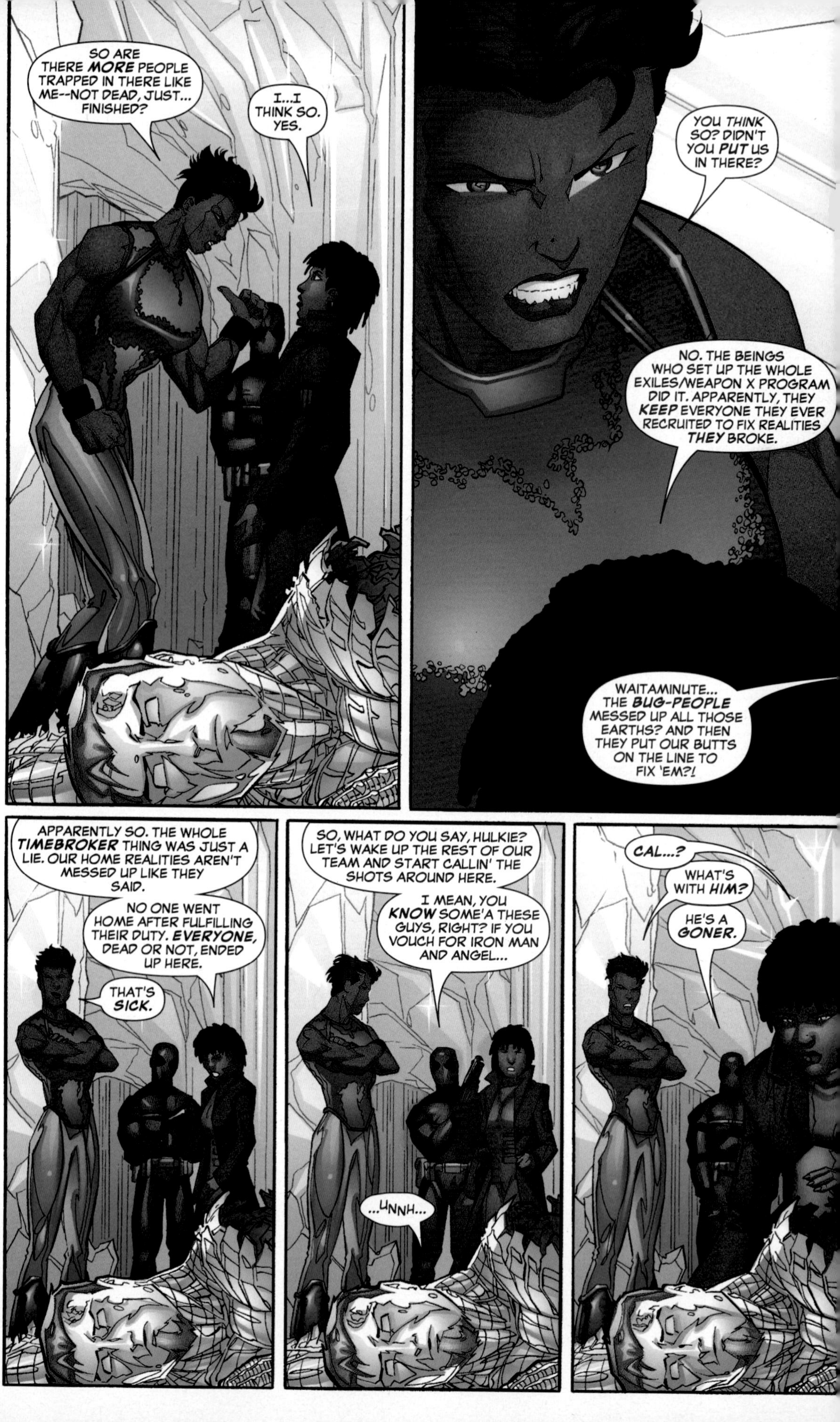
SO ARE THERE MORE PEOPLE TRAPPED IN THERE LIKE ME--NOT DEAD, JUST... FINISHED?
I...I THINK SO. YES.
YOU THINK SO? DIDN'T YOU PUT US IN THERE?
NO. THE BEINGS WHO SET UP THE WHOLE EXILES/WEAPON X PROGRAM DID IT. APPARENTLY, THEY KEEP EVERYONE THEY EVER RECRUITED TO FIX REALITIES THEY BROKE.
WAITAMINUTE... THE BUG-PEOPLE MESSED UP ALL THOSE EARTHS? AND THEN THEY PUT OUR BUTTS ON THE LINE TO FIX 'EM?!
APPARENTLY SO. THE WHOLE TIMEBROKER THING WAS JUST A LIE. OUR HOME REALITIES AREN'T MESSED UP LIKE THEY SAID.
NO ONE WENT HOME AFTER FULFILLING THEIR DUTY. EVERYONE, DEAD OR NOT, ENDED UP HERE.
THAT'S SICK.
SO, WHAT DO YOU SAY, HULKIE? LET'S WAKE UP THE REST OF OUR TEAM AND START CALLIN' THE SHOTS AROUND HERE.
I MEAN, YOU KNOW SOME'A THESE GUYS, RIGHT? IF YOU VOUCH FOR IRON MAN AND ANGEL...
...UNNH...
CAL...?
WHAT'S WITH HIM?
HE'S A GONER.

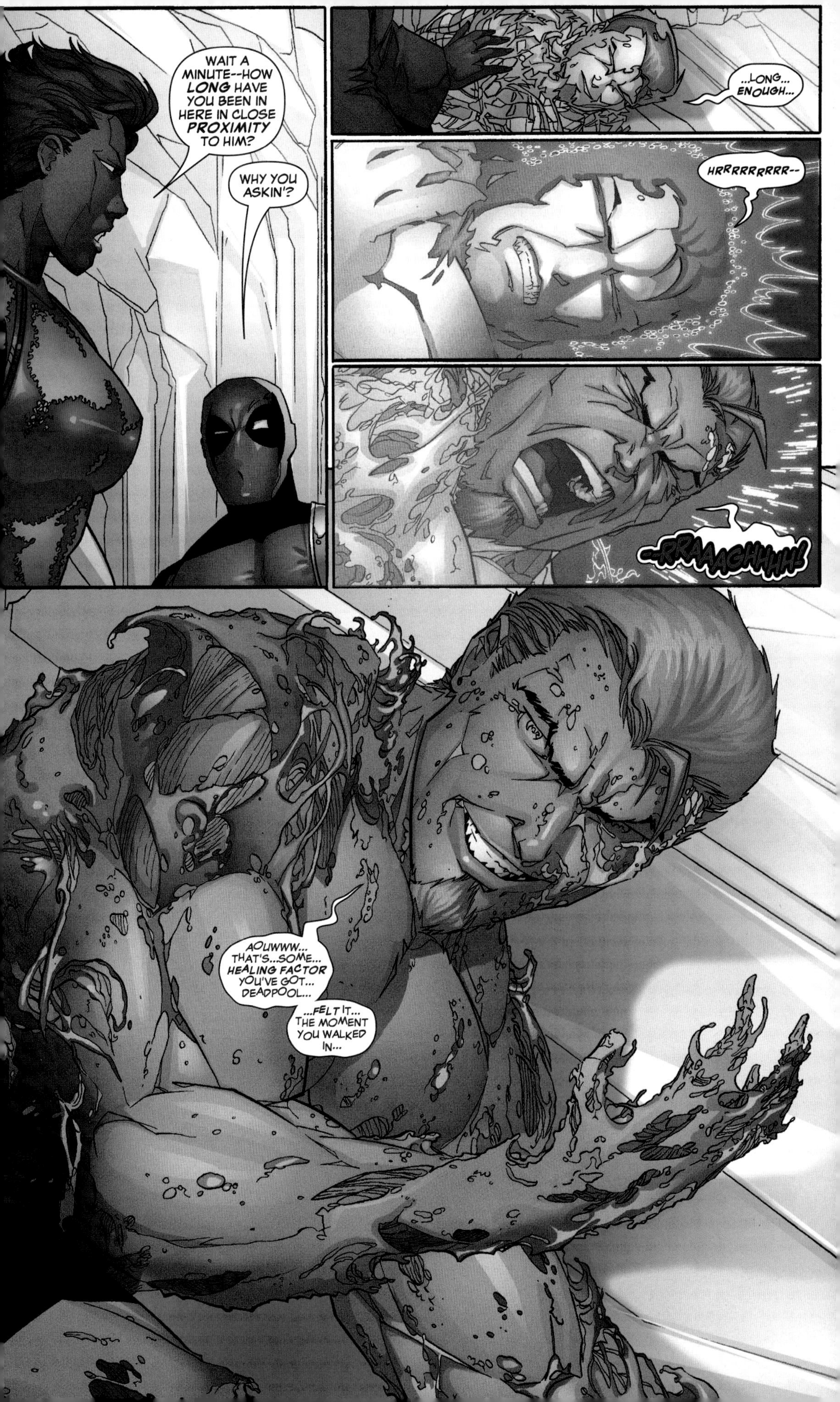

WAIT A MINUTE--HOW LONG HAVE YOU BEEN IN HERE IN CLOSE PROXIMITY TO HIM?
WHY YOU ASKIN'?
...LONG... ENOUGH...
HRRRRRRRR--
--RRAAAGHHHH!
AOUWWW... THAT'S...SOME... HEALING FACTOR YOU'VE GOT... DEADPOOL...
...FELT IT... THE MOMENT YOU WALKED IN...

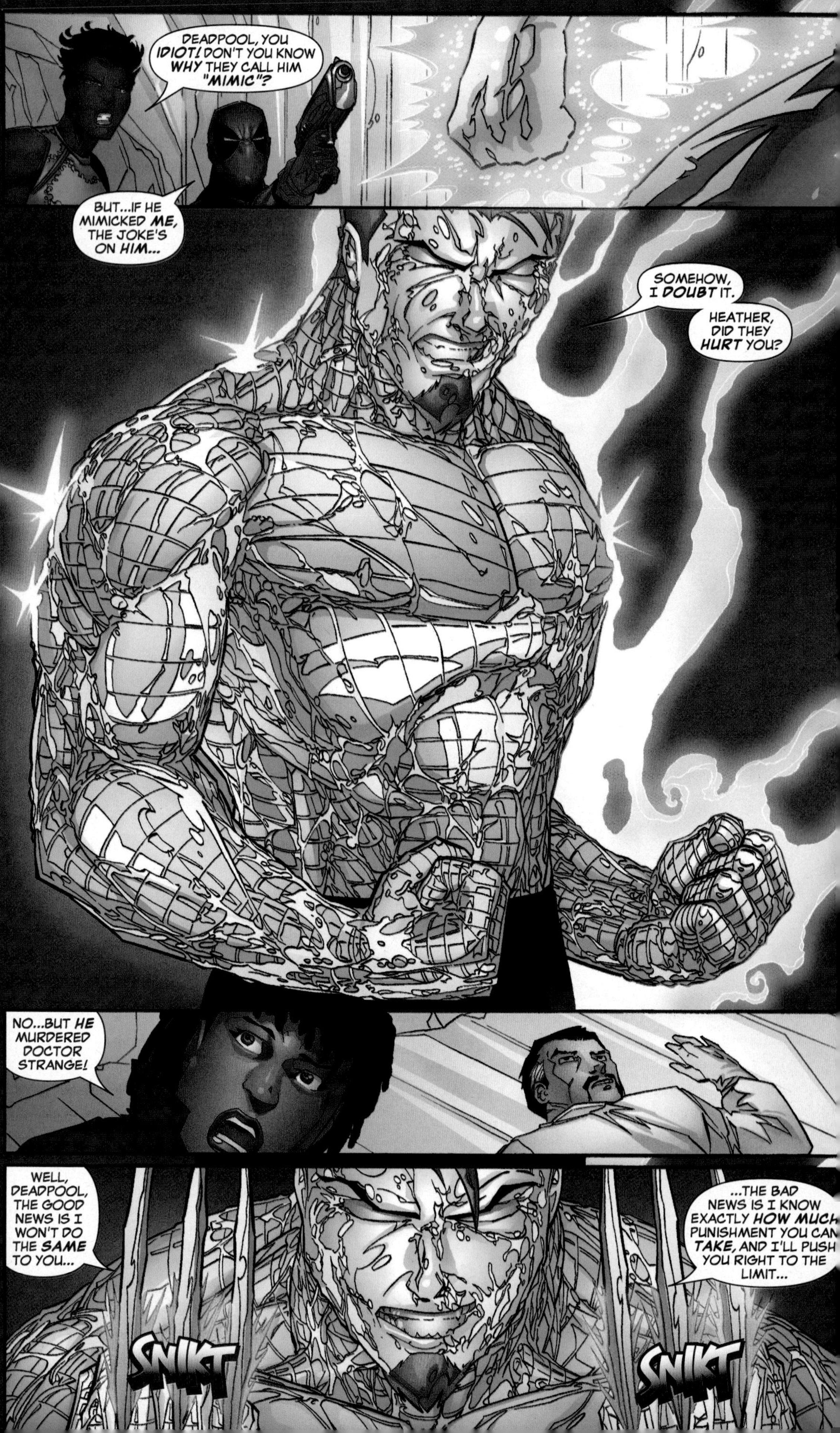
DEADPOOL, YOU IDIOT! DON'T YOU KNOW WHY THEY CALL HIM "MIMIC"?
BUT...IF HE MIMICKED ME, THE JOKE'S ON HIM...
SOMEHOW, I DOUBT IT.
HEATHER, DID THEY HURT YOU?
NO...BUT HE MURDERED DOCTOR STRANGE!
WELL, DEADPOOL, THE GOOD NEWS IS I WON'T DO THE SAME TO YOU...
...THE BAD NEWS IS I KNOW EXACTLY HOW MUCH PUNISHMENT YOU CAN TAKE, AND I'LL PUSH YOU RIGHT TO THE LIMIT...
SNIKT
SNIKT

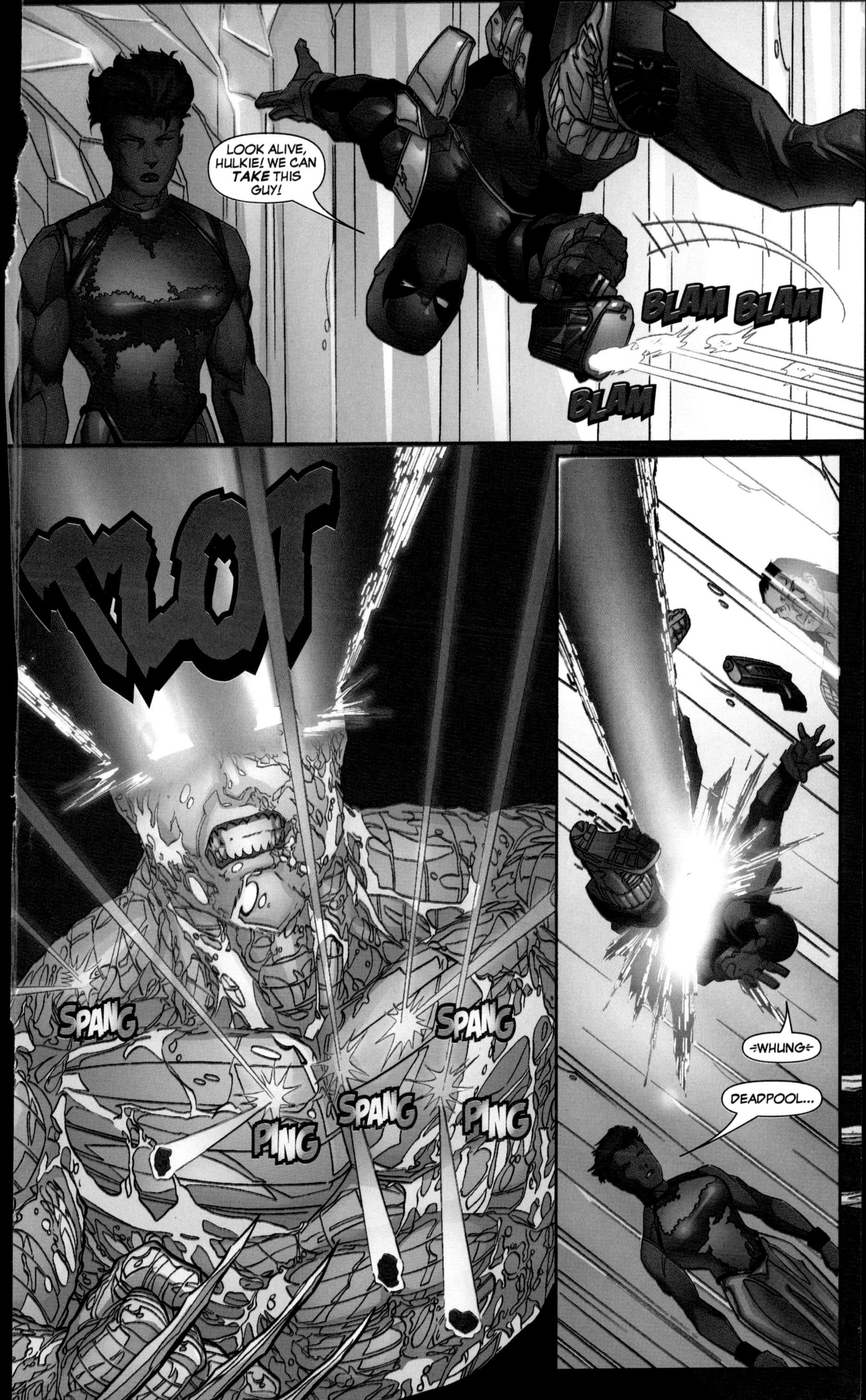
LOOK ALIVE, HULKIE! WE CAN TAKE THIS GUY!
BLAM BLAM
BLAM
ZZOT
SPANG
SPANG
PING
SPANG
PING
WHUNG
DEADPOOL...

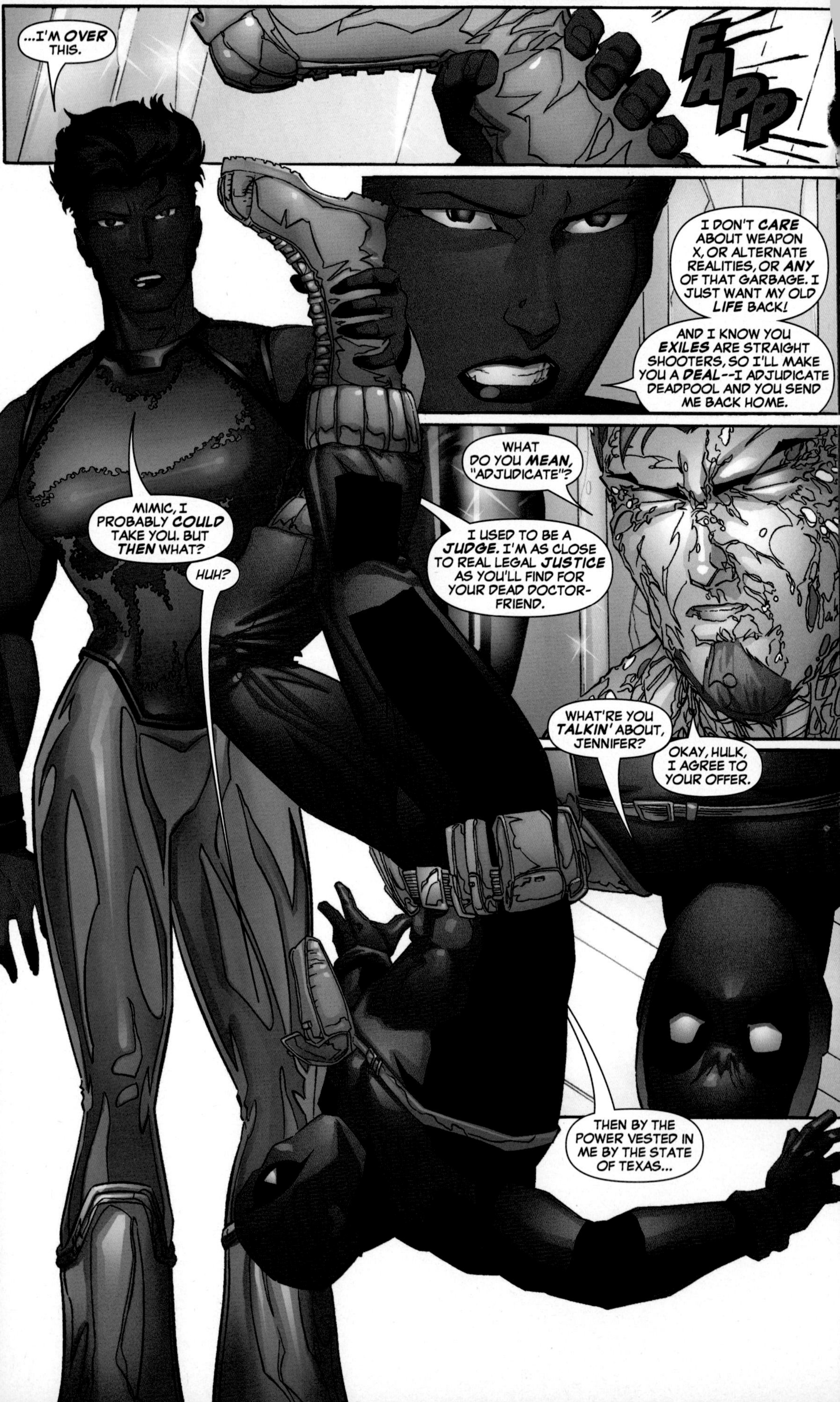
...I'M OVER THIS.
FAPP
I DON'T CARE ABOUT WEAPON X, OR ALTERNATE REALITIES, OR ANY OF THAT GARBAGE. I JUST WANT MY OLD LIFE BACK!
AND I KNOW YOU EXILES ARE STRAIGHT SHOOTERS, SO I'LL MAKE YOU A DEAL--I ADJUDICATE DEADPOOL AND YOU SEND ME BACK HOME.
MIMIC, I PROBABLY COULD TAKE YOU. BUT THEN WHAT?
HUH?
WHAT DO YOU MEAN, "ADJUDICATE"?
I USED TO BE A JUDGE. I'M AS CLOSE TO REAL LEGAL JUSTICE AS YOU'LL FIND FOR YOUR DEAD DOCTOR-FRIEND.
WHAT'RE YOU TALKIN' ABOUT, JENNIFER?
OKAY, HULK, I AGREE TO YOUR OFFER.
THEN BY THE POWER VESTED IN ME BY THE STATE OF TEXAS...

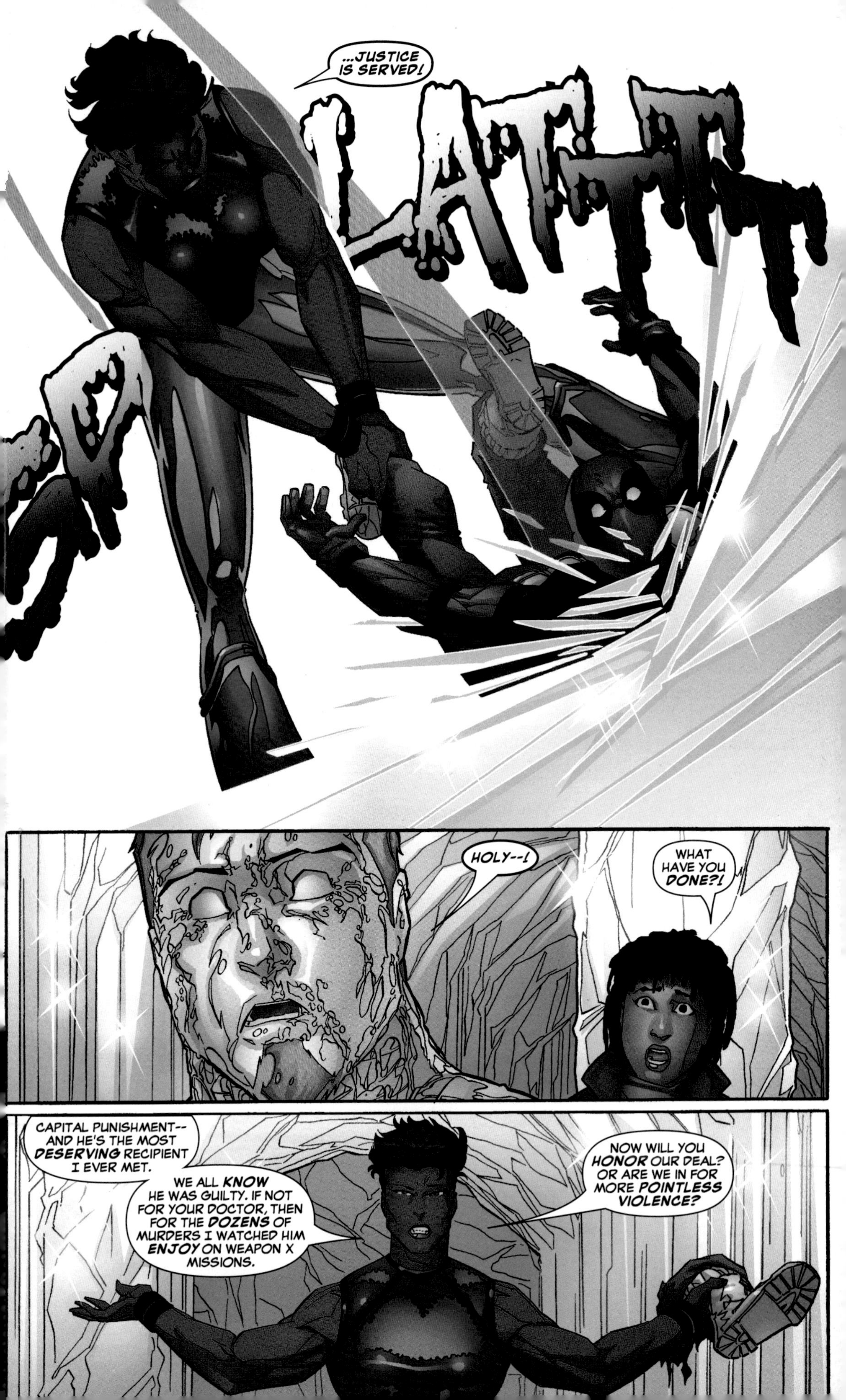
...JUSTICE IS SERVED!
SPLATTT
HOLY--!
WHAT HAVE YOU DONE?!
CAPITAL PUNISHMENT-- AND HE'S THE MOST DESERVING RECIPIENT I EVER MET.
WE ALL KNOW HE WAS GUILTY. IF NOT FOR YOUR DOCTOR, THEN FOR THE DOZENS OF MURDERS I WATCHED HIM ENJOY ON WEAPON X MISSIONS.
NOW WILL YOU HONOR OUR DEAL? OR ARE WE IN FOR MORE POINTLESS VIOLENCE?

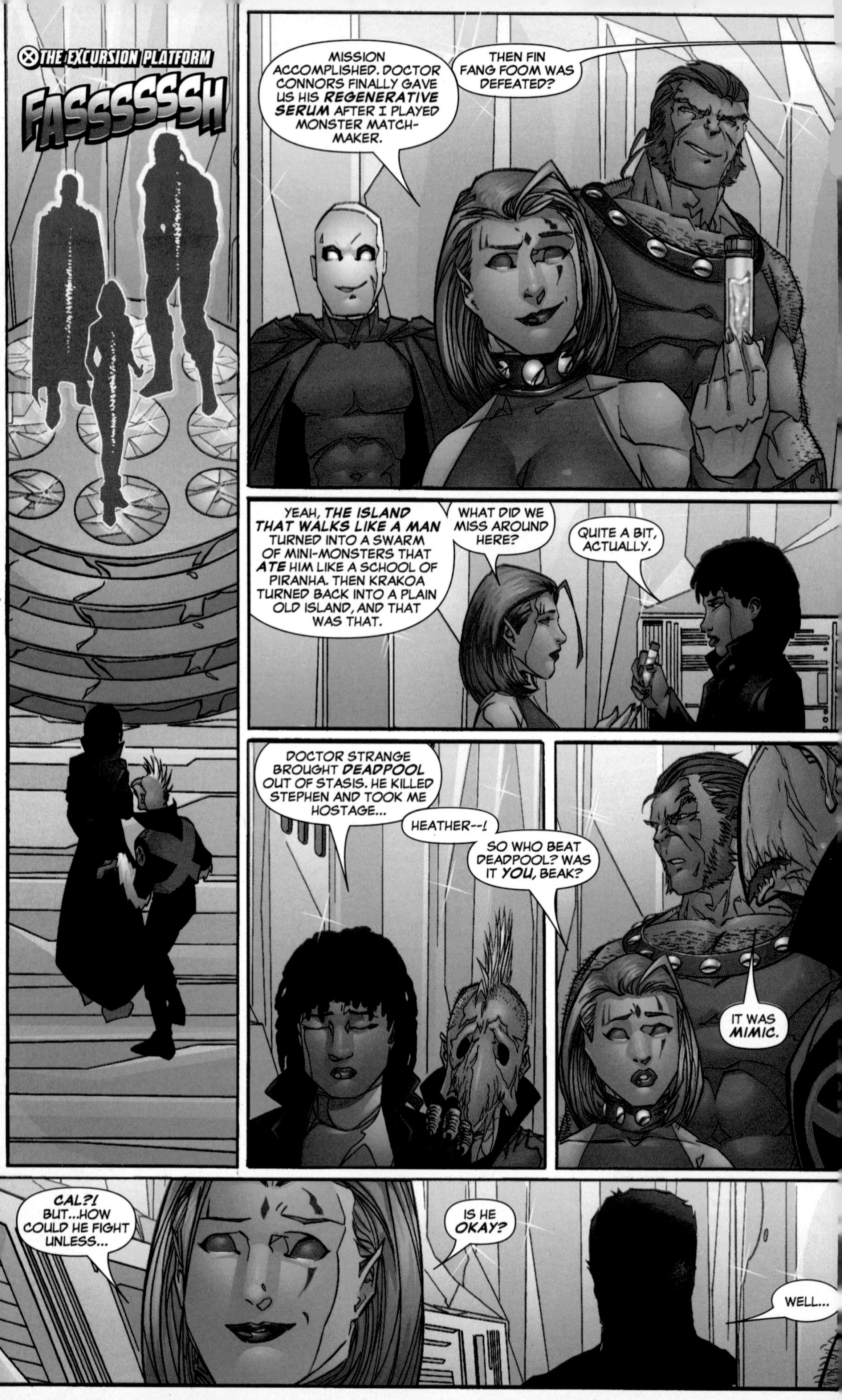
THE EXCURSION PLATFORM
FASSSSSSH
MISSION ACCOMPLISHED. DOCTOR CONNORS FINALLY GAVE US HIS REGENERATIVE SERUM AFTER I PLAYED MONSTER MATCH-MAKER.
THEN FIN FANG FOOM WAS DEFEATED?
YEAH, THE ISLAND THAT WALKS LIKE A MAN TURNED INTO A SWARM OF MINI-MONSTERS THAT ATE HIM LIKE A SCHOOL OF PIRANHA. THEN KRAKOA TURNED BACK INTO A PLAIN OLD ISLAND, AND THAT WAS THAT.
WHAT DID WE MISS AROUND HERE?
QUITE A BIT, ACTUALLY.
DOCTOR STRANGE BROUGHT DEADPOOL OUT OF STASIS. HE KILLED STEPHEN AND TOOK ME HOSTAGE...
HEATHER--!
SO WHO BEAT DEADPOOL? WAS IT YOU, BEAK?
IT WAS MIMIC.
CAL?! BUT...HOW COULD HE FIGHT UNLESS...
IS HE OKAY?
WELL...

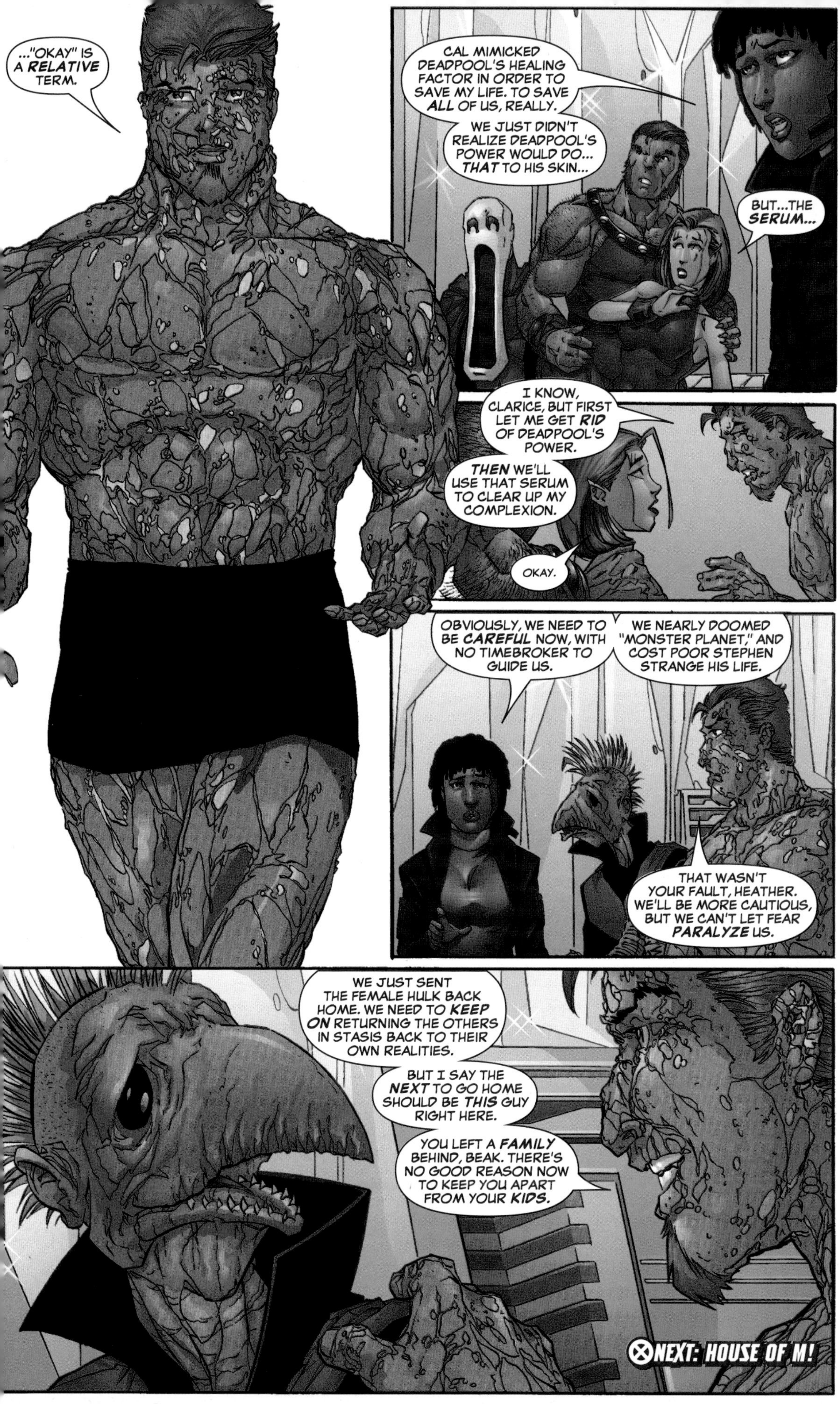
..."OKAY" IS A RELATIVE TERM.
CAL MIMICKED DEADPOOL'S HEALING FACTOR IN ORDER TO SAVE MY LIFE. TO SAVE ALL OF US, REALLY.
WE JUST DIDN'T REALIZE DEADPOOL'S POWER WOULD DO... THAT TO HIS SKIN...
BUT...THE SERUM...
I KNOW, CLARICE, BUT FIRST LET ME GET RID OF DEADPOOL'S POWER.
THEN WE'LL USE THAT SERUM TO CLEAR UP MY COMPLEXION.
OKAY.
OBVIOUSLY, WE NEED TO BE CAREFUL NOW, WITH NO TIMEBROKER TO GUIDE US.
WE NEARLY DOOMED "MONSTER PLANET," AND COST POOR STEPHEN STRANGE HIS LIFE.
THAT WASN'T YOUR FAULT, HEATHER. WE'LL BE MORE CAUTIOUS, BUT WE CAN'T LET FEAR PARALYZE US.
WE JUST SENT THE FEMALE HULK BACK HOME. WE NEED TO KEEP ON RETURNING THE OTHERS IN STASIS BACK TO THEIR OWN REALITIES.
BUT I SAY THE NEXT TO GO HOME SHOULD BE THIS GUY RIGHT HERE.
YOU LEFT A FAMILY BEHIND, BEAK. THERE'S NO GOOD REASON NOW TO KEEP YOU APART FROM YOUR KIDS.
NEXT: HOUSE OF M!

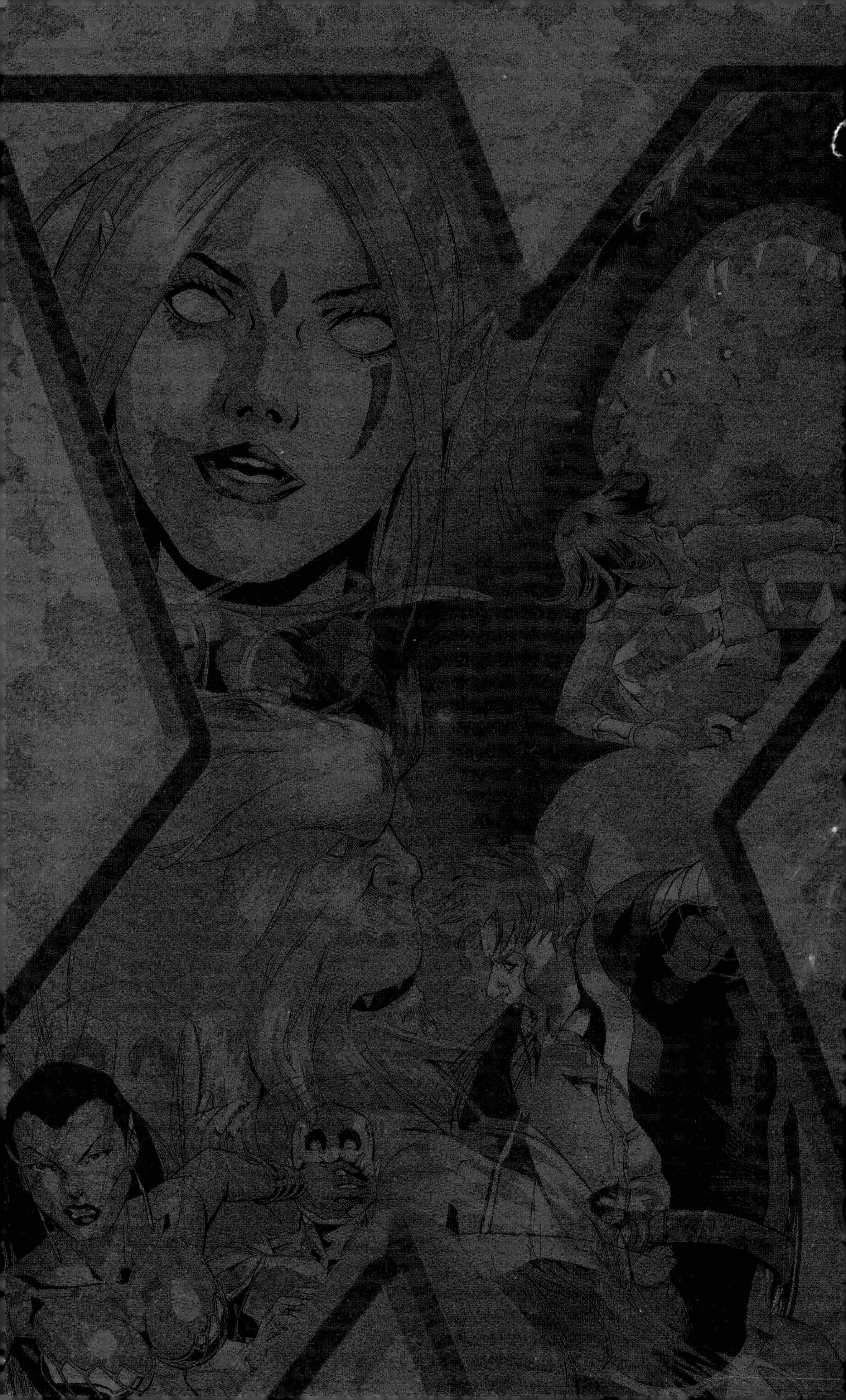